The Complete Galloping Gourmet Cookbook

Graham Kerr

Photographs by Neville Bell

GROSSET & DUNLAP

A FILMWAYS COMPANY

PUBLISHERS   NEW YORK

The Complete Galloping Gourmet Cookbook

To my children, Tessa, Andrew and Kareena,
with apologies for all those times that I had to say,
"Sorry—not now, I'm busy."

ACKNOWLEDGMENTS

The following people made invaluable contributions in the emergence of this book: Angela Lemaire for original woodcuts; Patricia Burgess and Willie Meemacker, my food assistants; Renate Schirmacher, my secretary; Ursula Laver for styling; New Zealand for my start in television; and my friend Wilbur Freifeld.

CONTENTS

André Simon with Graham Kerr

INTRODUCTION

Dear Reader:

I am today a composite of yesterday's beliefs. A mixture of hard-fought compromises and lost battles of conscience that I wish had never been joined. Yet with all this I'm now unfettered; no man has expectations of me other than myself. It is this state of mind that allows me the incredible good fortune of being a happy man. I don't want to bore you with a load of psychological cod-swallop or rags-to-riches clichés—for this you will have to read *between* the lines.

Food is my bread and butter. One way or another it has been so since I was born. Apart from the briefest of spells as an automotive engineer (grease monkey), and as a Drill and Weapons Training Instructor (murder by numbers), I have done nothing else. My food experiences have covered such an enormously wide area that I have to believe that what I may lack in specific depth, I certainly make up for in breadth.

Early on I was more of an "eater" than a cook; something that André Simon (see facing page) told me was his lifetime situation. He seldom cooked. He believed that a good cook has to be exposed to rich and varied gastronomic experiences in order to have a relative standard for his own, later, achievements. What a shame André never cooked—no man experienced more.

My eating wasn't exactly epicurean but it was varied. Here and there, where war rationing permitted, it was an inspiration. So I have a memory of all my food experiences, good and bad. In it lurks sights, smells and flavors. Unfortunately, the most joyous recollections become even better as they age. Consequently, when I try to duplicate a memorable eating occasion it becomes extremely difficult, but this at least keeps me from growing content. I said earlier that I am happy but I am not content. Contentment is a creative vacuum and I'm not ready to retire from the realm of innovation or refinement.

No matter how often people rave on about the evils of money, it is, in my opinion, an essential ingredient in life. If you don't have it there is a tendency to compromise. Compromise is only acceptable if done in small doses for strictly limited objectives. A compromise must have a clear-cut conclusion, otherwise it turns its user into a two-faced confidence man.

I have used compromise throughout my life but I have never wittingly let it lead me into dishonesty. Each compromise has been hard, each I have regretted making, each has stiffened my resolve to avoid them in the future.

One side of my life has come through unscathed by these commercial pressures—my major books. So what you read now we can share together for exactly what it is: an honest attempt to do the best I can within the limits of my ability. Every recipe has involved personal blood, sweat and even tears, and hours upon hours of research, testing and writing. They are not a collection copied from others; they are more of a conversion to suit my developing tastes. There is, in each recipe, a genuine and substantial slice of personal commitment.

While the thoughts and the recipes in this book represent my life to date, I really feel that my work has just begun. I am totally committed to the removal of dull repetitive activity in the kitchen and I shall attempt, using every modern device known to mankind, to replace boredom with interest, repetition with innovation, unhappiness with joy.

Until that time I remain,

with your future in mind,

Graham Kerr

Graham Kerr in his first TV kitchen, 1961

THE GROUND RULES

I can only hope that my wildest dreams come true and that you read these pages. Armed with the information contained in these short paragraphs you will be able to *use* this book—without it you stand a chance of failure, and at this price neither of us can afford it!

MEASUREMENTS

I have chosen to put measurements in a form least likely to be misunderstood. As you know I have done battle over the years with the *cup measurement:* this simply isn't accurate enough, and it doesn't take the place of an *efficient weighing scale.* Therefore I have used ounces and pounds; I have avoided pints and quarts due to the disparity between Imperial (20 fl oz = 1 pint) and U.S.A. (16 fl oz = 1 pint) by using fluid ounces.

Throughout the book you will notice immediately following a measurement its conversion to metric in brackets, i.e. 20 fl oz (6 dl). I have taken the metric to the closest reasonable figure for cooking purposes.

On the endpapers at each end of the book you will find a full page devoted to cup conversion if you feel you must.

COOKING TIMES AND TEMPERATURES

I hate excuses so I prefer to tell you that all the temperatures and times were worked out at the time of testing these dishes and double-checked during television. The equipment used was the very best, and it was checked by thermocouples twice a week. There should, as a result, be no way that you should not achieve a perfect result unless *your* oven is on the blink.

First Prepare

You will note that in all but the shortest recipes, I have included this direction. This means prepare everything up to the last possible degree before actual cooking. The French call this *mis en place,* and it is the reason why their restaurant techniques are followed throughout the world and called *a la carte.* This means you can be assured of good last-minute cooking and not food kept on the steam table as you expect from *table d'hôte* menus.

PLEASE use this technique yourself: it really does work and I have gone to a lot of trouble to make it easier to follow.

KEY TO MARGIN ILLUSTRATIONS

You will find that each recipe is graded by a strip of vertical symbols in the margin. This is what they mean.

$⊖ ECONOMY DISH — Should be within all basic budgets.

$◒ MODERATE COST — Within budget reach for entertaining.

$● EXPENSIVE — Could be most expensive for most budgets.

⊠◒ QUICK — Can be made within half an hour.

⊠● LENGTHY — Anywhere from an hour to four hours (no longer!).

CAN BE FROZEN — A good dish for precooking, careful wrapping and holding in the deep freeze.

HOT WEATHER DISH — Suitable for hot, sunny and/or humid weather when you don't want to cook or eat.

COLD WEATHER DISH — Great for days when the kitchen is a good place to be and appetites run high.

GG DESIGNED BY AUTHOR — My double G symbol is used on everything I do *actually*
65   design—the date is added as a matter of record.

✳ SEE APPENDIX — Everytime an asterisk appears in a recipe it is an indication to turn to the appendix for an explanation of the ingredient or, in the case of hard-to-find items, a substitution.

PARTY PLANNING

May I ask you to limit the number of people you invite to a party to eight.

Try not to exceed three courses plus cheese and fresh fruit.

Never undertake more than one course for the first time but *always* try one dish as an experiment.

If the main dish takes last-minute finishing, choose a first course and dessert that you can finish before the guests are seated.

If the main dish can be completely pre-prepared then let the dessert be your grand finale.

Never pre-prepare and precook everything; it takes away the magic and the feeling of receiving personal attention.

If red wine is consumed with the main dish, serve cheese before the dessert. This helps to use up the red and it's a good digestive.

Keep the portions small. Quantity, no matter how good, can never be as good as wanting more.

Avoid similar foods such as fish and shellfish for both first and main courses—or rich dishes that contain cream in all courses.

Unless the whole gathering is as thin as rakes, do your best to plan the least fattening menu.

With a three-course meal serve only two wines. Even wine lovers get confused with too much of a good thing.

Plan for plenty of time to talk afterwards over coffee. This is the host's reward.

No matter how much it hurts—please don't allow your guests to help clear up. It's their night out—let them enjoy it.

Most of the step-by-step photo sequences begin with a photograph like this showing the ingredients necessary for the particular recipe being done.

If a guest falls asleep early, let him put his head down and sleep.

If it's really hot, let the men remove their jackets. If it's stinking hot, then the ties can follow. Any higher temperature and you should cancel the party!

If you want to thank someone, send them a pot of homemade clarified butter in a beautiful reagent jar (see page 54 for the recipe).

Allow yourself (male or female) a good hour between getting everything ready and the arrival of your guests. Have a bath, relax; your food should never be allowed to upstage its creator.

Lastly, have fun!

MUTUAL ASSISTANCE PROGRAM

I give you my word that, for as long as this book is in print, I shall retain the services of an assistant who can be reached through the offices of my publisher:

Grosset & Dunlap, Inc.

51 Madison Avenue

New York, N.Y. 10010

Please address any queries, any criticisms and constructive suggestions, or any pleas for further assistance on purchasing any item named within these covers to:

Graham Kerr's After Sales Service

This is a large book and, even though its contents have been created over a period of over twenty-four years, there is always room to improve its contents and bring it up-to-date.

WHAT IS A MAN LIKE YOU
DOING IN A BOOK LIKE THIS?

I am, or rather have been, a constant paradox no matter where I have worked or at what level. I think you should know (if you don't already) that I used to have an inferiority complex. This was largely due to an upbringing in the postwar hotel business when England was still casting off the molds of ancient traditions and waging a modern "class" war. It was a time when the last surge of social status was felt in the British blood. Indebtedness to North America, loss of Empire, and worst of all—the repatriated officers trained only in the gentle art of murder. It was a time when men who returned to run hotels were regarded as one of the lower orders. My wife Treena's parents, for example, didn't want their daughter marrying the son of a hotel keeper.

I believe that everyone in the hotel and restaurant industry felt this undertow during the immediate postwar years. It was responsible for a huge swing to *La Cuisine Française*, with all the status that it bestowed upon the select who could both read and interpret its instructions. There was talk of Escoffier, Carême, Soyer, Saulnier while making the Shepherd's Pie. There was discussion about Estouffades and Demi-glace while the parsley sauce blooped.

Awards and medals, certificates and citations blew through the halls of newly opened technical colleges. All this in the cause of status. A status won at the cost of diluting British national cookery and making food a public mystery. But then, the greater the mystery the greater the status. Between 1948 and 1952, I swam along happily in this tidal stream of opinion, eager to share in the golden future of "status" that would warm my inferiority. I progressed through Technical Colleges and Kitchen Departments. My intention was to become a great hôtelier and run the Savoy or Claridge's.

In 1952 I was eighteen years old and ready to serve in Her Majesty's Armed Forces (she insisted). There followed five years of unusual activity for a classically trained "French" hôtelier. I was commissioned eventually as an S.M.O. (Specialist Messing Officer) in the Army Catering Corps—not much of a boost for an inferiority complex! I set out with complete zeal to prove to the army, and anyone else that mattered, how wrong they were to hold a caterer in disrepute!

The Army, thankfully I suspect, let me go in 1955 with the rank of Captain. I returned to the hotel business complete with a rather new wife, Treena, and a very new baby, Tessa. The hotel belonged to my parents. It was the Woolpack Hotel in Tenterden, Kent, England. A 15th-century pub with a sixty-seat restaurant—the latter my responsibility. If you are a student of history you may recall that the Suez Canal crisis took place in October/November 1956. The result was a great disaster for world trade and, as it turned out, for our local trade. When the 8-percent bankrate was applied, we were literally smothered by overdrafts and rather than go bankrupt we elected, as a family, to go off to work. By taking no more than four pounds per week ($10), we would repay our creditors. Treena worked as a cocktail barmaid, I was a waiter. We paid off our friends.

In 1958 Treena and I had scratched our way up the ladder to General Manager and Manageress of the Royal Ascot Hotel, Ascot, Berkshire. We were twenty-four. Treena lost our second child, and I nearly lost Treena from the complications that attended the birth. I was told that it was the life we led, the pressure. I tried to get a job of similar status where we could close our door. None. It looked like a return to the army, and in desperation I went for an interview. By a curious chain of circumstances I wound up as Chief Catering Adviser to the Royal New Zealand Airforce with the rank of Squadron Leader (Major). My small family set forth, with considerable faith, to cover half the world in search of a good life together. We *were* to find it.

On arrival in New Zealand we possessed less than one pound ($2.60). But I had a good job. I also had ten very interesting years of experience all directed toward *La Cuisine Française.* In 1958 New Zealand contained possibly ten people who were serious gourmets (in the fullest sense). Ninety-nine percent of the population knew nothing of the "finer" aspects of eating. I would talk about Sauce Béchamel, only to be greeted with such comments as "What's that, mate?" "Well it's a white roux-based sauce seasoned with onion, mace and. . .!" "Well, if it's a white sauce, why don't you bloody well call the flipping thing a white sauce and cut out the French crap!" This conversation actually happened between me and a Corporal Cook in an Army Officers' Mess at Fort Dorset in Wellington. I wish I could recall his name. I owe him a great deal, although I didn't appreciate it much at the time!

In 1959, I gave my first series of radio shows for the New Zealand Broadcasting Service called "Cook's Tour"—enough said! In 1961, mine was one of the very first live programs on New Zealand television at AKTV2, Auckland. By this time the hard edges of *La Cuisine Française* had become as softened as my accent had become broadened—both a godsend later! There followed many series of shows for the NZBC that continued after I left the Airforce in 1963. I became a sort of gastronomic entrepreneur. I was a consultant and adviser to many Government Primary Produce Boards and to dozens of private concerns. I organized the first National New Zealand Food and Wine Fair and established the National Food and Wine Centre in Wellington.

Forbidden as I was from directly endorsing anything, I was, during the latter part of 1963 to mid-1965, at the absolute height of my missionary zeal. I really believed in New Zealand as the *Switzerland of the Pacific.* A land of great beauty, enormous agricultural skills, and an unusually highly developed sense of fair play and the rightness of things. I still consider New Zealand a truly great country. Unfortunately a New Zealand theatrical entrepreneur, Harry M. Miller, based in Sydney, Australia, came on the scene. Harry M. proposed that I do a series of television shows in Sydney. Australian television, with its four-channel cities, is very big time against New Zealand's *one!* My overdrive instincts came to the fore, and I agreed for what I thought was a huge sum. It worked, but at what a cost!

I wasn't happy in Australia, nor was Treena. It was undeniably my fault. I suffered variously from big-headedness, compromise, acquisitiveness, boredom, envy—you name it—it happened! I lashed out at everyone near and dear to me and hurt a lot of people. For this, I am truly sorry. If it is any consolation to those who were upset or hurt by my behavior, let me say that I actually lost money on the deal. Every penny I saved during 1965 and 1969 was paid over to business associates of that era. I was actually in the red when Paul Talbot called me from New York with much the same proposition that Harry Miller had put to me—except this time it was for North America.

The "Galloping Gourmet" television series began in January 1969 on WCBS Channel 2, New York, the world's largest television station. What happened then is largely history, but let me add for the record, a short statement. Treena and I produced 600 shows in three years. The speed of production was not our decision; neither was it Paul Talbot's. It was dictated by an industry that uses talent with a frenzy unparalleled in the history of all media. Set our show against that of Julia Child's *"The French Chef"* on the National Educational Television Network. Julia would make 39 episodes a year against our

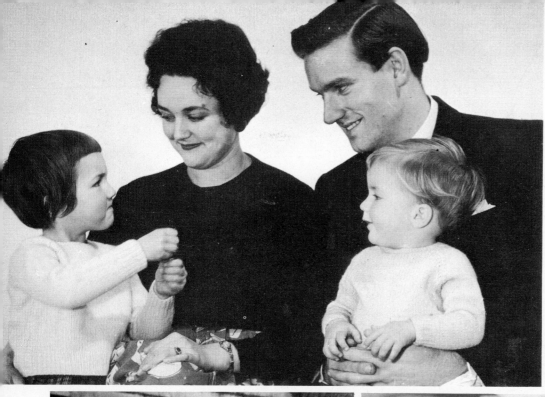

Left to right: Tessa (4), Treena, Graham Kerr and Andrew (18 months) in Wellington, New Zealand.

With first girlfriend, identity unknown (please write).

Sixteen years old, the Don Quixote of the Ashdonon Forest, England.

Graham, Treena and Anne Ramsden, Tenterden, Kent, England, 1955.

Corporal Kerr, Drill and Weapon Training Instructor, Aldershot, 1952.

Second Lieutenant Kerr married to Treena on 22 September 1955.

Officers Candidates Squad, 1952.

Officer in Charge of Catering, Tonfanan Garrison, Wales, United Kingdom.

200. Or put it this way—Julia will have to record her weekly show for over fifteen years to compete numerically! I am not suggesting competition because, if anything, I envy her. I envy her time and her lack of commercial involvement. I use the comparison only to highlight what we said would be an impossible task. It almost was.

Our last programs were made in Ottawa in 1971. We dismounted as "Galloping Gourmets" because we felt we owed our viewers a sincere compliment. We were glad they watched when we did the best we could, and when we felt tired we gave them credit for their ability to detect the change. We wanted to remain friends and not enter into a race that neither side would have wanted the other to lose.

So now I sit here with most every recipe I have ever cooked as the "Galloping Gourmet." Since 1948 they have been hatching—just waiting for this book and you, its reader.

It will never be done again—so here it is,

Just for you!

Reception at Hôtel Meurice, Rue de Rivoli, Paris, France. Graham Kerr and Raymond Olivier being invested as Ambassador des Vins de Cahors, Knight of the Black Truffle and the Grand Order of Rocamador.

FIRST CATCH YOUR APPRECIATION

Before Treena and I began our "Galloping Gourmet" television career, we were a small family of four in a very small apartment. Our days fell upon each other like leaves plucked by the cold wind of Budget. They contained one advantage that we lost for many years—the blessing of time.

We had *time* for each other, *time* for our children and *time* for our friends. The earning of a substantial income has many classic advantages but none can offset the inevitable loss of time. It takes time to cook for other people—one's family and friends. It is time enjoyed or time regretted and the deciding factor is success.

Giving (no matter how unchristian this may sound) isn't worth a tin of fish if there is no appreciation. Love is warmed when reciprocated, so why not the act of giving? Unfortunately, the creation of everyday meals does not always lend itself to congratulations or praise. It is only when guests join your table that you stand a better than even chance of receiving praise and, if I may express it as an equation:

WORK x TIME + PRAISE = SUCCESS OR ENJOYMENT.

Constant praise is, however, very limiting and raises doubts about the reality of success; hence one also needs criticism. This you stand a better than even chance of *not* receiving from your guests, but you can train your family to exercise this rarest form of courage.

Actually, by seeking out criticism of your daily efforts you gain in two ways. Firstly, your confidence increases to a level where you actually want to cook for company and secondly, you stand a better chance of attracting day-to-day praise for your time.

"Audience" reaction is therefore the single most important creative spur to the cook; without it there is little justification for the expenditure of time and it is better spent otherwise. There are individuals who see their culinary activities as unavoidable. They have no audience reaction—yet they spend the same time but receive no satisfaction.

It would be better for those people to adopt a completely different mode of eating based upon liquids and gut-extending roughage combined with a balanced intake of diet pills. They could then apply their timeless lives to other "timefull" pleasures. Apart from the medical drawbacks, this is not an altogether acceptable suggestion largely because of communication.

Whether sought deliberately or not, it is often true that the dining table is the only *tribal contact point* we, as modern men, possess. Visual mass media tend to be excluded from the dining table (with the understandable exception of the morning paper), and a gap is left that can only be filled with a good old-fashioned chat. At the table we actually communicate while we eat. The proposed "pill" people would lose this chance, and we would see the eventual elimination of the family as we accept it today.

The desire to convert time into pleasure is almost universal. Man is incredibly easy to please; all he needs is the opportunity to succeed and be recognized no matter how small the audience. With food, the opportunity is presented daily.

THE LOGICAL KITCHEN

The home kitchen is a confused and confusing place. It is the No Man's Land between liberation and nostalgia; an erratic sea of no opinion.

Confusion breeds commercialization, the impulse purchase overwhelms logic, at least while confusion reigns. I have chosen to pour a little oil on these erratic seas by introducing the element of logic.

It seems *logical* to me that, as the world population grows, we shall have to become accustomed to living closer together. Space on earth will be the most prized of possessions.

Every instinct I possess rebels against the misuse of space. As a cook I abhor material waste; as a designer, my war is with the unnecessary.

The first target is size. At one time it was considered desirable to increase the size of a product in order to justify its price. We now see that society is prepared to accept that good things can come in small packages. A perfect example is the acceptance of the small European car into the big-car-dominated market of North America.

Reduction of physical size does not automatically reduce confusion. The Japanese capitalized upon the transistor and introduced the micro-electric "look" of black and chrome. Because the size had diminished, they sought to give their products a *highly technical instrument* appearance in order to justify the price.

Designers are now moving on to simplicity as a "style" and justify the continued increases on their ability to "deconfuse."

I see all this movement as highly satisfactory and commercially sound. The whole trend is logical. It follows that, as everything gets smaller, we should need less space. The trend should therefore be to the smaller kitchen.

Small kitchens can be suffocating if contained in one small room. They can also become excellent conversation and family centers if combined with their natural partner, the dining room.

My kitchens are always designed to permit a *flexible* contact between guests and hostess. By flexible I mean that the kitchen can be shut off, or opened up as the home cook wishes.

Miniature working kitchens are totally *logical*. When you reduce size and confusion you also eliminate repetition. Implements are purchased because they fulfill more than one function. Service dishes are designed to stack and even the shapes are moving toward rectangles rather than the traditional round or oval.

Logical kitchens have a good food flow. Raw materials enter the kitchen and are sorted into storage adjacent to the preparation areas; *not* put away into larder areas miles from the chopping board.

The entire objective is to reduce bending, stretching and in fact all but the essential working movements.

One is left with an area that is viewed as *somewhat clinical* by those who still manage to peddle nostalgia. There is some truth in this, and this is where color, audio-visual equipment and a sofa can also play their part.

Color is easy. The markets are full of it. But be sure that impulse doesn't overcome logic. Many sets of cooking utensils are "garnished" to appeal, but they simply don't cook well. You can protect yourself by looking for thick bottoms and lids that fit. It's a generality, I know, but with these factors satisfied the rest are simply design details subject to constant change.

Given the natural color of food and the bright, light colors of enamels, I am happy to stay with a muted background of natural wood, stainless steel, parchment-textured white laminate, copper, tinted glass and a cork floor.

Music and television are luxury extras, but if space permits they should be fitted in an area adjacent to or facing the kitchen sofa. This may seem preposterous to you at first glance, but if you install a sofa in *your* kitchen your life immediately takes on another dimension. For me the placing of such a relaxing *conversation corner* in what has hitherto been kept as a straightlaced work area is the ultimate in design being used to redirect "attitude."

I wish to attack nostalgia, wasted space, confusion and bad workmanship because I believe that the future will be filled with more leisure time, and while cooking will almost always be work, I should like to narrow the gap by introducing pleasant surroundings and in so doing to attract people to spend some of their time in the pursuit of other people's pleasure—surely the greatest pleasure of all.

Graham Kerr's boatshed kitchen in Australia

THE DINING TABLE

There is absolutely no doubt in my mind whatsoever that the most significant piece of furniture in the world is the dining table.

It is the *tribal meeting place* for family and friends.

It forms a conference arena for discussing all the world's malfunctions (which I see as the prime motivation for dinner parties).

It is the largest flat area in the house upon which papers, maps, *et al*, can be studied.

It was at a table that Jesus was pictured at the Last Supper. King Arthur had a round one. Modern day politicians argue about the shape before they even begin to talk.

To me, the modern dining table is a *disaster*.

More bad, thoughtless and basically bad design has been lavished upon this vital piece of furniture than on any other material object I know.

It has legs that fight with your legs, undersides that splinter and snag trousers and stockings, surfaces that burn, mark, smear, blister, crack or just feel wrong. Areas impossible to reach to or pass from. Things get cold on it, spill on it. Some *need* covers and these need cleaning. The traditional oblong design causes architects to create dining rooms as "rectangles with ridiculous lighting."

Most home dining rooms have as much ambiance as a miniature warehouse.

All these faults conspire against one of the first essentials in the service of good food.

The French bless 'em, call it *ambiance*; an almost-able-to-be-touched sense of order and well-being and correctness in context with the overall surroundings.

Ambiance is easier to achieve in the restaurant business where a *theme* has been established; the Italian *trattoria*, the French *bistro*, the German *biergarten*. You can always cod up a few gimmicks to induce a feeling of being "in context."

Your home is quite different.

Last year you may have visited Spain or Japan. You may have enjoyed the scenery, the people and their food and wine but you would hardly start redecorating your home to suit!

Your ambiance is your own sense of family taste; the things your family likes. It isn't something delegated to a neglected housewife to placate her natural human drive to achieve.

It is a group decision for your whole family that will project an amalgam of your small world of likes and dislikes.

Your home is a real place in which several real people coexist, not a montage of pages snipped from *House and Garden*.

By all this I'm not exactly discounting a possible theme to be developed in terms of color or type of materials—I'm only suggesting that actual decorator ideas obtained from outside the family group are at best skin deep and almost always completely fail to establish the comfort, cooperation and support that the cook should get from her dining area.

The focal point of this area is the Dining Table. It has many needs, but the most important are: *Comfort; Conversation; Ease of Service;* and *Touch.*

COMFORT

This can be subdivided into chairs, under-table construction and lighting.

Chairs

More designers are involved with chairs than tables. To me, a dining chair should not be required to *double* for anything else. The design must suit the primary function first, second *and* third!

The temptation to rock back and forth on a four-legged chair is removed by the use of a single-based pedestal chair. Similarly four legs tend to negate the impression of space (my main enemy in design is misuse of space). I therefore opt for the generality of a fiber-glass-molded, light-colored, single-pedestal, well-padded, cool-covered, arm-rested chair, in which I can sit in total comfort for three hours. This has yet to be designed to my complete satisfaction (at time of writing).

Under Table Construction

More legs have spoilt more dinners than bad cooks.
As with the chair, so with the table.
No matter what its shape, it must be supported by only one central pedestal.
The undersides must be finished in a soft, smooth, washable, snagless material and have absolutely no projections whatsoever.

Lighting

Candles are so beautiful, so romantic and almost totally unacceptable because:

- They are messy.

- Unless they are raised above forehead level they obstruct visual contact.

- Unless they are at eye level (which clearly creates the worst visibility problem) there is a tendency for them to cast *unflattering* shadows.

- Quite often they simply smell and this is bad for both the food and the wine.

I subscribe to the overhead lighting console—an unobtrusive object not unlike a sea mine, suspended or fixed to the ceiling above the table. The console is lined with a highly reflective material, illuminated by a single high-powered bulb, controlled by a rheostat and provided with simple lens apertures that can be aimed at each dining area.

In this way you don't take up table space. You don't obstruct sight lines. You illuminate the area you need to see and you get "bounced" or diffused light reflected to the face (flattering!). The rheostat also helps to establish and control mood.

CONVERSATION

Long tables designed to keep husband and wife as far apart as possible seem to be a development of the banquet tables of royalty.

The round table has, however, been much more widely used by those who are anxious to communicate and haven't had their dining room made into a narrow rectangle.

The round table is also diplomatic in that there is no head. The curve, while allowing less *width* per place setting, gives far greater elbow room should the butcher have passed off some throbbingly beautiful, bright red (tough) steaks! So providing that the shape of the room permits—it's round for me everytime.

Graham Kerr and his first Galloping Gourmet audience in North America

EASE OF SERVICE

I mentioned on page 304 "The Main Course—Sight" that it is better to present a dish in one piece rather than serve up a lonely spoonful on a tepid plate. The same goes for vegetables. But my God, all that passing back and forth that goes on *and* those tepid plates!

An answer, only to be found with the round table, is to build in a "Lazy Susan heat pad." Essentially, this is a flush-fitted revolving central disc that can receive its heating source through the central pedestal, thereby eliminating the trailing wires of other heating devices.

There needs to be a carving area but this can be achieved by using the host's place setting and having him carve directly onto a platter set on the heated rotunda. Not all the central disc should be heated. One quarter should be insulated to keep the heat from a salad.

Using this technique it should be possible to serve a main dish, its garnish and/or sauce *and* three vegetables plus a salad without lifting one dish! It avoids so many of the "Dinner Party Body Blows" that it appears, if economically possible, to be an essential.

TOUCH

This almost seems like an afterthought whereas in fact it is of the utmost importance.

The use of plastic materials for surfaces has much to commend it but as a covering for a dining table it is, to my mind, absolutely out of court. It is cold, impersonal and cheap (in the worst sense of that word). Less expensive materials are far far better. Red check gingham is super, and so are other inexpensive linens and fiber materials.

Wood has a lovely feel and can be protected by special varnishes to preserve the grain from heat damage. Dark wood has always been favored because of its generally superior grain. Light woods remind people of the immediate postwar, "plain deal" furniture. However, the lighter the wood the less "bulk" it appears to have, and the less space it absorbs.

Figured sycamore has the advantage of being both beautiful and light. It also keeps its appearance by not showing the fine scratch marks that would show up on mahogany or rosewood.

I would therefore go for a sycamore edge with a darker central disc, the color of which could match the tablemats.

THE COST OF LEISURE

Cooking can be viewed as applying to two different groups, *family* and *friends*. Family cooking is part of the job of running the home, regardless of who is in charge. Friend cooking is a hobby, a relaxation. It is part of our leisure time. If you consider it a drag, then take your friends to a restaurant. Home hospitality is too precious to regret; let it come when *you* want to, don't force it! Back to the family.

I simply do not believe a person who tells me that they cook every day because it's their hobby. There are too many unrewarding, repetitive, noncreative tasks in the preparation of an average family meal for it to be a hobby. It's like a political prisoner in Siberia taking up salt carving. Leisure is precious because it allows time to think. People who fill their leisure full of activity *to stop being bored* have low opinions of themselves. More time to explore ways in which "self-opinion" can be increased is, in my view, a superb use of leisure. Once the methods are established, try to make the application short-term. University courses are great personal-opinion builders, but they conspire to defeat leisure, and reduce the time to think. I introduced this apparently random mini-thesis on leisure because I wanted to give some justification for my next idea.

There are times to work and times to enjoy one's leisure. To cook for a family is WORK. People who work are paid. A homemaker receives payment *in kind*—security, accommodation, possessions, love. There is a value to each of these fringe benefits. The homemaker is therefore paid. A nebulous payment per hour rests upon the homemaker's shoulders. She (or he) receives no overtime, no holiday bonus. The task fills a full twenty-four hour span, seven days a week. A cost per hour for labor must be computed. This labor cost should be set against the making of a recipe, especially when deciding upon the so-called low-cost peasant dishes. Had it occurred to you that those original peasants who created the dish had no time for leisure because of their overcrowded, dull, repetitive days? No leisure, no thought. No thought, no progress. No progress kept them exactly where they were!

Don't be a *peasant* in your own home. Figure in your time and make an allowance for leisure. Get to know yourself; it really can be a pleasant surprise for both you and your family.

CHOLESTEROL AND TENSION

This book is filled from end to end with butter, olive oil, cream, milk, cheese, eggs and other saturated animal fats. Obviously I need to make a statement concerning my position with regard to cholesterol. Please understand that I make these observations in anticipation of potential inquiry, and not as an evangelistic lay medical authority! It is my *opinion,* based upon a continuing concern regarding the use of animal fats.

I do agree that excessive consumption of animal fats does increase the cholesterol level, but it also appears that at least two other factors need to be present before this is a fact. The first, and deadliest, is tension—a high-pressure existence—and the second is an equally high carbohydrate intake with heavy concentrations of refined starches. Studies made of the Navaho Indians and the Eskimo people, both of whom ingest huge quantities of animal fats, show little or no cholesterol build-up. Yet when less fat is eaten the high-pressure Western male suffers from serious deposits. I venture to suggest that this equation is the reality:

ANIMAL FAT + TENSION + REFINED STARCHES = CHOLESTEROL

It is in all our interests to reduce each of these if we want to stay alive longer. Contentment and the time to digest need only be added to avoid concern on this matter. My advice is to try to make more time for meals and to take them at the same time each day. Eliminate refined flour and refined sugar altogether, and take animal fats in moderation. Again, please consult your own doctor before accepting this suggestion.

SHOPPING GUIDE

It is difficult to know whether this piece should be entitled "Shopping Guide" or "Human Relations." The truth of the matter is that good shopping is now, more than ever before, a matter of good relations. Last year, government statistics showed that over thirty-six million Americans moved.

We can assume that this means a flood of over ten million new customers, not counting the natural consumer increase. The chance of personal contact with a shopkeeper is becoming less likely. This is due to the population, the movers and retail techniques. The real point is: do we have to just lie back? Is there no way of getting personal service without going for broke? I firmly believe there is. In fact, I believe that it can be easier today than it was in the prime *corner store* days. Because so many people have become accustomed to *shopping by numbers* it is possible for the individualist to seek out and receive personal attention.

The supermarket manager is no less an expert on the goods he sells than "Old Man Crunch of the Corner Store." He has a great deal more to sell numerically, but he still knows what's good and what merely sells because of the price. Also, he is a human being who responds to honest pleas for help in much the same way as you or I would. He has pride, scruples and a sense of rightness. And he is, above all, a businessman who knows the value of the loyal customer who will remain untempted by the skin-deep "pennies-off" approach made by his competitors. I mention this so that you will have confidence to take the next step. If you have just moved, or are plain dissatisfied with your present retailers, ring up your local store and make an appointment to see the manager. Explain that you want to decide upon a suitable store and need only ten minutes of his time to become a possible customer for life! If the manager will not grant you this time, then it is the wrong store for you anyway! Jot down a short list of your past shopping problems, and use these as an agenda at your meeting. Using your list, simply ask how his store will help you solve these problems. Assuming that all is A.O.K. you could then decide to "have a go" for a month.

Be pleasant but firm and always confident that no matter how little you may spend you are a vital link in his pulling power. When you leave his office you have achieved 100 percent of your objective: to become known by the manager. From this moment on you have got your foot in his door. BUT be sure you use it sparingly; your personal contact is only of use when it is kept as insurance against a real rainy day problem. Use the same technique on all your retailers until you have assembled the best all-round marketing situation.

This is especially important with meat, fruit and vegetables, and seafood, and in these latter areas it is essential that you deal with specialists. Remember to adopt a *student* posture with a specialist, be he butcher or baker. The specialist always knows best—he's been at it longer and he has his trade pride. He loves to be able to pass on his knowledge. He is, or at least he can be, flattered. It really is an art to shop well, and like everything else it takes time and experience, plus these brief rules.

- Decide upon a supplier and stick with him.
- Don't chase bargains if you want real service.
- Be pleasant at all times.
- Remain confident that you are a very important customer.
- Ask for advice—don't instruct.
- Don't impulse-buy in excess of your budget.

A SHORT SLURP

I have mentioned elsewhere in the book the effect of population explosion upon the supply of "natural" foods. The effect of population affluence is already being felt within the wine industry and must become increasingly acute, at least at the quality end of the market.

New techniques are being successfully employed to hold wine in good condition in vacuum-packed plastic "bladders." Initially, ideas like these will help to keep wine at a relatively reasonable price but after that—well, the sky's the limit. A great many lovely people have developed a rosy mystique that now completely envelops the purchaser of wine.

There are three groups of wine-buyers:

The serious and dedicated wine-lover.

Those who enjoy a good drop with a meal.

Those who get drunk on it cheaper and/or quicker.

I have no time for the self-indulgence needed at either end of the scale. For me it is enough that I can jot down the names of moderately priced wines that I enjoy and endeavor to find them again (not so easy nowadays). The *initiated* will not be reading this Part so let us *uninitiated* agree on a few small pointers.

Taste appreciation starts with sweet white (Sauternes, Moselle, some Alsace) and gradually goes up the ladder via such steps as sparkling red Burgundy, soft Spanish reds, Chianti, dry whites, to red Burgundy and on to the so-called prince of wines, claret.

Because of the status enjoyed by "wine-lovers," you tend to get "wine fibbers," who want to bask in the same glory without the benefit of time and experience. Wine fibbers *start* on the classic dry red wines. They suck and gurgle away, murmuring quaint phrases about how *"this is a trifle young but it has the right balance to mature into a truly great wine."* This means that it is virtually undrinkable! It also means that the drinker doesn't like it. It can also mean that the drinker may not actually enjoy the taste of wine at all and would have been far happier had he started with an inexpensive sweet white wine. The moral of this little piece is: Don't drink anything just because someone says "it's the right wine" or because it "looks like it should be O.K. by the price." Drink only to quench your thirst with something that appeals to your tastebuds,

BUT

do it soon, before there is nothing left that's worth the drinking!

PART I
KITCHEN BASICS

PART I
KITCHEN BASICS

Certain processes, at least on the savory side, are standard to all recipes. Understanding them can have a widespread effect on almost every dish you cook. I have grouped here some ideas on Stocks, Aspics, Marinades, Thickenings and Butters.

STOCK

Auguste Escoffier is recognized by the culinary profession as a *Master Chef* largely because of his attitude to stocks. He describes them as the absolute basis of good cooking. He taught that any liquid, thin or thick, that was served with any food should contain the flavor of the food it garnishes. In this way the sauce *supports* rather than *masks* the food. It follows that the liquid flavor base (or stock) must have really fine flavor. If it is less than good, a few pennyworth of sauce may ruin the exceedingly expensive meat. A good stock is not, however, an easy thing to produce in the home. Escoffier addressed chefs, not home cooks. A home cook cannot produce multigallon liquids, and even when scaled down the classic stock (estouffade) never quite matches the supreme *reductions* made in huge steam-jacketed boilers.

There are four avenues open to the home cook who wants to grab a slice of glory and add stock. (All of them are better than tap water!)

1. *Scale down the classic estouffade.* This will give you the best result but you need at least a 3-gallon pot and a minimum of 12 hours. It will also be expensive.

2. *Make one of the short stocks that follow.* At this date I suspect that this will give you the most practical alternative to a classic estouffade.

3. *Prepared Stocks.* These come as solid cubes, powders and bottled or canned in liquid form. The *solids* contain monosodium glutamate, which must be used in minute quantities. Unfortunately most manufacturers overdo it. The *liquids* often contain dyed hydrolized protein and are burnt-bitter as a result. I prefer to use a low-mono-sodium-content powder.

4. *Mono-Power Stock Pot.* The equipment is not available at press time. I am currently involved in its design. Essentially it is a large size *stockpot* of greater height than breadth that operates on a coffee percolator basis. More than that I am not at liberty to discuss. (Walls have ears, you know!)

It is important to realize that any flavored liquid added to a sauce, soup, casserole or stew is a stock. Stock can be made from veal (bland taste) as well as from all other meats and poultry. The coconut also produces an exotic stock, especially good in curries. Fish and shellfish stocks are quick to make and very good. Even the water from low-moisture-cooked vegetables makes a valuable contribution. The only real rule is to consider the main "meat" as a close relative and the stock as an intruder. Protect your family and let the intruder support rather than dominate.

ASPIC

An aspic is simply a well-made classical stock using good knuckle bones as part of the recipe. It is then clarified and reduced in volume until, when cooled, it sets. The method of clarification shown for Beef Stock (page 49; Fig. 10 & 11) works well. There are also manufactured aspics that suffer from the overuse of monosodium glutamate. A passable aspic can be made by using pure gelatin powder in the quick stock recipe after careful clarification.

MARINADES

What a dreadful disappointment this can be! Early attempts sometimes put people off using wine in cooking for life. A good marinade serves several functions:

1. It softens tough tissue.
2. It flavors.
3. It can preserve for short periods.

Recipes calling for marinades use wine and/or vinegars, or citrus juices, and contain aromatic vegetables, herbs and a few spices. Like a good stock, marinades should support but obviously they cannot be *of the same family*. Therefore they must be considered as cologne or skin lotion in their bulk state and as perfume in their reduced form.

Only game and tough, cheap meat need to be marinated to make them tender. I think it is a mistake to waste a good wine on poor meat. By the time you get through with the marinade you might as well have bought better, more tender meat in the first place.

Therefore, apart from game, the need for the tenderizing marinade is not great. It is entirely unnecessary in the case of already tender meats, fish and poultry.

The so-called tenderizing agents in a marinade are the acids. The number-one taste enemy is therefore an over-acid wine-based steak marinade. The flavor is acid and completely out of balance. No wonder it turns people off! If the object is to flavor food then the marinade takes on a new look. Much less—if any—acid is needed. Vinegar and lemon or lime juice are banished. That leaves seasoned wine, which is fragrant and delicious—but why so much? Most recipes call for meat to marinate in the marinade. To lie there and soak it up. But meat is roughly 70 percent moisture already! This is where hypo-marinades come in.

HYPOMARINADES

Quite simply this is instant flavor marination. A nonacid, slightly oily, aromatically seasoned wine is injected into the steak, fish or fowl with a long, *blunt* needle fitted into a special kitchen hypodermic syringe. In this way the flavor is introduced into the center of the meat and not into the outer 1/16 inch (2 mm), from which it must be dried with a cloth to permit browning to take place. The quantity of wine needed is much less and the quality much higher.

The last use of marinades is for preservation. Here it combines with tenderizing. The older the meat the greater the enzyme breakdown. This breakdown creates a rapid increase in microorganisms that need to be suppressed. A good acid marinade does this, but the liquid should be drained off and boiled each day to prevent meat spoilage.

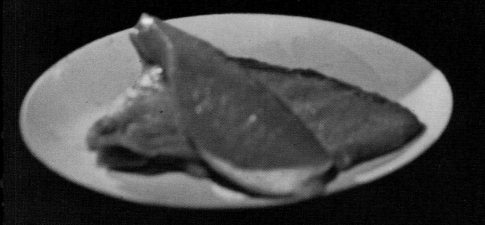

THICKENINGS

Here they are: st-*arch* criminals, all of them, if used poorly. Mastering the correct use of each thickening will eliminate at least *50 percent* of the common reasons for recipe failure.

1. *ROUX.* The classic thickener, using almost equal quantities of plain flour and butter combined over heat until grainy.

2. *LIAISON.* Egg yolks and cream combined and poured into hot but *not boiling* liquid.

3. *BLOOD.* Certain dishes can be thickened with fresh blood (usually chicken's). The same problem occurs as with liaison—it must not boil or it will curdle.

4. *BEURRE MANIE.* Kneaded butter is, like the roux, a combination of plain flour and butter but combined cold. It should be added to boiling liquid but taken off the heat immediately and stirred. Boiling will bring back a strong *flour* taste.

5. *ARROWROOT CREAM.* A paste made from fine-powdered arrowroot and water. When poured into boiling liquid it thickens and clears instantly.

FAILURE FACTORS

ROUX

- Too much roux to liquid. A roux will absorb six times its weight in liquid. Therefore 2 oz (57 g) roux (1 oz: 28 g butter + 1 oz: 28 g flour) x 6 = 12 fl oz (340 g) liquid.

- For a dark roux for brown sauces use clarified butter, as ordinary butter browns at temperatures in excess of 180-205°F (82-96°C).

- Too rapid addition of liquid. The roux forms a miniature dumpling and is almost impossible to break down unless passed through a sieve. Add the liquid gradually, beating at the same time (like a swift mayonnaise).

- Not enough time to cook out. The roux needs at least 15 minutes at a low heat to cook out the raw flour taste—more for a brown roux.

- Too high an initial heat when combining the flour and butter. The starch cell shrivels and will not absorb so much liquid. Therefore if too much roux is used it results in a "flour clog."

LIAISON

- Too much cream. The quantity should be 1 tablespoon per large egg yolk.

- Too hot a pan. Even if the liquid is not boiling the pan can retain heat high enough to curdle the liaison.

- Boiling. Any boiling will produce scrambled eggs!

- Insufficient mixing. Pockets can be missed and these will curdle. I use a 1-inch (2.5 cm) natural-bristle paintbrush—nothing escapes it! (see Sole Vermouth, page 232; Fig. 11).

- Egg white. If the whites are not entirely removed they can form white blobs and make the sauce lumpy. They can, however, be removed by sieving the sauce.

BLOOD

- Too high a temperature. Keep everything just below a simmer, otherwise it will curdle.

- Held too long. Add the blood, let it thicken—then serve instantly.

- Blood not fresh. The blood must be obtained and used the same day. Keep it refrigerated until used.

BEURRE MANIE

- Cooked too long. It only takes a couple of minutes after the introduction of the kneaded butter for it to thicken. Lengthy cooking simply brings back the flour taste.
- Too large pieces. The mixture (slightly more flour than butter) should go through a small hand sieve to keep its smooth, nonlumpy texture. Hard lumps will form dumplings.

ARROWROOT CREAM

- Cooked too long. The advantage of arrowroot is its *instant* ability to clear and leave no taste. If boiled for over 2 minutes it will begin to thin again.
- Too much. One level tablespoon of arrowroot should thicken 1 pint (60 cc) of liquid. More than this and the mixture looks like the last stages of making glue. Add a little, let it thicken, then add more if needed.
- Too shallow pan. If the cream is added to boiling liquid in a frypan the depth could be insufficient. The cream hits the bottom and jells instantly, forming lumps. Better to decant the frypan liquid into a small saucepan.

BUTTERS

I suggest that if you have not as yet used clarified butter for shallow frying then you can make the most immediate and satisfactory change in your food by preparing some. The techniques are given fully on page 54 in step-by-step detail. Sufficient evidence is available at press time to indicate that there are certain health benefits to be gained through its use. Certainly less clarified butter is needed than any other frying ingredient and it is not supposed to be absorbed into the food being fried. My reason for so determinedly supporting its use, however, is for its aroma and flavor. It is a superb kitchen basic. It has the merit of being simple to make and dramatic in use.

CHICKEN STOCK

1 oz (28 g) fresh ginger root*
½ lb (227 g) chicken feet, bones,
    neck, etc.
½ lb (227 g) pork bones
1 oz (28 g) lard or 2 tbs
    clarified butter*
120 fl oz (3.4 l) water

Freshly ground salt
Freshly ground pepper
½ oz (14 g) celery
1 bay leaf
Parsley stalks*
5 water chestnuts

Now cook!

Place clarified butter or lard into a pan and add ginger and chestnuts. Add chicken and pork bones, celery, bay leaf, parsley, seasonings and water. Bring to a boil and simmer for 1 hour. Strain. Makes about 96 fl oz (3 l).

BEEF STOCK

3 lb (1.4 kg) shin of beef meat
1 large onion
1 clove garlic
1 leek
1 carrot
2 parsley stalks*
1 stalk celery

1 tbs freshly ground salt
2 oz (56 g) clarified butter*
48 fl oz (1.5 l) water or
    vegetable broth
1 bay leaf
2 egg whites

First prepare:

Grind meat and vegetables. Beat egg whites until stiff.

Now cook!

1. Mix meat, vegetables and salt.
2. Heat butter and brown meat and vegetables.
3. Add water and bay leaf. Cover and simmer for 30 minutes to 1 hour.
4. Skim off excess fat.
5. Add beaten egg whites to stock. Bring to a boil, reduce heat and bring to a boil again.
6. Skim off egg whites and then strain broth through a double thickness of cheesecloth or muslin. Refrigerate until needed. Makes about 32 fl oz (1 l).

*Tradition is something you
build on—not escape into.*

1. BEEF STOCK. Try to forget the coconut.

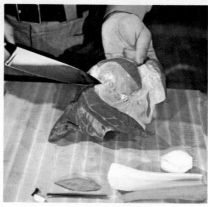

2. Choose beef with as much gristle and sinew as possible.

3. Put the meat and vegetables through a fine blade grinder.

4. Season with freshly ground salt to draw out juices.

5. Fry in very hot clarified butter. Add a little at a time.

6. Add the water or vegetable broth.

7. Cover and simmer for 30 minutes (a full hour if possible).

8. Skim off all surface fat and foam.

9. Pour off all liquid.

10. Add beaten egg whites. Bring to a boil; reduce heat twice.

11. Carefully skim off egg white particles.

12. Sieve once again into a jug ready for use.

FISH STOCK

1 red snapper head
1 medium onion
1 bouquet garni (2 sprigs thyme,
   3-inch stalk (7.6 cm) celery,
   1 bay leaf, 6 parsley sprigs)

20 fl oz (6 dl) water
2 fl oz (5.6 cl) dry white wine
Freshly ground salt
8 peppercorns

Now cook!

1. Place all ingredients into a saucepan. Bring to a boil and skim surface. Allow stock to boil gently for 25 minutes. Cool and then strain. Refrigerate until needed.

FISH FUMET

24 fl oz (7 dl) cold water
1 lb (0.5 kg) fish bones
1 small onion
1 bay leaf

1 small leek
4 white peppercorns
4 celery tops
Pinch of thyme

Now cook!

To the water in saucepan, add fish bones, onion, bay leaf, leek, peppercorns, celery tops and thyme. Place over moderate heat and bring to the boiling point, then simmer for 20 minutes skimming frequently. Strain and reserve liquid. Makes about 16 fl oz (4 dl). Can be used for poaching, for sauces or soups, in gelatin molds, for flavoring in any fish dish.

COCONUT STOCK

8 oz (227 g) dried unsweetened
   coconut

20 fl oz (6 dl) water
Muslin or cheesecloth

Now cook!

1. Boil water—stir in coconut. Place lid on top and steep for 30 minutes.
2. Squeeze out coconut stock through muslin. Makes about 16 fl oz (4 dl).

1. COCONUT STOCK AND CO-
CONUT CREAM.

2. Put grated meat into pan. Cover with boiling water.

3. Lid tightly. The meat now infuses like tea.

4. When the "stock" is cool, strain it into a jug.

5. Press all moisture out of meat. This makes Coconut Cream.

6. Using same meat, infuse again for a thin Coconut Stock.

VEAL JELLY

1 veal knuckle
1 onion
1 bouquet garni (2 sprigs thyme,
   3-inch stalk (7.6 cm) celery,
   1 bay leaf, 6 parsley sprigs)

Freshly ground salt
Freshly ground black peppercorns
Water to cover

Now cook!

1. Place all ingredients together in a saucepan and bring to a boil. Skim surface and allow to simmer for 6 hours until reduced to about 4 fl oz (1.2 dl). Strain and refrigerate. It will set like rubber and can be used as a base for many excellent sauces.

COURT BOUILLON

1 stalk celery
3 sprigs parsley
1 onion
2 lemons
Bones and head of 1 red snapper

64 fl oz (2 l) water
2 tsp freshly ground salt
10 peppercorns
1 bay leaf

First prepare:

Chop vegetables. Juice lemons.

Now cook!

In a saucepan combine all ingredients and simmer uncovered for 20 minutes. Strain liquid through a double thickness of cheesecloth. Cool and refrigerate until needed. Makes about 64 fl oz (2 l).

Clarified Butter

CLARIFIED BUTTER

1 lb (0.5 kg) butter

Now cook!

1. Place butter into at least a 1-quart saucepan over low heat.
2. When butter has melted in 5-6 minutes (depending on heat of element or gas) keep a careful eye on it. A milky substance will rise in small bubbles until entire surface is coated with it. Raise heat a little and this will turn to a foam; skim this off as it forms. Do not throw skimmings away.
3. Remove butter from heat when foam has been removed and allow to settle for a couple of minutes.
4. Pour off new clear butter slowly through muslin to remove sediment that will have fallen to bottom of pan.
5. Refrigerate clarified butter (or keep in a cool place) and use as required.
6. The sediment and butter foam can be used in baked potatoes in their jackets.

1. CLARIFIED BUTTER can be slightly converted to produce an excellent CHILI BUTTER.

2. Salted or unsalted butter is first placed over a low heat in a small saucepan.

3. Let the butter simmer for 10 minutes. During this time the water content steams off. Don't overheat or it will burn.

4. Using a bent soup spoon, skim the foam from the surface. Put these skimmings into a cup or bowl.

5. When the surface is free from foam pour the remaining *clear* butter into another bowl. Stop when the sediment shows.

6. Add the sediment to the foam skimmings and keep this for buttering vegetables.

7. Using very hot pickled chilies remove the "vicious" seeds. Wash your hands *immediately* — don't even *touch* your eyes during the seeding.

8. Cook the herbs, garlic and chili in the clarified butter to infuse their flavor.

9. Sieve and keep in a pot marked "danger."

LEMON PARSLEY BUTTER

4 oz (113 g) butter
1 oz (28 g) minced parsley
½ tsp cayenne pepper

1 fl oz (2.8 cl) lemon juice
1 clove garlic

Now assemble!

Add all ingredients to softened butter. Roll in wax paper to form long roll 1 inch in diameter. Refrigerate until firm. Cut into thin slices and place on meat or fish just before serving.

WHISKY BUTTER

2 fl oz (5.6 cl) whisky
2 oz (56 g) butter
2 oz (56 g) confectioners' sugar

Peel of ½ orange
½ tsp ground coriander

Now assemble!

1. Place finely chopped orange rind in a saucepan with whisky and set alight.
2. Mix softened butter with confectioners' sugar in a bowl and flavor with coriander. Beat in whisky and orange rind residue.
3. Stir to form a smooth sauce. Refrigerate.

ANCHOVY BUTTER

1½ oz (42 g) butter
1 tsp anchovy paste

1 tbs minced parsley

Now assemble!

Place butter, anchovy paste and parsley on a board and work together until smooth with a knife. Place in a bowl and refrigerate till needed.

ASPIC JELLY

Rabbit bones and carcass
Goose bones and carcass
(or other poultry bones)
1 onion
1 bay leaf

Bouquet garni
8 peppercorns
80 fl oz (2.3 l) water
2 envelopes unflavored gelatin
1 egg white

Now cook!

1. Place rabbit and goose bones into a large pot and cover with water. Add bay leaf, onion cut in half, bouquet garni and peppercorns. Bring to a boil; skim the surface and then allow to simmer 4 hours. Add salt to taste; strain through a fine sieve. Allow to cool and remove fat.
2. Place stock into a saucepan with egg white. Stir and bring to a boil; remove from heat. Replace on heat and allow to come to a boil once more. Remove from heat and strain liquid through muslin into a bowl.
3. Mix gelatin with a little cold water and add to hot stock. Stir until dissolved. Allow to cool. Chill.

DIAMOND HEAD SOLE

For 4 servings, you will need:

2 whole sole (4 fillets)
8 raw jumbo shrimp, shelled
 and deveined
2 hard-boiled eggs
Salt
White pepper
6 slices pimento (canned
 red capsicum)
2 tbs dill
1 tbs gelatin (1 envelope)

Lemon juice
Fish Stock:
1 large snapper head and
 sole trimmings
1 large onion
Bouquet garni
6 peppercorns
4 fl oz (1.2 dl) dry white wine
40 fl oz (1.2 l) water

First prepare:

Fish stock: Place all ingredients in saucepan and bring to a boil. Skim surface and then allow to simmer 25 minutes. Strain and clarify (see below). Fillet sole removing skin. Cook shrimp. Hard-boil eggs 10 minutes. Cut eggs into thin slices with egg slicer. Wash and finely chop dill. Finely slice 2 tbs of the pimento. Add a little cold water to gelatin and then mix with 20 fl oz (6 dl) of the warm fish stock. Add lemon juice, stir until dissolved and then allow to cool. Place a ½-quart aspic mold into refrigerator.

Now cook!

1. Take cold mold and pour a ¼-inch layer of the slightly jellied stock into the bottom. Place in refrigerator until firm. When set remove and garnish with 8 slices of egg. Add another thin layer of jellied stock and refrigerate again.

2. Make sure the entire sand tract is removed from shrimp. Roll shrimp in sole fillets and place in a large frypan containing 20 fl oz (6 dl) of the fish stock. Season with salt and pepper; cover with well-buttered paper and lid and place on low heat to poach 5 minutes. Remove fish and allow to cool on a dish.

3. Remove mold from refrigerator and cover egg base with 2 tbs pimento and 2 tbs dill and arrange cooled sole on top. Cover with thin slices of pimento. Add enough jellied stock to cover and then refrigerate again. When set (about 1 hour) remove and dip mold into a bowl containing hot water. Invert onto a service dish.

A special hint:

To clarify fish stock. Clarify by adding 1 raw egg white. Bring stock to a boil whisking all the time and then remove from heat when frothing. Place back onto heat, bring to the boil once more. Remove and pour cleared stock through a sieve covered by muslin.

LE DIPLOMATE

For 4 servings, you will need:

20 Boudoir Biscuits*	*Wine jelly:*
10 fl oz (3 dl) milk	Peel of 1 lemon
4 oz (113 g) sugar	3 fl oz (8 cl) lemon juice
3 egg yolks	30 fl oz (9 dl) cold water
¾ oz (21 g) unflavored	6 oz (170 g) cube sugar
gelatin	2 oz (56 g) unflavored gelatin
2 fl oz (5.6 cl) marsala	2 eggs
5 fl oz (1.5 dl) heavy cream	8 fl oz (2 dl) dry sherry
Glacé cherries*	2 fl oz (5.6 cl) brandy
Vanilla bean	Red food coloring
Angelica	Muslin or cheesecloth

First prepare:

Wine jelly: Peel rind from lemon. Juice lemon. Separate whites of eggs from yolks. Crush and keep eggshells. Measure gelatin, brandy and sherry. A large pan, a piece of muslin and ice cubes will be needed.

Cream filling: Trim biscuits to fit a deep round charlotte mold about 1½ quarts (make allowance for ½ inch of jelly on bottom). Crush remaining biscuits. Weigh dry ingredients, whip cream and soak crushed biscuits in marsala. Beat egg yolks in bowl.

Now cook!

1. In a saucepan place lemon peel in cold water. Stir in sugar and gelatin. Bring to a simmer but do not boil.

2. Place crushed eggshells into gelatin mixture. Beat the egg whites until frothy.

3. The gelatin will be close to boiling point now. Add lemon juice and whisk liquid until it rises to the boil again. Add sherry and brandy.

4. Bring back to boiling once again and whisk.

5. Remove pan from heat and allow to settle for a few minutes.

6. Place muslin over a hand sieve and rest it on a bowl. Pour liquid through and if it is still not clear—strain again. Add coloring to make a deep red and chill until slightly thickened.

7. Place mold in a bowl of ice and gently pour a little jelly down the sides. Roll it around the bottom until the sides and bottom are evenly coated in a thin layer (about 1/16 inch thick).

8. Decorate the bottom with cherries and angelica and cover with a thin layer of jelly to secure. Chill on ice until firm.

9. Line mold with precut biscuits and spoon over remaining jelly to keep them firmly in place. Refrigerate until firm.

10. Scald milk in a saucepan—add vanilla bean and sugar—bring to a boil.

11. Remove milk from heat and remove bean.

12. Gradually beat flavored milk into beaten egg yolks in a bowl.

13. Return this mixture to saucepan and stir over low heat until thick.

14. Stir in gelatin mixed with 2 tbs water until dissolved. Pour this into a bowl and refrigerate until slightly thickened.

15. Whisk again and fold in marsala and crushed biscuits. Fold in cream.

16. Pour this into center of mold and refrigerate until set.

17. To unmold—float mold in a bowl of piping hot water for a few seconds and turn upside down on a serving dish.

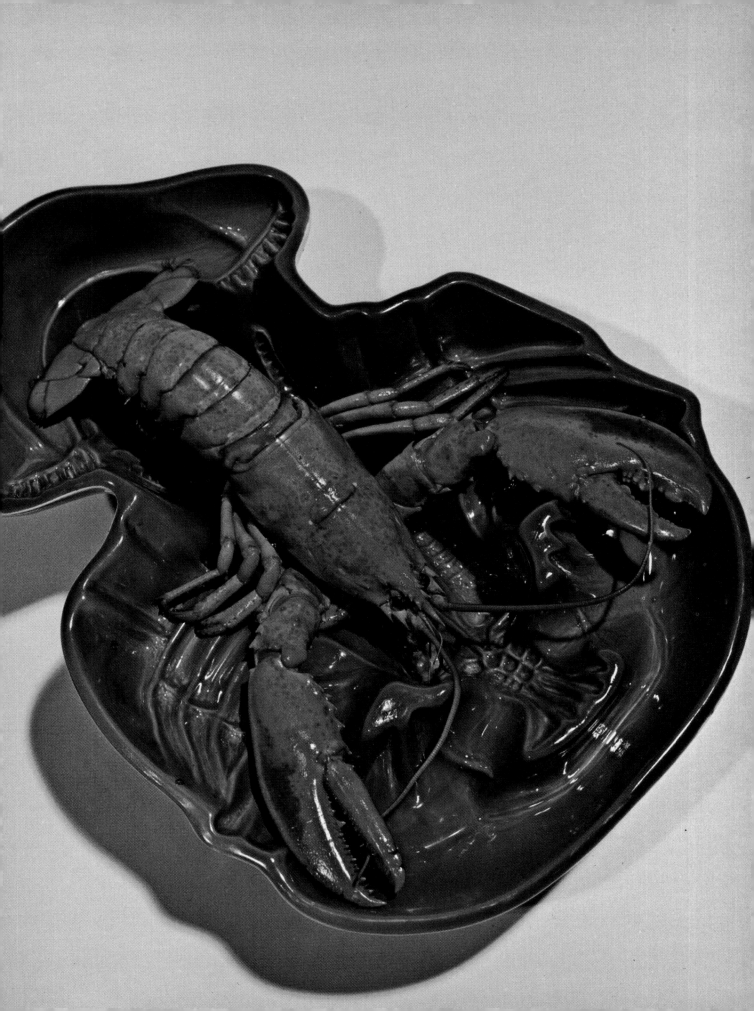

APPLE ANDY

For 6 servings, you will need:

22 fl oz (6.5 dl) apple cider
1 lemon
2 small apples
1 tbs Cointreau
1 tbs water
½ oz (14 g) unflavored
   gelatin

12 oz (339 g) cream cheese
1½ eggs
1 fl oz (2.8 cl) brandy
2 oz (56 g) sugar
Peel from ½ orange

First prepare:

Squeeze lemon. Slice peel *very* fine. Measure Cointreau, water, gelatin, cream cheese, brandy and sugar. Core apples. Measure cider. Cut about ¼ inch off top of apples.

Now assemble!

1. Pour cider and lemon juice into a pan, bring to a boil; then cool.
2. Dissolve gelatin in water over very low heat. Stir in Cointreau and apple cider.
3. Slice apples thinly.
4. Divide apples between 6 small serving bowls. They should be about ½ inch below the top of the bowl.
5. Pour cooled cider mixture over apples and refrigerate until set.
6. In a bowl, mix cheese, eggs, brandy, sugar and orange rind. Mash mixture together.
7. Whisk to ensure there are no lumps.
8. Pour cream mixture over set apple jelly and refrigerate until set.
9. When firm, unmold serving bowls. (Running a heated knife around the outer edge of the jelly will help.) If you find difficulty unmolding, place a hot towel around bowl to loosen mixture.

PART II
FIRST COURSES

PART II
FIRST COURSES

A leading and rather obdurate headwaiter I know always leans upon his guests with the command, "First decide on the main course, then choose the starter." This is good advice for a restaurant night out but it doesn't make much sense at home.

First courses should be tailor-made for the diner and the climate. The object should be to enliven the palate not kill it. Too rich and it will cause a revolution later in the meal. If your guest has a sedentary job, is over forty years of age and the weather is warm, then the first course should be light, cold and stimulating. On the other hand if your friend is active and the weather is cold, then let the first course be warming and substantial. Wise selection with your guests and the weather in mind will precondition their attitude to the star performance. I have collected in this section a pretty wide choice of *starters*. They include pâtés, snails, pasta, soups of most kinds, fondues and small seafood dishes as well as a collection of miscellaneous ideas.

PATES OR TERRINES

For my money a homemade *pâté* or *terrine* in an excellent starter. Only the portion size determines the effect upon the remaining appetite. The main difference between a pâté and terrine is its presentation. A pâté is cooked in a pastry or bread crust while a terrine is cooked in, and often served from, a china or enameled covered dish.

Of the two I prefer the terrine for both ease of cooking and serving. You can divide either type into another two categories—*smooth* and *rough*. (There are also terrines that have whole slices of meat or game set in layers with the forcemeat.) The very fine smooth "emulsified" texture is popular in the *haute cuisine* belt. The rough ground mixture is more farmhouse. I prefer the rougher texture because it makes a clear distinction between homemade and that revolting *pâté de foie gras*, a product made from the misery of force-fed geese.

SNAILS AND FROGS' LEGS

I call this "siege" food (food to be eaten when there is nothing else to be had) and frankly, I prefer to think that those whose tastes venture into the bizarre, do so more for the garlic butter than for the wet, slimy, calcium-encased slug!

PASTA

My choice for pure self-satisfaction would be to make and serve fresh my own pasta. It is hard work but not nearly so lengthy as bread making. The only trick, if you call it that, is to roll the paste as thin as tissue paper. Remember it almost doubles in size when boiled. Good tender pasta tossed in butter, bathed in cream, liberally dusted with Parmesan cheese and topped with thin slices of white truffle, is a dish among the absolute top ten.

SOUPS

Because of its great variety, soup is always the right choice as a starter. Some different kinds of soup are:

Bisques. Usually shellfish-based, thick, creamy and very rich.

Soup Stews. Again seafood, excellent for a meal-in-one.

Naturally Thick. These rely only upon their ingredients and reduction to create a solid, almost always highly nutritious, soup. Fine for really cold weather and heavy eaters.

Thickened. As a rule these are less nutritious than those that thicken naturally, but they are also excellent rib-sticking fare for bad weather.

Clear. A real appetite builder for those with jaded palates but great care needs to be exercised in its preparation. It must be absolutely clear and sufficiently viscous to *just* stick your lips together.

Cold. Either a jellied cold soup which has the same limitations as the hot clear soup, or a whole collection of raw vegetables and fish soups. All are excellent interest developers for bored, listless, uncomfortable people that you shouldn't have invited home in the first place.

One word of warning. The thicker or heavier the soup the greater the need to reduce cooking time. The longer vegetables cook the fewer vitamins survive. The thicker the soup the more appetite it satisfies. Therefore if the soup is overcooked and has only slight food value the appetite is being quenched by useless gut-stretching slush. (Think about this when serving pre-packaged soups: check the label for food value first.)

FONDUE

Not so much a first course as a traditional means of becoming constipated. I have given you a classical (and expensive) Swiss fondue together with some most unusual ideas for both a fish fondue and one that uses chicken stock in lieu of wine. Frankly this is round-the-fire-on-a-cold-night-food and not recommended as up-front inspiration!

SEAFOOD FIRSTS

Almost the number one choice in restaurants around the world is the Prawn or Shrimp Cocktail. There are also many other good first course ideas with seafood and I use them more often than any of the other headings. With the first course I strive for delicacy and real interest. You really must force the guest's attention away from the humdrum activities of his day and give him confidence in the delights to come.

Graham Kerr Pâté (page 66)

GRAHAM KERR PATE

GG
60

For 10 to 15 servings, you will need:

1 lb (0.5 kg) pork liver
½ lb (227 g) neck of pork
4 oz (113 g) bacon*
8 oz (227 g) bacon rashers*
2 shallots (or large spring
   onions)
2 eggs
1 tsp freshly ground black pepper
½ tsp nutmeg

½ bay leaf
½ tsp crumbled thyme
3 oz (85 g) mushrooms
2 to 3 cloves garlic
2 fl oz (5.6 cl) brandy
½ oz (14 g) parsley stalks*
8 fl oz (2 dl) white sauce
   (see page 491)
6 tbs clarified butter*

First prepare:

Preheat oven to 450ºF (232ºC). Remove sinews and dice liver. Cut pork into 1-inch (2.5 cm) cubes. Cut off bacon rind and cut into 1-inch (2.5 cm) cubes. Cut rind off bacon rashers. Break bay leaf into pieces. Peel and slice mushrooms. Peel and smash garlic. Finely chop parsley stalks. Slice shallots and mushrooms.

Now cook!

1. Put liver, 4 oz bacon and pork meat through fine blade of meat grinder, once and put in mixing bowl.

2. Add shallots (or spring onions), parsley stalks and mushrooms.

3. Break in eggs, add cold white sauce and season with ground pepper, nutmeg and garlic.

4. Blend together well and add brandy.

5. Take a 40 fl oz (1.2 l) earthenware or enamel ovenproof container and lay strips of bacon rashers to cover inside completely.

6. Fill with mixture and smooth surface. Place bay leaf pieces and thyme on surface, cover with lid and place in a roasting pan, half filled with water.

7. Place pan and container into heated oven 450ºF (232ºC) and bake for 1 hour; check that water in roasting pan does not evaporate; refill if necessary.

8. Test for "doneness" with a needle or skewer driven into center of mixture; if it comes out clean, it is cooked. (A meat thermometer can also be used—treat as for pork— well done 185ºF: 85ºC.)

9. Remove from oven and allow to cool for 30 minutes; then place a piece of board cut to shape of container on top of cooled mixture. Place a 2- to 3-lb (1 to 1½ kg) weight on board.

10. Leave weight in position until mixture is throughly cold. Loosen edges and unmold. Cut into slices to serve.

A special hint:

To keep pâté: unmold, take off bacon rashers, rinse mold clean replace pâté and cover with 8 tbs clarified butter. Tie on foil and store in refrigerator. Will keep at least 14 days.

GG

*You cannot buy hospitality
with a credit card.*

1. GRAHAM KERR PATE. My variation of a standard terrine.

2. Trim heavy rind from meat but don't remove too much fat.

3. The meat is first finely ground.

4. A very good stiff white sauce is made.

5. Season the sauce with peppercorns, nutmeg and garlic.

6. Slice mushrooms in ¼-inch (7 mm) thick pieces.

7. Add eggs to bind the mix.

8. Add brandy.

9. Finally beat in the stiff white sauce.

10. Set terrine with air hole in lid in waterbath. Top with herbs.

11. Cover and bake *or* use meat thermometer; done at 185°F (85°C).

12. When cooked, cover with board with heavy weights on top.

PHEASANT PATE

For 10 servings, you will need:

1 rabbit	Freshly ground salt
1 leg of goose	Freshly ground pepper
1 breast of goose	½ tsp allspice
3 bacon rashers*	1 tsp mace
1 lb 6 oz (623 g) pork liver	2 eggs
8 oz (227 g) ground pork sausage meat	1 fl oz (2.8 cl) brandy
5 oz (142 g) venison or elk	1 bay leaf
1 medium onion	6 bacon rashers to line mold*
1 clove garlic	30 fl oz (9 dl) aspic jelly
	1 tbs dill

First prepare:

Remove neck from rabbit, rinse and dry thoroughly. Spread out on a broiler rack in a baking dish. Cover with bacon rashers. Place goose leg and breast onto broiler rack, prick flesh, paint with a little clarified butter and roast both meats in a 350⁰F (177⁰C) oven (the rabbit for 1 hour and the goose for 1 hour 15 minutes). Remove from oven, allow to cool and slice finely 3 oz (85 g) goose and 3 oz (85 g) rabbit.

Put pork liver, pork sausage and venison through fine blade of a grinder. Grind onion. Line base and side of 1½-quart ovenproof mold with fat bacon. Preheat oven to 450⁰F (232⁰C). Finely chop dill. Make aspic jelly from goose and rabbit stock.

Now cook!

1. Place ground meats and onion into a bowl. Add smashed garlic and season with salt, pepper, allspice and mace. Mix with eggs and flavor with brandy. Fill bacon-lined mold. Place bay leaf on top, cover with a lid and put into a pan containing hot water and half cover. Bake for 1 hour.

2. Remove pâté. Take off lid and place a heavy weight on pâté and allow to cool. When cooled remove pâté from mold by placing in hot water for 5 seconds and inverting onto a dish. Cut pâté in half crosswise into 2 layers. Wash mold.

3. Spoon a ¼-inch (7 mm) layer of aspic jelly in mold, put in refrigerator and allow to set. When set, place a slice of pâté on top, barely cover with more aspic jelly and refrigerate until set. When second layer of jelly has set, cover it with a layer of goose slices, a layer of dill and then rabbit slices. Season with salt and pepper and cover with second layer of pâté. Add aspic jelly to just cover surface, lifting top layer of pâté to allow aspic to run into center of mold. Refrigerate and allow to set 4 hours.

4. Dip mold into hot water and then invert onto serving dish.

Aspic Jelly

Rabbit bones and carcass	Bouquet garni
Goose bones and carcass (or other poultry bones)	8 peppercorns
	80 fl oz (2.3 l) water
1 onion	2 envelopes unflavored gelatin
1 bay leaf	1 egg white

1. Place goose and rabbit bones into a large pot, cover with water, add bay leaf, onion cut in half, bouquet garni and peppercorns. Bring to a boil, skim surface and simmer 4 hours. Add salt to taste and strain through a fine sieve. Allow to cool and remove fat.

2. Put stock in a saucepan with 1 egg white. Stir stock, bring to a boil and remove from heat. Replace on heat and bring to a boil once more. Remove from heat and strain liquid through muslin into a bowl.

3. Mix gelatin with a little cold water and add to hot stock. Stir until dissolved. Allow to cool. Chill.

Service:

Can be used as a first course for 8 to 10 people. Or as a cold, but rich, main dish for 6 on a hot day.

A special hint:

Slice pâté in half lengthways in 1-inch (2.5 cm) slices. Trim edges very lightly.

SMOKED FISH PATE ·

For 6 servings, you will need:

3 lbs (1.4 kg) smoked haddock
1 lb (0.5 kg) tomatoes
2 red peppers (capsicum)
1 clove garlic
1 onion
6 tbs clarified butter*
2 eggs
6 oz (170 g) bread crumbs
   soaked in milk and then
   squeezed dry*
1 tsp each chives and basil
Freshly ground salt

Freshly ground black pepper
1 bay leaf
Pinch saffron
1 lb (0.5 kg) puff pastry*
2 tbs parsley
1 lemon
Court Bouillon:
2 fl oz (5.6 cl) white wine
   vinegar
40 fl oz (1.2 l) water
12 black peppercorns
3 bay leaves

70

First prepare:

Peel tomatoes and slice. Slice peppers finely. Make court bouillon. Finely chop chives. Roll out pastry. Preheat oven to 400°F (205°C). Juice lemon. Finely chop onion.

Place all ingredients together in a saucepan and bring to a boil. Simmer 10 minutes and cool.

Now cook!

1. Place fish in cold court bouillon, cover pan and bring court bouillon slowly to a boil. Drain fish, remove skin and crush with a fork.

2. Place clarified butter in a frypan to just cover bottom, add onion, garlic and peppers. Fry gently until wilted and add tomatoes. Season with salt and pepper. Add basil, chives, parsley and bay leaf. Fry gently for a few minutes and then add this mixture to mashed fish. Press mixture in a sieve to remove excess juices and reserve juice.

3. Beat eggs and add to fish mixture with bread crumbs and saffron. Adjust seasoning and allow to cool.

4. Roll pastry into a 12-inch circle. Place fish mixture in center and fold up the edges of the pastry to meet in the middle of top and dampen with water to secure edges, forming a large "pasty" with sealed edge on top. Paint with egg yolk. Make light incisions in diamond shapes across pastry with dull back of knife. Bake on a cookie sheet for 30 minutes.

5. Place reserved juices from vegetables into a saucepan, add lemon juice and heat but do not boil. Serve separately in a sauceboat.

A special hint:

Be sure to press all moisture from mix at end of Step 2, otherwise it will be hard to keep fish sealed in crust.

GAME TERRINE

For 10 servings, you will need:

1 lb (0.5 kg) pheasant meat
½ lb (227 g) rabbit
3½ oz (100 g) neck of pork
3½ oz (100 g) goose breast
3½ oz (100 g) veal fillet
2 oz (56 g) bacon*

Marinade:

2 oz (56 g) shallots
Skin from 1 Granny Smith apple*
1 tbs parsley stalks*
2 juniper berries
Sprig thyme
Sprig basil or ½ tsp dried basil
3 fl oz (8 cl) dry white wine
3 fl oz (8 cl) Madeira
2 fl oz (5.6 cl) cognac
Clarified butter*

2 oz (56 g) champignons (French mushrooms)
½ oz (14 g) dried morels (a special dried mushroom)
Rind of ½ orange
Rind of ½ lemon
1 oz (28 g) skinned pistachio nuts
½ oz (14 g) truffle*
3 fl oz (8 cl) dry red wine
Freshly ground salt
Freshly ground black pepper
2 tsp paprika
1 fl oz (2.8 cl) Calvados
2 eggs
4 fl oz (1.2 dl) heavy cream
1 bay leaf
Fat bacon to line terrine mold*

First prepare:

All meat should be boneless and skinless. Cut meat finely and place in a bowl. Lightly bruise shallots and add to meat. Add parsley stalks finely cut and the apple skin finely sliced. Put juniper berries, thyme and basil into a muslin bag, tie up and put with meat. Add wine, Madeira and cognac. Cover and leave to marinate 3 days in refrigerator. After 3 days remove herbs and shallots and dry meat well.

Soak dried morels in cold water for ½ hour and drain. Remove rind from orange and lemon with potato parer. Slice truffle finely. Measure wine. Line a 2-quart terrine mold with fatty overlapping bacon slices. Preheat oven to 425°F (218°C). Whip cream. Slice champignons.

Now cook!

1. Place some clarified butter in a large frypan to just cover bottom and when hot add dried meat and brown on all sides.

2. Into another pan put 2 tbs clarified butter and add champignons and morels. Fry lightly and add orange and lemon rind, pistachio nuts and truffle. Fry together for a few minutes.

3. Discard lemon and orange rind. Add champignon mixture to meat. Put through finest blade of grinder.

4. Deglaze frypan in which meat was browned with red wine and allow to reduce to 4 fl oz (1.2 dl). Add to meat, season with salt, pepper, paprika and Calvados and mix with eggs. Fold in cream and pour into lined terrine. Put bay leaf on top and cover.

5. Place terrine into a pan containing enough hot water to come halfway up sides, cover and cook 1 hour, or until meat thermometer reads 185°F (85°C).

6. Remove terrine from oven, remove lid, place a heavy weight on top and put in refrigerator to cool.

Service:

Unmold terrine, remove bacon slices, wash terrine and replace mixture. Seal top with clarified butter. It can be served with buttered or plain toast fingers.

STUFFED CHICKEN NECKS

For 2 servings, you will need:

4 oz (113 g) veal tenderloin
4 oz (113 g) pork tenderloin
4 oz (113 g) chicken livers
4 oz (113 g) chicken fat
1 truffle and truffle juice*
   (from the can)

16 fl oz (4.7 dl) veal or chicken
   stock
12 chicken necks (or 3 goose necks)
Freshly ground salt
Freshly ground black pepper

71

First prepare:

Remove skin from chicken necks. Keep bones for stock. Make sure muscular pipe is also taken out. Grind meats together. Finely slice truffle and add it and truffle juice to ground meat. Measure chicken fat removed from top of chicken stock. Small wooden skewers will be required.

Now cook!

1. Season ground meats and truffle generously with salt and black pepper. Stir in chicken fat.
2. Close one end of chicken neck skins with a wooden skewer.
3. Fill little sacs with seasoned meats.
4. Secure other end of filled pouches with wooden skewers and tie with a piece of string.
5. Place in a pot of veal or chicken stock and cook gently for ½ hour.
6. Then cool in stock and cut into slices. They are ready to serve as an hors d'oeuvre when thoroughly chilled.

SMOKED HADDOCK MOUSSE

For 2 servings, you will need:

1 lb (0.5 kg) smoked haddock
   fillet
4 fl oz (1.2 dl) milk
2 hard-boiled eggs
2 oz (56 g) softened butter

½ tsp cayenne pepper
½ tsp nutmeg
½ tsp mace
Freshly ground salt
Freshly ground white pepper

71

First prepare:

Remove skin and bones from fish and cut into small pieces (1 inch: 2.5 cm cubes). Hard-boil eggs. Measure milk.

Now cook!

1. Place fish with milk in a pan, cover and poach fish for 5 minutes. Remove fish with a slotted spoon and put in blender. Add eggs, butter, ⅜ of poaching milk, nutmeg, mace and cayenne pepper. Add salt and pepper. Blend until very smooth.
2. Place mousse into 2 small 1-cup pots, cover with a piece of plastic film and allow to set in refrigerator overnight.
3. Remove from refrigerator, dip into hot water for 5 seconds and invert onto serving dishes.

Service:

Serve in very small portions with hot toast fingers and lemon wedges. It is eaten by spreading mousse on toast and adding lemon juice to taste.

SMOKED SALMON CORNETS

71

For 6 servings, you will need:

8 oz (227 g) smoked salmon cut
   in 4-inch (10 cm) square
   slices (very thin)
12 oz (340 g) medium raw
   shrimp (shelled weight)
3 oz (84 g) butter
1 oz (28 g) all-purpose flour

2 tbs clarified butter*
1 bay leaf
3 black peppercorns
8 fl oz (2 dl) milk
8 fl oz (2 dl) heavy cream
Freshly ground salt
Freshly ground white pepper

First prepare:

You will need 6 tinplate French Cream Horn molds for this dish. Cut smoked salmon into 6 squares, peel raw shrimp. Measure cream and milk. A large bowl containing ice cubes will be required.

Now cook!

1. Pour enough clarified butter to just cover bottom into a hot frypan. Add shrimp, stirring constantly until evenly coated.

2. Season with salt.

3. In a second pan melt 1 oz (28 g) butter and then add flour. Cook stirring for 3 minutes. Gradually stir in milk and add bay leaf and peppercorns. Blend all ingredients with wooden spoon. Increase heat to boiling point and stir until mixture thickens. Reduce heat and simmer.

4. Grind white pepper over shrimp and add 2 oz (56 g) butter.

5. Sieve the sauce into a bowl removing bay leaf and peppercorns. Add sauce to buttered shrimp.

6. Add 4 fl oz (1.2 dl) cream to sauce and pour everything into blender. Whirl at low speed, slowly adding 2 fl oz (5.6 cl) cream. Increase speed and slowly add remaining 2 fl oz (5.6 cl) cream. Season with salt and pepper.

7. Pour sauce into a bowl and place over a bowl of ice to cool. Stir this superb creamy mixture to speed cooling.

8. Line a cream horn mold with a piece of salmon. Spoon creamy cooled mixture into a pastry bag and, using a ½-inch (1.2 cm) rose nozzle, pipe it into the center of smoked salmon and let it cool under refrigeration.

9. Remove smoked salmon cornets from refrigerator, slide them gently from molds to a plate and serve.

A special hint:

In Step 6, add cream slowly, otherwise mix may curdle.

Waste more than taste marks the poor cook.

TERRINE DE HOMARD MOUSSELINE

For 4 servings, you will need:

5 oz (142 g) lobster meat
  1½ lb (680 g) live weight lobster
9 oz (255 g) pike (meat
  weight only)
6 oz (170 g) mushrooms
1 medium onion
1 clove garlic
2 large tomatoes
1 fl oz (2.8 cl) brandy

8 fl oz (2 dl) dry white wine
8 fl oz (2 dl) heavy cream
2 eggs
Parsley
1 tsp arrowroot
1 tbs heavy cream
Clarified butter*
Freshly ground white pepper
Freshly ground salt

First prepare:

Place live lobster in a sink of blood heat water (it is at this temperature that scientists say all edible shellfish die with the least discomfort). Remove and crack open and take out meat. Reserve shells. Wash mushrooms, blanch in a pan of boiling water and drain. Slice tomatoes into thick rings, then cut these pieces in half. Finely slice onion, smash garlic. Measure brandy, wine and cream. Separate whites from egg yolks and set aside. Wash and chop parsley, blend arrowroot with 1 tbs cream. Heat a serving platter in warm oven. Assemble a grinder with a very fine blade. Preheat oven to 300ºF (149ºC).

Now cook!

1. Put both pike and lobster meat through grinder. Keep in a bowl set in another bowl of ice.

2. Into a hot frypan place enough clarified butter to just cover bottom and add onion and garlic. Pop in lobster shells and simmer gently.

3. Add 1 fl oz (2.8 cl) brandy and set it alight. Pour in white wine, cover and continue cooking over a low heat.

4. Put blanched mushrooms through grinder and add to chilled fish. Carefully blend in 8 fl oz (2 dl) cream and season generously with salt and white pepper.

5. Beat two egg whites and fold into fish. Pour this mixture into 2 to 3 cup molds, cover with foil and set them in a "bain-marie" (bath of hot water).

6. Bake in preheated oven 300ºF (149ºC) for 30 minutes. Remove foil after this period and bake uncovered for another 30 minutes.

7. Strain stock from lobster shells (approximately 6 fl oz: 1.6 dl will be left), pour into a heated pan, increase temperature and add tomatoes. Simmer.

8. Remove baked fish molds from oven and unmold onto heated serving platter.

9. Sieve tomato stock mixture into a saucepan pushing through as much tomato flesh as possible. Stir 2 egg yolks and blended arrowroot into this sieved stock. Return to heat and stir until sauce thickens—it shouldn't boil. Pour sauce over fish molds, dust with chopped parsley and serve.

ESCARGOT TRUFFIERE

For 6 servings, you will need:

2 cans snails (48 large)
2 tbs clarified butter*
1 oz (28 g) all-purpose flour
3 oz (85 g) tomato paste
Bouquet garni (celery stalk,
 bay leaf, sweet basil, parsley,
 thyme, black peppercorns)

12 fl oz (3.2 dl) red Burgundy wine
2 oz (56 g) fresh ham
1 truffle*
Freshly ground salt
Freshly ground black pepper

First prepare:

Drain snails and rinse them under cold running water. Sift flour. Measure butter, wine and tomato paste. Cut ham into tiny cubes. Dice truffle. Tie herbs in small piece of cheese-cloth to make bouquet garni. Place snail shells in a dish on a bed of rock salt. Preheat oven to 400°F (205°C).

Now cook!

1. Heat a pan and melt clarified butter. Stir in flour and cook two or three minutes over moderate heat.
2. Add tomato paste and slowly stir in wine. Add bouquet garni. Allow to cook gently for 30 minutes, stirring occasionally.
3. Add ham to bubbling sauce and season with salt and black pepper.
4. Add snails. Simmer over low heat for 10 minutes.
5. Add truffle and stir thoroughly.
6. Sieve snails—reserving the rich sauce—and place snails into shells and top shells with sauce.
7. Place in preheated 400°F (205°C) oven until sauce in shells starts to bubble, about 5 minutes.

A special hint:

Snails are much easier eaten with proper snail "holders" and snail forks. Look for some in a good kitchenware shop.

SNAILS

For 2 servings, you will need:

1 dozen snails, plus 1 dozen
 snail shells
2 spring onions*
2 oz (56 g) butter
¼ tsp dry mustard
3 cloves garlic

1 tsp Worcestershire sauce
Freshly ground salt
Freshly ground black pepper
2 tsp parsley
2 oz (56 g) bread crumbs*

First prepare:

Place snails into shells. Preheat oven to 350°F (177°C). Finely slice spring onions. Measure butter. Peel garlic and finely chop. Finely chop parsley.

Now cook!

1. Place butter, mustard, spring onions and garlic in a bowl and work together with a wooden spatula. Add Worcestershire sauce and parsley. Season with salt and pepper.
2. Now work garlic butter on a board with the back of a knife until it forms a smooth paste.
3. Put a snail and 1 heaped teaspoonful of butter into each shell and sprinkle with bread crumbs. Press mixture well into shell with your finger.
4. Cover bottom of an ovenproof dish with coarse salt and arrange filled snail shells on dish. Bake in oven for 15 minutes.

FROGS' LEGS CALVADOS

For 4 servings, you will need:

4 pairs of frogs' legs
Clarified butter*
Flour
Freshly ground salt
Freshly ground black pepper
2 tbs parsley
2 cloves garlic
1 tbs fresh basil or 1 tsp
   dried

1 tbs fresh chives or 1 tsp dried
1 tbs fresh tarragon or 1 tsp dried
2 fl oz (5.6 cl) Calvados
2 fl oz (5.6 cl) dry white wine
1 large Granny Smith apple*
2 tbs sour cream
2 tbs Worcestershire sauce
2 tsp capers
2 tbs dry white wine

First prepare:

Cut parsley roughly. Finely chop chives, tarragon and basil if fresh. (If dried herbs are used tie these in a muslin bag.) Measure Calvados and dry white wine. Measure sour cream and Worcestershire sauce. Measure capers. Cut apple in half and scoop out center with a teaspoon leaving ¼ inch (7 mm) of flesh around outside. Heat broiler unit. Separate frogs' legs and dry thoroughly with a cloth. Lightly flour. Finely smash garlic.

Now cook!

1. Place enough clarified butter in a heated frypan to just cover bottom. Add floured and seasoned frogs' legs and fry gently. Smother frogs' legs with garlic and turn legs after 2 minutes.
2. Add herbs to pan and then pour over heated Calvados and set alight. Give pan a good shake and add dry white wine. Reduce heat, cover and allow to cook gently for 4 minutes.
3. Place apple under broiler for 10 minutes.
4. To frogs' legs add sour cream, Worcestershire sauce, capers and 2 tbs dry white wine. Stir gently to combine. Season to taste with salt and pepper.
5. Place frogs' legs on a heated serving dish, coat with a little of the sauce and serve the rest of the sauce in broiled apple halves.

STUFFED MUSHROOMS "NEUCHATEL"

For 4 servings, you will need:

8 mushrooms (2 inches: 5 cm
   in diameter or even size)
16 snails
Lemon juice
1 large clove garlic
2 spring onions*
Worcestershire sauce

1 tsp dry mustard
1 tbs parsley
Freshly ground salt
Freshly ground black pepper
2 oz (56 g) softened butter
1 large bunch watercress

First prepare:

Preheat broiler unit. Smash garlic. Finely chop spring onions and parsley. Measure butter.

Now cook!

1. Combine garlic, spring onions, Worcestershire sauce, mustard, parsley and softened butter. Mix to a paste and season with salt.
2. Sprinkle lemon juice over veins of mushrooms. Place 2 snails on each mushroom and cover with garlic butter. Place in an ovenproof dish and broil for 5 minutes.
3. Place mushrooms on individual plates on a bed of chilled watercress.

1. CANNELONI is made from these ingredients.

2. The vegetables are ground separately from the meats.

3. Fry the vegetables on their own, and then add the meats.

4. Bind the mixture with an egg and place on the prepared pasta sheet (see page 80).

5. The filling is then rolled into a fat cigar shape.

6. Add the Bolognaise Sauce (see page 497) to some bechamel sauce to lighten its texture.

7. The canneloni are then completely covered.

8. Add a line of Parmesan to point up each parcel. These are then broiled.

Canneloni (page 78)

CANNELONI

For 4 servings, you will need:

12 pieces of pasta 6 inches
x 5 inches (15 cm x 12 cm)

Pasta:
1 lb (0.5 kg) all-purpose flour
3 whole eggs
Freshly ground salt
6 fl oz (1.6 dl) ice water

Filling:
4 tbs clarified butter*
3 oz (85 g) onion
1 clove garlic
2 oz (56 g) carrot
1 oz (28 g) celery
1 oz (28 g) green pepper
4 oz (113 g) rump steak
4 oz (113 g) breast of chicken
4 oz (113 g) veal fillet
4 oz (113 g) bacon
3 fl oz (8 cl) dry white wine
Oregano
Freshly ground salt
Freshly ground black pepper
2 eggs
6 tbs béchamel sauce

Béchamel sauce:
2 oz (56 g) butter
2 oz (56 g) all-purpose flour
30 fl oz (9 dl) milk
Freshly ground salt
Freshly ground white pepper
Nutmeg

Bolognaise sauce:
2 tbs clarified butter*
12 oz (340 g) ground steak
4 oz (113 g) finely chopped
shoulder bacon*
2 bay leaves
1 oz (28 g) celery
3 oz (85 g) onion
2 oz (56 g) carrot
1 clove garlic
3 tbs tomato paste
3 fl oz (8 cl) dry white wine
12 fl oz beef stock
Freshly ground salt
Freshly ground white pepper
2 oz (56 g) Parmesan cheese

First prepare:

Finely chop onion, celery, carrot and green pepper. Peel garlic clove. Finely chop all meats. Measure wine. Make béchamel sauce.

1. *Bolognaise sauce:* Grind bacon and meat. Finely chop carrot, celery and onion. Peel and smash garlic. Measure wine and beef stock. Grate cheese.

2. Heat butter in a frypan and when hot add onion and garlic. When golden add meat and brown.

3. Stir in carrot, celery and white wine.

4. Add tomato paste and moisten with beef stock. Add bay leaves and season with salt and pepper.

5. Simmer in an open pot 1 hour. Discard bay leaves.

1. *Béchamel sauce:* Place butter into a pan on heat and when melted add flour. Stir to form a roux and cook 1 minute over low heat.

2. Add milk slowly whisking to mix. Bring to a boil, season with salt, pepper and nutmeg, and allow sauce to simmer for 20 minutes, stirring from time to time.

1. *Pasta:* Place sifted flour on a board. Make a well in center and add 3 eggs and salt. Mix quickly with the hands, adding water to form a smooth dough. Knead well for at least 5 minutes.

2. Roll out dough on a floured board until paper thin. Cut into 6 inch x 5 inch (15 cm x 12 cm) pieces and place into plenty of salted boiling water. Cook 8 minutes, remove, rinse under cold water and drain.

Now cook!

1. To prepare filling, melt butter in a pan and when hot add onion and carrot and fry till lightly browned. Add garlic, celery and green pepper.

2. Add meats and brown. Season with 1 tbs crumbled oregano, salt and pepper.

3. Add wine and cook gently in an open pot for 30 minutes.

4. Put mixture through the finest blade of a grinder and mix with eggs.

5. Stir in 6 tbs of the béchamel sauce.

6. Place 2 tbs of mixture into center of each piece of cooked pasta and roll up. Place canneloni into a buttered shallow baking pan. Mix remaining béchamel sauce with Bolognaise sauce. Spoon evenly over canneloni.

7. Dust canneloni with Parmesan cheese and bake in a 400°F (205°C) oven for 20 minutes.

1. VARIOUS PASTA. A crinkle-edge cutter is used.

2. Some examples of fancy-edged pasta from ravioli to lasagna.

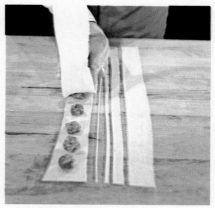

3. The egg-brushed ravioli strip is covered with another strip.

4. Edges are trimmed with a *sealer trimmer*.

5. The crinkle edge gives ravioli its classic shape.

6. Ravioli in back and tortellini or "navel" in front.

1. PASTA FOR CANNELONI.

2. Combine salt, water and egg yolks. Bring in flour gradually.

3. When liquids form a stiff cream—bring in sides and mold.

4. The molding is carried out for at least 15 minutes.

5. Use the heel of the hand—push down and away from you.

6. Roll out into a very long, thin tongue.

7. Measure exactly 6 by 5 inches (15 cm x 12 cm) and very thin.

8. Here you see how the cooked one (left) has expanded.

9. Work the pasta off the bench with a palette knife.

10. Drop into swiftly boiling water.

11. Have a bowl of ice water standing next to boiling pan.

12. When *just* firm to bite lift out; drop into water to set.

TORTELLINI

For 6 first-course servings, you will need (to produce 3 dozen tortellini):

30 fl oz (9 dl) chicken stock
4 fl oz (1.2 dl) heavy cream
Freshly ground salt
Freshly ground black pepper
Grated Parmesan cheese
Pasta:
  1 lb (0.5 kg) all-purpose flour
  Freshly ground salt
  Freshly ground pepper
  5 eggs
Filling:
  3 oz (85 g) lean pork

2 oz (56 g) veal
2 oz (56 g) chicken or turkey breast
2 oz (56 g) ham
1 oz (28 g) mortadella sausage
2 oz (56 g) veal brains
2 tbs clarified butter*
Freshly ground salt
Freshly ground black pepper
Freshly grated nutmeg
2 eggs
3 oz (85 g) grated Parmesan

First prepare:

Heat chicken stock. Measure cream.

Filling: Finely chop meats. Soak brains in salted water for 1 hour. Heat clarified butter in a pan and brown pork, veal and chicken meat gently. Add ham, mortadella and brains and season with salt, pepper and nutmeg. Grind mixture very fine. Combine with eggs and grated cheese and heat until fine and smooth.

Pasta: Place sifted flour into a bowl and season with salt and pepper. Make a well in the center and add the eggs. Stir until dough is stiff and sticky. Knead dough on a floured surface until smooth and elastic. Allow dough to stand covered for 30 minutes. Roll out thinly on a floured surface. Cut small rounds of pasta 1½ inches (4 cm) in diameter.

Place 1 tsp of filling in the center of each round. Brush edges with water. Fold in half to form a half circle and press edges together. Bring the two points of the half circle together curling the tortellini around the finger to form a little "ring," pinching the edges together and sealing with water.

Arrange tortellini in lightly floured dish, cover with a cloth and leave until the next day.

Now cook!

1. Bring chicken stock to the boil. Toss tortellini in the boiling stock and allow to cook for 8 minutes. The cooking time depends on how thinly you have rolled the pasta. After 8 minutes test one, and continue to cook if it doesn't melt in your mouth.

2. Pour the cream into a frypan, bring to a boil and season with salt and pepper. With a slotted spoon place tortellini into the cream and heat until well coated.

3. Place tortellini on a heated serving dish and grate Parmesan cheese over them.

SPAGHETTI KAREENA

69

For 4 servings, you will need:

1 lb (0.5 kg) spaghetti
1 medium onion
4 rashers bacon*
2 cloves garlic
1 medium carrot
1 oz (28 g) celery
4 fl oz (1.2 dl) dry white wine
2 bay leaves
3 tbs tomato paste

20 fl oz (6 dl) kangaroo tail soup*
4 oz (113 g) butter
4 oz (113 g) Parmesan cheese
4 fl oz (1.2 dl) heavy cream
Parsley
2 tbs clarified butter*
Freshly ground salt
Freshly ground black pepper

First prepare:

Slice bacon thinly. Slice onion finely. Open cans of kangaroo tail soup. Smash garlic. Slice celery and carrots very thinly. Grate cheese, measure wine and cream, chop parsley finely. Heat a deep serving platter. Prepare 4 cups ice water.

Now cook!

1. Into 40 fl oz (1.2 l) of boiling salted water drop spaghetti and cook for 10 minutes.

2. Meanwhile in another pan add enough clarified butter to just cover bottom and pop in bacon. Fry until crisp.

3. Add onion and garlic to bacon—superb aroma!

4. At this point stir in carrots, celery and tomato paste.

5. Now pour in kangaroo tail soup and simmer for ½ hour in an open pot. Gradually blend in wine and drop in bay leaves. Continue cooking over low heat.

6. Remove bay leaves from sauce and whirl sauce in a blender until smooth.

7. Add the cream slowly while sauce is blending. Reheat but do not boil.

8. Meanwhile test spaghetti to see if it is cooked—remove a strand and cut it in two—there should be a little grain of starch in the center (it is now "al dente"—to suit the tooth)—this being so, pour in ice water.

9. This will free spaghetti from surface starch and it will not clog or knot together.

10. Drain through a sieve and reheat in a buttered pan set on low heat. Season to taste with salt and black pepper and stir in cheese.

11. Pour sauce over buttered spaghetti and turn onto a heated serving dish. Dust with freshly chopped parsley and serve piping hot.

Service:

A good tossed salad on the side and crusty French bread—this makes a delicious supper.

A special hint:

(Refer to Steps 8/9 above). By adding the 4 cups of ice water to the boiling spaghetti you achieve instant cleansing of surface starch—it works well.

SPAGHETTI CARBONARA

For 4 servings, you will need:

8 oz (227 g) spaghetti
2 eggs
2 tbs clarified butter*
4 oz (113 g) shoulder bacon*

Freshly ground salt
Freshly ground black pepper
Parmesan cheese

First prepare:

Finely dice bacon into ¼-inch (7 mm) cubes. Place pot of salted water on high heat. Have 20 fl oz (6 dl) of ice water ready in refrigerator.

Now cook!

1. Drop spaghetti into boiling salted water and cook 7 minutes until al dente. Pour ice water into pan and drain spaghetti in a colander.
2. Heat clarified butter in a casserole. When hot add bacon cubes and fry until crisp.
3. Add drained spaghetti to bacon and toss well. Season with salt and pepper.
4. Break eggs into a bowl, beat with a fork, season with salt and pepper and add to spaghetti. Toss spaghetti to cover with egg mixture.
5. Serve immediately with grated Parmesan cheese.

A special hint:

When you add beaten eggs be sure to toss spaghetti until well mixed or eggs will become watery instead of creamy.

SPAGHETTI CON SALSE DI VONGOLE

For 6 servings, you will need:

1 lb (0.5 kg) spaghetti
Sauce:
10 oz (283 g) can clams
3 tbs parsley
1 tbs capers

Freshly ground salt
Freshly ground black pepper
1 lb (0.5 kg) tomatoes
3 tbs olive oil
1 clove garlic

First prepare:

Bring large pot of salted water to a boil and place spaghetti on end in pot. Push spaghetti deeper into water as it softens. Make sure strands are separated by prodding gently with a fork. Cook spaghetti for 7 minutes. Pour 20 fl oz (6 dl) ice water onto spaghetti in pot. Remove from heat and pour into a colander. Return spaghetti to pan with olive oil and keep warm. Peel and smash garlic. Finely chop capers. Finely chop parsley. Skin, seed and chop tomatoes.

Now cook!

1. Place oil in a frypan and when hot add capers and garlic. Fry gently—don't brown.
2. Add tomatoes and parsley and cook 5 minutes over low heat.
3. Add clams to tomato sauce, season with salt and black pepper, and cook uncovered until hot. Do not boil or clams will toughen.
4. Reheat spaghetti in oil. Place on serving dish and pour sauce over.

A special hint:

Please note method of cooking spaghetti—especially ice water—it works!

TORTELLI REGGIO EMILIA

For 12 tortelli (4 small servings), you will need:

Pasta:
1 lb (0.5 kg) all-purpose flour
5 eggs
Freshly ground salt
Freshly ground pepper
2 tbs heavy cream
100 fl oz (2.8 l) chicken
  stock

Parmesan cheese
Filling:
2 oz (56 g) cottage cheese
2 oz (56 g) finely chopped cooked
  spinach
Nutmeg
Freshly ground salt
Freshly ground pepper

Now cook!

1. Place sifted flour in a bowl and season it with salt and pepper. Make a well in center and add eggs. Knead dough with hands for 5 minutes until spongy. Allow dough to stand 30 minutes. Roll out thinly on a floured surface until it is 12 inches x 24 inches (30 cm x 60 cm). Trim edges and fold dough in half into a 12-inch square. Top half of dough should be 1 inch (2.5 cm) larger than bottom half. Press the fold to mark and open pasta flat on board.

2. To prepare filling, squeeze out all moisture from spinach. Mix with cheese. Season to taste with nutmeg, salt and pepper.

3. Place teaspoonfuls of filling on bottom half of pasta 2 inches (5 cm) apart and 1 inch (2.5 cm) from outside edges. Fold top half of dough over and seal edges by lightly pressing in between mounds of filling, working from border into filling. Cut with scalloped edged pastry cutter forming tortelli.

4. Place tortelli in a sieve and lower into boiling chicken stock. Cook gently 20 minutes. Drain and put in cream in frypan. Grate 1/3 cup Parmesan over top and toss to coat with cheese and cream. Serve immediately.

A special hint:

I hope the description on folding the pasta is clear. The extra 1 inch (2.5 cm) required on top sheet allows enough dough to cover mounds of filling and have bottom edges of dough even with top piece.

TAGLIATELLE VERDI

For 4 servings, you will need:

8 oz (227 g) green tagliatelle*
4 oz (113 g) prosciutto*
6 oz (170 g) fresh peas (cooked)
8 fl oz (2 dl) heavy cream
2 tbs Parmesan cheese

Freshly ground black pepper
2 tbs clarified butter*
1 quart chicken stock
20 fl oz (6 dl) ice water

First prepare:

Cook peas, cut prosciutto into ½-inch (1.5 cm) squares, measure cream, grate Parmesan cheese.

Now cook!

1. When chicken stock is boiling, add salt to taste and pasta. Continue to keep stock boiling for 5 minutes. Remove pot from range and add ice water. Drain tagliatelle in a sieve.

2. Melt clarified butter in a large pan and when hot add tagliatelle and toss with a spoon and fork until well coated in butter and separated. Add prosciutto and peas.

3. Pour in the cream and toss. Add cheese, toss and season with black pepper. Place on heated serving dish.

BUTTERED EGG NOODLES

For 4 servings, you will need:

12 oz (340 g) medium egg noodles
2 oz (56 g) butter
1 clove garlic
Pinch of freshly ground nutmeg

2 oz (56 g) Parmesan cheese
2 fl oz (5.6 cl) heavy cream
Freshly ground salt
Freshly ground white pepper

First prepare:

Drop noodles in boiling salted water and cook in accordance with directions on package. Drain and plunge into ice water to refresh them. Grate cheese, smash garlic, measure cream, grate nutmeg. Warm a serving dish.

Now cook!

1. Put butter into a heated pot and add garlic stirring it thoroughly into melted butter.

2. Season and add nutmeg. Simmer for a few moments over low heat.

3. Add drained cooked noodles and stir until evenly coated with butter. Increase heat.

4. Stir in cheese and finally pour cream over top, toss well and serve at once piping hot on a heated serving dish.

TOHEROA SOUP

For 4 servings, you will need:
½ oz (14 g) butter
½ oz (14 g) all-purpose flour
10 fl oz (3 dl) fish stock
5 fl oz (1.5 dl) milk
4 oz (113 g) ground toheroas*
Lemon juice
Freshly ground salt
Freshly ground white pepper
Chopped parsley
1 fl oz (2.8 cl) heavy cream

Fish stock:
1 fish head—snapper, 1 lb
  (0.5 kg) minimum
1 onion
Bouquet garni (small piece of
  celery, two pieces each of
  thyme, parsley, bay leaf)
16 fl oz (4 dl) water
2 fl oz (5.6 cl) dry white wine
8 black peppercorns

First prepare:

Make fish stock. Measure milk, butter and flour. Finely chop parsley.
Place fish head in a saucepan. Add chopped onion, bouquet garni, peppercorns, water and wine and bring to a boil. Skim surface and then allow to simmer 30 minutes. Strain.

Now cook!

1. Melt butter and stir in flour to form a roux. Add fish stock, milk heated to boiling, and toheroas. Whisk until smooth. Simmer for 5 minutes, stirring occasionally.
2. Add lemon juice and cream.
3. Season to taste with salt and pepper. Serve dusted with parsley.
4. Serve chilled watercress with or without salad dressing on the side.

From top left counterclockwise: Jamaican Fish Chowder (page 90), Mushroom Soup Alfredo (page 105), Gazpacho (page 116), Artichoke and Oyster Soup, (page 93), Crema de Tomate con Ova (page 98), Soupe au Pistou (page 110).

SCALLOP CHOWDER

69

For 8 servings, you will need:

6 bacon rashers*
1½ lbs (680 g) scallops
2 medium onions
2 green peppers (capsicum)
3 small carrots
2 tbs all-purpose flour
1 lb (0.5 kg) peeled tomatoes
14 fl oz (3.4 dl) fish stock

Freshly ground salt
Freshly ground black pepper
Bouquet garni (3 parsley stalks,
   1 bay leaf, 1 sprig thyme)
12 fl oz (3.2 dl) water
Worcestershire sauce
1 lb (0.5 kg) potatoes
4 oz (113 g) celery

First prepare:

Cut bacon into small cubes. Finely slice onions and peppers. Slice carrots into ½-inch (1.5 cm) thick slices. Peel and cut tomatoes into chunks. Measure water and fish stock. Peel potatoes and cut into ½-inch (1.5 cm) cubes. Cut celery into ½-inch (1.5 cm) slices.

Now cook!

1. Place diced bacon in a large saucepan on high heat. Add onion and saute gently in bacon fat. Add peppers, carrots and celery and fry until onion is soft, but not colored.

2. Stir flour gently into vegetables and cook on low heat for 2 minutes.

3. Add fish stock, water and potatoes and season with salt and pepper. Add bouquet garni and a dash of Worcestershire sauce. Bring chowder to a boil, lower heat, cover pan and allow soup to simmer 20 minutes.

4. Remove bouquet garni, add tomatoes and scallops. Raise heat under saucepan until chowder comes to a boil once more and allow to boil gently for 3 to 5 minutes or until scallops are just cooked and tender.

A special hint:

Be careful when you boil the scallops at Step 4. It is wise to test one after 3 minutes. They should be soft and delicate. They become hard if overcooked.

---

*Processed foods are only acceptable
as long as we remember they are second best.*

CIOPPINO

For 6 servings, you will need:

1 cooked lobster with head,
    2½ lb (1.2 kg)
24 mussels
4 fl oz (1.2 dl) dry white wine
4 fl oz (1.2 dl) water
3 fl oz (8 cl) olive oil
1 large onion
2 cloves garlic
½ lb fresh mushrooms
Freshly ground salt
Freshly ground black pepper

8 oz (227 g) tomato puree
1 green pepper (capsicum)
8 oz (227 g) spring onions*
2 bay leaves
4 oz (113 g) crab meat
8 oz (226 g) sole fillets
8 fl oz (2 dl) dry white wine
Parmesan cheese
Sprig thyme
Oregano

First prepare:

Detach head and claws from lobster. Wash "mustard" from head. Measure wine in 2 portions. Measure water. Scrub and beard mussels. Cut lobster tail meat into 1-inch (2.5 cm) thick slices. Finely slice onion. Finely slice green pepper. Slice spring onions into 2-inch (5 cm) pieces. Slice mushroom caps finely. Measure tomato puree. Cut sole fillets into 2 inch x 1 inch (5 cm x 2.5 cm) pieces. Slice crab into chunks.

Now cook!

1. Place lobster head, carcass and claws in large pan on high heat, add mussels and 4 fl oz (1.2 dl) dry white wine and water. Cover and cook 5 minutes.

2. Remove mussels to a bowl, remove lobster carcass and claws. Break carcass into decorative pieces, crack claws and reserve lobster. Discard lobster head. Boil liquid to half its original volume and reserve.

3. Heat olive oil in a frypan and fry onion and bruised garlic cloves until wilted. Add green pepper and spring onions. Raise heat under pan and add bay leaves, thyme and oregano. Stir constantly to prevent scorching.

4. Remove garlic cloves from pan, stir in mushrooms and season with salt and pepper. Add tomato puree, fish pieces and 8 oz (2 dl) white wine. Cover pan and allow fish to poach for 2 minutes.

5. Add reserved mussel and lobster liquid to vegetable and fish mixture together with lobster meat and crab. Bring to a boil, remove herbs and spoon into soup tureen. Arrange mussels on top in a decorative fashion and garnish with lobster claws and pieces of carcass. Grate cheese over top and serve immediately.

Service:

I have a large copper dish that looks well. You can serve fresh sliced (or torn) pieces of hot Italian bread on side.

A special hint:

Don't cook mussels longer than five minutes.

JAMAICAN FISH CHOWDER

For 4 to 6 servings, you will need:

1½ lb (680 g) red snapper
   (gutted weight, with head on)
4 oz (113 g) celery
½ tbs clarified butter*
4 oz (113 g) onion
4 oz (113 g) carrot
4 oz (113 g) peeled potatoes
¼ tsp powdered thyme
1 bay leaf
2 oz (56 g) spring onions*

Fish stock:
32 fl oz (10 dl) water
4 oz (113 g) onion
4 oz (113 g) celery
4 oz (113 g) carrot
4 parsley stalks*
½ tsp thyme
2 bay leaves
Pinch sage

First prepare:

Fillet red snapper and strip off skin making sure no scales or bones remain on fillets. To make fish stock, put skin, bones and head in a pan with finely chopped onion, celery, carrot, parsley, thyme, sage and bay leaves. Add water, bring to boil, skim, reduce to medium heat and simmer 20 minutes. Strain but reserve one bay leaf. Finely chop fish fillets. Finely dice onion, celery, carrot, potatoes and spring onions.

Now cook!

1. Shallow fry onion and carrot in clarified butter for 2 minutes over medium heat.
2. Add celery, potatoes and spring onions.
3. Stir in strained fish stock, add bay leaf and powdered thyme.
4. Add red snapper and boil gently for 6 minutes.
5. When vegetables are tender season to taste with salt and possibly some pepper.
6. Skim once more and serve after removing bay leaf.

SHRIMP AND OYSTER GUMBO

For 4 servings, you will need:

10 oz (283 g) raw shrimp (8 jumbo
   shrimp frozen, uncooked, in
   shell, head off)
2 tbs clarified butter*
1 clove garlic
1 medium onion
1 oz (28 g) celery
1 bay leaf
1 sprig thyme
1 sprig parsley
32 fl oz (10 dl) water
Freshly ground salt
Freshly ground white pepper

1 cup long grain rice
3 tbs spring onions*
¼ tsp gumbo filé*
4 oz (113 g) pimento
8 oz (226 g) long grain rice
2 oz (56 g) soft butter
48 fl oz (1.4 l) water
½ tsp gumbo filé*
1 tsp Worcestershire sauce
2 fl oz (5.6 cl) heavy cream
2 tsp arrowroot
1 dozen oysters
2 tsp freshly ground salt

First prepare:

Peel shells off shrimp (keep shells). Devein shrimp by lightly cutting into curved back and removing the sand tract. Crush garlic and finely chop. Peel and slice onion. Finely slice celery. Measure water. Slice spring onions and finely chop pimento.

Now cook!

1. Add clarified butter to a large frypan over low heat. Add garlic, shrimp shells, onion, celery, bay leaf, thyme and parsley. Fry for 4 minutes while stirring.

2. After 4 minutes add 32 fl oz (10 dl) water, bring to a boil and allow this "quick stock" to cook for 20 minutes. When cooked, strain and discard solids. Reserve liquid.

3. Cook rice. First rinse grains under cold running water. Place 48 fl oz (1.4 l) water into a large saucepan. Add 2 tsp salt and bring to a boil. Sprinkle in rice so that water never stops boiling. Boil for 10 minutes.

4. When rice has cooked 10 minutes, remove from heat and pour into a colander. DO NOT RINSE IT. Pour 2 inches (5 cm) of water into a saucepan and place colander over boiling water. Add spring onions and pimento. Stir and season witn ¼ tsp gumbo filé.

5. Cover vegetable-flavored rice and allow it to steam for 5 minutes. (Keep an eye on the water; it must boil gently to create steam.)

6. Bring reserved stock to a boil and add *raw* shrimp; cook for 4 minutes at a boil.

7. Remove cooked shrimp, chop them finely and return them to soup.

8. Mix cream and arrowroot. Bring soup to a boil and dribble in arrowroot mixture very slowly stirring all the time. You may not need all the arrowroot mix—don't overdo it! It should be the consistency of thin cream.

9. Mix ½ tsp gumbo filé to a paste with a little water and add this with Worcestershire sauce. Add oysters, stir and heat (DO NOT BOIL) for 1 minute and serve.

10. Add soft butter to rice at last moment and serve on side with soup.

SYDNEY HARBOR PRAWN SOUP

68

For 6 servings, you will need:

2 oz (56 g) onion
10 spring onions*
1 clove garlic
10 oz (283 g) tomatoes
2 parsley stalks*
1 bay leaf
Dried peel from ¼ orange
24 fl oz (7 dl) fish stock
4 tbs clarified butter*
Freshly ground salt

Freshly ground white pepper
Pinch of saffron
10 oz (283 g) fillets of sole
15 mussels in shells
½ lb (227 g) cooked, shelled and
    deveined jumbo shrimp 1 lb
    (0.5 kg) raw
½ lb (227 g) cooked shelled lobster
1 loaf French bread, butter,
    garlic
8 oz (227 g) snapper (fillets)

First prepare:

Slice onion finely, cut tops from spring onions (leaving about 5 inches: 12.7 cm of stalk). Peel garlic clove. Skin, seed and dice tomatoes. Make fish stock. Cut fish into 2 inch x 1 inch (5 cm x 2.5 cm) pieces. Peel shrimp and cut lobster meat into chunks. Prepare garlic bread. Slice loaf into thick slices, but don't sever completely. Butter between each slice and spread with a little smashed garlic. Place in a 375°F (190°C) oven for 15 to 20 minutes wrapped in aluminum foil.

Now cook!

1. Place clarified butter in a deep pan, add onion, spring onions, tomatoes, smashed garlic, parsley stalks, bay leaf and orange peel. Sauté gently for 2 minutes only. Add fish (snapper and sole) and mussels in shells. Season with salt and pepper.

2. Cover mixture with fish stock in which saffron has been dissolved. Bring mixture to a boil, reduce heat. Add shrimp and lobster and heat through.

3. Strain liquid into a serving bowl. Arrange shellfish, fish and mussels in a decorative manner on a serving dish (removing bay leaf and parsley). Surround seafood with slices of garlic bread. When ready to serve, spoon broth into bowls and add pieces of seafood.

ARTICHOKE AND OYSTER SOUP

For 4 servings, you will need:

1 fl oz (2.8 cl) olive oil
1 large green pepper (capsicum)
1 small onion
1 clove garlic
1 small leek
12 canned artichoke hearts

12 fl oz (3.2 dl) artichoke juice
8 fl oz (2 dl) chicken stock
2 tsp arrowroot
5 fl oz (1.5 dl) dry white wine
1 dozen oysters

First prepare:

Slice off top of green pepper, remove seeds and finely chop. Finely slice onion and leek. Slightly bruise garlic (this lets the juices out, but makes it easy to remove garlic later). Drain and reserve liquid from the artichokes. (Taste it before you use it, it may be over-salted. If it is, don't add salt to the dish.) Make chicken stock. Measure arrowroot and wine.

Now cook!

1. Pour olive oil into a large frypan. Heat over low heat. Stir in green pepper and onion until all pieces are coated.
2. Add garlic.
3. Add finely sliced leek and stir. Season this mixture with salt and white pepper.
4. Add artichoke juice to vegetables. Also add 8 fl oz (2 dl) good chicken stock.
5. Let simmer over low heat for 10 minutes. Then place artichoke hearts into soup bottom side down.
6. Add 4 fl oz (1.2 dl) dry white wine and allow artichokes to warm through. Remove garlic.
7. Make a paste of arrowroot and 1 fl oz (2.8 cl) dry white wine and pour this into boiling soup over high heat. Stir all the time taking care not to crush the artichokes, and add arrowroot mixture little by little until smooth and thickened.
8. It will thicken instantly. Add oysters. Taste and adjust seasoning to your taste. Stir once and serve. (Please don't cook oysters too long. It is enough to have them warmed through.)

A special hint:

Refer to Step 7. Arrowroot is a splendid thickening, but be careful to mix paste well (it settles to bottom quickly). Use only a little at a time; it can be awful if overdone.

Artichoke and Oyster Soup (page 93)

FARMHOUSE VEGETABLE SOUP

For 4 servings, you will need:

6 oz (170 g) carrots
3 oz (85 g) parsnips
4 oz (113 g) onions
4 tbs clarified butter*
1 clove garlic
20 fl oz (6 dl) beef stock

4 fl oz (1.2 dl) heavy cream
Freshly ground salt
9 black peppercorns
3 bay leaves
4 parsley stalks*
3 thyme sprigs or powdered thyme

57

First prepare:

Wash and peel vegetables. Measure stock and cream. Tie herbs in muslin bag.

Now cook!

1. Slice vegetables into thick slices.
2. Melt clarified butter in a frypan. Add vegetables and cook gently for 4 minutes.
3. Add stock and herbs and allow to simmer 20 minutes or until the vegetables are tender. Remove herbs.
4. Place liquid and vegetables in a blender. Blend until smooth and add cream. Reheat but do not boil. Season to taste and serve.

POTAGE PARMENTIER

For 6 servings, you will need:

4 leeks
1 onion
4 tbs clarified butter*
1 lb (0.5 kg) potatoes
Sprig thyme
24 fl oz (7 dl) water

2 tsp freshly ground salt
24 fl oz (7 dl) hot milk
2 egg yolks
2 fl oz (5.6 cl) heavy cream
Freshly ground black pepper
Nutmeg

First prepare:

Chop leeks roughly. Chop onion finely. Peel and roughly chop potatoes. Measure water and milk.

Now cook!

1. Put leeks and onion in a saucepan with butter. Cover and cook over low heat a few minutes until they are soft, but do not allow to brown.
2. Add potatoes, water, thyme and salt. Bring to a boil and cook slowly 45 minutes. Strain through a fine sieve. Return strained puree to pan, bring to a boil and add milk, pepper and nutmeg.
3. Beat yolks and cream together and whisk into hot soup. Stir constantly until thickened. Do not boil after this addition.

A special hint:

Restrain yourself from putting this lot through a blender. This is one job it cannot do!

COCKIE LEEKIE SOUP

For 4 servings, you will need:

¾ lb (340 g) leeks
Clarified butter*
½ lb (227 g) potatoes
1 medium onion
½ tsp mixed herbs*

40 fl oz (1.2 l) chicken stock
8 fl oz (2 dl) heavy cream
Freshly ground salt
Freshly ground white pepper

First prepare:

Chop leeks roughly after washing thoroughly. Cut peeled potatoes into ¼-inch (7 mm) slices. Finely slice onion. Measure chicken stock. Measure cream.

Now cook!

1. Place some clarified butter into a large saucepan to just cover bottom and when hot add leeks and allow to fry gently 2 minutes. Add onion and potatoes and toss in the butter. Season vegetables with salt and pepper and add mixed herbs.

2. Stir in chicken stock. Bring soup to a boil, lower heat and simmer uncovered for 1½ hours.

3. Pass soup through a sieve and replace in saucepan. Bring soup to a boil and stir in cream. Remove from heat and place into a soup tureen.

A special hint:

Many leek dishes suffer because of grit. To wash them perfectly you have to slice them in quarters lengthways and then rinse well in warm water.

ERWTENSOEP

For 6 servings, you will need:

16 oz (453 g) split green peas
120 fl oz (3.6 l) cold water
1 pig's ear*
2 pig's trotters*
1 lb (453 g) potatoes
6 oz (170 g) shoulder bacon*

4 frankfurters
4 oz (113 g) celery
2 leeks
2 medium onions
Freshly ground salt
Freshly ground black pepper

First prepare:

Wash peas and soak in 120 fl oz (3.4 l) of water for 12 hours. Scald pig's ear with boiling water to clean it thoroughly. Have butcher split one trotter lengthways and cut second into four pieces. Peel potatoes and place in cold water with a piece of washed charcoal (to keep them white). Chop celery. Slice leeks thinly. Quarter onions and slice them thinly. Slice frankfurters thinly. Cube shoulder bacon.

Now cook!

1. Pour peas and water in which they soaked into a large pan (120 fl oz: 3.6 l) size if possible) and allow to cook, boiling gently for 1 hour.
2. After 1 hour remove 20 fl oz (6 dl) of soup with a ladle and keep it ready for use.
3. Add pig's ear, trotters and bacon and cook for one hour longer.
4. Thinly slice potatoes and add to bubbling stock. These will disintegrate in soup.
5. Now add celery, leeks and onions.
6. Once again remove 20 fl oz (6 dl) of soup and reserve.
7. Cook for another hour. The stock will be gradually reducing in quantity. Stir in soup you removed.
8. Remove trotters and pig's ear.
9. At this point season with salt.
10. The texture of soup should be thick and smooth.
11. Finally add frankfurters 10 minutes before serving.
12. When leftover soup is cold and thick enough to cut you will find that flavor will have improved on reheating.

Service:

Serve in soup plates or bowls. It should be just able to be poured!

A special hint:

From Step 8 you must exercise (after this you'll need to exercise!) great care to avoid scorching soup—it is very thick. The bottom of pan should be heavy and heat low.

CREMA DE TAMATE CON OVO

For 12 servings, you will need:

2 cloves garlic
1½ lbs (679 g) celery heart
32 fl oz (10 dl) tomato puree
32 fl oz (10 dl) chicken stock
4 tbs mashed potato
3 medium onions
3 oz (85 g) chorizo sausage
   (spiced Spanish style sausage)

Freshly ground salt
Freshly ground black pepper
Sprig oregano (or ¼ tsp dried)
2 tbs parsley stalks*
12 eggs
8 fl oz (2 dl) dry white wine
Nutmeg
Olive oil

First prepare:

Finely slice sausage and celery heart. Cook and mash potato. Roughly chop parsley stalks. Measure tomato puree and chicken stock. Peel and finely dice onion. Measure dry white wine.

Now cook!

1. Place enough olive oil to cover bottom of a large 4-quart (4 l) pan and add smashed garlic, onion and sausage. Stir and gently fry for 5 minutes. Add celery heart, tomato puree and hot chicken stock reserving 4 fl oz (1.2 dl) of stock. Add oregano and parsley stalks. Season with salt and pepper.

2. Whip mashed potatoes with reserved chicken stock and add to soup. Simmer 20 minutes in an open pot. Stir white wine into soup. Ladle boiling soup into warmed soup bowls. Drop a raw egg into each bowl and add a dash of nutmeg. Serve immediately.

A special hint:

If oregano is dried, tie it in a small square of muslin so it can be easily removed.

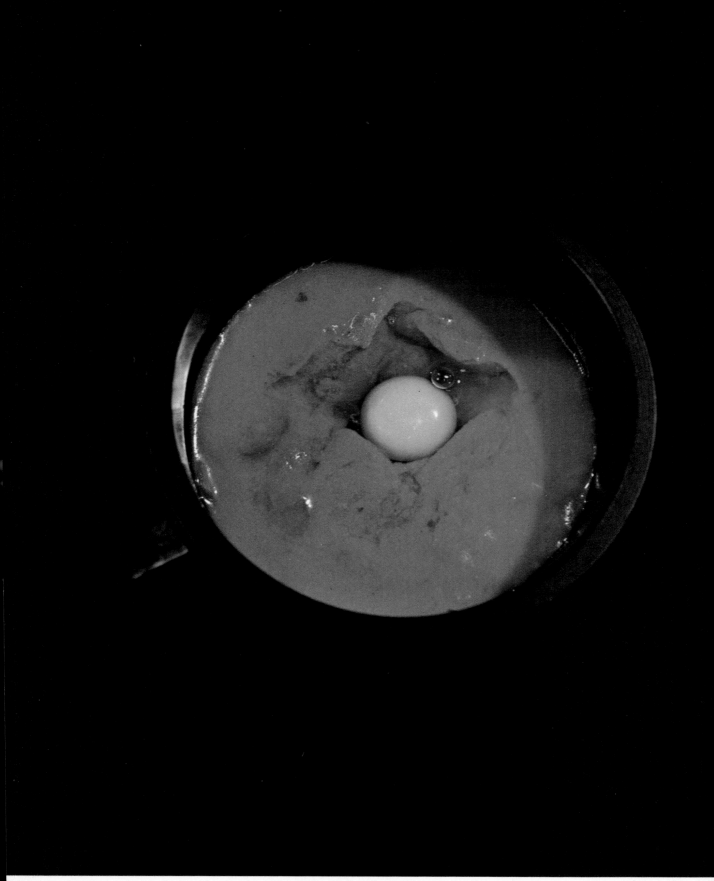

Crema de Tomate con Ova

RED PEA SOUP

For 6 servings, you will need:

1 lb (0.5 kg) dried red beans
2 pig's tails*
1 lb (0.5 kg) salt beef*
1 lb (0.5 kg) meat scraps
130 fl oz (3.7 l) water
1 lb (0.5 kg) yams
1 lb (0.5 kg) coco*
8 oz (227 g) sweet potato
3 spring onions*

1 large onion
1 tsp dried thyme (heaped)
Spinners:
2½ oz (71 g) all-purpose flour
2½ oz (71 g) butter
Freshly ground salt
Freshly ground black pepper
1 egg

First prepare:

Rinse red beans (called peas in the Islands) in fresh cold water—no need to soak them. Scrub pig's tails and chop them into 1-inch (2.5 cm) pieces. Cube salt beef into 1-inch (2.5 cm) pieces and also cube meat scraps. Peel and finely dice yams, coco, sweet potato, onion and spring onions. Measure flour and butter for Spinners.

Now cook!

1. You will need a large pot that holds at least 160 fl oz (4.6 l) of water. Place this on the heat and add red beans. Cover with 130 fl oz (3.7 l) of water.

2. Add tails, salt beef and meat scraps. Cook at a slow boil for 1 hour.

3. Add root vegetables: yams, sweet potato and cocos. Continue to cook for another ½ hour over low heat.

4. *Spinners:* Meanwhile, make small spinners by mixing flour, salt and pepper. Cut in butter until particles are fine. Stir in egg.

5. Knead dough for a couple of minutes on a floured surface and roll into a 1 inch (2.5 cm) in diameter cylinder. Cut into 8 equal pieces and shape like small footballs.

6. When soup has cooked for 1½ hours, add 32 fl oz (1 l) of ice water and skim congealed fats that will form. Bring soup back to a boil and drop in spinners.

7. At the same time add onion and spring onions.

8. Simmer another 30 minutes. Sample soup, adjust seasoning and serve.

A special hint:

With this recipe I prefer that the thyme leaves are powdered or at least rubbed fine with the palms of your hands.

JAMAICAN PEPPER POT SOUP

For 6 large servings, you will need:

2 lbs (0.9 kg) pig tails*
1 lb (453 g) salt beef (silverside)*
130 fl oz (3.7 l) water
1 lb (453 g) yams
1 lb (453 g) coco*
12 okra
8 oz (226 g) Indian kale*

3 spring onions*
1 large onion
1 tsp powdered thyme
1 14 oz (397 g) can callaloo*
Freshly ground salt
Freshly ground black pepper
32 fl oz (10 dl) ice water

First prepare:

Scrub pig tails and rinse in cold water, then cut into 1-inch (2.5 cm) pieces. Cut salt beef into ½-inch (1.2 cm) cubes. Peel and chop yams and coco into 1-inch (2.5 cm) cubes. Rinse okra but leave whole. Trim heavy stalks from Indian kale and slice. Finely chop spring onions. Peel and finely slice onion. Open can of callaloo. Use both juice and leaf vegetable.

Now cook!

1. You will need one large pot that holds at least 160 fl oz (4.6 l) of water. Place pig-tail pieces into pan over low heat and allow lard to ooze out.

2. When sufficient drippings have formed, add cubed salt beef and fry these until brown on all sides (beef cubes must be dried with a towel just before being added).

3. Add water and allow to simmer for 1 hour. Skim surface completely clear of all foam and clean sides of pot.

4. Add yams and cocos and ice water to congeal fats. These will float to surface. Skim fat.

5. Reheat and cook another 30 minutes. Add okra and Indian kale, chopped onion and spring onions. Simmer another 30 minutes.

6. Add callaloo and allow it to heat through (if callaloo is not available add 1 lb (0.5 kg) of fine shredded spinach and boil for 3 minutes). Serve hot.

7. Don't be disappointed at the first taste. Many Jamaican families pass on their cast iron Pepper Pot as an heirloom with *soup intact*. It just boils and has more meat pieces and root vegetables added each day.

8. Fresh green vegetables go in just before serving time. Why not try it for a week and see how it goes—but boil it at least 20 minutes each day. A great catchall in the kitchen; the flavor changes and improves with each cooking.

MULLIGATAWNY SOUP

For 8 servings, you will need:

1 chicken, 3 lb (1.4 kg)
Clarified butter*
2 medium onions
4 tbs clarified butter*
1 clove garlic
½ tsp freshly ground salt
1 tbs curry powder
8 fl oz (2 dl) coconut stock

24 fl oz (7 dl) chicken stock
12 fl oz (3.2 dl) lentils
 (soaked weight)
2 bay leaves
Freshly ground black pepper
1 tsp cayenne pepper
Juice of ½ lemon
8 oz (227 g) long grain rice

First prepare:

Remove wings from chicken and cut bird into 16 pieces (thighs into 2, legs into 2 and breasts into 4 pieces). Skin and bone pieces. Finely slice onions. Smash garlic clove. Make coconut stock. Make chicken stock. Soak lentils overnight in cold water and then drain and measure. Boil rice.

Now cook!

1. Place clarified butter in large saucepan to just cover bottom and when hot add chicken meat and allow to fry until brown. Season with pepper and cayenne. Cook for 12 minutes. Remove and reserve.

2. Add chicken carcass and skin to saucepan. Allow to fry gently until golden.

3. In a large frypan place clarified butter and when hot add onions and garlic and allow to fry until tender but not brown.

4. Place salt in small bowl, add a little hot butter from onions and combine with curry powder. Pour over onions and allow spice to fry for 1 minute.

5. Add curried onions to chicken carcass and skin in saucepan, coconut stock, chicken stock and lentils. Add bay leaves. Allow soup to boil gently 1 hour.

6. Remove carcass and skin from soup and remove bay leaves. Add fried chicken pieces to soup together with lemon juice. Skim any surface fats.

7. Serve with a bowl of boiled rice.

OYSTER SOUP

For 4 servings, you will need:

Fish stock:
8 oz (227 g) fish bones
1 small onion
1 small carrot
2 parsley stalks✱
3 black peppercorns
½ tsp freshly ground salt
Small piece lemon peel
1 fl oz (2.8 cl) dry white wine

20 fl oz (6 dl) water
Garnish:
16 fresh oysters
4 oz (113 g) fillets of sole
2 fl oz (5.6 cl) dry white wine
2 oz (56 g) beurre manie
1 oz (28 g) each flour and butter
    mixed together

First prepare:

Stock: Chop onion and carrot finely, put with parsley stalks, peppercorns, salt and lemon peel, wine and water into saucepan, bring to a boil, skim and simmer 30 minutes. Strain through cheesecloth. Fillet sole, remove skin and slice fillets into small thin strips 1 inch x ¼ inch (2.5 cm x 7 mm). Prepare beurre manie.

Now cook!

1. Add wine and sole to stock.
2. Poach sole for 6 minutes. Drop beurre manie into soup and stir until thick. Do not allow soup to boil after this addition.
3. Put oysters in warmed soup bowls and pour hot soup over.

SOLDOUTS SOUP

For 4 servings, you will need:
2 avocados
30 fl oz (9 dl) chicken stock
2 tsp arrowroot
2 oz (56 g) chicken meat

2 oz (56 g) crabmeat
Freshly ground salt
Freshly ground black pepper

First prepare:

Measure chicken stock. Peel and seed avocados. Shred chicken meat and crabmeat.

Now cook!

1. Bring chicken stock to a boil. Thicken with arrowroot mixed with a little cold chicken stock.
2. Place avocados and hot chicken stock in blender and blend.
3. Reheat but do not boil. Season to taste with salt and pepper. Serve garnished with chicken and crabmeat.

A special hint:

The avocados must be very ripe to make this a success. Try shredding the chicken and crab with a fork—it's easier.

BISQUE CHATAIGNE

For 8 servings, you will need:

16 oz (0.5 kg) natural chestnut puree, canned
36 fl oz (11 dl) chicken stock
20 fl oz (6 dl) milk
Freshly ground white pepper
Freshly ground salt
½ tsp nutmeg
¼ tsp cayenne
1 tsp paprika

½ tsp cumin
3 pieces lemon peel
4 egg yolks
2 tbs parsley
2 tbs dry sherry
1 tbs chives
1 tbs heavy cream per serving
2 lemons for garnish
Whole nutmeg

First prepare:

Make chicken stock. Separate eggs. Roughly chop parsley. Finely chop chives. Measure cream. Cut lemon peel and bruise with back of knife. Cut 2 lemons into wedges. Measure milk.

Now cook!

1. Place chestnut puree in a large saucepan and whisk in hot chicken stock and milk. Season with nutmeg, cumin, cayenne, and paprika. Stir until soup comes to a boil. Skim soup and add lemon peel.

2. Add a little of the hot soup to egg yolks and beat. Whisk this mixture into remaining soup. Stir until thickened, but do not allow to boil again.

3. Add parsley, chives and dry sherry. Remove lemon peel. Season to taste with salt and pepper.

4. Ladle soup into hot bowls or a hot tureen and add 1 tbs cream to each serving.

5. Accompany with lemon wedges and a whole nutmeg with grater so that each guest can season his own soup.

A special hint:

Be careful to avoid boiling the soup after egg yolks are added. It is easy to curdle.

MUSHROOM SOUP ALFREDO

For 4 servings, you will need:

1 lb (0.5 kg) mushrooms
3 tbs tomato paste
2 tbs sweet Italian vermouth
2 tbs clarified butter*
1 fl oz (2.8 cl) olive oil
2 cloves garlic

1 medium onion
24 fl oz (7 dl) chicken stock
4 egg yolks
2 tbs parsley
2½ tbs grated Parmesan cheese
3 slices white bread

First prepare:

Slice mushrooms finely. Measure tomato paste, vermouth and chicken stock. Finely dice onion. Separate eggs. Finely chop parsley. Cut bread into ½ inch (1.2 cm) cubes and fry in clarified butter until golden.

Now cook!

1. Add oil and butter to a large saucepan. Heat and add bruised garlic and allow to sweat. Add onion and gently sauté.

2. Remove garlic. Raise heat and add tomato paste and finely sliced mushrooms stirring all the time to prevent burning. Add hot chicken stock and vermouth, bring to a boil, lower heat and simmer 2 minutes.

3. Skim off fat from surface of soup.

4. Whisk egg yolks with parsley and Parmesan cheese and then beat in a little hot soup. Whisk this mixture into remaining soup. Stir until thickened but do not boil. Serve immediately with bread croutons.

A special hint:

In Step 4 be careful to cook the soup only until it thickens. Pour it immediately into tureen otherwise it could curdle.

MEHLSUPPE AND BUTTERROSTI

For 8 servings, you will need:

60 fl oz (1.7 l) chicken stock
4 oz (113 g) bacon rind*
4 oz (113 g) all-purpose flour
2 oz (56 g) celery
2 oz (56 g) carrot
2 oz (56 g) leek
½ clove garlic
1 large onion
6 tbs clarified butter*

Freshly ground salt
Freshly ground black pepper
4 fl oz (1.2 dl) dry red wine
¼ tsp nutmeg, freshly grated
Butterrosti—For 2 servings
1 lb (0.5 kg) potatoes
2 oz (56 g) butter
Freshly ground salt
Freshly ground black pepper

First prepare:

Mehlsuppe: Sift flour, make chicken stock, cut bacon into tiny pieces with a pair of scissors. Dice carrot, leek, celery, and lightly smash the garlic. Measure wine, grate nutmeg.

Butterrosti: Wash and scrape potatoes (preferably long, new potatoes) and parboil for 5 minutes in salted water. Drain thoroughly and allow to cool.

Now cook!

1. *Mehlsuppe:* Pour clarified butter into a saucepan, heat and beat in the flour with a wooden spoon. Turn heat high to cook flour. Continue to stir briskly; mixture must gradually deepen in color without actually burning flour.

2. Pop bacon rind into another pan and allow to sizzle on high heat until fat oozes out freely. Add mirepoix (finely chopped) of vegetables and cook for 3 minutes.

3. Add this to flour mixture and sauté them for 2 minutes while stirring.

4. Now pour in chicken stock, about 16 fl oz (4 dl) at a time, and whisk together briskly. Increase color and flavor by adding red wine. Bring all this to a boil and add another 16 fl oz (4 dl) of stock.

5. Boil once again and as it thickens, continue to add stock. Reduce heat and simmer for 1½ hours. Stir often to prevent soup sticking on the bottom of pan.

6. Adjust seasoning to taste. Not too much salt as bacon will add some, but a good dash of pepper and a grating of nutmeg.

7. Serve at once piping hot.

8. *Butterrosti:* Grate parboiled potatoes onto a plate lengthwise. Keep grated "strands" as long as possible.

9. Melt butter in an omelet pan over high heat.

10. Into this, put potatoes, season very generously with salt and pepper, mix well and shallow fry.

11. Cook potatoes without stirring over moderate heat.

12. When underside is brown, flip over like an omelet onto dinner plate the same size as pan.

13. Add more butter to pan and replace potatoes.

14. Brown other side. They should now look like a beautifully browned omelet pancake.

15. Carefully slide it from pan onto a serving platter and serve at once.

PUMPKIN AND OYSTER SOUP

For 6-8 servings, you will need:

2 lb (0.9 kg) Jamaican pumpkin*
  (peeled weight)
4 tbs clarified butter*
4 oz (113 g) onion
14 oz (396 g) beef bone (marrow)

40 fl oz (12 dl) cold water
6 oz (170 g) oysters
8 fl oz (2 dl) beef stock
Freshly ground salt
Freshly ground white pepper

First prepare:

Remove green outer skin from pumpkin and discard inner seeds. Roughly cut into cubes. Finely slice onion. Measure water and stock, oysters and clarified butter. Heat a soup tureen.

Now cook!

1. Pour clarified butter into a large saucepan over moderate heat.
2. Stir in onion and allow natural juices to "sweat" out.
3. Add chopped pumpkin and beef bone and allow to fry together. Season with salt and white pepper.
4. Cover ingredients with cold water and cook gently for 1 hour, letting liquid reduce gradually. Stir occasionally.
5. Just before end of cooking period stir in beef stock and remove beef bones.
6. Press soup through a sieve into a tureen and add oysters and their juices. Serve hot.

CREAM OF LETTUCE SOUP

For 4 servings, you will need:

1 lb (453 g) Boston lettuce
1 large onion
2 oz (56 g) butter
2 oz (56 g) all-purpose flour
6 tbs clarified butter*
4 slices white bread

2 cloves garlic
16 fl oz (4 dl) milk
16 fl oz (4 dl) chicken stock
Freshly ground salt
Freshly ground white pepper

First prepare:

Thoroughly rinse lettuce and remove cores. Finely slice onion. Measure dry and liquid ingredients. Smash garlic and chop to a pulp. Heat a soup tureen. Decrust bread and cut slices into cubes.

Now cook!

1. Place lettuce leaves in a large, dry saucepan and cook over medium heat for 6 minutes.

2. Into another pan on low heat, place butter, stir in onion and let cook until soft. Stir in flour, making a roux. Cook 3 minutes while stirring.

3. Stir 16 fl oz (4 dl) of milk into roux and add 8 fl oz (2 dl) chicken stock.

4. Remove cooked lettuce from pot, puree in a blender and add to soup. Add remaining 8 fl oz (2 dl) of chicken stock and cook while stirring for 7 minutes or until thickened. Season to taste with salt and pepper.

5. Pour 4 tbs clarified butter into a small frypan and when heated add cubes of bread, occasionally shaking pan to prevent them from getting too brown. Add another 2 tbs clarified butter and garlic cloves.

6. Drain garlic bread "croutons" on a paper towel. Place on heated serving dish.

7. Strain lettuce soup through a sieve into soup tureen and serve at once with croutons.

CONSOMME LADY CURZON

For 2 servings, you will need:

16 fl oz (4 dl) turtle soup
   (canned)
¼ lemon
2 egg yolks
3 oz (85 g) butter

½ tsp curry powder
Pinch nutmeg
1 fl oz (2.8 cl) heavy cream
Freshly ground salt
Freshly ground white pepper

First prepare:

Open can of soup, remove turtle meat and chop it into small pieces. Squeeze lemon juice, grate nutmeg, cut butter into three even pieces, measure curry powder. A double boiler will be required.

Now cook!

1. Pour soup into a pan and heat. Add thinly sliced turtle meat and simmer.
2. Into top of double boiler heated over simmering water place lemon juice and a little salt and white pepper.
3. Beat in egg yolks and gradually beat in cubes of butter stirring constantly.
4. Whisk in curry powder and nutmeg and continue beating.
5. Slowly beat in cream thoroughly. The sauce will now thicken very fast; lower heat under double boiler.
6. Pour hot soup into soup cups and top with thick cream sauce. Serve at once.

A special hint:

Refer to end of Step 5. If sauce curdles, add an ice cube and whip it, away from heat, until it becomes smooth.

SOUPE AU PISTOU

For 6 servings, you will need:

1 small carrot
1 small leek
1 stick celery
1 small zucchini
(baby marrow)
4 oz (113 g) fresh green
beans
1 small potato
2 medium tomatoes
1 large clove garlic
2 tbs parsley

1 tsp dried basil (preferably fresh
leaves)
2 oz (56 g) Cheddar cheese
4 oz (113 g) fine noodles
1 can (14 oz: 396 g) red kidney
beans
2 fl oz (5.6 cl) olive oil
48 fl oz (1.4 l) cold water
4 tbs clarified butter*
Freshly ground salt
Freshly ground black pepper

First prepare:

Scrape and cube carrot. Wash leek very thoroughly and slice thinly. Slice celery and beans. Cube zucchini, potato and tomatoes. Open can of kidney beans. Measure parsley and basil. Grate Cheddar cheese. Heat a soup tureen in warming oven. Measure clarified butter and olive oil. Smash garlic.

Now cook!

1. Into a heated saucepan pour clarified butter and olive oil.
2. Fry carrots in hot oils. Add potatoes, green beans and garlic. Stir well together and add zucchini. Cook gently for 5 minutes to release natural vegetable oils.
3. Transfer vegetables to boiling salted water.
4. Add noodles.
5. To boiling soup, add beans and stir well. Add parsley and basil, freshly ground salt and pepper to taste. Cook until vegetables are tender, approximately 12-15 minutes.
6. Finally, add tomato cubes and Cheddar cheese. Stir until cheese is melted.
7. Pour into heated soup tureen and serve piping hot.

Service:

Crusty French bread can be partially cut and buttered with garlic butter, then heated until crisp and served hot with the soup.

A special hint:

Remove soup from heat the moment the carrot is *just* tender and let it cool quickly under normal refrigeration. Reheat next day and serve. This technique increases flavor but regrettably reduces vitamins.

Soupe au Pistou

CEVICHE

For 6 servings, you will need:

2 lbs (0.9 kg) whole sea bass
    (whole weight gutted)
7 limes
1 oz (28 g) onion
8 fl oz (2 dl) tomato juice
10 oz (283 g) tomatoes
1 oz (28 g) chili pepper

1 level tbs coriander, fresh
1 clove garlic
1 tbs olive oil
4 whole cloves
½ tsp oregano
Freshly ground salt
Freshly ground white pepper

First prepare:

Scale fish under water, using back edge of knife. Then, with a sharp knife, slit down back of fish and carefully remove fillets from bone. Trim skin off fillets. (No bones allowed! Save the scraps for stock—see a special hint.) Squeeze juice from limes. Dice onion. Blanch tomatoes in boiling water, cool, peel off skin and remove seeds. Measure tomato juice and oil. Wash, dry and finely chop coriander. Smash garlic. Carefully remove seeds from pepper.

Now cook!

1. Place fillets of fish into a grinder and when ground pour lime juice over it and season with salt and white pepper. Set aside in a cool place overnight or for 4 hours in refrigerator.
2. After marinating, strain off excess lime juice, pressing fish to drain thoroughly.
3. Stir in diced onion, then tomato juice.
4. Chop tomatoes, add to fish mixture and stir.
5. Finely chop chili pepper and add.
6. Mix in coriander.
7. Into a small bowl pour olive oil, garlic and oregano.
8. Push this mixture through a very fine sieve and beat into ceviche ingredients. Make sure every drop of oil and herb juice is blended in.
9. Chill very thoroughly and serve when required.

A special hint:

Fish is always best when purchased in a whole fresh piece or at least when you have seen whole fish filleted in front of you (obviously some fish are too large to have this done!). The point is, don't throw away the bones. Make a fish stock regardless of whether you need it or not. Then freeze it, label it and it's ready when you want a good base for a fish sauce or soup.

1. CEVICHE is a colorful and delicious dish.

2. Striped sea bass is first filleted and skinned.

3. And put through a fine bladed grinder.

4. This little gadget helps to juice the limes.

5. Soak the finely ground fish in lime for 4 hours and then drain.

6. Use large, very red tomatoes. Make a cut at the stalk area.

7. Place tomato in boiling water until skin peels back.

8. Place the hot tomato into a bowl of iced water.

9. When cold remove skin, seeds and chop flesh finely.

10. Crush the oregano and garlic into the oil.

11. Pass the herb oil through a sieve into the fish.

12. Add the tomato juice and serve really cold.

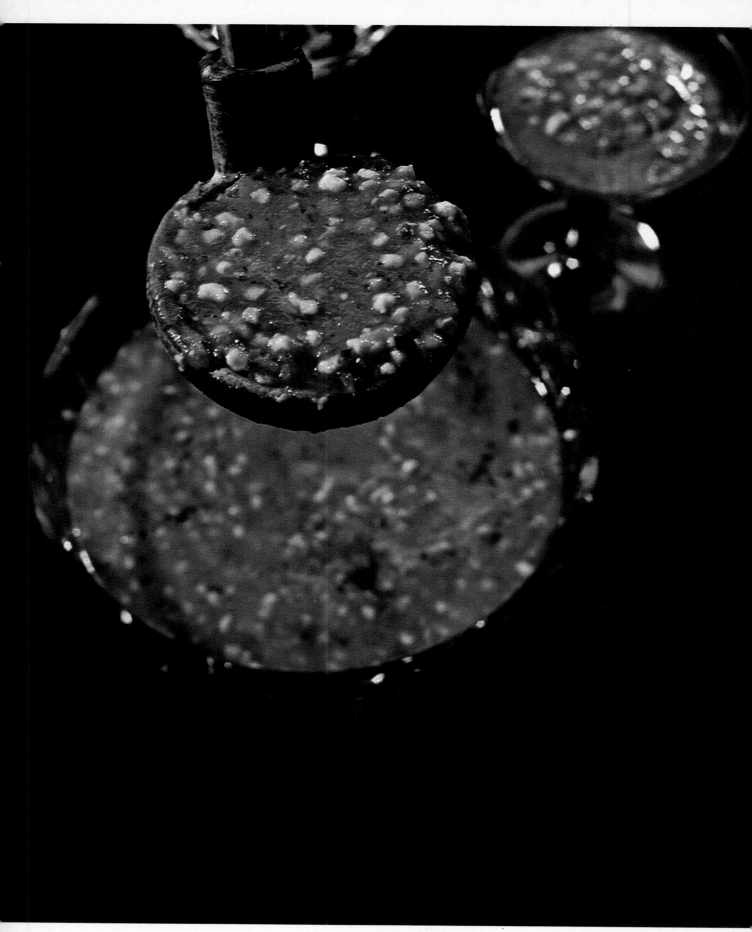

Ceviche (page 112)

ICED CUCUMBER AND MINT SOUP

For 4 servings, you will need:

4 cucumbers
Spring onions*
24 fl oz (7 dl) water
Freshly ground salt
Freshly ground black pepper

3 tbs fresh mint
12 fl oz (3.2 dl) light cream
Clarified butter*
Chili sauce
Sprig fresh thyme

First prepare:

Finely chop mint. Peel cucumbers and slice thinly. Finely slice about 8 spring onions. Measure water and cream.

Now cook!

1. Melt a little clarified butter in a saucepan to just cover bottom and fry spring onions gently. When soft stir in cucumber but do not allow to brown. Season cucumber and spring onions with salt and pepper.

2. Add water and thyme and cook very slowly until cucumber and onions are soft. Put through a fine strainer or food mill. Season again if necessary. Stir in chili sauce and mint.

3. Stir in cream. Chill. Garnish with a little chopped mint or a few cucumber slices.

A special hint:

In Step 2, do not use a blender, the cucumber seeds taste bitter when blended.

GAZPACHO

For 4 servings, you will need:

1 clove garlic
2 lbs (0.9 kg) ripe tomatoes
4 oz (113 g) spring onions*
4 oz (113 g) radishes
4 oz (113 g) green pepper (capsicum)
4 oz (113 g) red canned pimento
4 oz (113 g) cucumber
4 oz (113 g) black olives, pitted
¼ tsp dried basil
¼ tsp dried tarragon

2 fl oz (5.6 cl) dry red wine
2 tsp paprika
1 tbs parsley
Freshly ground salt
Freshly ground black pepper
3 hard-boiled eggs
2 tbs lemon juice
2 tbs white wine vinegar
2 tbs olive oil

First prepare:

Skin and sieve tomatoes. Finely dice radishes, spring onions, cucumber (leave on skin), green pepper, pimento and olives. Separate whites from yolks of hard-boiled eggs. Finely dice white and lightly scrape egg yolks with knife. Squeeze lemon juice, measure wine, vinegar and oil. Roughly chop parsley.

Now cook!

1. Rub earthenware bowl with cut garlic clove.
2. Place sieved tomatoes in bowl and add radish, spring onions, cucumber, green pepper, pimento and olives. Season with basil and tarragon (rubbed between palms of hands to bring out flavor). Add paprika, parsley, wine, lemon juice, vinegar and oil. Stir to combine. Season to taste with salt and pepper.
3. Gently fold in egg white and then yolks. Chill for 2 hours.

A special hint:

Try to dice every piece of vegetable exactly the same size. It adds to the beauty of this colorful dish.

Gazpacho

OKROSHKA

For 6 servings, you will need:

20 fl oz (6 dl) hard cider
8 fl oz (2 dl) sour cream
8 oz (227 g) skinless and boneless
   cooked chicken breasts
5 oz (142 g) cucumber
2 hard-boiled eggs
2 tsp dill
4 spring onions*

Freshly ground salt
Freshly ground white pepper
2 tsp tarragon wine vinegar
Garnish:
4 slices white bread
4 slices lean bacon
4 tbs clarified butter*
2 tbs chopped parsley

First prepare:

Soup: Measure cider and sour cream. Chop boiled breast of chicken and cucumber into even ½ inch (1.27 cm) cubes. Sieve hard-boiled egg white and crumble yolk. Finely chop dill and spring onions.

Garnish: Cut bread into ½ inch (1.27 cm) cubes. Chop bacon into fine strips across the grain. Finely chop parsley.

Now cook!

1. Set a large bowl on crushed ice.
2. Pour cider and sour cream into chilled bowl and mix.
3. Stir in chicken, cucumber, egg white and egg yolk.
4. Stir in dill and spring onions.
5. Add tarragon wine vinegar slowly to taste.
6. Season with salt and white pepper.
7. Allow soup to rest on ice for 2 hours before serving. This helps to blend the flavors.
8. Just before serving add the chopped bacon to clarified butter and fry 1 minute. Now add bread cubes and toss until crisp and golden brown.
9. Add parsley to toasted bread and pour into a heated bowl. Sprinkle toasted bread on each serving of cold soup.

TEARAWAY SOUP

For 6 servings, you will need:

16 fl oz (4 dl) chicken stock
2 lbs (0.9 kg) tomatoes
1 large leek
4 oz (113 g) celery
1 medium onion
2 tsp chives

2 tsp sweet basil
1 tsp Tabasco
Freshly ground salt
Freshly ground white pepper
Clarified butter*

68

First prepare:

Measure chicken stock. Finely chop celery, onion and leek. Slice tomatoes. Measure herbs.

Now cook!

1. Strain chicken stock and remove every trace of fat (it need not be clear).
2. In a large deep pot put celery, onion and leeks. Sprinkle with herbs and shallow fry in a little clarified butter for 4 minutes. Add tomatoes.
3. Add chicken stock and cover.
4. Boil for 15 minutes stirring from time to time. Season with salt and white pepper.
5. Press soup through a sieve, taste and add Tabasco as required. Chill.

A special hint:

Please don't use a blender to sieve cooked vegetables. The ground tomato seeds give it a bitter taste.

FISCHE FONDUE

For 2 servings, you will need:

4 oz (113 g) turbot
12 raw shrimp
4 oz (113 g) sole
4 oz (113 g) salmon
4 oz (113 g) scallops
2 eggs
¼ tsp dry mustard
8 fl oz (2 dl) oil
1 clove garlic
2 sweet gherkins
2 tsp capers

1 tbs parsley
Pinch tarragon
Pinch chervil
1 tsp sliced almonds
½ tsp curry powder
½ tsp tomato paste
½ tsp brandy
3 anchovy fillets
Freshly ground salt
Freshly ground white pepper
Deep oil

First prepare:

Remove all tiny bones from fish, shell and devein raw shrimp, cut fish into large bite-size cubes. Separate whites from yolks and beat whites until stiff. Measure oil, smash garlic, chop gherkins finely. Wash and chop parsley, cut anchovy fillets into small pieces. A fondue pot and wooden skewers will be needed, also a fondue plate for sauce served per person.

Now cook!

1. Make basic sauce—mayonnaise.
2. Put egg yolks into a bowl placed over a pot of warm water. Beat with an electric mixer until light and creamy. Remove from heat.
3. Add mustard and salt—continue beating—gradually start adding 2 fl oz (5.6 cl) oil drop by drop (if mayonnaise should curdle and lose its bulk beat in some stiffly beaten egg white).
4. Continue to add remainder of oil until mixture is smooth and creamy. 2 tsp of boiling water can now be slowly beaten into mixture.
5. Set aside mayonnaise. Have several little bowls ready for mixing.
6. To 1 tbs of mayonnaise in a bowl, add garlic and mix together. Place this in fondue sauce tray. Place almonds in a small bowl.
7. Place 1 heaped tbs of mayonnaise into each of the 6 small bowls and add separately to these. 1. Chopped gherkins and capers; 2. Chopped parsley; 3. Chopped tarragon and chervil; 4. Dry mustard and curry powder; 5. Tomato paste and brandy; 6. Chopped anchovies.
8. Pour these sauces into fondue sauce trays.
9. Heat oil in fondue pot and arrange fish cubes and shrimp attractively on a serving platter. Spear fish and fry in hot oil. Dip hot fish into desired cold sauce to cool it quickly. Eat immediately.

FONDUE

For 6 servings, you will need:

10 oz (283 g) Emmenthal cheese
10 oz (283 g) Gruyère cheese
1 clove garlic
16 fl oz (4 dl) dry white wine
2 tsp lemon juice

1 heaped tsp potato flour or·starch
2 fl oz (5.6 cl) kirsch
Freshly ground pepper
Nutmeg

First prepare:

Cut cheese into ½-inch (1.27 cm) cubes. Peel garlic. Measure wine. Warm wine with lemon juice.

Now cook!

1. Rub inside of earthenware casserole with garlic. Pour in wine and lemon juice. Heat until juice just starts to bubble. Add cheese one handful at a time, stirring constantly.

2. Bring to a boil, then add kirsch mixed to a smooth paste with potato flour.

3. Continue to cook for a short time, whisking fondue all the time in form of figure "8".

4. Set fondue over a warmer and continue to simmer it gently. The creamy cheese mixture is eaten by spearing a cube of French bread on a fork, and dunking it in fondue.

BLACK DIAMOND FONDUE

69

For 6 servings, you will need:

1 small loaf bread
2 tbs cornstarch
3 tbs brandy
12 oz (340 g) Edam or
Elbo cheese

4 oz (113 g) Black Diamond
Cheddar cheese*
8 fl oz (2 dl) dry white wine
2 Granny Smith apples*

First prepare:

Cut bread in 1¼-inch .(3 cm) cubes. Mix brandy with cornstarch until smooth. Cut cheese into ¼-inch (7 mm) cubes. Cut apple into 1-inch (2.5 cm) cubes just before serving.

Now cook!

1. Place cheese and wine in a small saucepan and cook over low heat stirring constantly until it looks like a smooth soup.

2. Pour in brandy and cornstarch paste and stir over heat until mixture thickens. Season with salt, white pepper and a touch of nutmeg.

3. Pour immediately into a serving dish and place on warmer on table.

4. The apple pieces and bread cubes are placed on dishes in front of guests to dunk in fondue.

CHICKEN AND CHEESE FONDUE

For 4 servings, you will need:

1½ oz (42 g) all-purpose flour
1½ oz (42 g) butter
16 fl oz (4 dl) chicken stock
1 lb (0.5 kg) Cheddar cheese
2 fl oz (5.6 cl) cognac

2 Granny Smith apples*
1 loaf French bread
1 lemon
Freshly ground black pepper

71

First prepare:

Measure butter, flour, cognac and chicken stock. Chop cheese into small pieces. Cube bread into bite-size portions. Cube apples, and cover with lemon juice to prevent their turning brown.

Now cook!

1. In a heated saucepan, melt butter over moderate heat.
2. Stir in flour and cook while stirring for 3-4 minutes.
3. Add chicken stock, whisking constantly until mixture thickens.
4. Add cheese to sauce and allow to melt.
5. Season with black pepper.
6. Pour bubbling fondue into fondue pot, place over a warmer.
7. At the last moment, stir in cognac and serve at once.
8. Dip into fondue cubed bread and pieces of apple speared on fondue stick or fork.

---

*Neither threats nor commands
should be used to force a child to eat.
Assuming no secret hoard of sweets exists,
he will soon be beating down the kitchen door.*

POTTED SHRIMP

For 2 servings, you will need:

8 oz (227 g) cooked, shelled
and deveined shrimp
3 oz (85 g) butter
¼ tsp mace

1 tsp nutmeg
Cayenne pepper
Clarified butter*
Lettuce leaves

First prepare:

Measure butter, grease small 4-ounce pots.

Now assemble!

1. Melt butter, add mace, nutmeg and good dash of cayenne pepper.
2. Add shrimp and coat in aromatic butter. Place into pots and when cool pour over a little clarified butter to just cover shrimp. Refrigerate.
3. Loosen edges. Turn out shrimp onto a lettuce leaf. Serve with thin slices brown bread and lemon wedges.

PRAWN AND OYSTER COCKTAIL

69

For 4 servings, you will need:

6 oz (227 g) cooked, shelled and
deveined shrimp
12 oysters
¼ iceberg lettuce
4 oz (113 g) mayonnaise
1 oz (28 g) tomato paste

1 tsp lemon juice
Cayenne pepper
Parsley
Lemon cut into quarters
1 fl oz (2.8 cl) heavy cream

First prepare:

Cut shrimp into small pieces. Slice lettuce finely. Measure mayonnaise. Whip cream. Juice lemon. Finely chop parsley.

Now assemble!

1. Toss lettuce in lemon juice and place equal quantities into 4 coup glasses. Half fill.
2. Place seafood on bed of lettuce and refrigerate.
3. Make sauce by stirring cream and tomato paste into mayonnaise.
4. Place spoonful of sauce over seafood and dust with cayenne pepper and chopped parsley. Place a lemon wedge on side of glass and serve.

Potted Shrimp

AUSTRIAN LOBSTER COCKTAIL

For 10 servings, you will need:

Tartarkraut:

1 medium onion
2 anchovy fillets
2 tsp capers
2 sweet gherkins
1 tbs parsley
1 hard-boiled egg
1½ lbs (680 g) cooked
    lobster tail meat
16 fl oz (4 dl) mayonnaise
2 tbs tomato sauce
1 tsp Worcestershire sauce
Tabasco
1 tbs orange juice
2 tbs lemon juice
Freshly ground salt

Freshly ground pepper
2 tsp French mustard
2 tsp horseradish
1 tsp paprika
½ tsp cayenne
1 tbs dry sherry
1 tbs cognac
1 tbs Cointreau
1 head Boston lettuce
Lemon juice
Paprika
Parsley
10 lemon slices
20 shrimp, cooked, shelled and
    deveined

First prepare:

To prepare tartarkraut, finely dice onion, finely chop capers, anchovy fillets, gherkins, parsley and egg white. Shave egg yolk with side of knife. Mix all ingredients together in a bowl. Measure mayonnaise. Roughly chop lobster tail meat. Finely slice lettuce and season it with salt, pepper and lemon juice and place into bottom of 10 champagne glasses. Finely chop parsley.

Now cook!

1. Place mayonnaise in a bowl and stand it on crushed ice. Add tomato sauce and 9 oz (225 g) of the lobster meat. Add tartarkraut and season with Worcestershire sauce, 6 shakes of Tabasco sauce, orange juice, lemon juice, mustard, horseradish, paprika, cayenne, dry sherry, cognac and Cointreau. Combine all ingredients carefully and season to taste with salt and pepper.

2. Place remaining lobster pieces in glasses on bed of lettuce and cover with lobster mayonnaise mixture. Garnish with 2 shrimps, chopped parsley, and sprinkle of paprika. Place a lemon wedge on rim of each glass. Chill. Serve cold.

A special hint:

To hang a wedge of lemon on the glass cut lemon into quarters. Trim ends flat for easy squeezing and cut under yellow skin halfway up lemon wedge. Slip this cut flap onto glass.

CANADIAN ROLLS

For 48 servings, you will need:

6 oz (170 g) thin sliced
  boiled ham
6 oz (170 g) thin slices
  smoked salmon
Dill Butter:
4 oz (113 g) butter

4 tbs chopped dill (blend
  together)
Horseradish butter:
4 oz (113 g) butter
3 tbs grated horseradish
  (blend together)

68

Now assemble!

1. Spread ham with horseradish butter. Spread smoked salmon with dill butter.
2. Roll up into small rolls. Wrap rolls in aluminum foil and refrigerate.
3. Cut rolls into 1 inch (2.5 cm) thick slices before serving.

A special hint:

Keep these in refrigerator until last moment.

DOLMADES

For 4 servings, you will need:

1 lb (0.5 kg) ground beef
4 oz (113 g) raw long grain rice
2 tbs parsley
4 oz (113 g) butter
1 egg
20 grape leaves (canned)
1 tbs dill
Freshly ground salt

Freshly ground black pepper
Sauce:
10 fl oz (3 dl) plain yogurt
2 cloves garlic
1 cucumber
2 tbs olive oil
Freshly ground black pepper

First prepare:

If using grape leaves in brine, wash well. Measure butter and rice. Roughly chop parsley. Finely chop dill. Place yogurt in muslin and hang over a bowl to drain. Smash garlic, peel cucumber and grate.

Now cook!

1. Place ground meat, rice, parsley, dill and egg in a bowl. Season with salt and pepper and mix all ingredients.
2. Place 1 tbs of mixture in center of each grape leaf, fold in sides and roll up leaf.
3. Place dolmades in a pan with water to cover and add butter. Put a plate on top of dolmades, pressing down lightly, and put a lid on pan. Simmer over low heat 30 minutes.
4. *Sauce:* Place yogurt curds in a bowl, add garlic and cucumber. Season with black pepper. Measure liquid drained from yogurt and replace it with the same quantity of olive oil. Stir into yogurt mixture and spoon over well drained dolmades.

A special hint:

Step 3. The plate must be put *inside* pan directly on top of bundles. If this is not done they could unwrap (ghastly mess!).

EELS ON TOAST

For 4 servings, you will need:

1 smoked eel (about 2 lbs: 0.9 kg)
3 oz (85 g) butter
2 fl oz (5.6 cl) heavy cream
2 tsp horseradish sauce*

½ tsp Dijon mustard
1 tsp parsley
Freshly ground salt
Freshly ground white pepper

First prepare:

Remove head, outer skin and tail from smoked eel. Gently ease flesh from bones, starting down back. Measure mustard and butter. Wash, dry and finely chop parsley. Preheat broiler. Measure cream.

Now cook!

1. Take loaf of bread and cut 4 slices. Place under broiler and toast both sides.
2. Spread toast with 1 oz (28 g) butter, trim crusts.
3. Place pieces of smoked eel on top of toast—two fillets per piece.
4. Mash mustard and 2 oz (56 g) butter. Stir in cream, horseradish sauce and parsley.
5. Spoon this mixture down the center of eel fillets and spread along sides of open face sandwiches.

BEEF AND CAVIAR

For 4 servings, you will need:

4 oz (113 g) beef tenderloin
2 tbs Danish lumpfish roe
4 fl oz (1.2 dl) sour cream
Dill

Freshly ground black pepper
1 small onion
1 tbs horseradish
1 lemon

70

First prepare:

Trim all fat from tenderloin and freeze slightly until firm for easier slicing. Wash roe well in bowl of water, drain thoroughly. Grate onion. Chop dill.

Now assemble!

1. Cut paper thin slices of meat, flatten with back of knife and spread with ¼ tsp grated onion. Season heavily with black pepper, spread sparingly with grated horseradish and sprinkle with a little fresh dill. Spoon over two tsp roe and add squeeze of lemon juice.

2. Using knife blade turn over opposite ends of meat, rolling beef from both sides tightly to meet in center. Trim edges.

3. Place meat on thin slice of rye bread (cut to same size as meat roll) and garnish with small sprig of parsley placed in center.

A special hint:

Use horseradish sparingly regardless of one's taste for hot things. Too much and you destroy the other, more subtle, flavors.

MELON TREENA

For 2 servings, you will need:

1 small cantaloupe
2 tbs sour cream

1 oz (28 g) preserved ginger
2 tbs ginger syrup

69

First prepare:

Finely chop ginger into slivers. Cut cantaloupe in half and remove seeds.

Now assemble!

1. Fill cantaloupe halves with sour cream, decorate with ginger slivers and pour over a little ginger syrup. Chill.

A special hint:

Trim a slice off each rounded end of melon; helps it to sit steady on plate.

GRAPEFRUIT AND ORANGE COCKTAIL

For 4 servings, you will need:

2 grapefruit
2 oranges
2 tbs castor sugar*

Chopped mint
1 fl oz (2.8 cl) light rum

First prepare:

Halve grapefruit and remove sections. Reserve shells. Peel oranges and cut into segments. Finely chop mint.

Now assemble!

1. Combine orange and grapefruit segments. Stir in sugar and rum.
2. Spoon mixture into grapefruit shells, garnish with mint and chill.

A special hint:

Try your hand at making serrated edges on grapefruit. It gives shells a better appearance.

BROILED GRAPEFRUIT

For 2 servings, you will need:

1 pink grapefruit
1 sprig mint

1 tsp finely packed brown sugar
½ fl oz (1.4 cl) Calvados (or kirsch)

First prepare:

With a sharp knife, cut grapefruit in half. Wash and dry mint. Measure Calvados and sugar. Preheat broiler.

Now cook!

1. Loosen and remove center cores of grapefruit halves with a grapefruit knife and cut around loosened segments.
2. Place grapefruit on a heatproof plate, sprinkle with brown sugar and Calvados, and let stand for about 10 minutes to marinate.
3. Slide under broiler about 2 inches (5 cm) from heat and cook for 4 minutes.
4. Place grapefruit on serving dishes and garnish with mint.

MRS. ENID SMALL'S BRANDIED PRUNES

For 6 servings, you will need:

18 large dessert prunes in
  syrup*
2 fl oz (5.6 cl) brandy

4 oz (113 g) Philadelphia
  cream cheese
2 oz (56 g) preserved ginger

Now assemble!

1. Pit prunes and allow to marinate with syrup and brandy for 1 hour. Drain.
2. Cream cheese until soft, finely chop ginger and mix into cheese.
3. Use a small quantity of cream cheese mixture to stuff each prune.

CHEESE AND ANCHOVY CROSTINI

For 4 servings, you will need:
    8 thin slices white bread
    32 anchovy fillets
    8 oz (227 g) Mozzarella cheese

    8 tbs clarified butter*
    Oregano

Now cook!

1. Remove crusts from bread and cut each slice into 4 fingers. Place a thin slice of Mozzarella cheese on each and top with an anchovy fillet. Add a little oregano. Top with another finger of bread. Press together.
2. Heat butter in pan and fry sandwiches on both sides until golden brown. Serve warm.

A special hint:

Keep cheese slices very thin, ¼ inch (7 mm) thick. Use only butter not oil.

ROQUEFORT AND NUT CANAPES

For 4 servings, you will need:
    2 oz (56 g) Roquefort cheese
    2 oz (56 g) butter
    Cayenne pepper
    12 walnuts

    8 toasted rounds of bread
        (1½ inches: 3.7 cm diameter)
    8 walnut halves

First prepare:

Soften cheese, roughly chop 12 walnuts. Butter bread on both sides and bake in 350°F (177°C) oven about 10-15 minutes or until golden.

Now assemble!

1. Beat cheese with butter. Season with cayenne. Stir in nuts. Spread on toasted bread.
2. Serve garnished with walnut halves.

A special hint:

Add chopped nuts gradually to suit your taste.

CUSCINETTI FILANTI

For 4 servings, you will need:

8 slices white bread
8 slices prosciutto ham*
4 fresh sage leaves
8 slices Mozzarella cheese
Black peppercorns
Milk

Flour
1 egg
1 tsp paprika
20 fl oz (6 dl) olive oil
Parsley
Deep oil

First prepare:

Trim crusts from bread slices. Thinly slice Mozzarella. Mix egg with paprika. Heat oil to 380⁰F (193⁰C). Roughly grind peppercorns.

Now cook!

1. Place 1 slice of prosciutto on a bread slice and cover with a slice of Mozzarella. Season with pepper and place ¼ of sage leaf on each corner of cheese. Cover with another slice of prosciutto and second slice of bread.

2. Press sandwich firmly and cut into quarters. Dip into milk, then flour and paint on both sides with egg mixture.

3. Deep fry for 30 seconds on each side, turning with long pronged fork. Drain on absorbent paper and serve hot.

PARMESAN PALMIERS

For 6 servings, you will need:

1 lb (0.5 kg) puff pastry*
  (page 254)
Cayenne pepper
8 oz (227 g) grated Parmesan
  cheese
1 egg yolk

Filling:
2 oz (56 g) grated Parmesan cheese
1 oz (28 g) butter
Cayenne
2 tbs chopped chives

First prepare:

Filling: Mix cheese, butter and chives together, add dash of cayenne.
Pastry: Roll out into a rectangle 8 x 10 inches (20 x 25 cm). Sprinkle with half of Parmesan cheese and a dash of cayenne. Fold pastry into thirds and turn pastry so that long side is facing you. Roll pastry out into a rectangle once more, powder with rest of cheese and a dash of cayenne. Fold dough again into thirds. Roll out dough to an 8 x 10 inch rectangle. Preheat oven to 475⁰F (246⁰C).

Now cook!

1. Fold each 8 inch side pastry to meet in the center. Fold 2 rolls together in center. Cut pastry into ½ inch (1.2 cm) thick slices. Place on a buttered cookie sheet and brush them with beaten egg yolk.

2. Cook for 7 minutes in preheated 475⁰F (246⁰C) oven until golden.

3. Sandwich 2 palmiers with Parmesan flavored butter and serve on a dish lined with a paper doily.

A special hint:

Keep everything as cool as possible when cutting and rolling pastry.

NEW YORKER ONION SANDWICH

For 2 servings, you will need:

4 rounds brown bread
1 tbs mayonnaise
4 thin slices onion
Freshly ground salt

Freshly ground black pepper
2 slices tomato
Parsley

First prepare:

Slice onion, cut rounds of bread. Slice tomato, finely chop parsley.

Now assemble!

1. Lightly spread 2 rounds of bread with mayonnaise.
2. Place onion slices on remaining rounds of bread, and season with salt and pepper. Sandwich bread together.
3. Spread sides of sandwich with mayonnaise, roll in parsley.
4. Garnish with slice of tomato and sprig of parsley.

GURKAS NORGE

For 6 servings, you will need:

6 small cucumbers
12 fillets anchovies
1 tbs dill
1 tbs chives
6 oz (170 g) cream cheese
2 tbs sour cream

Freshly ground salt
Freshly ground black pepper
Lemon
Parsley
1 tsp sour cream, for each serving
1 tsp caviar, for each serving

First prepare:

Scrape cucumbers lengthwise with fork to make long grooves in skin. Cut in 2 inch (5 cm) sections and remove seeds, leaving cucumber rings. Measure cream cheese and sour cream. Finely chop chives and dill. Cut lemon into wedges.

Now assemble!

1. Mash anchovies and mix with dill, chives, cream cheese and sour cream. Season to taste with salt and pepper.
2. Stuff cucumber rings with cheese mixture and refrigerate for 2 hours.
3. Place 1 tsp sour cream and caviar on top of each cucumber ring.
4. Serve accompanied by lemon wedges and parsley.

MUSHROOMS SUR CLOCHE

For 4 servings, you will need:

1 lb (0.5 kg) mushrooms (weight with stalks removed)	3 egg yolks
8 fl oz (2 dl) cold water	3 fl oz (8 cl) heavy cream
4 fl oz (1.2 dl) dry white wine	1 lemon
4 oz (113 g) butter	1 tbs chives
1½ oz (42 g) all-purpose flour	Freshly ground salt
4 slices bread	Freshly ground black pepper
	Freshly ground white pepper

First prepare:

Wash and dry mushrooms. Measure dry and liquid ingredients. Juice lemon. Wash and finely chop chives. Separate eggs.

Now cook!

1. Pour cold water into a saucepan. Add wine, 1½ oz (42 g) butter and mushrooms and cook over high heat for 10 minutes.
2. When this mixture comes to a boil, reduce heat to medium and simmer 5 minutes. Strain, reserving liquid.
3. In another saucepan over medium heat, melt 1½ oz (42 g) butter, stir in flour and cook for a few minutes, stirring. (This is called a roux.)
4. Slowly stir reserved mushroom juice into roux. Stir briskly and bring mixture to a boil.
5. When roux has boiled add drained mushrooms, lemon juice and chives.
6. Mix cream with egg yolks.
7. Gradually stir in egg and cream mixture. Reheat but do not boil. Season to taste with salt and pepper.
8. Toast bread.
9. Cut crusts off toast and spread with remaining 1 oz (28 g) butter. Place on a serving platter and spoon mushroom mixture over. Serve piping hot.

CHILI CUCUMBER

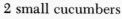

For 2 servings, you will need:

2 small cucumbers	2 limes
1 tsp chili powder	Freshly ground salt

First prepare:

Peel cucumbers. Squeeze juice from limes. Measure chili powder. Waxed paper will be required.

Now assemble!

1. Quarter cucumbers lengthwise all but for the last inch (2 cm) (this holds it together).
2. Fold a piece of waxed paper around base of cucumbers.
3. Season cucumbers with lime juice and salt.
4. Finally dust with chili powder and serve.

MUSHROOMS RIVOLI

For 4 servings, you will need:

8 oz (227 g) button mushrooms
2 oz (56 g) sultana raisins
Clarified butter*

3 fl oz (8 cl) ketchup
3 fl oz (8 cl) dry white wine

First prepare:

Measure dry white wine and ketchup. Wash mushrooms.

Now cook!

1. Into a saucepan containing enough clarified butter to just cover bottom, gently fry mushrooms over moderate heat. Then add white wine, tomato ketchup and sultanas. Simmer 1 minute.
2. Pour mushroom mixture into a bowl and chill.

COLD CUCUMBER WITH PROVENCALE DRESSING

For 4 servings, you will need:

1 seedless cucumber
    (European type)
Provençale dressing:
4 fl oz (1.2 dl) wine vinegar

1 tsp thyme
1 tsp rosemary
1 bay leaf
5 fl oz (1.5 dl) heavy cream

First prepare:

Slightly blanch cucumber in boiling water. Slice.

Now assemble!

1. Place all ingredients for dressing, except cream, into a pan and simmer for 10 minutes.
2. Strain and chill.
3. Stir gently into cream so as not to curdle.
4. Place sliced cucumber in bowl and pour over dressing. Chill.

GUACAMOLE

For 6 servings, you will need:

3 avocado pears
8 oz (227 g) tomatoes
1 medium onion
1 tbs cilantro*
1 serrano chili*
1 tbs light oil

1 tsp white wine vinegar
2 tortillas
2 tbs clarified butter*
Freshly ground salt
Freshly ground white pepper
¼ tsp cayenne pepper

First prepare:

Blanch tomatoes in boiling water for 2 minutes. Remove, cool, peel, cut into quarters and scrape out seeds. Finely chop tomato and onion. Remove seeds from chili and discard. Wash, dry and finely chop cilantro. Measure oil and vinegar. Lastly, slice avocado pears in half keeping one of the seeds for marinade. Reserve avocado shell halves. Quarter tortillas (see recipe page 552).

Now cook!

1. Scoop avocados from skin. Reserve skins. Puree avocado in a blender and pour into a bowl.
2. Add tomatoes and onion to puree. Season to taste with salt and pepper.
3. Mix cilantro and chili pulp.
4. Mix oil and vinegar together in a small bowl.
5. Pour into avocado mixture.
6. Place one avocado pear seed in bowl (this prevents the avocado flesh from discoloring).
7. Cover with a clean cloth and chill.
8. Into a large frypan pour clarified butter and when hot, fry quartered tortillas for 2 minutes until crisp.
9. In the meantime, scoop marinated avocado mixture into the avocado skins. Discard the seed.
10. Drain fried tortillas on absorbent paper and dust with cayenne pepper. Serve with guacamole.

SALSA VERDE AND GOAT CHEESE

For 4 servings, you will need:

4 serrano chilies*
4 oz (113 g) green tomatoes
3 tbs cilantro*
2 oz (56 g) celery
3 cloves garlic
1 tsp white wine vinegar
1 tbs olive oil

2 fl oz (5.6 cl) white wine
1 level tsp mint
14 tortillas, canned or frozen
8 oz (227 g) goat cheese
Freshly ground salt
1 level tsp freshly ground
  black pepper

First prepare:

Remove seeds from serrano chilies and discard. Chop flesh very finely. Repeat with tomatoes. Finely dice celery and garlic. Cut goat cheese into narrow sticks. Measure dry and liquid ingredients. Wash, dry and finely chop cilantro and mint.

Now cook!

1. Mix tomatoes, chilies, cilantro and celery in a bowl.
2. Season with salt and pepper. Add garlic.
3. In a small bowl mix olive oil and white wine. Pour over vegetables.
4. Stir in vinegar and mint and set aside to chill.
5. Arrange goat cheese sticks in a small serving dish, on top of "green sauce."
6. Boil some water in a large frypan and place tortillas over it on a wire rack for 30 seconds (4 at a time).
7. Arrange them in a napkin in a basket and serve with goat cheese and Salsa Verde.

MANTAY

For 8 servings, you will need:
Pastry:
12 oz (340 g) all-purpose flour
1 tsp baking powder
3 eggs
½ eggshell cold water
Filling:
1½ lbs (680 g) boneless
   mutton (ground)
4 oz (113 g) onion

2 tbs chopped parsley
Freshly ground black pepper
Freshly ground salt
2 tsp dried dill
1 small onion
Clarified butter*
Egg white to seal
12 fl oz (3.2 dl) chicken stock
3 tbs sour cream

First prepare:

Make dough by placing sifted flour and baking powder on a board, forming a well in the center and adding eggs and water. Work the flour into the eggs gradually with fingertips to form a firm dough. Knead dough well and then allow to rest for 30 minutes under a bowl. Finely grind the mutton. Finely dice all the onion and finely chop parsley. Measure chicken stock. Measure sour cream.

Now cook!

1. Mix meat, onion and parsley together and season with lots of pepper and salt. Add dill and mix thoroughly.
2. Roll out pastry until very thin and cut into 3 inch (7.6 cm) squares. Paint with slightly beaten egg white. Place 1 tbs of the meat mixture in the middle of the pastry square, bring all 4 corners to the center and press together to seal.
3. Place a little clarified butter into a saucepan to just cover bottom and add finely chopped onion. Allow to fry gently. Add chicken stock and place mantays into saucepan. When the chicken stock comes to a boil, cover pot and simmer for 35 minutes. Drain mantays and place on a heated serving dish.
4. Add sour cream to the chicken stock but do not allow to boil or it will curdle. Pour sauce over mantays.

BELGIAN ENDIVE

For 2 servings, you will need:

2 Belgian endive	Freshly ground black pepper
1 cucumber	Oil
Freshly ground salt	Vinegar

First prepare:

Wash endive, peel and cube cucumber. Place a pan of cold water on to boil.

Now cook!

1. Blanch endive in boiling water and add cubes of cucumber.
2. Drain and cool, season with salt and pepper.
3. Put ingredients in a bowl and sprinkle with oil and vinegar dressing.

BEANOVSKI

71

For 6 servings, you will need:

1 can (1 lb) red kidney beans	12 fl oz (3.2 dl) cold water
1 medium onion	½ tsp chili powder
4 oz (113 g) bacon	Clarified butter*
1½ tbs all-purpose flour	Freshly ground salt
8 fl oz (2 dl) sour cream	Freshly ground white pepper
8 fl oz (2 dl) dry white wine	

First prepare:

Open can of beans. Dice onion and bacon. Measure flour, water, chili powder and sour cream. Heat a serving dish in warming oven.

Now cook!

1. Fry bacon in a pan and add 2 tbs clarified butter.
2. Stir in onion and cook until soft.
3. Add flour and chili powder. Cook for 3 minutes.
4. Add beans and 8 fl oz (2 dl) of cold water. The mixture will thicken almost immediately. Cook over low heat for 1 hour, stirring occasionally.
5. Gradually blend in dry white wine and remaining 4 fl oz (1.2 dl) of cold water.
6. Finally stir in sour cream and simmer for another 10 minutes.
7. Pour into heated serving dish and serve at once.

A special hint:

Refer to Step 5. Add only sufficient wine and water to keep mixture from sticking.

VEAL BRAINS IN MARINADE

For 4 servings, you will need:

2 veal brains
2 oz (56 g) sugar
4 fl oz (1.2 dl) white wine vinegar

2 fl oz (5.6 cl) olive oil
¼ tsp cayenne pepper

First prepare:

Soak brains (after rinsing very thoroughly) in cold water for 1 hour. Measure white wine vinegar and olive oil. A bowl of ice water will be required.

Now cook!

1. Drain water from veal brains and cover with fresh cold water in a saucepan. Place over moderate heat and bring to a boil. Remove brains from boiling water and plunge into bowl of ice water until required.

2. Into a blender place sugar, wine vinegar, olive oil and cayenne pepper (a quick vinaigrette).

3. Drain brains and place into a bowl (see hint). Pour over dressing. Chill for 1 hour before serving.

A special hint:

Strip all fat from blanched (and stiffened) brains and cut into 1 inch (2.5 cm) pieces.

BABY ONIONS IN SAUCE

For 4 servings, you will need:

4 yellow onions
3 fl oz (8 cl) dry white wine
3 fl oz (8 cl) tomato ketchup

2 oz (56 g) sultana raisins
Clarified butter*

First prepare:

Cut onions into quarters and peel petals off separately. Measure white wine and ketchup.

Now cook!

1. Pour some clarified butter into a frypan to just cover bottom and place over moderate heat. Pop in petals of onions and gently fry.

2. To onions add white wine, ketchup and sultanas. Fry together for a few moments.

3. Pour onion mixture into a bowl and chill.

PART III
EGGS

PART III
EGGS

Recently a number of obviously well-intentioned experts have been suggesting that the cholesterol content in egg yolks is so high that we should cut down or even eliminate eggs from our diet. But the egg must have been one of the earliest forms of protein consumed by man. It is a superb piece of advanced packaging and best of all it is converted almost instantly into hundreds of easily digested dishes. Bad for one? See Cholesterol and Tension, page 36.

My life begins each day with a really superb breakfast. Bacon and eggs when I'm at my right weight; bacon and poached eggs when the weight is going up; and poached or boiled eggs when I'm up there! Lunches consist, now and again, of omelets, scrambled eggs or eggs baked in small pots. At night it's a soufflé or filled pancakes or, even better, a combination of both. It's not quite as bad as it sounds. I'm neither broody nor egg-bound, but I'm happy to have been the author of the slogan "Where would we be without eggs!"

In a previous book, *The Graham Kerr Cookbook,* published variously by A. H. & A. W. Read (Australia, New Zealand), Doubleday (U.S., Canada), W. H. Allen (Great Britain) and by my present publishers in the paperback edition, I give detailed methods of all egg-cooking techniques. In this Part, I have restricted comment to boiled and poached eggs, omelets and soufflés. Elsewhere in this book, you will find recipes for pancakes, soufflé pancakes, soufflé omelets and egg custards. Enough to get you broody, perhaps?

BOILED

A useful hint for hard-boiling eggs is to drain off the hot water the instant they are cooked and then rustle them around the empty pan to gently crack the shells all over. Put under cold, running water and just twist the whole shell away. Leave them in the cold water to cool rapidly and you will avoid that dark sulphur ring around the yolk.

POACHED

I once wrote on my first typewriter, "Anything I write shall be the whole truth as I know it. Should I be proved wrong then I shall say so." I was wrong with my poached egg idea. The one where tired old eggs can have their albumen stiffened by plunging them into boiling water in their shells for 10 seconds. It is a great deal of effort for little result and it's far, far better to buy really fresh eggs! See Eggs Meurette (page 150; Fig. 7) for the new technique.

OMELETS

I am an omelet fanatic. If I ever go into the restaurant business it will be an Omelet Emporium. Great food, wonderfully sustaining, and the potential for variety is endless. The great secret is to set up the cooking area and serve them with minimum delay. The following sketch plus notes gives you a good plan.

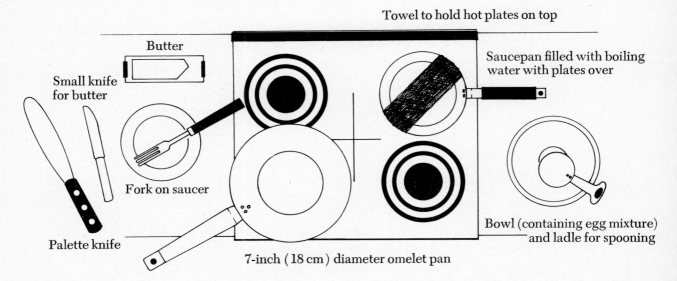

The idea here is that everything is at hand. The plates are heated and the cloth is there to hold them. The eggs are mixed and seasoned, for however many omelets are to be made. The 8 oz (227 g.) ladle transfers enough for a three-egg omelet. Butter and knife are side by side. A fork (for stirring) is on a saucer to save dropping a dirty fork on the counter top. The palette knife is there to help lever the omelet from the pan.

SOUFFLES

The fact that a soufflé is largely hot air is interesting when you consider that most comments about its preparation are equally inflated. A well-made cheese soufflé makes a good meal for a family. It is filling, contains good food value and is delicious. At a party I prefer to serve a cheese soufflé after a simple dessert, when there is no time deadline. The baking time for soufflés (about 40 minutes) is so critical that enormous tension can result if you live in dread of its birth throughout the meal. The moral is to serve it as a first course (a bit tricky if guests are late). As a main dish, put it in when they arrive— this gives you half an hour for drinks plus 10 minutes for the first course. Or, do as I do and put it in after the main course and simply serve it after dessert in place of cheese.

EGGS MAYONNAISE

For 4 servings, you will need:

4 eggs
2 oz (56 g) can of flat
 anchovy fillets
4 fl oz (1.2 dl) mayonnaise

1 lettuce heart
1 tbs capers
1 tbs parsley
Cayenne pepper

First prepare:

Hard-boil eggs. Halve lengthwise and lay each half on a crisp lettuce leaf. Refrigerate. Measure mayonnaise. Finely chop parsley. Strain oil from anchovy fillets into a bowl and split fillets in two lengthwise.

Now assemble!

1. Mix mayonnaise with oil from anchovies.
2. Cover each egg half with a spoonful of mayonnaise and garnish with two anchovy fillets. Dust with parsley and cayenne pepper. Scatter capers around eggs.

PLOVERS' EGGS

For 4 servings, you will need:

4 small eggs (as newly laid
 as possible)
4 sticks of celery
16 radishes

1 bunch of watercress
Freshly ground salt
Freshly ground white pepper

First prepare:

Prick wide base of eggs with an egg pricker (or pin). Wash celery and watercress. Wash radishes, trim off tops and tails.

Now cook!

1. Put eggs in a pan of boiling water and boil for 8 minutes.
2. Remove from heat and drain. Run cold water over eggs and gently shake in pan to crack shells. Remove shells under water.
3. Set peeled eggs aside (keep them warm).
4. Now place warm eggs one at a time, between the palms of the hands and gently apply pressure. Eggs will slowly flatten out into a small round white "cake."
5. Season eggs in the hand with salt and pepper, and eat alternately with celery, radishes and watercress.

EGGS HUSSARDE

For 6 servings, you will need:

6 eggs	7 oz (198 g) butter
1 medium onion	6 fl oz (1.6 dl) beef stock
3 shallots	12 fl oz (3.2 dl) dry red wine
2 cloves garlic	6 Holland rusks
1 oz (28 g) mushrooms	2 tbs parsley
10 oz (284 g) cooked smoked ham	¼ tsp paprika
2 tbs all-purpose flour	4 tbs clarified butter*
8 oz (227 g) tomato	Freshly ground salt
1 tsp lemon juice	Freshly ground black pepper
½ tsp nutmeg	Freshly ground white pepper
¼ tsp cayenne pepper	

First prepare:

Leave 2 eggs whole then separate remaining 4 into yolks and whites (these can be kept for meringues, etc.). Mince onion, shallots, garlic and mushrooms. Also mince 4 oz (113 g) of ham. Slice tomato in ½-inch (1.2 cm) thick rounds. Measure spices and liquid ingredients. Preheat broiler. Divide butter into four portions: three 2-oz (56 g) portions and one 1-oz (28 g) portion.

Now cook!

1. Into a casserole on medium heat pour 2 fl oz (5.6 cl) clarified butter and stir in mixture of onion, shallots, mushrooms, garlic and ham. Fry for about 2 minutes.

2. Stir in flour and cook on medium heat. Season with salt and black pepper and stir to get a good brown color.

3. Stir in beef stock and 8 fl oz (2 dl) red wine. Stir and simmer over low heat 10 minutes.

4. Add another 4 fl oz (1.2 dl) red wine to vegetables and simmer over low heat.

5. Into top of a double boiler (the water should just be bubbling underneath) pour lemon juice, nutmeg, cayenne pepper and season with salt and white pepper.

6. With a whisk stir in 4 egg yolks and 2 oz (56 g) butter.

7. Whisk another 2 oz (56 g) butter into sauce in double-boiler.

8. Whisk another 2 oz (56 g) butter to the thickened egg sauce.

9. Place tomato slices on an ovenproof dish, season with salt and slide under broiler. Stir vegetables and ham once more.

10. Remove tomatoes from broiler.

11. Cut remaining cooked ham into slices to cover top of Holland rusks. Brown lightly under broiler.

12. Pour a little water into a frypan over medium heat and when slightly bubbly add 1 oz (28 g) butter and melt. Take off heat and break eggs into water. Return to heat and spoon a little of the hot water over eggs and lightly poach.

13. Remove ham-covered rusks from broiler.

14. Sprinkle parsley into vegetable sauce and pour 1 tbs over each slice of ham. Pop slice of broiled tomato on top of ham, then drain poached eggs and crown with these.

15. Stir the hollandaise sauce and pour 2 tsp over each egg.

16. Dust with a little paprika.

Eggs Hussarde

CHICKEN EGGS

For 4 servings, you will need:

4 hard-boiled eggs
1 chicken, 3 lbs (1.4 kg)
2 oz (56 g) dill pickles
1 tsp cardamon
3 tsp horseradish
Freshly ground salt
1 egg
Flour
1 egg yolk beaten with 1 tbs
   clarified butter*

4 oz (113 g) bread crumbs*
8 peppercorns
1 onion, cut in half
Sprig of thyme
Sprig of parsley
Deep oil
Sauce:
4 fl oz (1.2 dl) mayonnaise
½ tsp curry powder
2 sweet gherkins

70

First prepare:

Hard-boil eggs for 10 minutes and put in cold water. Place chicken in a large pot, cover with water, add peppercorns, onion, thyme and parsley. When water has come to the boil, cover and allow to simmer for 1 hour. Remove chicken and refrigerate. When chicken has cooled, skin and strip off flesh and put flesh into finest blade of grinder. Grind dill pickles along with chicken. Put bread crumbs in a bowl. Mix egg yolk with clarified butter. Heat oil to 350⁰ F (177⁰ C).

Now cook!

1. Combine ground chicken and pickles with cardamon and horseradish. Season with salt and mix well with an egg. Place on wax paper and press out with fingers until the mixture is ½ inch (1.2 cm) thick.
2. Shell hard-boiled eggs. Cut some of the chicken mixture to fit eggs and press around, enclosing them. Roll in flour. Paint with beaten egg yolk and roll around in a bowl of bread crumbs to coat.
3. Place eggs into basket of deep fryer and fry for 4 minutes, 30 seconds. Drain on absorbent paper.
4. Cut eggs in half with a sharp knife, place on a serving dish and accompany with sauce.
5. *Sauce:* Mix mayonnaise, curry powder and finely chopped gherkins.

POACHED EGGS WITH BACON AND CHEESE

For 4 servings, you will need:

8 eggs
3 lbs (1.4 kg) baking potatoes
1 egg
1 oz (28 g) butter
Freshly ground salt
Freshly ground white pepper

Nutmeg
8 bacon slices
8 slices of mild Cheddar cheese
   cut thinly
½ oz (14 g) butter

First prepare:

Bake potatoes in their jackets in 350ºF (177ºC) oven for 1 hour. Peel potatoes and mash. Cut bacon into fine strips. Slice cheese finely. Preheat broiler.

Now cook!

1. Beat 1 egg and butter into mashed potatoes and season with salt, pepper and nutmeg.
2. Pipe a ring of mashed potatoes onto 4 individual ovenproof dishes.
3. Fry bacon in its own fat until crisp.
4. In a frypan filled with boiling salted water place ½ oz (14 g) butter. When melted, break in 8 eggs. Remove pan from heat and allow eggs to just set. Drain in a slotted spoon and place 2 eggs into each potato ring. Pour bacon fat over eggs. Add bacon strips. Season with pepper and cover eggs with cheese slices.
5. Place under broiler for 5 minutes until cheese is melted and browned.

POACHED EGGS IN MAPLE SYRUP

For 2 servings, you will need:

4 eggs
4 back bacon slices*

12 fl oz (3.2 dl) maple syrup

First prepare:

Measure maple syrup.

Now cook!

1. Place ½ tbs of maple syrup in a pan on heat and add bacon slices. When bacon is crisp, remove and keep hot. Add rest of maple syrup to drippings. When syrup is frothy break in the eggs and allow them to poach over low heat. Spoon froth over the eggs.
2. When the eggs are set, place on a serving dish surrounded by the bacon.

A special hint:

The time of addition is critical. You must add eggs when syrup froths for first time. The syrup can be strained and reused.

OEUFS EN MEURETTE

For 4 servings, you will need:

6 large shallots
3 cloves garlic
4 fresh eggs
12 fl oz (3.2 dl) Burgundy
1 lump sugar
3 slices fat bacon*
8 fl oz (2 dl) beef bouillon
3 tbs red wine vinegar
4 slices white bread

Bouquet garni: 1 bay leaf, 4 parsley
   stalks,*1 sprig thyme and 3 inch
   (7.6 cm) celery stick
Fresh chopped parsley
1 oz (28 g) butter
1½ oz (42 g) all-purpose flour
Freshly ground salt
Freshly ground black pepper
Clarified butter*

First prepare:

Remove outer skin of shallots and cut each one into three pieces. Peel and crush garlic. Open wine. Chop bacon fat into ½ inch (1.2 cm) cubes. Tie bouquet garni with string if fresh or in a muslin bag if dried herbs are used. Cut bread slices into rounds. Boil water for eggs. Place serving dishes in warming oven.

Now cook!

1. Pour 1½ oz (42 g) clarified butter into a pan and heat until smoking, 400°F (205°C).
2. Stir in shallots to allow natural juices (oils) to ooze out.
3. Add fat bacon and brown lightly.
4. Add 2 cloves garlic.
5. Sprinkle flour over this mixture and stir over heat until golden brown, about 4 minutes.
6. Add Burgundy and whisk off heat.
7. Add bouillon and stir thoroughly.
8. Now add lump of sugar.
9. Pop in bouquet garni, salt and pepper. Simmer on heat covered for 1½ hours. Stir occasionally.
10. After one hour add vinegar.
11. At the end of 1½ hours add 1 oz (28 g) butter to sauce.
12. Sieve sauce scraping every last drop of it into clean pan. Cook gently over low heat.
13. Put a little clarified butter to just cover bottom of a skillet, and cook remaining garlic to release natural juices.
14. Drop rounds of bread into garlic butter adding a little more clarified butter if necessary. Fry until crisp and golden brown.
15. Prick wide end of eggs with an egg pricker or needle, place in a wire basket and lower it into pan of boiling water. Count 10 seconds, remove eggs and break each one into a cup. (You will find by boiling eggs for 10 seconds, fresh quality of egg white will be retained.)
16. Add a pinch of salt to water and lower heat to simmering. Add eggs and gently poach.
17. Meanwhile remove fried bread rounds from pan and place in small heated serving bowls.
18. Have ready a slotted spoon to drain eggs.
19. Place lightly poached egg on bread and pour sauce around egg leaving some white showing. Garnish with parsley.

A special hint:

To prevent eggs from cracking when cooking prick them with an egg pricker. This makes a hole in the shell and equalizes the pressure of the air in the egg as it heats and expands in the hot water.

1. OEUFS EN MEURETTE are basically poached and served in a red wine sauce.

2. Like all relatively quick sauces the flavor is improved if the ingredients are cut very small.

3. Fry shallots, bacon and garlic first and then add flour to make the roux.

4. Stir well until the flour has had time to cook—about 4 minutes.

5. Add a rather long slurp of good red Burgundy!

6. Brush a small frypan with melted butter and fill it with hot water.

7. Bring the water to a boil and reduce the heat to a simmer. Add the eggs from a dish or saucer.

8. Poach until firm. Use a slotted spoon to lift the egg to the ramequin.

9. Put a slice of fried bread in the ramequin. Add the egg, and coat with strained sauce. Reheat and garnish with parsley.

ARNOLD BENNETT OMELET

For 4 servings, you will need:

4 oz (113 g) smoked cod (blue)*
4 eggs
½ oz (14 g) butter
Garlic salt

Freshly ground white pepper
4 tbs heavy cream
1 tbs grated cheese
10 fl oz (3 dl) milk

First prepare:

Poach fish gently in milk. Grate cheese, measure cream. Drain fish and flake.

Now cook!

1. Break eggs into a bowl, add cream and season with garlic salt and pepper. Add fish and mix.
2. Heat 8-inch (20 cm) omelet pan and add the butter. Allow butter to brown at edges.
3. Add half the egg mixture, stir rapidly with a fork moving the pan at the same time. This ensures that eggs cook evenly. Leave center slightly runny.
4. Sprinkle center of omelet with half the grated cheese.
5. Turn out, brush with melted butter.
6. Repeat for remaining omelets.

MEXICAN OMELET

For 2 servings, you will need:

1 red pepper (capsicum)
1 green pepper (capsicum)
2 fl oz (5.6 cl) olive oil
3 oz (85 g) onion
2 cloves garlic
1 oz (28 g) pitted green olives
4 tbs fresh parsley
1 medium tomato
1 serrano chili*

6 eggs
½ tsp cold water
6 oz (170 g) potatoes
¼ tsp powdered oregano
2 fl oz (5.6 cl) heavy cream
2 oz (56 g) butter
Freshly ground salt
Freshly ground white pepper

First prepare:

Peel potatoes and boil in salted water until cooked. Slice top from red and green peppers, remove seeds and dice coarsely. Dice onion. Smash garlic and finely chop. Slice olives in half crosswise. Wash, dry and finely chop parsley. Cut tomato in half, remove seeds and cut the flesh into thin strips. (Do not peel.) Very carefully slice serrano chili in half, discard seeds and chop finely. Separate eggs and place in separate mixing bowls. Measure remaining dry and liquid ingredients. Heat a serving platter in warm oven and preheat broiler. Quarter and dice cooked potatoes.

Now cook!

1. Into a small frypan on medium heat, place olive oil and add red and green peppers. Season generously with salt and pepper.
2. Add onion, garlic and halved olives.
3. Add tomato and stir mixture constantly. The serrano chili can now be stirred in.
4. Stir diced potatoes, oregano and parsley into frying vegetables. Cook over low heat.
5. Into a mixer on low speed, pour in egg whites and season with salt. Add ½ tsp cold water. Beat on high speed until egg whites are "peaky" but not "dry."

6. Beat cream into egg yolks.

7. Turn off mixer and with rubber scraper fold egg yolks through stiff egg whites until thoroughly blended.

8. Check that broiler is really hot.

9. Into a large 10-inch (25 cm) frypan on high heat melt 1 oz (28 g) butter and stir in ¾ of the omelet mixture. Spoon fried vegetables evenly over omelet. When underside is cooked (less than 60 seconds) pour remaining quarter of mixture over vegetables, smooth it out and slide pan under broiler.

10. After approximately 2 minutes it should be ready.

11. Invert savory omelet onto a heated serving platter and glaze with remaining 1 oz (28 g) fresh butter.

A special hint:

To butter-glaze an omelet I always draw a piece of butter over the open face. The butter seals in the moisture and gives the omelet a great glossy look. It tastes good too!

OMELET MEERAKKER

For 2 servings, you will need:

1 clove garlic	1 oz (28 g) butter
4 slices bacon	3 eggs
6 oz (170 g) cooked kidney beans	1½ fl oz (4.2 cl) heavy cream
1 tsp sambal oelek*	Clarified butter*

First prepare:

Chop bacon finely. Beat eggs gently with heavy cream. Smash clove of garlic.

Now cook!

1. Pour some clarified butter into a small saucepan. Add garlic. Add bacon and season with sambal oelek. Stir in beans and let simmer.

2. Place fresh butter in omelet pan and let it melt over moderate to high heat. When butter starts to brown add eggs and stir vigorously with a fork, moving pan at the same time.

3. When the eggs are cooked but still moist on top, spoon bean mixture into middle of omelet. Fold outer edges in and turn onto a serving dish.

PETER RODENBURG OMELET

60

For 4 servings, you will need:

6 oz (170 g) shrimp
   (cooked and peeled)
6 oz (170 g) white cabbage
1 oz (28 g) white cabbage core
1 tbs green chili
1 tsp parsley stalks*
1½ oz (42 g) onion
8 eggs

6 fl oz (1.6 dl) heavy cream
2 tbs butter
3 tbs soya sauce
4 tbs clarified butter*
Garlic
Freshly ground salt
Freshly ground white pepper

First prepare:

Cut cabbage into fine slices. Cut cabbage core into matchstick slivers. Finely chop chili and parsley stalks. Finely slice onion. Measure butter. Beat eggs with cream. Place each item on a separate dish.

Now cook!

1. Mix cabbage core, garlic, parsley stalks and chili with soya sauce in a bowl and allow to stand at least 1 hour.

2. Place clarified butter in frypan. Stir in onions and cabbage and cook 1 minute. Add soya sauce mixture. Stir until soya sauce is well distributed. Add shrimp, stir lightly with a fork, cover saucepan tightly and remove from heat.

3. Mix eggs with cream, season with salt and pepper.

4. Heat an 8-inch (20 cm) omelet pan, add butter and ¼ of the egg and cream mixture. Stir well and when evenly cooked but still moist and runny on top, add ¼ of prepared filling. Turn omelet onto dish, place a small piece of butter on top and garnish with parsley. Continue until all 4 omelets are made.

A special hint:

You can measure eggs from bowl with a ladle; about 6 fl oz (1.6 dl) equal 1 omelet.

1. PETER RODENBURG OMELET.

2. To eggs add pepper, salt and a knife point of garlic.

3. Cream is also added to keep the richness and succulence.

4. The eggs and cream are beaten to a pale yellow—no froth.

5. Add whole butter to a hot pan. Wait until the edges *just* brown.

6. Add a ladleful of egg mixture (note that filling is close by).

7. Stir mix vigorously, moving pan. This is a one-hole spurtle.

8. While center is moist add hot filling at right angle to handle.

9. Fold back the handle edge of omelet to the middle.

10. Then fold the opposite edge to the center.

11. Hold hot plate in left hand and bring omelet over.

12. It will fall neatly in place. Brush with butter and serve.

GRAHAM KERR OMELET

59

For 4 servings, you will need:

12 eggs
12 fl oz (3.2 dl) heavy cream
1 clove garlic
Freshly ground white pepper
Freshly ground salt

Filling:
12 oz (340 g) tomatoes
8 oz (227 g) bacon slices
1 oz (28 g) parsley stalks*
4 fl oz (1.2 dl) dry white wine

First prepare:

Mix eggs with cream and pepper. Mash garlic with salt, and add to eggs. Skin, seed and chop tomatoes. Finely slice bacon. Chop parsley stalks. Measure wine.

Now cook!

1. Heat finely sliced bacon slowly in a small saucepan to release natural fats.
2. Add tomatoes and dry white wine. Simmer uncovered for 4 minutes.
3. Add parsley stalks and keep warm.
4. Make omelets as shown in basic method (page 152).
5. Fill each omelet before folding with a good spoonful of tomato mixture. Serve very hot.

A special hint:

Serve direct from the pan. A tepid omelet is a waste of your energy and your guest's time!

------------------ ------------------

*Children who won't eat well-cooked natural food
should be allowed to go hungry.*

TROUCHA

For 6 servings, you will need:

3 lbs (1.4 kg) spinach
8 oz (227 g) bacon
8 fl oz (2 dl) water
½ tsp freshly grated nutmeg
4 oz (113 g) butter

9 eggs
2 tsp butter
Freshly ground salt
Freshly ground white pepper

First prepare:

Remove stalks from spinach leaves, wash carefully at least 7 times. Finely dice bacon. Measure butter and water. Grate nutmeg. Break eggs into a bowl.

Now cook!

1. Heat a frypan and fry bacon gently until brown and crisp. Drain.
2. Sprinkle water over spinach, season with salt and pepper, sprinkle with grated nutmeg.
3. Place a large pan (or 2 smaller pans) on the heat and melt 4 oz (113 g) of butter.
4. Add seasoned spinach and cover tightly with a lid (it may not fit at first but the bulk will reduce in 2-3 minutes).
5. After spinach has reduced and cooked about 5 minutes, cool and squeeze out surplus liquid (keep this for soup broth). Repeat 3 times.
6. Add bacon.
7. Grease a 10-inch (25 cm) diameter bowl with 2 tbs butter and add ¼ of the drained spinach and bacon.
8. Whisk eggs.
9. Pour some beaten egg over the hot spinach mixture in bowl (this should cook eggs). Cover with more hot spinach, more eggs, more spinach until all is used, finishing off with spinach.
10. Put a weight on top and place bowl into a large pan containing about 2 inches (5 cm) hot water.
11. Let simmer for 20 minutes.
12. Remove bowl from water and again place weight on top to press while it cools.
13. When it is completely cold, loosen edges, tap to unmold and serve.

A special hint:

It is vital that you use three pressings to rid spinach of as much water as possible at Step 5. You don't have another chance to press it after this step.

Peter Rodenburg Omelet (page 154)

LANGOUSTE SOUFFLE ERNIE'S

For 2 servings, you will need:

2½ lb (1.1 kg) raw lobster
½ tsp paprika
4 fl oz (1.2 dl) corn oil
2 tbs shallots
1 tbs tarragon
1 clove garlic
2 fl oz (5.6 cl) brandy
8 fl oz (2 dl) white wine
2 medium tomatoes
1 bay leaf

Pinch thyme
20 fl oz (6 dl) fish stock
Freshly ground salt
Freshly ground black pepper
3 oz (84 g) butter
3 tbs all-purpose flour
3 egg yolks
4 egg whites
2 oz (56 g) mushrooms

First prepare:

Make fish stock. Split lobster in half lengthwise. Season both halves with paprika, salt and pepper. Measure brandy and wine. Finely chop shallots. Peel and crush garlic. Skin and seed tomatoes, cut into quarters. Measure butter. Preheat oven to 425ºF (218ºC). Chop mushrooms and cook in 1 oz butter until all moisture is absorbed.

Now cook!

1. Place oil in a large pan over medium heat. Sauté lobster in pan until shell turns red. Add shallots and garlic.

2. Heat brandy, pour over lobster and flame. Add wine, tomatoes, tarragon, thyme, bay leaf and fish stock. Season with salt and pepper. Cover pan and allow to cook gently 8 minutes. Take off heat and remove lobster. Cool.

3. Remove cut lobster meat from shell and dice. Strain poaching liquid through muslin. Cool.

4. Place 2 oz (56 g) butter in a saucepan and when melted stir in flour. Cook over low heat for 3 minutes and slowly whisk in 12 fl oz (3.2 dl) of the poaching liquid. Bring to boil and remove pan from heat to cool sauce.

5. Beat egg yolks into cooled sauce. Fold in lobster meat and mushrooms. Check seasoning and lightly fold in stiffly beaten egg whites.

6. Fill cleaned lobster shells with soufflé mixture and place on a cookie sheet.

7. Bake 15 minutes in a preheated oven 425ºF (218ºC) or until puffed and brown. Serve immediately on folded napkins.

A special hint:

To heat brandy: Pour brandy into a ladle and warm to lukewarm over low heat.

68

BRISBANE PRAWN SOUFFLE

For 4 servings, you will need:

6 oz (170 g) raw shelled and deveined shrimp	1 tbs Scotch whisky
2 tbs butter	1 tbs clarified butter*
2 oz (56 g) all-purpose flour	2 tbs Scotch whisky
8 fl oz (2 dl) milk	Freshly ground salt
4 eggs	Freshly ground pepper
6 oz (170 g) Cheddar cheese	Nutmeg
	Cayenne pepper

First prepare:

Measure butter, flour and milk. Separate eggs and whip whites stiffly. Grate cheese, measure whisky. Cut shrimp into ½ inch (1.2 cm) pieces. Grease a 1½ quart (1.5 l) soufflé dish. Preheat baking sheet in oven at 375°F (190°C). Warm whisky.

Now cook!

1. Melt butter, add flour to make a roux. Stir milk in gradually and whisk until smooth. Allow to cool.

2. Beat egg yolks and cheese into cooled roux.

3. Finely chop 1 oz (28 g) of shrimp and add to roux with 1 tbs of whisky. Season with salt, pepper, nutmeg and cayenne. Fold in stiffly beaten whites carefully.

4. Sauté remaining shrimp in clarified butter for 1 minute, then add 2 tbs of warmed whisky and set alight.

5. Place half the soufflé mixture in soufflé dish. Put sautéed shrimp in center and cover with more mixture.

6. Place on baking sheet in oven and bake 40 minutes.

A special hint:

When folding in whites add a large spoonful of beaten egg whites to sauce and fold in well before folding in remaining whites.

1. BRISBANE PRAWN SOUFFLE.

2. A good roux with a sandy texture is vital.

3. The sauce base is carefully made and *highly* seasoned.

4. It must be beaten absolutely smooth.

5. And poured out on a plate to cool quickly.

6. Egg whites are beaten until stiffly peaked but not dry.

7. Beat yolks, fold into cooled sauce. Beat in grated cheese.

8. Add a large spoonful of egg white to sauce and beat in thoroughly.

9. Fold remaining whites in very lightly.

10. Butter fry shrimp between Step 5 & 6. Flambé in whisky; cool.

11. Half fill soufflé. Add shrimp. Top with rest of mixture.

12. Wrap dish with buttered paper collar and place in oven.

HUEVOS RANCHEROS

For 4 servings, you will need:

4 eggs
1 green pepper (capsicum)
2 pimentos
28 fl oz (8 dl) canned Italian plum
    tomatoes
2 tsp chili powder
Freshly ground salt

Freshly ground black pepper
20 leaves of oregano
2 medium onions
1 clove garlic
2 pinches cumin
8 tbs grated mild Cheddar
    cheese
1 tbs clarified butter*

First prepare:

Seed and slice green pepper into fine strips and cut pimento into strips. Press tomatoes through a sieve. Finely slice onions. Grate cheese. Peel garlic. Preheat oven to 450°F (232°C).

Now cook!

1. Heat clarified butter in frypan and add garlic. Allow garlic to sweat to release oil and then discard. Add green pepper and onions. Toss in butter and allow to fry gently. Add tomatoes, cumin, chili powder and oregano. Cook until the mixture has thickened (approximately 2 minutes). Season to taste with salt and pepper.

2. Place vegetable mixture into an 8-inch (20 cm) square baking pan. Make 4 hollows and break an egg into each. Decorate eggs with crisscross strips of pimento and cover entire surface with cheese. Bake in preheated oven 450°F (232°C) for 7½ minutes. Serve immediately.

CHAMP

For 2 servings, you will need:

1 lb (0.5 kg) potatoes
1 medium leek
4 fl oz (1.2 dl) milk
5 oz (141 g) butter
4 fl oz (1.2 dl) heavy cream

4 eggs
1 tbs parsley
Freshly ground salt
Freshly ground white pepper

First prepare:

Boil potatoes and drain. Measure milk, cream and butter. Chop parsley. Break eggs into a bowl. Wash and finely slice leek.

Now cook!

1. Pour milk into a pan, add leek and poach until tender. Strain milk into a bowl. Reserve leek.
2. Mash potatoes and beat in strained milk.
3. Melt 4 oz (113 g) of the butter.
4. Place potatoes in serving bowl, make a well in center and pour butter into it.
5. Mix half the cream (2 fl oz: 5.6 cl) with eggs, season generously with salt and pepper.
6. Melt remaining 1 oz (28 g) of butter in a pan, pour egg and cream mixture into it and cook stirring all the time. When eggs are just set stir in remaining cream. Take off heat and beat cream into eggs.
7. Place reserved leeks in center well of potatoes and cover with scrambled eggs.
8. Sprinkle with chopped parsley and serve.

A special hint:

See Step 6 above. Adding cold cream at point at which scrambled eggs set helps to keep them creamy and prevents overcooking.

(Overleaf)
Brisbane Prawn Soufflé (page 160)

PART IV
FISH AND SHELLFISH

PART IV
FISH AND SHELLFISH

Fish isn't cooked to make it tender—the object is to promote flavor. Considering the enormous interest in quick cooking it surprises me that the fishing industry and the consumer have never really hit it off. It has to be a "cold touch" problem.

"Cold touch" describes the feeling you get from handling fish. Perhaps it is this feeling that is responsible for its reduced use in the home. The enormous consumption, relatively speaking, of seafood in restaurants suggests an appreciation of the finished dish—so it has to be something to do with handling.

The first hurdle to overcome is at the retail level. I am absolutely certain that a pouch pack, containing the completely prepared fillets in one side and some stock bones in an opaque pouch on the other, would be of immediate interest to potential seafood cooks. It is vital to remove all bones from the fillets and to permit the home cook to slip the fillet from pack to pan without touching it.

Obviously there are techniques that require intermediate handling such as egg washes, seasoned flour and the good old bread crumbs. However, all these are coverings and insulate the cook from the cold touch. When once the retail problems are solved we shall only need to create suitable recipes.

In this Part, I have attempted to touch most bases. There are recipes for all of the twelve themes that follow. In addition you will find fish pies in Part IV, soups and first courses in Part III and filled pancakes in Part VI.

DEEP FRYING

The secret is in the batter. An absolute seal has to be made so that the fish virtually *steams*. All the natural juices are retained and, in my opinion, it is the best possible method.

There are, of course, some problems that have yet to be solved by home kitchen designers. First, you need a large fryer to accommodate sufficient fish for, say, a family of six: too large and too expensive to justify purchase. Because of the size you need too much oil—a waste unless you deep-fry often, and frankly I don't believe that too much fried food is good for one. But on the other hand, this can largely be avoided by breaking the batter off before eating the tender steaming fish.

Lastly, there is the real problem of coating small fish pieces so that there are no holes and also ensure that several portions can be cooked together. As a designer I am trying to cure these faults. As you read this I may in fact have done so. Without the cure, home deep-frying is something of a drag.

SPICING

Soused fish is well known but the use of somewhat vigorously spiced mixes is less popular due simply to their rarity. I believe that there is a great future for such spice mixtures as the one used for Shrimp Watts (page 178) and would urge you to try it on sole fillets and other small local fish.

SHALLOW FRYING

The most popular home fish-cooking technique and the most abused! For some reason cooks decide that a piece of fish has to receive the same pan temperature as a steak. Above all else, the heat must be kept low. Let the butter soak up gently into the soft flesh, without driving off the moisture. The only exception to this rule is in the Chinese kitchen's preparation of raw peeled shrimp (Cornprawn, page 546). Here quick high heat is used to "crisp" the shrimp.

UNCOOKED

The term *green* is sometimes used to describe uncooked fish and shellfish, not because the uncooked color is always green but because it is a tradition among professional cooks. It is curious to examine the relationship between an oyster and an uncooked fish fillet. Both are born and live in the sea, yet the oyster is happily eaten raw, while the poor old fish is shunned with revulsion by the self-same oyster fancier. The answer lies in the pickling of the fish—an acidic mixture that turns the color *white* and adds a "punchy" flavor. When handled in this fashion raw fish can become an easy-to-make favorite.

CASSEROLES

Because of the necessarily short cooking times involved it follows that the liquid in which chopped seafood is cooked must be at full flavor strength before adding the fish. Meat casseroles can be expected to give up their own juices and come to the aid of the flavor, but seafood is another kettle of fish.

For the same reason there are a number of thickenings used that require little if any boiling (to boil fish is gastronomic death). You can use a liaison (page 46) or beurre manie (page 47); I like to use an egg and cream liaison with a touch of arrowroot to hasten the thickening in cream-based casseroles.

BROILED LOBSTER

The term *broiled* is being used in deference to the need for an international language of the kitchen. One stands out "under the broiling sun," so why not relate this to overhead radiant heat? Then a grill can literally mean *underneath* radiant heat and a lightly greased metal sheet can then be called a griddle. Anyway, lobsters are usually broiled or grilled with equally unfortunate results.

The high radiant heat produced by broiler or grill is too much for the lobster meat and the result is either exceedingly tough or dry. There *is* a point midway that can be excellent, but it takes skill and very good equipment to get to it. The best advice I can give is: take it easy, don't use too high a heat and always serve a soft buttery sauce like Hollandaise (see page 500) or utilize the head, shell and legs, and make a Sauce Armoricaine (page 202).

BOILED LOBSTER

This is the tender way, and obviously the best. I put the lobsters to sleep by dropping them into 98.6°F (37°C) *court bouillon.* All edible crustacea die drowsily at this temperature and I cannot believe that plunging them into boiling water or putting a hot steel needle through the eyes or simply tearing them apart are acceptable killing methods. The

Governor's Fried Fish (page 172)

shellfish is removed when dead and the water brought to the boil. I undercook lobster unless it is to be served cold for salad. Six minutes at the boil for a 1½ pounder (680 g) is enough but it must be plunged directly into ice cold water; otherwise, it continues to cook from the heat retained in the shell. Slightly undercooked boiled lobster is, in my opinion, better used fried or in a casserole dish than the raw pieces. It has a neater appearance, more flavor, a great deal more tenderness and needs an extremely short cooking time. If cooked too long, it becomes dry and tough.

BAKED

A fisherman's technique, this one. Best suited to round-bodied game fish like the salmon. The real problems are in the turning and heat penetration. I have solved the turning problem in the recipe Salmon St. Gotthard (page 215; Fig. 9 & 10). This recipe gives one way of shortening the heat penetration. The constant worry with a round-bodied fish is that the outside will be slightly overcooked and yet the inside may remain raw. By slashing the flanks you expose a greater area to more direct heat, thus reducing the problem.

HERB FLAMBEED

An exotic idea born along the Côte d'Azur where the use of local herbs tends to be overdone. Basically it is achieved by first cooking your fish or shellfish and then setting fire to some dried fennel while the seafood is suspended above it on a trivet. A short slurp of cognac helps to promote a healthy blaze. At the dinner table I frankly feel that the whole business is a bit chi-chi. At a barbecue it can be both fun and quite rewarding, as anything that sets out to overpower the frequently hideous tastes of briquettes is all right in my book.

BROILED

The only important point I'd like to make here is that the fish must not be completely skinned before it hits the broiler. Fish skin has a layer of natural oil just beneath the surface that melts out and bastes the flesh in its *own natural flavor.* No added butter or oil can match its value.

Should the fish have scales then these must, of course, be removed first. Do this with the fish, your hands and the back of a kitchen knife all underwater. Scale from tail to head. The water prevents the scales from flying everywhere. If you don't watch it, you wind up looking like Liberace playing the lead from "The Old Man of the Sea."

POACHED

Here you have a technique second only to deep frying for finished excellence. Much despised because of its universal use as a palliative to ulcers, I find it among my Top Ten favorite culinary techniques. Poached fish is generally accompanied by a sauce. The sauce should be derived from the liquid in which the fish is cooked. BUT, if the liquor is removed after poaching, the fish dries out while the sauce cooks. SO, make the *roux* first and add sufficient milk or white wine to make it very thick but still able to despumate (cook out the flour taste). When the raw taste has gone, poach the fish in a mixture of wine and fish stock or fish stock and milk, or a combination of all three, and when the fish is cooked drain off the liquor into the sauce. The sauce will then be ready to use and the old stigma of "gluey parsley" is removed.

STEAMBOAT

Please turn to page 242 where the fullest details are given about this remarkable Swiss-styled oriental social occasion that was probably the starting point for fondues bourguignonnes of all kinds.

60

STRIP DIP

For 6 servings, you will need:
    1½ lb (680 g) squid
    6 oz (170 g) all-purpose flour
    10 fl oz (3 dl) frying batter
    100 fl oz (2.8 l) peanut oil
    6 oz (170 g) ketchup
    2 cloves garlic
    Parsley
Frying batter:
    8 oz (227 g) all-purpose flour

    ¼ tsp freshly ground salt
    3 fl oz (8 cl) steaming liquor
    ¼ oz (7 g) compressed yeast*
    3 fl oz (8 cl) flat beer
        (bitter type)
    1 tbs olive oil
    ½ egg white

First prepare:

Cut squid down back of hood, lay it open, remove ink sac and cut off just above eyes. Rub purple-tinted skin from outside with coarse salt, or strip it off under cold running water. Remove membrane spine from hood. Cut tentacles from head, just below beak. Remove serrated edge from suckers.

Frying batter: Warm a mixing bowl with hot water. Throw away water and dry. Add sifted flour and salt and make a well in center. Place yeast in well and add stock, beer and olive oil. Mix in flour gradually until batter is smooth. Place batter in a warm place and cover with a cloth. Leave for 4 hours. Remove cloth and fold in stiffly beaten half egg white. If it is still too thick add a little more beer.

Now cook!

1. Place both sections of cleaned squid in top of a double boiler. Cover and allow to cook gently for 45 to 60 minutes over simmering water until it gives easily to touch. Remove, cool, slice into bite-size pieces and dredge with flour seasoned with salt and pepper. Reserve steaming liquor in top of double boiler.

2. Place smashed garlic in ketchup and stir in squid liquid. Place this mixture into a small bowl in center of serving dish. Place paper doily on serving dish.

3. Heat oil to 380°F (193°C). Place floured squid into batter and then transfer to hot oil. Fry until crisp and golden. Place on serving dish, dust with salt and garnish with parsley.

71

GOVERNOR'S FRIED FISH

For 4 servings, you will need:

1 lb (0.5 kg) haddock fillets
3 tbs freshly shredded coconut
  (or packaged)
1 lemon
3 oz (85 g) all-purpose flour
Batter:
  1 tbs olive oil
  3 fl oz (8 cl) fish stock

3 fl oz (8 cl) beer
¼ oz (7 g) compressed yeast*
8 oz (227 g) all-purpose flour
½ egg white
Freshly ground salt
Freshly ground white pepper
Deep fat or oil

First prepare:

Batter: Into a bowl place flour, crumble compressed yeast into tiny pieces. Moisten with beer. Stir in oil and fish stock. Beat well and allow to rise for 4 hours. Squeeze juice of lemon and pour over haddock fillets. Allow to soak for ½ hour. Heat a serving platter in warming oven. Beat egg white. Heat oil in the deep fat fryer to 380°F (193°C).

Now cook!

1. Fold beaten egg white into risen batter. If batter is too stiff to use as a coating add a little extra flat beer.
2. With a paper towel dry fish and coat fillets with flour mixed with salt and pepper.
3. Fold coconut into batter and coat fish lightly with batter.
4. Put coated fish into hot oil and fry for 5 minutes until golden brown on all sides.
5. Remove fish and drain on absorbent paper. Place on heated platter and serve.

A special hint:

The best instrument to use to hold fish when dipping into batter is your fingers. Sharper objects can tear flesh and make a hole in the batter coating.

1. GOVERNOR'S FRIED FISH.
A completely unique flavor.

2. Soak coconuts for 5 minutes in hot water for easier splitting.

3. With a serrated knife make a shallow "saw" start.

4. Tap the shell all around with the back of a heavy knife.

5. Give a hefty tap and Bingo— it's open! Finely grate meat.

6. Mix the yeast completely before incorporating the flour.

7. Make a good beer batter.

8. Combine with your hands— you've got them wet already.

9. Add egg white to the batter, then grated coconut.

10. Coat each piece of fish completely.

11. Place into a deep fryer.

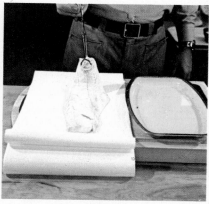

12. Drain cooked fillets on absorbent paper before serving.

LOBSTER CUTLETS

For 6 servings, you will need:

1 raw lobster, 4 lb (1.8 kg)
Clarified butter*
1 medium onion
3 oz (85 g) celery
10 parsley stalks*
2 tbs brandy
2 fl oz (5.6 cl) dry white wine
16 fl oz (4 dl) water
1 tbs tomato puree
24 black peppercorns
1 tbs mixed herbs
4 oz (113 g) all-purpose flour

4 oz (113 g) butter
6 fl oz (1.6 dl) dry white
  wine
2 egg yolks
Freshly ground salt
Cayenne pepper
8 oz (227 g) all-purpose flour
1 egg
Bread crumbs*
Sole trimmings (bones, etc.)
4 parsley stalks*
Deep oil

First prepare:

Place sole trimmings with 2 tbs clarified butter into a large saucepan. Add finely chopped onion, celery and parsley stalks. Remove meat from lobster tail and claws. Crush lobster shell and add to sole trimmings. Add brandy, white wine, water, peppercorns, tomato puree and mixed herbs. Cover and allow to simmer 15 minutes. Strain stock and reserve. Cut lobster meat into pieces and put through fine blade of grinder. Measure butter and flour. Measure dry white wine. Make bread crumbs. Heat oil in deep fryer to 375°F (190°C).

Now cook!

1. Melt butter in a pan and add 4 oz (113 g) flour to form a roux. Cook while stirring for 1 minute over low heat. Gradually stir in stock and wine. Add lobster, season with salt and cayenne pepper. Cook stirring constantly for 5 minutes. Beat in egg yolks and pour mixture into a 10 x 6 inch (25 x 15 cm) Pyrex dish and place in refrigerator to cool.

2. Using a 3 inch (7.5 cm) round cutter cut cold mixture into 6 rounds. Dip into flour, beaten egg and then bread crumbs and shape into cutlets. Place in hot oil and cook 3 minutes until golden. Drain on absorbent paper.

3. Place well-washed and dried sprigs of parsley into hot oil. Remove with a slotted spoon when crisp. Drain on absorbent paper.

4. Serve cutlets on a heated dish garnished with fried parsley.

FAIRFIELD FLOUNDER FILLETS AND LEGAL SAUCE

For 4 servings, you will need:

4 flounder fillets
8 oz (227 g) large mushrooms
2 fl oz (5.6 cl) dry white wine
Juice of ½ lemon
Freshly ground salt
Cayenne pepper
1 egg yolk
All-purpose flour
4 oz (113 g) Cheddar cheese

12 oz (340 g) bread crumbs*
Deep corn oil
Legal sauce:
    4 oz (113 g) cooked, shelled
        and deveined shrimp
    8 black olives
    1 tbs dill
    4 fl oz (1.2 dl) mayonnaise
    Freshly ground black pepper

First prepare:

Measure wine. Juice lemon. Make bread crumbs and place on a dish. Place flour on a dish. Grate cheese finely and place on dish. Heat oil in deep fryer to 350ºF (177ºC). Pit olives. Finely chop dill. Measure mayonnaise.

Now cook!

1. Place wine in a saucepan and allow to reduce over high heat to 1 tbs.
2. Mash mushrooms with a fork and then chop with 2 knives until a paste is formed. Add to reduced wine with lemon juice and season with salt and cayenne pepper. Fry for 1 minute. Remove from heat, add egg yolk and stir all ingredients together.
3. Dry fish fillets, season with salt. Dip in flour and spread with mushroom paste. Dip fish into grated cheese and finally bread crumbs.
4. Place fish in hot oil and fry 2½ minutes. Drain on absorbent paper.
5. *Sauce:* Combine olives, shrimp and dill with mayonnaise, season with pepper.
6. Place on serving dish covered with a paper doily and serve with Legal Sauce.

AVOCADO FRENCHMAN'S COVE

71

For 4 servings, you will need:

2½ lbs (1.2 kg) red snapper
2 ripe avocados
2 limes
2 tsp dark brown sugar, firmly packed
8 oz (227 g) small cooked, shelled and
    deveined shrimp
5 oz (142 g) red pimento

1 clove garlic
1 oz (28 g) Parmesan cheese
2 fl oz (5.6 cl) rum
2 tsp dill
2 oz (56 g) butter
2 tbs clarified butter*
Freshly ground white pepper

First prepare:

Scale fish under water by running back of a knife against scales. With a very sharp knife cut from just below the head through to the tail lengthwise along spine of fish. Cut fillets from both sides of spine and trim off skin. Rinse under cold water and dry with a clean cloth. Finely dice pimento. Rinse shrimp. Crush garlic. Wash, dry and finely chop dill. Measure dry and liquid ingredients. Remove pits from avocados by cutting through skin and flesh lengthwise. Scoop out pits at last possible moment. Squeeze limes and pour over avocados to prevent discoloration. Preheat broiler. Keep fish bones for stock.

Now cook!

1. With back of a fork mash through avocado flesh right to skin. Place avocado halves under preheated broiler for 2 minutes.
2. Cut fish fillets into small bite-size pieces and then pour 1 fl oz (2.8 cl) of clarified butter into a large frypan over high heat and add fish.
3. Season with pepper. Add no salt.
4. Stir in brown sugar to give it a sweet glaze.
5. Remove avocado from under broiler and set aside in a warm place.
6. Stir tiny shrimp into frypan.
7. Stir in pimento and garlic.
8. Pour rum into frypan shaking pan constantly. Add dill.
9. Stir in 2 oz (56 g) butter and take pan off heat, letting butter melt into "sauce."
10. Spoon this mixture into broiled avocado halves and sprinkle with a little grated cheese. Place under broiler 1 inch (2.5 cm) away from source of heat for about 3 minutes to allow cheese to brown.

Avocado Frenchman's Cove

71

SHRIMP WATTS

For 4 servings, you will need:

1 lb (0.5 kg) raw shelled and
   deveined shrimp
1 lb (0.5 kg) tomatoes
5 oz (142 g) onion
1 clove garlic
3 Belgian shallots
8 fl oz (2 dl) white wine vinegar
4 Serrano chilis*

½ tsp cayenne pepper
2 fl oz (5.6 cl) olive oil
2 bay leaves
1 tbs parsley
2 tbs clarified butter*
Freshly ground salt
Freshly ground white pepper

First prepare:

Blanch tomato in boiling salted water, cook for 2 minutes, remove, cool, skin and remove seeds. Finely slice onion. Smash garlic. Finely slice shallots. Remove seeds from Serrano chilis and discard. Finely chop chilis. Measure dry and liquid ingredients. A bowl of crushed ice will be needed.

Now cook!

1. Pour clarified butter into a large frypan on high heat. Add onion, garlic, shallots and fry.
2. Stir in white wine vinegar and season with salt and white pepper.
3. Stir in Serrano chilis, cayenne pepper, olive oil and bay leaves.
4. Add shrimp to pan and stir into bubbling marinade. Reduce heat to medium and cook for 2 minutes.
5. Finely chop tomato pulp and add to shrimp.
6. Sprinkle with parsley. Drain off liquid.
7. Increase heat and bring to a boil to evaporate excess liquid.
8. Remove pan from heat, pour mixture into a bowl over crushed ice and stir gently for about 5 minutes until well chilled.

A special hint:

Refer Step 4. It is vital not to leave shrimp cooking in marinade longer than 2 minutes or they will be too vinegary.

1. SHRIMP WATTS is a simple example of an instant spice pickle. This one has quite a bite.

2. It is garnished with thin slices of raw potato laid in a shallow dish and lightly salted.

3. Soak the potato liberally in lime or lemon juice.

4. The various onions, garlic and shallots are used to create an unusually pungent taste.

5. A low heat pan is used so that the onions release their oils but don't brown.

6. Stir in a good quality chili powder.

7. Wine vinegar is then added to make up this super spiced *court bouillon*. Add the shrimp, and cook with lid off.

8. Finally tomato flesh is finely chopped—having removed all seeds and skin.

9. Strain off the surplus vinegar and add the chopped tomato. Cool quickly and serve cold.

ABALONE SWEET AND SOUR

For 4 servings, you will need:

4 abalone steaks
Freshly ground black pepper
1 medium onion
1 tbs light brown sugar, firmly packed
1 cucumber
1 tbs wine vinegar

1 fl oz (2.8 cl) vodka
1 tsp sugar
4 fl oz (1.2 dl) chicken stock
2 fl oz (5.6 cl) soya sauce
Clarified butter*

First prepare:

Combine vodka and sugar. Measure chicken stock and soya sauce. Cut a slice from each side of cucumber lengthwise and then slice finely. Finely slice onion. Trim tough pieces from abalone and beat steaks a few times with a meat tenderizing hammer.

Now cook!

1. Place some clarified butter into pan to just cover bottom and when hot add onion and cucumber. Stir to coat in butter and gently fry. Add brown sugar and wine vinegar. Season with pepper.

2. Add chicken stock and soya sauce to vodka and sugar to form "Warashita" and pour into cucumber and onion mixture. Heat for 2 minutes.

3. Place a little clarified butter in another pan to just cover bottom and when hot add abalone steaks previously seasoned with salt and pepper. When they commence to curl after 1 minute, turn them and cook for 1 minute. Remove steaks and place into onion and cucumber mixture. Mix and spoon onto a serving dish. Accompany with fried hair noodles.*

A special hint:

Do not overcook abalone. It only requires 2 minutes (1 minute either side). If steaks are left in sauce for more than 2-3 minutes they will toughen.

Fillet of Fish Macadamia (page 182)

66

FILET OF FISH MACADAMIA

For 2 servings, you will need:

2 steaks, barramundi* or halibut or salmon,
    6 oz (170 g)
2 oz (56 g) macadamia nuts
Freshly ground white pepper
Freshly ground salt
1 egg yolk

2 tbs clarified butter*
1 fl oz (2.8 cl) dry sherry
1 oz (28 g) butter
1 tbs parsley stalks*
Juice of ½ lemon

First prepare:

Mix egg yolk, clarified butter and half of the lemon juice. Chop parsley stalks finely. Grate nuts. Warm sherry.

Now cook!

1. Season fish with pepper and salt, brush with egg yolk mixture and press nuts into each side.
2. Melt clarified butter in frypan. When hot add fish and fry 3 minutes on each side. Add heated sherry and set alight. Add chopped parsley stalks. Place fish on serving dish. Add butter and remaining lemon juice to frypan, stir to loosen all particles and pour sauce over fish.

A special hint:

The egg, butter, lemon juice combination is essential to success of dish. Without it the nuts scorch.

1. FILLET OF FISH MACADA-MIA. Any good solid fish will do.

2. Macadamia nuts should be fresh grated. A fiddly job.

3. The dried fillets are well season-ed.

4. Melted butter and egg yolk makes an excellent adhesive.

5. Combine butter, yolk and lem-on juice.

6. Brush the fillets with the but-tered yolks.

7. Press fillets down into the nuts— be gentle!

8. Shake off surplus nuts. Fry in butter over moderate heat.

9. When the fish flakes easily— flame in sherry.

10. Lift the fish onto a warmed serving platter.

11. Add butter to the pan, stir and lightly brown.

12. Deglaze pan with sherry. Pour sauce over fish.

SOLE MEUNIERE

For 1 serving, you will need:

1 whole sole, trimmed and cleaned
4 oz (113 g) butter
Juice of 1 lemon
Parsley

Flour
Freshly ground salt
Freshly ground black pepper

First prepare:

Remove black skin from sole, cut off tail and head. Measure butter. Chop parsley finely.

Now cook!

1. Season fish with salt and pepper and lightly coat with flour.
2. Place 2 oz (56 g) butter in a pan on moderate heat and when hot cook fish for 2 minutes on each side.
3. Place parsley in tea towel, dampen towel and ring out excess moisture.
4. Remove sole and bone carefully. Place boned fish fillets on serving dish. Sprinkle with parsley.
5. Add rest of butter and lemon juice to pan, heat until just browned and pour over fish. Serve immediately.

A special hint:

When fillets come cleanly from bone when loosened with a knife fish is done. Don't overcook.

SOLE WITH CAFE DE PARIS SAUCE

For 2 servings, you will need:

2 sole, 1 lb (0.5 kg)
All-purpose flour
Freshly ground salt
Freshly ground white pepper
4 tbs clarified butter*
Café de Paris sauce
2 tbs spring onions*
2 anchovy fillets
3 oz (85 g) butter

1 tbs parsley
5 sage leaves
Pinch of dried tarragon
1 small clove garlic
1 tsp lemon juice
2 tsp mild French mustard
Paprika
Freshly ground white pepper
1 tsp cognac

First prepare:

Remove head, fins and tail from sole. Peel off black skin on one side. Make a 3 inch (7.5 cm) incision down backbone (this is in the center of the skinned side of the fish) and slit pockets in either side of the cut. Season flour with salt and pepper. Flour fish. Finely chop spring onions. Finely chop anchovy fillets. Allow butter to soften. Finely chop parsley and sage. Crush garlic.

Now cook!

1. Heat clarified butter in a large frypan and place fish skinned side down into the hot butter. Allow fish to fry gently 4 minutes on each side.
2. Place softened butter in a bowl and add spring onions, anchovy fillets, parsley, sage leaves, tarragon, garlic, lemon juice, mustard, paprika and pepper. Flavor with cognac.
3. Place fish on a heated serving dish, skinned side uppermost, and spread with sauce.
4. Accompany with pommes sautées (fried potatoes) garnished with pimento strips and spring onions.

SHRIMP MACADAMIA

For 2 servings, you will need:

24 jumbo shrimp
3 oz (85 g) macadamia nuts
1 clove garlic
2 fl oz (5.6 cl) dry sherry
2 oz (56 g) butter
½ lemon

¼ tsp paprika
1 lb (0.5 kg) potatoes
Clarified butter*
Freshly ground salt
Freshly ground white pepper

First prepare:

Remove shells and devein shrimp. Measure sherry and butter. Squeeze lemon into a shallow dish. Boil potatoes, drain, mash and cream them with butter, milk, salt and pepper. A pastry bag with a rosette tip and 2 scallop shells will be required. Finely chop nuts. Crush garlic.

Now cook!

1. Coat shrimp with cold clarified butter and roll them in chopped nuts.
2. Heat clarified butter in a frying pan to just cover bottom.
3. Fry garlic gently for 2 minutes.
4. Drop in coated shrimp, remove garlic and cook shrimp for 2 minutes on each side.
5. After 4 minutes add sherry and flame.
6. Stir in butter and lemon juice.
7. Pipe creamed potatoes in a border around rim of scallop shells.
8. Pour shrimp into center of shells, decorate each with a sprig of parsley and a dusting of paprika.

SOLE WITH ANCHOVY SAUCE

For 4 servings, you will need:

2 whole lemon sole
Freshly ground salt
Freshly ground black pepper
Flour
6 tbs clarified butter*
1½ oz (42 g) butter
2 tsp parsley

2 tsp chives
12 fresh oregano leaves or
  ¼ tsp dried
3 tsp blanched almonds
4 fl oz (1.2 dl) dry white
  wine
1 tbs marsala
4 anchovy fillets

First prepare:

Fillet sole, removing black skin and head. Finely chop parsley and chives. Finely chop almonds. Measure wine and marsala.

Now cook!

1. Season fish with salt and pepper and roll in flour. Place clarified butter in heated pan, add floured fish skin side up and cook gently for four minutes.
2. Place butter in a saucepan and add anchovy fillets. Mash anchovies into butter and allow butter to foam, remove from heat and mix anchovies well into butter.
3. Stir in chives, parsley, oregano leaves, blanched almonds, white wine and marsala. Bring to a boil, and pour sauce over fried fish.

70

SHRIMP POVLIK

For 2 servings, you will need:

12 raw jumbo shrimp	2 fl oz (5.6 cl) dry sherry
2 cloves garlic	1 oz (28 g) butter
1 medium onion	1 lemon
1 tsp rosemary	1 tbs parsley
8 fl oz (2 dl) dry white wine	Clarified butter*
1 fl oz (2.8 cl) vodka	Freshly ground salt
	Freshly ground white pepper

First prepare:

Lightly crush garlic. Finely slice onion. Measure sherry, dry white wine, vodka. Shell shrimp. With a pair of scissors, cut through back of shrimp to the tail, starting from where head was removed. With a knife blade deepen the gash to cut the flesh but don't go through the membrane on the under side. Remove coral and sand tract. Open out shrimp. Measure rosemary and butter. Preheat a serving platter in warm oven. Chop parsley.

Now cook!

1. Pour some clarified butter into heated frypan to just cover bottom and fry onion gently.

2. Add garlic. Simmer.

3. Season with rosemary, salt and pepper. Moisten with 6 fl oz (1.6 dl) dry white wine.

4. Allow sauce to bubble gently over moderate heat and add shrimp flesh side down. Place a small pan on top to flatten them while cooking. Poach for four minutes.

5. Lift out shrimp onto a heated plate. Keep hot.

6. Pour 2 fl oz (5.6 cl) dry white wine over onion and herb mixture. Strain and discard cooked onions and herbs.

7. Place a clean pan over moderate heat and pour in strained liquid. Reduce over high heat until only a "syrup" is left on the bottom of the pan.

8. Lower heat and stir in cooked shrimp. Add butter.

9. Increase temperature, pour vodka over mixture and flame. When flame has died, add dry sherry and flame once more.

10. Arrange shrimp on a serving platter, pour pan drippings over them. Garnish with a piece of lemon and serve lightly dusted with chopped parsley.

SHRIMP MOSKA

For 4 servings, you will need:

2 lb (0.9 kg) raw jumbo shrimp	Freshly ground black pepper
2 fl oz (5.6 cl) olive oil	3 bay leaves
1 small sprig oregano (fresh)	6 cloves garlic
1 small sprig rosemary (fresh)	4 fl oz (1.2 dl) dry white wine
Freshly ground salt	

First prepare:

Measure oil. Peel garlic cloves and chop finely. Measure wine. Finely chop herbs or use dried.

Now cook!

1. Heat oil in a large pan and when hot add unpeeled shrimp, oregano, rosemary, pepper, salt, bay leaves and garlic. Sauté gently for 5 minutes. Add white wine and cook gently for another 5 minutes or until wine is reduced to a syrup.

2. Place shrimp on a serving dish. Remove bay leaves from sauce and spoon over shrimp.

Shrimp Moska

GREEN PRAWNS—GINGER AND GARLIC SAUCE

68

For 4 servings, you will need:

2 lb (0.9 kg) small school prawns*
2 tbs freshly ground salt
1 piece fresh ginger root*
6 shallots

2 cloves garlic
2 fl oz (5.6 cl) chicken stock
Monosodium glutamate
Freshly ground pepper

First prepare:

Shell prawns, cover with salt and marinate 10 minutes. Wash salt from prawns and dry well. Slice garlic and ginger thinly, and chop shallots coarsely.

Now cook!

1. Sauté garlic, ginger and shallots in peanut oil. Add prawns and cook 2 minutes, stirring constantly.

2. Add stock and season with monosodium glutamate and pepper. Thicken with cornstarch mixed with a little chicken stock, and serve with rice noodles*. (The rice noodles are fried in extremely hot fat until crisp.)

KONA COAST SHRIMP

70

For 4 servings, you will need:

2 small coconuts
1 small clove garlic
Clarified butter*
1 lb (0.5 kg) raw jumbo shrimp
3 oz (85 g) onion
Freshly ground salt
Freshly ground pepper
1 tbs soya sauce

6 fl oz (1.6 dl) coconut stock
1½ tsp arrowroot
1 oz (28 g) coconut fat from
  surface of coconut milk
Coconut stock:
4 oz (113 g) fresh coconut
16 fl oz (4 dl) water

First prepare:

Split coconuts in half by making a ¼-inch (7 mm) deep cut into side with a fine saw. Then take a large knife, rest blade in cut, tap knife gently with a hammer and coconut will split into two. First place coconut on a dish to collect the milk. Using a melon baller, scrape thin slices of coconut from shell until only ¼-inch (7 mm) rim of meat remains. Trim rounded sides of coconuts so they will sit evenly.

Finely chop onion. Preheat broiler unit. Place coconut shells in oven to warm through. Make coconut stock by placing scraped coconut into a bowl and pour over 16 fl oz (4 dl) of boiling water. Cover and allow to stand 30 minutes. Strain through muslin squeezing to press out all liquid. Cool in refrigerator.

Now cook!

1. Place some clarified butter into a frypan to just cover bottom and when hot add garlic. Add shrimp, season with salt and pepper and allow shrimp to fry gently 5 minutes. After 3 minutes add onion.

2. Strain excess butter from shrimp and stir in soya sauce. Remove fat from top of refrigerated coconut stock. Stir fat into shrimp. When melted add remainder of coconut stock. Allow to come to a boil.

3. Mix arrowroot with a little water and stir into shrimp, thickening sauce immediately. Remove shrimp from heat and fill warmed coconut shells. Place shells on an ovenproof dish. Decorate shrimp with a coconut rose shaped from curled coconut shavings and place under broiler for 1½ minutes or until coconut is golden brown.

SCALLOPS WHAKATANE

For 4 servings, you will need:

1 lb (0.5 kg) scallops
All-purpose flour
Freshly ground salt
Freshly ground white pepper
Juice of ¼ lemon
Clarified butter*

Garnish:
8 oz (227 g) mushrooms
8 oz (227 g) spring onions*
8 oz (227 g) tomatoes
2 oz (56 g) green pepper (capsicum)
2 tbs parsley
1 clove garlic

65

First prepare:

Dry scallops well, season and lightly dust with flour. Finely slice mushrooms and green pepper. Chop spring onions. Roughly chop parsley. Peel and cut garlic into 4 pieces. Cut peeled tomato in eighths.

Now cook!

1. Melt 1 tbs clarified butter in a pan, add garlic and allow it to sweat. Stir in spring onions, reduce heat and remove garlic pieces. Stir in green pepper.

2. Stir in mushrooms and coat with butter. Stir in lemon juice and tomatoes. Season with salt and pepper.

3. In a separate pan place enough clarified butter to coat the bottom. Add scallops and shallow fry for 4 minutes tossing them over several times. Add chopped parsley. Serve scallops on a warmed platter topped with vegetable garnish.

ABALONE VICTORIA

For 4 servings, you will need:

8 sliced abalone**steaks
  (freshly sliced and frozen)
Freshly ground salt
Freshly ground white pepper
2 tbs parsley
8 oz (227 g) bread crumbs*

4 oz (113 g) butter
1 tbs sherry
1 egg yolk
1 tsp lemon juice
2 tsp clarified butter*
Flour

69

**Hard to get even in good markets. For information regarding 20 lb (9 kg) boxes, frozen, write to Abalone, P.O. Box 185, North Sydney, Australia.

First prepare:

Finely chop parsley and mix with bread crumbs. Mix egg yolk with cooled clarified butter and lemon juice. Place flour on a dish. Thaw abalone steaks.

Now cook!

1. Season one side of abalone steaks with salt and pepper. Lightly flour abalone and then paint with egg mixture. Dip in bread crumb and parsley mixture.

2. Melt butter in a frypan and when it starts to foam add abalone steaks. Cook 1 minute on each side, add sherry and set alight.

3. Remove to a serving dish and cover with pan juices.

A special hint:

Please don't overcook. The times given/should be regarded as maximum or abalone will toughen.

FILETE DE ROBALO A LA VERACRUZANA

For 2 servings, you will need:

2 lbs (0.9 kg) sea bass
1 lemon
1 tsp Worcestershire sauce
8 tbs clarified butter*
1 medium onion
1 green pepper (capsicum)
2 tomatoes

7 oz (198 g) jar pimento
12 stuffed green olives
1 tsp butter
Dusting flour
Freshly ground salt
Freshly ground white pepper

First prepare:

To fillet fish, make a cut just behind the head of the bass cutting down to the backbone on both sides of the fish. Cut around gills and slice away each fillet along backbone in one piece. Remove skins from fillets.

Juice lemon. Have ready Worcestershire sauce, salt and pepper. Measure clarified butter. Finely slice onion and pepper. Cut tomatoes into eighths but don't skin, only remove core. Drain pimento and chop fine, drain olives. Have butter ready.

Now cook!

1. Lay two fillets on a medium-sized plate. Spoon lemon juice over fish. Sprinkle with Worcestershire sauce and season with salt and pepper. Turn fish over several times and allow to marinate for 6 minutes only. Drain fish and reserve marinade.

2. Melt 4 tbs clarified butter in a large frypan over high heat. Add onion, green pepper and tomato wedges (seeds and all!).

3. Allow this mixture to fry over medium heat for 4 minutes. Please don't crush tomatoes—they should hold their shape.

4. In a separate frypan, heat another 4 tbs clarified butter over low heat. Dry fillets with a paper towel and dust with flour. Cook for 3 minutes on either side until browned.

5. After vegetables have cooked 4 minutes reduce heat to low. Add pimento and olives. Taste and adjust seasoning.

6. Lay fish on a platter.

7. Pour pan drippings from fish into vegetables together with 1 tbs reserved marinade. Add butter, remove from heat and stir in butter until it melts.

8. Cover cooked bass with sauce—it's super!

TROUT ORLEANS

For 2 servings, you will need:

2¼ lbs (1 kg) trout
2 eggs
3 oz (85 g) fresh bread crumbs*
2 tbs lemon juice
4 oz (113 g) butter
2 medium bananas
4 oz (113 g) tomato

1 lemon
2 egg yolks
1 tbs chives
Flour
2 tbs clarified butter*
Freshly ground salt
Freshly ground white pepper

70

First prepare:

Wash fish thoroughly. Chop off head and tail (can be used for stock). With a small sharp knife cut down close to one side of backbone. With light strokes scrape flesh away from bone. Repeat on other side. Remove little fins. Leave skins on both fillets. Rinse under running cold water and dry. Crack eggs on a platter, mix with clarified butter and season with salt and white pepper. Sift some flour onto another platter and on yet another, spread bread crumbs. Measure butter and soften. Remove hard core from tomato and cut into thin slices. Remove skin and pits from lemon and cut into thin circles. Preheat broiler and serving platter. Wash, dry and finely chop chives.

Now cook!

1. Dip each fillet into flour seasoned with salt and pepper, then into egg and then bread crumbs. Cover fillets evenly. Press firmly and then shake to remove excess crumbs.

2. Pour enough clarified butter into a large baking dish to just cover bottom ¼-inch deep. Fry fish flesh side down on high heat.

3. After 2 minutes turn fish with pancake turner or spatula.

4. Pour 2 tbs lemon juice into top of a double boiler (the water should be just bubbling away underneath). Stir in egg yolks and season with salt and white pepper.

5. Add 2 oz (56 g) butter to the egg mixture and whisk until smooth (do not overheat or the sauce will curdle). Remove from heat and keep over hot water.

6. Stir remaining 2 oz (56 g) butter into this "hollandaise" sauce.

7. Peel bananas, cut in half lengthwise and lay around the fish.

8. Turn bananas after cooking for 2 minutes.

9. When fish has had 4 minutes on second side take a spatula and lift fillets onto a serving platter; arrange bananas alongside. Overlap tomato and lemon slices alternately down the full length of fillet. Season with salt and white pepper.

10. Place under broiler for 4 minutes, 3 inches (7.6 cm) from heat until brown.

11. Stir chives into sauce. Remove fish from under broiler, cover with sauce and serve at once.

A special hint:

This so-called hollandaise-type sauce is purposely made much thicker than usual for this dish.

HERRING MOUSSE

For 4 servings, you will need:

5 pickled herrings, boned
2 large green apples
2 fl oz (5.6 cl) heavy cream
2 fl oz (5.6 cl) Calvados
2 envelopes unflavored gelatin

4 fl oz (1.2 dl) cold water
2 egg whites
Freshly ground salt
Freshly ground white pepper

71

First prepare:

Measure cold water, Calvados and heavy cream. Beat egg whites. Core and peel apples and dice. Chill mold for mousse in freezer.

Now cook!

1. Place herring (one at a time) into a blender and allow to puree. Then pass through a hand sieve to get a smooth texture. (Wash blender.) Pop apples into blender and pour in Calvados. Add this puree to blended herring, and stir in heavy cream. Season with freshly ground salt and white pepper.

2. Place gelatin in cold water in a saucepan and then heat stirring until gelatin dissolves (never allow gelatin to boil). Cool this liquid.

3. Fold gelatin into herring and apple puree and fold in beaten egg whites. Pour into chilled 1-quart (1 l) mold and place in refrigerator until firm.

4. Unmold herring mousse by dipping mold for a few seconds into lukewarm water. Cut into slices and arrange on serving platter.

DANISH HERRINGS

For 4 servings, you will need:

4 fresh herrings (filleted)
5 fl oz (1.5 dl) white wine vinegar
1½ tbs granulated sugar
Freshly ground black pepper

1 bay leaf
1 small onion
Dill

First prepare:

Soak herrings in water for 24 hours. Finely slice onion. Measure vinegar and sugar.

Now assemble!

1. Drain herrings and dry. Marinate in vinegar, sugar, pepper, bay leaf and sliced onion. Allow to stand for 12 hours.

2. Drain and cut herrings in half lengthways. Place a few sprigs of fresh dill in center of strip and roll fish around dill.

3. Serve herrings on a bed of ice.

HUNTER OYSTERS

For 2 servings, you will need:

12 oysters
Lemon wedges

Dry white wine
Small triangles of brown
    bread and butter

68

Now assemble!

1. Sprinkle oysters in half shell with dry white wine. Marinate in wine under refrigeration for 20 minutes.

2. Serve on a dish with lemon wedges and small triangles of brown bread and butter.

Hunter Oysters

GG
65

MORWONG CRU

For 6 servings, you will need:

1½ lbs (680 g) haddock or bream*
   fillets
2 small onions
Juice of 6 lemons

4 oz (113 g) cucumber
4 oz (113 g) carrot
4 oz (113 g) celery
Coconut cream mayonnaise

First prepare:

Cut fish into ½-inch (1.2 cm) cubes, removing bone. Slice onions finely. Juice lemons. Finely dice cucumber, carrot and celery. Make coconut cream mayonnaise by adding coconut cream to mayonnaise to taste.

Now assemble!

1. Place fish, onions and lemon juice in a bowl. Cover with a cloth and refrigerate for 12 hours.
2. When fish becomes white and opaque strain off lemon juice and stir in chopped vegetables.
3. Serve this mixture chilled, with coconut mayonnaise dressing in a separate bowl.

SEAFOOD CASSEROLE COTE D'AZUR

For 4 smallish servings, you will need:

6 oz (170 g) jewfish* or haddock
6 oz (170 g) scallops
6 oz (170 g) raw shrimp, shelled
   and deveined
1 clove garlic
2 tbs clarified butter*
2 tbs olive oil
4 fl oz (1.2 dl) Chablis
2 tsp Dijon mustard

1 tbs fresh lemon juice
2 tbs parsley
2 tsp arrowroot
2 tbs heavy cream
Dill
Cayenne pepper
Freshly ground salt
Freshly ground black pepper

First prepare:

Slice fish into slivers. Cut shrimp into round slices crosswise, cut scallops into halves. Peel and crush garlic. Measure butter, Chablis and cream. Measure lemon juice. Mix arrowroot with a little white wine and mustard.

Now cook!

1. Place clarified butter and oil in a pan and when hot add fish, scallops and shrimp. Fry quickly, cover and cook over low heat for 5 minutes.
2. Stir in garlic, Chablis and lemon juice. Stir in arrowroot mixture until sauce thickens. Stir in parsley and cream. Season to taste with salt and pepper. Sprinkle with dill and cayenne.

A special hint:

Raw shrimp are essential for this dish. Cooked shrimp get very tough in their second cooking.

1. SEAFOOD CASSEROLE COTE D'AZUR is a specialty of Hawaii.

2. Cut up the back of shrimp. Remove sand tract and shell.

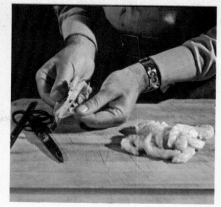

3. Here you can clearly see the sand tract.

4. The fish is cut into slivers. The scallops cut in half.

5. Half olive oil, half clarified butter for this unique taste.

6. Shallow fry the fish over a very low heat.

7. Add wine.

8. Cover and allow to poach— again slowly.

9. Dijon mustard is mixed with arrowroot and cream.

10. Pour mustard thickening into the just-boiling mixture.

11. Stir casserole gently until the sauce has thickened.

12. Add cayenne and dill.

POTTS POINT FISH POT

66

For 6 servings, you will need:

40 fl oz (1.2 l) white fish sauce (page 208)
4 fl oz (1.2 dl) dry white wine
1½ lb (680 g) flounder fillets
4 tbs clarified butter*
12 oysters
1½ lb (680 g) cooked shelled
    lobster
2 tbs brandy
All-purpose flour

4 oz (113 g) button mushrooms
8 oz (227 g) tomatoes
4 oz (113 g) cooked, shelled
    and deveined shrimp
2 tbs lemon juice
1 tbs parsley
Cayenne pepper
2 oz (56 g) Cheddar cheese

First prepare:

Make sauce, measure wine, cut fish (skin removed) into fingers 2 inches x 1 inch (5 cm x 2.5 cm). Cut lobster into 1-inch (2.5 cm) pieces, warm brandy, season flour with salt and pepper, slice mushrooms finely. Skin, seed and chop tomatoes, slice cheese, chop parsley.

Now cook!

1. Heat white sauce and stir in wine.
2. Coat flounder with flour and shake off excess.
3. Melt clarified butter in large frypan, add fish, lobster, tomatoes and oysters. Toss gently and push food to one side. Pour brandy into pan and set alight.
4. Pour sauce over seafood to douse flames and to bind. Fold in shrimp. Season to taste with salt and pepper.
5. In separate pan toss mushrooms in 1 tbs butter with lemon juice and touch of cayenne. Spoon over seafood. Cover with thin slices of cheese and brown under broiler. Garnish with parsley and cayenne pepper and serve.

VOL AU VENT FRUITS DE MER

For 4 servings, you will need:

2 lbs (1 kg) puff pastry*
4 sole fillets
24 mussels
10 oz (283 g) button mushrooms
4 tbs clarified butter*
Freshly ground salt
Freshly ground white pepper
Juice ¼ lemon
12 scallops
1 shallot
12 fl oz (3.2 dl) fish stock, plus
    4 fl oz (1.2 dl)
2 fl oz (5.6 cl) dry white wine
1 tbs butter

2 oz (56 g) all-purpose flour
1 egg yolk
2 fl oz (5.6 cl) heavy cream
1 tbs butter
6 jumbo shrimp, cooked,
    shelled and deveined
2 fl oz (5.6 cl) dry white wine
Nutmeg
Fish stock:
1 snapper head
Bouquet garni
20 fl oz (6 dl) water
1 onion

First prepare:

Preheat oven to 425°F (218°C). Roll out puff paste to a circle 8½ inches in diameter and 1 inch thick. With a sharp knife trim edges to an 8-inch circle. With a sharp knife make another incision 1½ inches (4 cm) from edge of pastry about ½ inch deep. Place round of pastry on a baking sheet, brush with cold water and bake 30 minutes. Remove center section of top and scoop out the doughy center to form a pastry case. Set aside. Place mussels in a pan on a high heat with white wine, cover, shake pan and cook for 2 minutes. Allow to cool and remove mussels from shells. Cut sole fillets into quarters. Finely chop shallot. Measure fish stock and 2 fl oz (5.6 cl) dry white wine. Sift flour. Separate egg yolk. Measure cream and add to egg yolk. Slice shrimp crosswise into round slices.

Fish stock: Simmer fish head with water, onion and herbs for 30 minutes and then strain. Reserve 16 fl oz (4 dl) liquid.

Now cook!

1. Heat half of the clarified butter in a pan and add shallot. Fry gently and then place fish fillets and scallops on top. Stir in 4 fl oz (1.2 dl) of fish stock and 2 fl oz (5.6 cl) dry white wine. Season with salt and pepper and poach for 5 minutes.

2. Melt 1 tbs butter in a saucepan and stir in flour. Stir gently to cook roux but do not allow it to color. Remove from heat and stir in warmed 12 fl oz (3.2 dl) fish stock a little at a time, beating well after each addition. Place sauce back on heat, season with salt and pepper and simmer 10 minutes, stirring from time to time.

3. In a separate pan place remaining clarified butter and when hot add mushrooms. Season with salt, pepper, nutmeg and a squeeze of lemon juice. Fry gently for 1 minute.

4. With a slotted spoon remove fish fillets and scallops and place into a bowl. Add shrimp, mussels and mushrooms.

5. Beat yolk with cream and stir into fish stock sauce. Stir in 1 tbs butter and when smooth fold in seafood, being very careful not to break fish. Correct seasoning.

6. Spoon seafood mixture into pastry case placed on a cookie sheet. Heat in a 350°F (177°C) oven for 10 minutes.

A special hint:

A common cause of failure with vol au vent is due to the incomplete removal of the doughy center. This must be totally removed.

SHRIMP JONGHE AND OKRA PILAF

For 4 servings, you will need:

24 raw jumbo shrimp
1 oz (28 g) celery
Clarified butter*
1 oz (28 g) carrot
2 small onions
1 bay leaf
3 sprigs fresh parsley
30 fl oz (9 dl) cold water
6 spring onions*
2 fl oz (5.6 cl) brandy

16 fl oz (4 dl) sour cream
4 oz (113 g) red pimento
8 oz (226 g) long grain rice
1 bay leaf
1 tsp tarragon (dried)
4 slices white bread
1 tsp gumbo filé
7 oz (198 g) okra
Freshly ground salt
Freshly ground white pepper

First prepare:

Run tip of a knife down the back of the rinsed shrimp, peeling away the shell and at the same time opening the back and removing sand tract. Reserve shells. Finely slice white ends of spring onions and put green parts in stock. Chop pimento. Remove bread crusts and cube bread. Drain okra and rinse under cold water. Measure dry and liquid ingredients. Preheat oven 450°F (232°C). Heat a serving platter.

Now cook!

1. Pour 1 tsp clarified butter in a saucepan and place over high heat. Stir in celery, carrots and half the onions and fry.

2. Stir in shrimp shells, bay leaf, parsley and cold water. Season with salt and white pepper. Bring to a boil, reduce heat to low and cook for 20 minutes. Strain and reserve liquid. Reserve bay leaf.

3. Pour clarified butter into a casserole to just cover bottom and place on medium heat. Stir in remaining onions and cook for 2 minutes.

4. Stir in long grain rice. Moisten with 20 fl oz (6 dl) of fish stock Add reserved bay leaf. Place on middle shelf of preheated oven set at 450°F (232°C) for 20 minutes.

5. Into a large frypan, pour 1 tbs clarified butter and place on medium heat. Stir in white part of spring onions and shrimp.

6. After 2 minutes pour in brandy and flame, shaking pan at same time. Season with salt and white pepper. Stir in sour cream, turn up heat and let mixture boil.

7. Season with tarragon leaves. Stir in bread cubes and reduce heat to medium.

8. Remove pilaf from oven and discard bay leaf. Stir in okra and pimento. Spoon onto serving platter in a ring.

9. Sprinkle gumbo filé into simmering shrimp mixture at last moment.

10. Pour shrimp mixture into rice ring and serve!

A special hint:

When making a shellfish stock don't fry shells. The calcium will scorch and give the dish an "off" flavor.

Seafood Casserole Côte D'Azur (page 194)

GARNALEN BROOD

For 4 servings, you will need:

1¼ lb (566 g) small raw shrimp	8 fl oz (2 dl) heavy cream
1 medium onion	4 tbs Parmesan cheese
2 fl oz (5.6 cl) brandy	2 tsp arrowroot
6 fl oz (1.6 dl) dry white wine	Parsley
4 medium tomatoes	Freshly ground salt
10 fl oz (3 dl) fish stock	Freshly ground white pepper
1 large unsliced loaf of	1 bay leaf
firm white bread	Clarified butter*
2 tsp tomato paste	

First prepare:

Shell shrimp and reserve shells. Thinly slice onion, measure brandy and wine, cut to-matoes into thin slices. Blend arrowroot with a little white wine, measure cream, wash and chop parsley. Remove crusts from bread. Preheat oven to 400°F (205°C). Heat a serving platter in warm oven.

Now cook!

1. Make 4 bread cases by cutting bread with a sharp knife into 4 blocks, 3 inches (7.6 cm) square. Cut out center of bread, leaving shell ¼ inch (7 cm) thick. Brush inside and out with clarified butter. Place on a baking sheet and bake in preheated oven for 12 minutes.

2. Pour some clarified butter to just cover the bottom of a heated pan. Add onions and shallots and fry for one minute.

3. Add shrimp shells, cover and simmer over low heat.

4. Stir shrimp shells and onion mixture, add brandy and set alight. Blend in dry white wine before shells get a chance to brown!

5. Stir in bay leaf and fish stock. Add ¼ cup chopped parsley. Adjust seasoning, continue cooking with lid on over moderate heat.

6. Add tomato paste to the shells and stock. Keep covered for a few moments and then pour the stock through a fine sieve, pushing soft solids through sieve with a wooden spoon into another empty pan on a low heat. Reduce this stock by letting mixture bubble uncovered.

7. Heat another pan and add some clarified butter to just cover bottom. Throw in raw shelled shrimp, stir to coat with butter and season with salt and white pepper. Simmer over low heat until cooked—about 5 minutes.

8. Drain buttered shrimp and remove as much excess butter as possible. Return to a clean pan.

9. Pour cream over shrimp and stir well. Stir in 2 tbs of grated Parmesan cheese and bring mixture to a boil to reduce it.

10. Remove bread cases (croustades) from oven. They should be a crisp, golden brown.

11. Now check reducing shrimp stock and stir 3 fl oz (8 dl) of it into shrimp. Stir in remainder of stock. Thicken with arrowroot, stir until sauce thickens. Season to taste with salt and pepper mixture.

12. Spoon shrimp sauce into croustades. Sprinkle other 2 tbs Parmesan cheese over top and pop under broiler for a few minutes to brown.

BOUZY EEL

For 4 servings, you will need:

2 eels (medium size, skinned)
Freshly ground salt
Freshly ground white pepper
4 tbs clarified butter*
2 tbs spring onions*
4 oz (113 g) celery
4 oz (113 g) mushrooms
2 cloves garlic
1 bay leaf
3 parsley stalks*
8 small onions
10 fl oz (3 dl) dry red wine

Juice of 1 lemon
Cayenne pepper
1 heaped tbs arrowroot
Court Bouillon:
120 fl oz (3.4 l) water
3 fl oz (8 cl) wine vinegar
1 oz (28 g) rock salt
6 oz (170 g) carrots
8 oz (227 g) onions
Bouquet garni
12 black peppercorns

First prepare:

Cut eel into 2-inch (5 cm) chunks. Peel onions, dice celery, chop spring onions finely, slice mushrooms, juice lemon.

Court Bouillon: Place all ingredients for court bouillon into a pan, bring to a boil and allow to simmer 1 hour.

Now cook!

1. Soak eels in salted water with dash of vinegar for 10 minutes. Drain.
2. Place eels into court bouillon and bring slowly to a boil. Remove and dry. Discard bouillon.
3. Heat 4 tbs clarified butter in large pan, add eel and brown. Add crushed garlic, spring onions and celery. Fry gently and then add red wine with bouquet garni of parsley and bay leaf. Simmer, covered, for 30 minutes.
4. Fry tiny onions in 1 tbs clarified butter until golden. Remove with a spoon and add to eels. Add mushrooms to pan drippings. Season with lemon juice and cayenne pepper and add to the eels.
5. When eels are cooked remove bouquet garni. Mix arrowroot with a little red wine, stir into sauce and cook until thickened.
6. Serve dusted liberally with chopped parsley.

BROILED LOBSTER TAIL WITH SAUCE ARMORICAINE

For 4 servings, you will need:

1 raw lobster, 6 lb (2.7 kg)
2 oz (56 g) onion
1 oz (28 g) spring onions*
 (white part only)
1 clove garlic
4 parsley stalks*
2 oz (56 g) carrot
1 bay leaf
2 sprigs thyme or ½ tsp
 dried thyme

2 fl oz (5.6 cl) brandy
4 fl oz (1.2 dl) dry white wine
5 fl oz (1.5 dl) fish stock
10 oz (283 g) tomatoes
1 tsp curry powder
2 egg yolks
2 tbs heavy cream
Clarified butter*
Freshly ground salt
Freshly ground black pepper

First prepare:

Split lobster (see below). Remove lobster head, clean and pull off claws and legs. Remove meat from claws and cut up roughly. Break up lobster shell. Reserve tail. Finely dice onion and carrot. Finely slice spring onion. Crush garlic. Finely chop parsley stalks. Measure brandy, white wine and fish stock. Skin and coarsely chop tomatoes. Mix egg yolks with cream. Preheat broiler.

Now cook!

1. Place some clarified butter in a large casserole to just cover bottom and add onion, spring onions, garlic and carrot. Fry gently for a few minutes. Add parsley, bay leaf, thyme and lobster head, claws and legs. Stir until shells turn red and then flambe with brandy. Douse flames with wine and fish stock. Add tomatoes and season with salt and pepper. Bring sauce to a boil and boil gently for 20 minutes.

2. Place split lobster tail shell side up on broiler rack. Paint cut surface with clarified butter and broil for 8 minutes. After this time turn, drizzle with clarified butter and cook another 6 minutes. Remove, pull out meat from shell and cut into crosswise slices. Place on a heated serving dish.

3. Pass sauce through a sieve into a clean pan. Add curry powder. Remove sauce from heat and whisk in egg and cream mixture stirring briskly to avoid curdling.

4. Cover lobster slices with sauce and accompany with herb pilaf.

A special hint:

To cut lobster. Cut through hard shell with a serrated knife. Make this cut lengthways through center of back. Stop cutting when you get to fine membrane on underside of tail. Insert your fingers into deep cut and open out lobster until cut surface lies flat.

1. BROILED LOBSTER TAIL WITH SAUCE AMORICAINE.

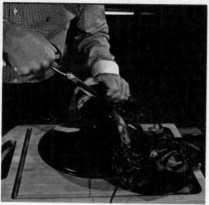

2. Snip tail from body.

3. Cut through *first* heavy under-rib.

4. With curved, serrated blade, saw through shell down center.

5. Cut down to underribs then STOP. Open center cut.

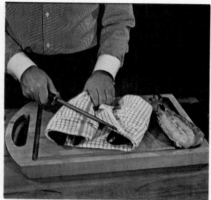

6. Wrap claws in a towel and break with a steel or hammer.

7. Use heavy scissors to remove the raw flesh.

8. Baste open tail with clarified butter. Broil flesh up.

9. Baste again when cooked and turn to cook second side.

10. This is what a "broken-down" lobster looks like.

11. Remove green sack and lungs from head; sand tract from tail.

12. When you flambé shells don't let them actually catch fire.

Broiled Lobster Tail with Sauce Armoricaine (page 202)

BROILED LOBSTER TAILS AND LEMON BUTTER SAUCE

For 2 servings, you will need:

2 raw lobster tails each
  10 oz (283 g)
Clarified butter*
Freshly ground salt
Freshly ground white pepper
Lemon butter sauce:
  2 egg yolks
  Freshly ground salt

Freshly ground white pepper
Nutmeg
½ tsp lemon juice
4 oz (113 g) softened butter
1 tbs water
1 tbs horseradish sauce*
1 tbs chopped chives

First prepare:

Lay lobster tail flat on board, shell uppermost. With serrated knife cut hard shell lengthways down center. Cut almost through. Put thumbs into cut and open shell out flat. The soft shell on the underside will hold halves of tail together. Remove digestive tract. Preheat broiler. Put rack on top rung.

Now cook!

1. Brush meaty cut surface and shell side of tails with melted clarified butter and season with salt and pepper.

2. Place, shell side up, under broiler for 5 minutes, then turn. Brush meaty surface again with melted butter and broil for 8 minutes more.

3. Cover lobster meat with lemon butter sauce and dust with parsley before serving.

4. *Sauce:* Place lemon juice, salt, pepper, grated nutmeg and water in top of double boiler over simmering water.

5. Add egg yolks with 1 oz (28 g) soft butter and whisk together. When blended and smooth, add another 1 oz piece of butter beating well. The sauce at this stage will have thickened considerably. Add remaining butter, 1 ounce at a time beating after each addition. Take pan from over water and whisk for 1 minute.

6. Replace pan over warm water and add chives and horseradish sauce. Keep over warm water until ready to serve. Water in lower pan must be just warm or sauce will overcook.

BROILED LOBSTER WITH CHORON SAUCE

For 4 servings, you will need:

2 raw lobster tails,
   2½ lb (1.2 kg)
2 fl oz (5.6 cl) tarragon vinegar
2 shallots
2 tbs chives
2 tbs parsley

4 egg yolks
8 oz (227 g) butter
Clarified butter*
Freshly ground salt
Freshly ground black pepper
2 fl oz (5.6 cl) tomato puree

First prepare:

Cut lobster tails through hard shell in half lengthwise. Don't sever completely and leave soft undershell in one piece. Open out tails. Preheat broiler unit. Finely chop chives and parsley. (I have not recommended fresh tarragon and chervil because they are difficult to obtain.) Measure vinegar. Separate eggs. Cut butter into four equal pieces. Measure tomato puree. Finely chop shallots.

Now cook!

1. Place lobster tails shell side up on a broiler rack. Brush with clarified butter. Broil for 6 minutes. Turn lobster tails over to meaty side and brush with clarified butter. Season with salt and pepper and broil for a further 8 minutes.

2. Heat vinegar, shallots, chives and parsley in a saucepan and boil mixture until reduced to a syrup.

3. Put syrup in a double boiler placed over boiling water. Add 2 oz (56 g) butter and 4 egg yolks, whisking until mixture thickens. Whisk in another 2 oz (56 g) butter and continue until all butter is absorbed. Season with salt and pepper and whisk in tomato puree. Sieve sauce. Stir in 1 tbs each finely chopped chives and parsley and replace sauce over warm water to keep warm. Do not allow water in bottom pot to boil.

4. Remove lobster tails from broiler, place on a heated serving dish, cover with sauce.

A special hint:

Should sauce curdle, drop an ice cube into it and whisk until cube melts completely. The sauce will become smooth.

66

YARRADARRA

For 4 first course or 2 main course servings, you will need:

10 fl oz (3 dl) white fish sauce
2 fl oz (5.6 cl) dry white wine
4 oz (113 g) cooked lobster meat
1 oz (28 g) mushrooms
1 tsp lemon juice
1 tbs parsley
8 oz (227 g) potatoes
1 oz (28 g) butter
2 fl oz (5.6 cl) milk
Freshly ground salt
Freshly ground white pepper

2 tbs Cheddar cheese
Chopped parsley
Cayenne pepper
Fish sauce:
6 fl oz (1.6 dl) fish stock
6 fl oz (1.6 dl) milk
1 oz (28 g) butter
1 oz (28 g) all-purpose flour
Freshly ground salt
Freshly ground white pepper
Nutmeg

First prepare:

Measure wine. Slice lobster meat thinly. Chop mushrooms and parsley finely. Cook potatoes, peel and mash, beat in butter and milk until creamy. Season with salt and pepper. Grate cheese. Preheat broiler. Prepare 4 scallop shells or 2 half lobster tail shells.

Fish sauce: Melt butter and stir in flour. Cook gently 1 minute then gradually stir in hot milk and fish stock. Cook stirring all the time to make a smooth sauce. Season with salt, pepper and nutmeg. Cook gently for 15 minutes, stirring from time to time.

Now cook!

1. Add wine to sauce and place 1 tbs of sauce in each shell. Cover with lobster meat. Mix mushrooms, lemon juice and parsley and sprinkle over lobster. Spoon over more sauce.

2. Using a pastry bag with ½-inch (1.5 cm) rosette tip pipe potato in a border around shells. Dust top of sauce with cheese and place under hot broiler for 2 minutes to brown.

3. Serve garnished with chopped parsley and a little cayenne pepper.

A special hint:

Pipe a little potato on the plate. Press scallop shells into potato to keep them from rocking and sliding.

1. YARRADARRA. Drown lobster in lukewarm water 98.6°F (37°C).

2. Place perforated disc in pot of boiling water. Add lobster.

3. Perforated disc keeps lobster from direct pot heat contact.

4. After 6 minutes remove to bowl of ice water to *arrest* cooking.

5. When cold remove claws and legs. Cut through *shell only*.

6. Use a knife to cut through the rest of the way.

7. Remove tender tails by hand. Discard sand tract.

8. Chop into very fine dice.

9. Coat shell base with a good fish sauce.

10. Cover sauce with chopped lobster meat.

11. Cover meat with mushrooms, cayenne, lemon juice and parsley.

12. Coat again with the sauce. Broil and serve hot.

CHEVRON CRAYFISH (LOBSTER)

For 2 servings, you will need:

1 large lobster, cooked
3 oz (85 g) onion
1 clove garlic
1 tsp mild curry powder
12 fl oz (3.2 dl) coconut milk
1 banana

8 oz (227 g) pineapple
2 tbs heavy cream
1 tbs brandy
2 tsp arrowroot
Parsley
2 tbs clarified butter*

First prepare:

Make coconut milk by infusing 4 oz (113 g) coconut in 12 fl oz (3.2 dl) boiling water. Allow to stand 20 minutes and then strain coconut milk through muslin, pressing out all liquid. Slice onion thinly. Peel garlic. Cut pineapple into chunks. Measure cream. Measure brandy. Remove head of lobster and reserve. With scissors remove thin undershell on inside of tail, remove meat and reserve tail shell. Cut lobster meat into chunks. Chop parsley.

Now cook!

1. Heat clarified butter in a pan, fry sliced onion until soft and golden. Add crushed garlic and curry powder and fry for a few minutes.

2. Add coconut milk to onion mixture and allow to simmer 10 minutes.

3. Mix arrowroot with brandy and slowly pour, stirring, into hot sauce to thicken it.

4. Fold in banana, sliced, pineapple, lobster and cream. Heat only until bubbly.

5. Arrange lobster head with tail shell (forming a receptacle) on a serving dish. Fill with lobster curry and decorate with finely chopped parsley.

A special hint:

Only *just* heat lobster through at Step 4. It will toughen if left to cook.

LOBSTER PLOV

For 4 servings, you will need:

1 lobster, 2½ lb (1.1 kg)
4 medium onions
2 oz (56 g) tomato ketchup
1 fl oz (2.8 cl) Worcestershire
   sauce
4 fl oz (1.2 dl) sour cream
8 oz (227 g) long grain rice
1 green pepper (capsicum)
1 red pepper (capsicum)

32 fl oz (1 l) cold water
1 bay leaf
¼ tsp thyme
¼ tsp cayenne
1 tsp arrowroot
Clarified butter*
Freshly ground salt
Freshly ground white pepper

First prepare:

Drown lobster in warm water 98.6⁰F (37⁰C). It will just fall asleep. Fill a large pan with water and bring to a boil. A bowl of ice cold water will be required. Finely slice onions, dice peppers. Measure tomato ketchup, sour cream, Worcestershire sauce and rice. Mix arrowroot with a little cold water in a bowl. Set aside herbs. Heat a platter in a warm oven. Preheat oven to 450⁰F (232⁰C).

Now cook!

1. Drop lobster into pot of boiling water and cook for 4 minutes. Remove and plunge into bowl of ice cold water. Remove meat from the shells, put the shells in blender with cold water and blend. Dice lobster meat.

2. Remove shells and water from blender, season with salt and white pepper. Pour into a pot, add bay leaf and thyme and cook for 20 minutes over a moderate heat (makes a quick stock). There should be 20 fl oz (6 dl) of stock. Strain and reserve.

3. Heat a little clarified butter to just cover bottom of saucepan, add half the onions, cayenne pepper, tomato ketchup and Worcestershire sauce.

4. Stir in sour cream and simmer gently over low heat.

5. Into 1½ quart casserole pour clarified butter to just cover bottom and add remaining onions. Stir and cook until opaque. Stir in rice and fry briefly until rice is golden. Stir in peppers.

6. Pour strained stock over rice mixture, place in preheated oven and bake for 20 minutes, uncovered.

7. Thicken sauce with arrowroot mixture.

8. Stir lobster into simmering sauce and heat through.

9. Remove rice pilaf from oven and spoon it onto heated serving dish. Pour lobster sauce over rice and serve at once piping hot.

A special hint:

Refer to Step 1. The ice water treatment stops lobster from overcooking.

LOBSTER MIRANDA HILL

For 2 servings, you will need:

2 lb 4 oz (1.1 kg) fresh lobster
30 whole allspice
2 bay leaves
4 fl oz (1.2 dl) rum
1 shallot
2 cloves garlic
12 oz (340 g) tomatoes
3 fl oz (8 dl) dry white wine
2 oz (56 g) butter
1 tsp lime juice

4 oz (113 g) small shrimp, cooked, shelled and deveined
2 tbs sour cream
1 bunch watercress
4 oz (113 g) mushrooms
1 fl oz (2.8 cl) oil
1 fl oz (2.8 cl) white wine vinegar
Freshly ground salt
Freshly ground white pepper
Clarified butter*

First prepare:

Place live lobster into a large bowl of water at 98.6°F (37°C) and it will fall asleep and drown (most humane way of killing it). A large bowl of ice water is required. Measure dry and liquid ingredients. Wash and dry watercress. Mix oil and vinegar together. Wash and dry mushrooms. Crush garlic and finely slice shallot. Boil a large pan of water. Roughly slice tomatoes.

Now cook!

1. Into large pan of boiling water throw in 12 allspice and bay leaves.
2. Rip claws and legs from lobster. Place whole lobster into boiling water, cover pot and cook for 3 minutes to the pound (0.5 kg). Drain and cool.
3. Into a small pan place 18 allspice and 2 fl oz (5.6 cl) light rum and heat through at low heat. Strain.
4. Place lobster legs and strained rum into a blender and whirl until smooth, making a beautiful stock base.
5. Into a frypan over medium heat pour 1 tbs clarified butter and add shallot and garlic. Lay tomatoes on top and season generously with salt and white pepper.
6. Strain mixture from blender through a fine sieve over tomatoes. Add white wine and bring to a boil.
7. After 6 minutes lift out lobster and plunge into ice water to arrest cooking.
8. Stir tomato stock sauce mixture.
9. Sieve stock sauce ingredients into a clean pan over high heat and let it reduce to about 3 fl oz (8 cl).
10. Put butter in a small frypan over low heat and stir in button mushrooms and lime juice.
11. Add shrimp to mushrooms.
12. Cut cooked lobster in half lengthwise and rinse. Take out the edible meat from tail and claws.
13. Cut meat into small pieces and add to mushrooms.
14. Push sautéed vegetables, shrimp and lobster mixture to one side of pan, pour over 2 fl oz (5.6 cl) rum and flame.
15. When flames die, stir in sour cream and reduced tomato stock and reduce again. You can add 1 tbs of arrowroot blended to a paste with rum if you wish to speed thickening of sauce.
16. Rinse out body shell and warm on a platter in hot oven.
17. Take warmed shells out of oven and spoon lobster mixture into them.
18. Toss watercress with oil and vinegar. Serve immediately with lobster.

LOBSTER WITH WHITE BUTTER

For 4 servings, you will need:

1 lobster, 7 lb (3.2 kg) or
    4 lobsters, 1½ lb (680 g)
Clarified butter*
½ medium onion
Freshly ground salt
4 fl oz (1.2 dl) dry white wine

½ tsp tarragon
2 tbs dry sherry
1 tbs butter
1 whole artichoke
1 small onion

First prepare:

Place lobster in warm water (98.6°F) (37°C). It will fall asleep and drown. Remove lobster head and claws. Using a large knife cut tail shell crosswise between natural joints into 1-inch (2.5 cm) thick slices. Remove flippers from last slice. Mince onion. Measure white wine and sherry. Poach artichoke until tender in boiling water with lemon juice or vinegar added to prevent darkening.

Now cook!

1. Place clarified butter in heated pan to just cover bottom. Add lobster medallions. Sauté for 1 minute and turn. Add onion, salt, white wine and tarragon. Cover pan, reduce heat and cook for 2 minutes.

2. Strain juices from pan in which lobster was cooked into a saucepan. Stir in butter, sherry and lobster medallions. Cover and poach 5 minutes.

3. Place lobster onto a serving dish with red part of shell on top and cover with sauce. Decorate with one whole artichoke in center.

A special hint:

Times given are for a large lobster. If four small lobsters are used, reduce poaching time in Step 2, to 3 minutes. Test and extend time if necessary.

LANGOUSTE CHEVRE D'OR

For 2 servings, you will need:

1 raw lobster, 2 lb (0.9 kg)
4 oz (113 g) mushrooms
1 bay leaf
2 shallots
1 fl oz (2.8 cl) brandy
1 small onion
1 large clove garlic
2 large tomatoes
2 fl oz (5.6 cl) dry white wine
Paprika
1 black truffle*
Parsley
1 fl oz (2.8 cl) cream

2 tsp arrowroot
Freshly ground salt
Freshly ground white pepper
Clarified butter*
Hollandaise sauce:
¼ tsp mace
4 egg yolks
8 oz (227 g) butter
1 tbs water
1 tsp lemon juice
Freshly ground salt
Freshly ground white pepper

First prepare:

Place lobster in water at blood heat for about 30 minutes. This is the most humane killing method as lobster falls asleep and drowns. Cut lobster in half lengthwise and discard intestinal tract and "mustard" in head. Pull meat from body using a fork and keep shell halves. Break off claws, crack them open and remove meat. Slice truffle. Finely chop parsley. Crush garlic. Thinly slice onion, mushrooms, tomatoes and shallots. Measure brandy and white wine. Blend arrowroot with cream in a small bowl. Heat a serving platter in a warm oven.

Hollandaise sauce: In the top part of a double boiler, mix lemon juice, salt, white pepper and mace. Add water. Gently stir in egg yolks and 4 tbs butter. Place over simmering water. Beat with a whisk. Slowly beat in remaining 12 tbs butter in three additions, beating in each 4 tbs completely before adding next. The sauce will thicken. Remove from heat and whisk for 1 minute. Replace over warm water and add a little extra lemon juice to taste. Set aside for a few minutes until required.

Now cook!

1. Place shell halves and claw shells into a hot dry frypan. Pour over a little clarified butter.

2. Pour over brandy and flame.

3. Tip pan to one side and add onion, garlic and tomatoes. Pour in dry white wine, add bay leaf and cover pan. Reduce heat to simmer and cook for 15 minutes. Strain and reserve shells and liquid.

4. Pour a little clarified butter to just cover bottom into another saucepan and add lobster meat and shallots. Add mushrooms. Continue cooking over low heat until lobster just turns white. Remove from heat.

5. Place shell halves on heated serving platter. The claw shells can also be used as decoration.

6. Pour reserved liquid into a clean pot. Add blended arrowroot and stir until sauce thickens. Add lobster and vegetables in saucepan.

7. Stir in hollandaise sauce.

8. Spoon sauce and meat into shells. Sprinkle with chopped parsley and garnish with slices of truffle. Serve at once.

1. SALMON ST. GOTTHARD. Serve with its own salad (page 217).

2. Smoked salmon mashes easily after skin and bones are removed.

3. Combine with firm unsalted butter to a soft paste.

4. Cut diagonal incisions down into each flank.

5. Fill incisions with smoked salmon butter. Don't overpack.

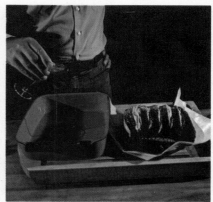

6. When filling second side use wax paper to protect side one.

7. Baste once just before the oven.

8. After 16 minutes place wire rack over dish. Pour off juices.

9. When pan is dry, hold rack against dish and invert.

10. If your 7th vertebra is all right you won't stay this way!

11. Looks good but from where I am, it *smells* better.

12. Slide back to cook side two. Use rack system to dish up.

SALMON ST. GOTTHARD

71

For 8 servings, you will need:

5 lbs (2.3 kg) fresh salmon
(center cut)

5 oz (141 g) smoked salmon

2 oz (56 g) butter

¼ tsp cayenne

Freshly ground salt

Freshly ground white pepper

Clarified butter*

Garnish:

3 lbs (1.4 kg) tiny, new
potatoes, boiled

Salad:

4 radishes

5 oz (141 g) smoked salmon
(thinly sliced)

Watercress

Dressing:

2 fl oz (5.6 cl) olive oil

4 fl oz (1.2 dl) white wine vinegar

1 tbs sugar

½ tsp English mustard (dry mustard
mixed with water to a paste)

1 small clove garlic

Freshly ground salt

Freshly ground white pepper

Dash cayenne pepper

First prepare:

The salmon: Make sure all scales are scraped from fish, and board on which it is resting is also free of scales. Cut smoked salmon into thin slices and with your knife blade mash salmon until it feels like butter. Mix butter with mashed salmon and add cayenne, salt and pepper. Make five incisions in flank of fish, increasing depth as you move from tail to shoulder. The incisions should be diagonal, slanting at 30⁰ to tail and between 1¼ inches (3.3 cm) to 1 inch (2.5 cm) deep—about 2 inches apart. Repeat on other side. Preheat oven to 350⁰F (177⁰C). Place a large oval serving platter in oven.

The salad: Slice radishes into thin rounds. Slice smoked salmon into fine strips and wash watercress. Have on hand a salad bowl.

The dressing: Measure oil, vinegar, sugar, mustard, finely slice garlic and place in a container or bottle with a lid or cork.

Now cook!

1. Into each incision in salmon press in firmly a large knob of prepared salmon butter.
2. Do this on both sides.
3. Brush clarified butter on bottom of a shallow baking pan to keep salmon from sticking.
4. Put salmon on pan and place uncovered in preheated oven 350⁰F (177⁰C) for 16 minutes.
5. After 16 minutes remove fish and pour off drippings into another pan. Run a spatula under length of fish to loosen, place another buttered baking pan over top of salmon and turn it over.
6. The underside is now uppermost. Pour pan drippings back over salmon and return to oven for another 16 minutes.
7. Meanwhile, put watercress in a salad bowl and sprinkle with fine strips of smoked salmon and rounds of radish. Refrigerate.
8. When salmon is fully cooked remove once again from oven and pour off drippings. Place oval serving platter over salmon and invert so that top side is showing.
9. Carefully scrape off silver gray skin. Scrape off center band of dark meat carefully with a knife and expose light pink flesh of cooked salmon. The salmon butter will appear darker pink in slashes—very colorful! Leave skin on the underside of the salmon. Wipe off platter.
10. Surround salmon with tiny new buttered potatoes (which have been kept warm without water in a pan covered with a towel). Serve at once.
11. Shake the salad dressing thoroughly and pour over the smoked salmon salad. Serve promptly with baked salmon.

1. ST. GOTTHARD SALAD goes with Salmon St. Gotthard.

2. Use soft brown sugar for health reasons.

3. Mix two parts vinegar to one part oil for a light dressing.

4. Here we have sliced smoked salmon, radishes and watercress.

5. Thoroughly shake dressing and add at last moment.

G
64

GOURMET GROUPER

For 6 servings, you will need:

3 lb (1.4 kg) shoal grouper*
10 fl oz (3 dl) water
Small piece parsley
3 celery leaves
½ bay leaf
2 lb (0.9 kg) large white potatoes
Freshly ground salt
Freshly ground white pepper

2 spring onions*
6 tbs clarified butter*
1 celery heart
10 tbs heavy cream
1½ tsp arrowroot
1 tbs capers
12 stuffed olives
2 tbs parsley

First prepare:

Trim tail from grouper. Measure water. Peel potatoes. Finely slice spring onions. Measure butter and cream. Quarter celery heart. Mix arrowroot with a little milk. Cut olives into halves. Chop parsley. Preheat oven to 350°F (177°C).

Now cook!

1. Boil potatoes for 10 minutes in salted water.
2. Place tail in saucepan with water, celery leaves, bay leaf and parsley head. Simmer for 30 minutes.
3. Make ½-inch (1.2 cm) diagonal cuts on flanks of fish and season inside and out with salt and white pepper.
4. Cut potatoes in ½-inch (1.2 cm) thick slices, lay in roasting pan.
5. Strain fish stock over potatoes and place fish on top. Place celery heart on top of fish.
6. Brush with butter, place on top shelf of oven and bake 10 minutes per lb (0.5 kg). Brush with butter each 10 minutes.
7. Place fish onto serving dish, surround with potatoes. Mix cream with pan juices, bring to a boil and thicken with arrowroot mixture. Stir in olives, capers and parsley.

A special hint:

The fish is cooked when flesh, gently lifted with a knife point, comes cleanly from bone.

SOLE GASCOGNE

For 2 servings, you will need:

2 whole sole (4 whole fillets)
Freshly ground salt
Cayenne pepper
1 tbs chopped chives
1 tbs chopped parsley
2 fl oz (5.6 cl) melted butter
Lemon juice
Clarified butter*
Freshly ground salt.
Freshly ground black pepper
2 oz (56 g) mushrooms
1 egg yolk
1 oz (28 g) bread crumbs*
2 tbs sweet white wine

Juice of ¼ lemon
3 oz (85 g) Gruyère cheese
Paprika to garnish
Sauce:
2 tbs butter
1 tsp spring onions*
½ tsp mild French mustard
1 tsp parsley
1 tsp tomato paste
2 tbs tarragon vinegar
Freshly ground salt
Freshly ground black pepper
4 fl oz (1.2 dl) sweet white wine
1 clove garlic

First prepare:

Cut fillets from sole, remove head and black skin. Finely chop parsley and chives. Melt butter, cut mushrooms into quarters. Measure wine, grate cheese, smash garlic.

Sauce: Measure butter, finely chop spring onions and parsley. Measure vinegar and tomato paste. Measure wine. Preheat oven to 350°F (177°C).

Now cook!

1. *Sauce:* Heat butter gently in saucepan. Add spring onions, mustard, parsley, tomato paste, tarragon vinegar, wine and season with salt and pepper. Add garlic and cook on gentle heat for 2 minutes.

2. Dry sole fillets and sprinkle with salt, cayenne pepper, chives and parsley. Brush with melted butter.

3. Place 1 fish fillet on top of the other (forming a sandwich) and lay in a well-buttered ovenproof dish. Pour over sauce and place in oven for 20 minutes.

4. Place enough clarified butter to just cover bottom in a frypan. Add mushrooms and a squeeze of lemon juice and salt and pepper. Fry gently for 2 minutes.

5. Remove fish from oven and keep warm on a platter. Pour juices into a pan. Add a little of the juice to egg yolk, beat well and then mix with rest of sauce. Stir over low heat until sauce thickens. Drain mushrooms and add to sauce.

6. Mix bread crumbs with wine, lemon juice and grated cheese.

7. Spoon sauce over sole and sprinkle with bread crumb mixture. Place under broiler and cook until top is brown and crisp.

SOLE WITH CHIVE SAUCE

For 2 servings, you will need:

2 sole
Egg yolk mixed with a little oil
2 oz (56 g) fine bread crumbs*
Flour
Freshly ground salt
Freshly ground white pepper
Clarified butter*
1 large shallot
1 tbs veal jelly
2 fl oz (5.6 cl) dry vermouth
2 fl oz (5.6 cl) fish stock
2 tbs heavy cream
1 oz (28 g) butter
1 tbs finely chopped chives
Juice ½ lemon
2 fl oz (5.6 cl) dry white wine
1 fl oz (2.8 cl) fish stock

Fish stock:
Sole trimmings
1 medium onion
1 bouquet garni
20 fl oz (6 dl) water
2 fl oz (5.6 cl) dry white wine
Freshly ground salt
8 peppercorns

Veal Jelly:
1 veal knuckle
1 onion, sliced
1 carrot, sliced
1 bouquet garni (parsley, bay leaf, celery leaves)
Freshly ground salt
Black peppercorns
Water to cover

First prepare:

Veal jelly: Bring all ingredients to a boil in a saucepan, skim surface and simmer 6 hours until reduced to about 4 fl oz (1.2 dl). Strain and refrigerate. It will set like rubber and can be used for many excellent sauces.

Sole: Remove black skin from sole by making an incision across the tail and carefully pulling off skin. Cut off head and remove fin and tail. Reserve for fish stock. Make bread crumbs. Mix egg yolk with a little oil. Finely slice shallot and chives. Measure dry vermouth and wine. Measure butter. Preheat oven to 425°F (218°C).

Fish stock: Place all ingredients into a saucepan, bring to a boil and skim surface. Allow stock to boil gently 25 minutes. Strain and reserve liquid.

Now cook!

1. Dip sole into flour, then egg and then bread crumbs—only on side from which skin was removed. Place in an ovenproof dish bread-crumbed side up and add dry white wine and fish stock to just cover bottom of dish. Season fish with salt and pepper. Drizzle a little clarified butter over fish and bake in oven 15 minutes.

2. Place a little clarified butter in a frypan to just cover bottom, add finely sliced shallot and allow to fry gently. Add veal jelly and when melted add vermouth and 2 fl oz (5.6 cl) fish stock. Season with salt and pepper, bring to a boil and allow to reduce to a syrupy consistency. When sauce has reduced to a syrup stir in cream. Remove pan from heat and whisk in butter, chives and lemon juice.

3. Remove fish from oven, place pan under broiler and brown for 2 minutes.

4. Pour sauce onto a heated serving platter and lay sole on sauce.

A special hint:

This is an unusual method of cookery—coating only one side of fish. It combines advantages of poaching with that of broiling and even that of bread-crumbing. It can only succeed if bread-crumbed side isn't saturated with stock and wine at Step 1.

LANGOUSTE (OR LOBSTER) FLAMBE

For 2 servings, you will need:

1 raw lobster, 2 lb (0.9 kg)
1 tsp thyme
1 tsp rosemary
1 tsp oregano
1 tsp tarragon
1 tbs parsley
2 fl oz (5.6 cl) brandy

4 fl oz (1.2 dl) white wine
2 oz (56 g) butter
2 fl oz (5.6 cl) heavy cream
1 tsp arrowroot
Freshly ground salt
Freshly ground white pepper
Clarified butter*

First prepare:

Saw through hard shell of uncooked lobster lengthwise. Measure herbs, wine and brandy. Bend a wire cake rack in half at an angle of 90º. Blend arrowroot with cream in a small bowl. Chop parsley. Heat a serving dish in a warm oven.

Now cook!

1. Pour enough clarified butter to just cover bottom of large heated skillet (or heavy roasting pan).
2. Add lobster halves, meat side down, and allow to sizzle gently in hot butter.
3. Turn lobster halves over and continue to cook side by side. Season with salt and pepper.
4. When both are heated through remove from skillet and put on a plate. Put bent rack into skillet and lay lobster halves on either side, meat side facing up.
5. Sprinkle herbs over lobsters, pour brandy over all and set alight.
6. Remove lobsters and place on a plate in warm oven.
7. Take rack out of skillet and stir in white wine. Let this cook gently over low heat for 5 minutes.
8. Strain everything through a sieve and pour into a clean pot. Add butter, bring to a boil. Stir in blended arrowroot until sauce thickens. Remove from heat and stir in parsley.
9. Remove lobster from warm oven and discard burnt herbs.
10. Place lobster on a serving dish, pour sauce over it and serve at once.

A special hint:

This dish is very much improved by the use of herbs dried on the branch. Some spice or food specialty stores do sell dried bunches of these herbs.

Salmon St. Gotthard (page 216)

SALMON STEAKS WITH HERB BUTTER

66

For 4 servings, you will need:

4 salmon steaks each 1 inch
   (2.5 cm) thick
Butter
Freshly ground salt
Freshly ground black pepper
2 shallots
Fish bones
Large piece of dried fennel

2 fl oz (5.6 cl) cognac
2 fl oz (5.6 cl) dry white wine
Herb butter:
8 oz (227 g) butter
1 small clove garlic
1 tsp fennel
1 tsp cayenne pepper

First prepare:

Butter an ovenproof casserole large enough to hold salmon steaks side by side. Prepare herb butter by softening butter and adding remaining ingredients. Peel shallots and chop finely. Warm cognac.

Now cook!

1. Season salmon steaks on both sides. Place in well-buttered casserole dish and sprinkle with shallots and wine. Cover with fish bones. Place lid on dish and cook over low heat for 10 minutes.

2. Place salmon steaks carefully on a trivet (a raised metal grid that elevates fish at least 3 inches [7.6 cm] from dish). Put fennel on a heated fireproof dish and place trivet over fennel. Pour warmed cognac over fennel and set aflame. When flames die, place salmon on a platter.

3. Serve salmon with a side dish of herb butter.

A special hint:

To prepare fennel. When it runs to seed cut off full length branches and hang them upside down in a warm part of kitchen. Takes about 7 days to dry.

Salmon Steaks with Herb Butter

57

TROUT WOOLPACK

For 4 servings, you will need:

1 trout, 2½ lb (1.1 kg)
Freshly ground salt
Freshly ground white pepper
8 oz (227 g) mushrooms
4 tbs clarified butter*
Juice 1 lemon

½ lb (227 g) canned cooked shrimp
Parsley
Cayenne pepper
Lemon cut into quarters
1 tbs parsley stalks*
4 tbs olive oil

First prepare:

Cut fish and wipe out inside with plenty of salt. Finely slice mushrooms. Juice lemon. Dice shrimp. Cut fish right down belly from head to tail, cutting not quite all the way through to shape a large pocket in trout. Heat oven to 375°F (190°C).

Now cook!

1. Season inside of trout with pepper and salt.
2. Place clarified butter in a frypan and add mushrooms. Add lemon juice and season with cayenne pepper. Fry gently until mushrooms are cooked. Add parsley stalks and shrimp. Mix and spoon half the mixture into trout and keep remainder moist and warm. Place trout on a buttered shallow baking pan.
3. Brush trout with mixture of melted butter and olive oil. Incise flanks diagonally about ¼ inch (7 mm) deep at ½-inch (1.2 cm) intervals to help cook trout quicker.
4. Bake trout in oven 20 minutes. It is done when flesh is opaque. Place trout on a serving dish. Reheat remaining mushroom and shrimp mixture with a little additional butter. Pour this over trout. Serve garnished with parsley and accompanied by lemon wedges.

A special hint:

Suggest you place trout onto a broiler (grill) rack in your baking pan. There is no need to turn when air can circulate. Drain pan juices. Place serving dish upside down on cooked fish and quickly invert.

1. TROUT WOOLPACK. Any good round-bodied fish will do.

2. Wipe out the inside of the fish with a gauze crusted in salt.

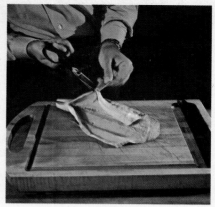

3. Remove the head and tail. Snip out the gills.

4. Season the filling of shrimp and mushrooms with plenty of lemon.

5. Toss well in butter but don't overcook the shrimp.

6. Cut ¼-inch (7 mm) incisions diagonally down each flank and season well.

7. Put half the filling into the fish.

8. Brush the fish well with melted butter and roll it firmly in foil to keep its shape under the heat.

9. Broil 3-4 inches (8 cm) from the heat. Unwrap before it gets to the table. You may wish to brown the cooked skin lightly under direct heat.

FISH AND BACON ROLLS

64

For 6 servings, you will need:

6 bacon rashers*
Juice of 1 lemon

Freshly ground black pepper
12 small sole fillets

First prepare:

Squeeze lemon. Remove rind from bacon rashers. Trim fillets. Preheat oven to 375ºF (190ºC).

Now cook!

1. Season fish fillets with lemon juice and pepper and roll up. Cut bacon into 12 strips and wrap around fish.

2. Arrange rolls in a lightly greased heatproof dish and cook quickly under a hot broiler until sole is white and opaque.

A special hint:

Keep rolls 3 inches (7.6 cm) from broiler heat. Don't overcook, bacon should not be crisp.

COQUILLES ST JACQUES AU CIDRE

For 4 servings, you will need:

1 lb (0.5 kg) scallops
4 fl oz (1.2 dl) hard cider
1 can 14 oz (396 g) small button
    mushrooms
2½ lbs (1.2 kg) potatoes
1 tbs dill
2 tbs parsley
3 tbs Parmesan cheese
½ tsp paprika
1 lemon
1 oz (28 g) butter
1½ oz (42 g) all-purpose flour
Celery leaf

4 fl oz (1.2 dl) milk
Clarified butter*
Freshly ground white pepper
Fish Fumet:
1 lb (0.5 kg) fish bones
1 small onion
1 bay leaf
1 small leek
4 white peppercorns
4 celery tops
Pinch of thyme
24 fl oz (7 dl) cold water

First prepare:

Measure cider and allow to become flat. Measure milk. Peel potatoes and let stand in cold water (with a piece of washed charcoal) until required. Grate cheese. Wash and dry dill and parsley very thoroughly, then finely chop. Drain mushrooms and squeeze juice of lemon over them. Rinse fish bones. Chop onion. Shred leek after washing it thoroughly. Measure water and pour it into a saucepan. Heat an ovenproof serving dish. A pastry bag with a large rosette tip will be required.

Now cook!

1. *Fumet:* To water in saucepan, add fish bones, celery tops, leek, onion, bay leaf, peppercorns and thyme. Place over moderate heat, bring to a boil, then simmer for 20 minutes, skimming frequently. Strain, reserving liquid.

2. Place peeled potatoes in salted water, bring to a boil and cook for 20 minutes. When easily pierced, drain off water. Return pan to low heat to dry excess moisture. Remove potatoes from heat and mash thoroughly. Add a knob of fresh butter, white pepper and moisten with some warm milk. Beat in dill, parsley and paprika. Cover until required.

3. *Sauce:* Melt butter in a slightly warmed saucepan, remove from heat and stir in flour. Return to heat and cook stirring constantly for 3 minutes over low heat.

4. Gradually stir in milk and cider. Cook for 3 minutes, then reduce heat. Cook while stirring until sauce bubbles and thickens.

5. Place scallops in a frypan and cover with 6 fl oz (1.6 dl) of reduced fish fumet. Poach them gently in liquid for 6 minutes.

6. When the scallops are done, drain and stir liquid into cider sauce. Reduce heat and simmer gently.

7. Pour some clarified butter into a frypan to just cover bottom and fry mushrooms. Sprinkle with lemon juice and white pepper. Drain off excess pan juices after mushrooms are hot.

8. Stir sauce into mushrooms. Fold in scallops.

9. Place mashed potatoes in a pastry bag.

10. Pipe potatoes around the edge of the heated serving dish. Pour scallops into center of dish.

11. Sprinkle with cheese and place under broiler to brown for approximately 4 minutes.

12. Serve at once, bubbling hot.

A special hint:

A washed lump of charcoal will add "iron" to water and help to keep peeled raw potatoes white. It can be used over and over, unlike a lemon, which serves the same purpose but can only be used once.

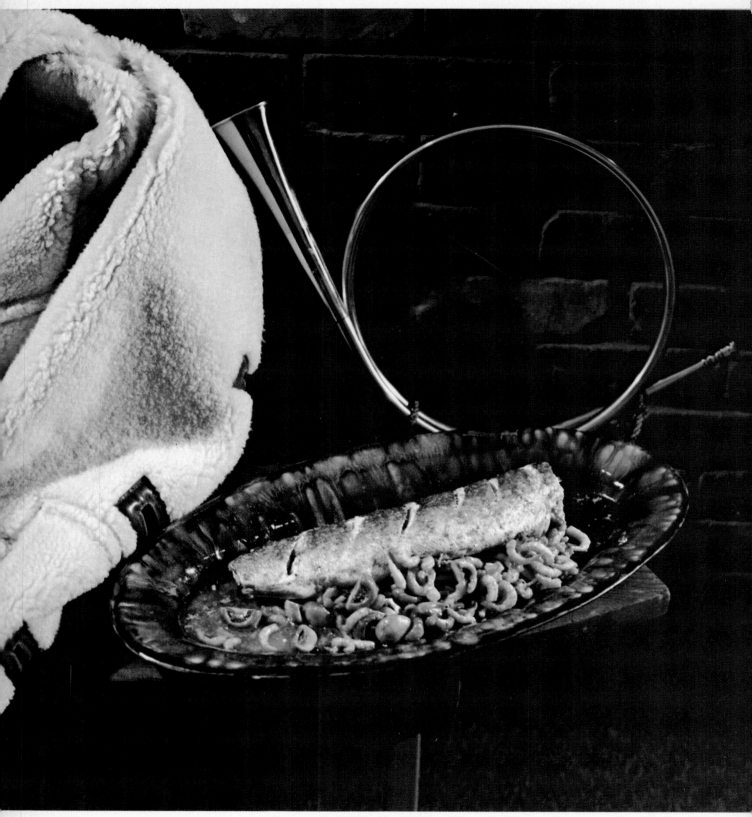

Trout Woolpack (page 224)

DEVILED CRAB

For 2 servings, you will need:

2 crabs each 1 lb (0.5 kg)
  (6 oz (170 g) crabmeat)
2 tbs lemon juice
1 tbs capers
1 tsp onion
½ tsp Tabasco sauce
Freshly ground black pepper
½ avocado
1 oz (28 g) mushrooms

¼ tsp dry mustard
Pinch mace
Pinch dry basil
½ egg yolk
1 tsp butter
1 tbs dry sherry
2 tbs fresh white bread crumbs*
Clarified butter*
Parsley

First prepare:

Remove crab shell from legs. Throw away lungs and feed sack. Reserve yellow "mustard" and remove all meat from body and claws. Scrub shell clean and dry out in a 350°F (177°C) oven. Finely chop capers. Finely chop onion. Remove avocado flesh with a teaspoon and mash. Finely chop mushrooms. Soften butter. Make bread crumbs. Preheat oven to 350°F (177°C).

Now cook!

1. Combine lemon juice, capers, onion, Tabasco sauce, avocado flesh and mushrooms. Season with black pepper. Stir in mustard, mace, basil, egg yolk, softened butter and dry sherry. Fold in crabmeat, being careful not to break up flesh.
2. Remove crab shells from oven and fill with mixture. Sprinkle with bread crumbs and drizzle some clarified butter over top. Bake in oven 20 minutes.
3. Serve garnished with parsley sprigs.

A special hint:

When once you have crab shells they can be scrubbed thoroughly in really hot water and saved for another dish. On the second go round I would recommend you use a first-quality canned crabmeat. It is so much easier and really almost as good.

HOT CRACKER CRAB

For 4 smallish servings, you will need:

12 oz (340 g) crabmeat
2 oz (56 g) celery
2 oz (56 g) green pepper
  (capsicum)
2 oz (56 g) shallots
2 tbs parsley

2 oz (56 g) soda crackers
Dry mustard
Freshly ground salt
¼ tsp cayenne
8 tbs clarified butter*
4 fl oz (1.2 dl) heavy cream

First prepare:

Slice crabmeat. Slice celery, shallots and green pepper finely. Finely chop parsley. Crush crackers roughly. Melt butter. Preheat oven to 350°F (177°C).

Now cook!

1. Melt one-half of the clarified butter in pan and add shallots. Fry gently and then add pepper, celery and crabmeat. Season with salt, mustard and cayenne.
2. Add cracker crumbs, cream and parsley. Place in a shallow 1-quart casserole dish. Top with remaining clarified butter.
3. Place in oven and bake for 25 minutes.

RENWICK CRAB

For 4 servings, you will need:

1 clove garlic	5 tbs mayonnaise
4 tbs clarified butter*	¼ tsp ground cardamon
3 oz (85 g) onion	½ tsp celery salt
1 green pepper (capsicum)	2 lbs (0.9 kg) peeled potatoes
2 tsp tomato paste	(peeled weight)
1 oz (28 g) Jamaican peppers*	1 tbs fresh chives
1 lb (0.5 kg) Alaskan king crab	2 oz (56 g) butter
3 oz (85 g) bacon	Freshly ground white pepper

First prepare:

Crush garlic. Finely slice and dice onion. Skin pepper by holding over heat. Strip off skin. Slice top from pepper, remove seeds and roughly dice. Very carefully remove seeds from Jamaican peppers and discard them. Measure tomato paste, cardamon, celery salt and mayonnaise. Chop chives. Peel potatoes, boil in salted water, drain, mash with milk and butter, season with chives and white pepper and set aside until required. Flake crabmeat. Cut each bacon strip into 4 pieces. Heat serving dishes. Preheat broiler.

Now cook!

1. Into a saucepan over moderate heat pour clarified butter. Add garlic and allow natural juices to "sweat out."
2. Stir in onions and green pepper, blend in tomato paste. Add Jamaican peppers (terribly hot) and cook for 3 minutes.
3. Place flaked crabmeat in equal portions on serving dishes.
4. Arrange bacon over crabmeat and place under broiler—3 inches (7.6 cm) away—until crisp, approximately 8 minutes.
5. Pass pepper sauce mixture through a sieve into a bowl. Discard mush. You should get about 1 tbs pepper puree.
6. Stir mayonnaise, cardamon and celery salt into puree.
7. Remove serving dishes from under broiler, drain off excess fat and pour a little sauce over each serving.
8. Pipe with border of hot mashed potatoes.

"C" PIN-TROUT

For 2 servings, you will need:

2 rainbow trout each	3 oz (85 g) butter
9 oz (255 g)	Sprig parsley
4 oz (113 g) Scottish oatmeal*	Freshly ground salt
½ lemon	Freshly ground white pepper

First prepare:

Gut trout. Measure oatmeal and butter. Preheat oven to 450°F (232°C). Heat a serving platter.

Now cook!

1. Place oatmeal on a plate and dip trout into it, covering them thoroughly.
2. Melt 1 oz (28 g) butter in a frypan.
3. Dip trout into butter and then into oatmeal once again.

4. Place remainder of the butter—2 oz (56 g)—in frypan and melt. Fry trout quickly on both sides.

5. Cover bottom of an oval casserole with a little of the hot melted butter in frypan and lay trout in it. Pour remainder of butter over them. Season with salt and white pepper.

6. Bake in preheated 450°F (232°C) oven for 10 minutes.

7. Remove trout from oven and serve garnished with a sprig of parsley and ½ lemon cut into 2 wedges.

FILETS DE SOLE VERMOUTH

For 4 first course servings or 2 main dish servings, you will need:

4 sole each 14 oz (396 g)
(or 8 fillets and ask for the
bones)
6 fl oz (1.6 dl) Italian dry
vermouth
1 black truffle*
Freshly ground salt
Freshly ground white pepper
Fish stock:
24 fl oz (7 dl) cold water
Bones from sole

4 fl oz (1.2 dl) white wine
1 medium onion
1 medium carrot
1 medium leek
3 fl oz (8 cl) Italian dry
vermouth
4 fl oz (1.2 dl) heavy cream
4 egg yolks
Freshly ground salt
Freshly ground white pepper

First prepare:

Fish: Fillet sole (8 fillets). Cut truffle into very thin pieces. Measure 6 fl oz (1.6 dl) of vermouth. Heat a serving dish in a warm oven.

Fish stock: Pour water into a pan, measure dry white wine. Finely slice onion, carrot, leek. Measure vermouth. Separate eggs and set aside yolks. Have heavy cream ready.

Now cook!

1. To cold water add sole bones, white wine, carrots, onion and leek. Simmer for 30 minutes over a low heat. Strain and discard bones and vegetables. Season stock and allow it to boil down to half its volume.

2. Put fillets into a large skillet and cover them with 3 fl oz (8 cl) of vermouth and 6 fl oz (1.6 dl) of stock. Cover and poach gently over low heat for 10 minutes.

3. Drain off most of stock from poached fillets. Bring stock to a boil. Sprinkle fish with a little vermouth, lower heat and season. Set aside. Strain boiling stock once again through a fine sieve, place in a clean pan and continue to reduce over high heat.

4. Mix 4 fl oz (1.2 dl) of stock and cream. Bring to a boil.

5. Place fillets of sole on a serving platter.

6. Beat egg yolks in a bowl and beat cream sauce into yolks. Pour back into pan and stir over low heat until thickened. Do not boil or you will definitely curdle eggs and ruin sauce.

7. Coat fillets with sauce and arrange sliced truffle over fish.

Service:

In my opinion two fillets is an ideal first course. The sauce can be made up to Step 7 ahead of serving time and finished in less than 60 seconds. The sole can be cooked and covered with a little stock and buttered paper.

A special hint:

I suggest that you tuck about ½ inch (1.2 cm) of sole fillets (at each end) underneath. Makes for a neater appearance.

1. FILETS DE SOLE VERMOUTH.

2. Tuck fillets in at both ends— neater and easier to handle.

3. Fish stock with vermouth is a superb poaching liquid.

4. Cover tightly. Note the well-fitting lid.

5. Slow and easy with the heat. The idea is to *infuse* fillets.

6. Lay the fillets into a heated dish.

7. Sprinkle with vermouth and keep warm in oven.

8. Boil poaching liquid to reduce volume and concentrate flavor.

9. Combine cream with yolks.

10. Pour egg and cream *liaison* back into cooled pan.

11. Brush sauce together over low heat.

12. Sieve sauce over fillets. Garnish with slices of truffle.

FILETS DE SOLE MEURICE

For 2 servings, you will need:

2 sole each about 14 oz (396 g)
2 fl oz (5.6 cl) dry white wine
1 eggplant
4 shallots
1 green pepper (capsicum)
1 red pepper (capsicum)
4 oz (113 g) mushrooms
2 fl oz (5.6 cl) heavy cream
1 tbs chives
Clarified butter*

Lemon sauce:
32 fl oz (1 l) veal stock
   reduced to 2 fl oz (5.6 cl)
1 tbs butter
1 egg yolk
2 fl oz (5.6 cl) heavy cream
½ lemon

Pilaf:
8 oz (227 g) long grain rice
20 fl oz (6 dl) fish stock
1 bay leaf
Freshly ground salt
Freshly ground white pepper

Veal stock:
2½ lb (1.2 kg) veal knuckle
   or veal bones
Enough water to cover
120 fl oz (3.6 l) cold water
6 oz (170 g) onion
6 oz (170 g) carrot
1 stalk celery
Bouquet garni
Sprinkle of crystallized salt
4 white peppercorns

First prepare:

Veal stock: Cover bones with cold water and bring to a boil, removing any scum which rises. Add vegetables and seasonings. Let it all boil together. Lower heat and simmer 1 hour. Strain liquid and boil until it is reduced to 32 fl oz (1 l). Strain. Boil again until reduced to 2 fl oz (5.6 cl).

Fish: Fillet soles (or have them filleted at your market and ask for the bones and head). Pop bones and head into a pan, add cold water to cover and bring to a boil to make fish stock (don't cook longer than 20 minutes). Strain and reserve fish stock, measure wine, finely chop shallots. Slice, then cube peppers removing all seeds (add all vegetable trimmings to fish stock). Finely slice mushrooms and chives. Cut eggplant in half lengthways and scoop out center leaving a shell 1 inch thick. Place shells in a pot of boiling salted water and cook until tender (approximately 10 minutes), then drain thoroughly. Heat a serving platter in the warm oven (the eggplant can be kept warm on this dish).

Sauce: Squeeze lemon, measure cream.

Pilaf: Weigh rice. Preheat oven to 400°F (205°C).

Now cook!

1. In bottom of a small heated casserole place some clarified butter to just cover bottom, and pop in rice to shallow fry for a few minutes until golden. Add bay leaf and 20 fl oz (6 dl) strained fish stock. Season generously and put uncovered casserole on middle shelf of preheated oven 400°F (205°C) for 20 minutes until tender, and rice has absorbed all the stock.

2. Into a large heated frypan pour a little clarified butter to just cover bottom. Add the fillets of sole and season generously with freshly ground salt and white pepper. Add dry white wine, cover and simmer 10 minutes over a moderate heat.

3. Pour fish stock into a saucepan and allow it to gently bubble away, reducing all the time.

4. In another heated pot add a little clarified butter to just cover bottom and shallow fry finely chopped shallots.

5. Add finely diced peppers and sliced mushrooms. Lower heat and simmer.

6. Inspect fish—don't overcook. Also check simmering vegetables. They should just be tender.

7. Remove pilaf from oven and stir into mixed vegetables.

8. Remove fillets of sole from heat. Drain juices into rice. Cover fish and keep warm. Add cream to rice.

1. FISH FILLETING. Make a center line down flat fish.

2. Fillets come away with light strokes of a small, flat blade.

3. Scaled fish such as this snapper can be descaled under water.

4. Cut round-bodied fish through the top, either side of backbone.

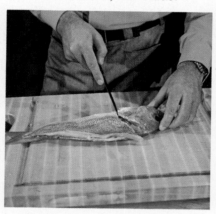

5. The head is best removed when the side is completely detached.

6. Bones left in will indict you! Get them out for your own sake!

9. Remove eggplants from warm oven and fill with rice mixture. Gently lay fillets of sole over rice. Moisten with a little reduced veal stock and cover.

10. Place reduced veal stock in a small saucepan. When it is boiling take it off heat and quickly whisk in butter and egg yolk, lemon juice and cream. Continue beating until smooth and creamy. (This all happens very quickly and should be prepared just before you serve it.)

11. Pour sauce over stuffed eggplant. Dust with freshly chopped chives and pop under a very hot broiler to brown lightly.

Service:

It looks good and tastes good. I usually use it for at least 8 people as a first course, in which case reduce the sole to only 2 fillets per eggplant.

A special hint:

The reduction of the veal stock from 32 fl oz (1 l) to 2 fl oz (5.6 cl), produces a very stiff, delicious glaze.

Filets de Sole Vermouth (page 232)

FILETS DE SOLE BAUMANIERE

For 2 servings, you will need:

1 whole sole (cut into 4 fillets)
Freshly ground salt
Cayenne pepper
4 fl oz (1.2 dl) dry vermouth
1 bay leaf
Pinch of saffron
2 fl oz (5.6 cl) dry vermouth
1½ tbs melted butter

Sprig thyme
5 fl oz (1.5 dl) poaching liquid
3 egg yolks
1 tsp brandy
1 dozen mussels
1 lb (0.5 kg) raw shrimp
2 fl oz (5.6 cl) dry white wine
8 fl oz (2 dl) heavy cream

First prepare:

Cut fillets from sole, remove black skin and head. Measure vermouth. Melt butter. Separate eggs. Cook shrimp, shell and devein. Place shrimp shells on a tray in a 300°F (149°C) oven for 30 minutes to dry. Remove. Remove beard from mussels and scrub well.

Now cook!

1. Place 4 fl oz (1.2 dl) of dry vermouth in a casserole pan on low heat, add fish fillets and season with salt and cayenne pepper. Cover pan and poach fish for 5 minutes.

2. Place shrimp shells in a blender with 2 fl oz (5.6 cl) dry vermouth and melted butter. Blend to a thick paste.

3. Place sole fillets on a heated serving dish and keep warm. Reserve fish poaching stock.

4. Place shrimp shell paste in top of a double boiler over simmering water and add 5 fl oz (1.5 dl) fish poaching stock, bay leaf, thyme and pinch of saffron and allow mixture to infuse for 5 minutes.

5. Sieve shrimp shell mixture into scalded cream and mix. Beat egg yolks with a little sauce and then mix with rest of sauce. Stir over low heat until thickened and stir in brandy.

6. Place mussels and shrimp in a pan on high heat with dry white wine and cover pan. Cook 2 minutes, shaking pan from time to time. Remove mussels from shells. Remove shrimp.

7. Garnish fish with hot mussels and shrimp and cover with sauce.

A special hint:

Be careful not to boil sauce after you add eggs at Step 5 or the eggs will scramble and make sauce lumpy.

WALLEYED PIKE PIE

For 4 servings, you will need:

1 lb (0.5 kg) walleyed pike
　　fillets (or halibut, haddock,
　　flounder, snapper)
4 fl oz (1.2 dl) dry white wine
10 fl oz (3 dl) milk
1 lb (0.5 kg) spinach
Freshly ground salt
Freshly ground white pepper

2 lbs (0.9 kg) potatoes
1 egg
6 cooked asparagus spears
1 lemon
4 oz (113 g) butter
Parsley
Paprika

First prepare:

Walleyed pike is a classic local specialty of Minnesota. If not available other solid white fleshed fish can be used. Marinate fish in mixture of wine and milk for 30 minutes. Wash spinach thoroughly. Trim stems and slice into 1-inch (2.5 cm) strips. Puree asparagus. Peel and boil potatoes. Mash, adding 2 oz (56 g) butter, 1 egg, pureed asparagus and season with pepper and salt. Roughly chop parsley. Preheat broiler. Butter an ovenproof dish.

Now cook!

1. Place spinach in a large saucepan with 2 oz (56 g) of butter. Season with salt and pepper. Put lid on pan and set over low heat for 5 minutes, giving spinach a good shake after 2 minutes to distribute butter.

2. Place pike fillets with marinade in another pan, season with salt and white pepper, bring to a boil, cover and allow to poach gently for 8 minutes.

3. Drain spinach and place half of it in ovenproof dish. Add drained fish, and sprinkle with juice of ½ lemon. Cover with rest of spinach.

4. Cover spinach with half of the potato, smoothing it with a spatula and then place the rest of the potato in a pastry bag (with a star-shaped nozzle) and pipe potato decoratively around dish.

5. Slide under broiler for 6 minutes. Remove, dust with parsley and paprika.

A special hint:

Be sure to puree the asparagus well. Any "strings" left will clog pastry tube.
The colder the milk and wine "marinade" the better. It should almost have ice flakes on top.

SNAPPER TAURANGA

For 2 servings, you will need:

1 red snapper, 2 lb (0.9 kg)
5 fl oz (1.5 dl) fish stock
5 fl oz (1.5 dl) milk
2 oz (56 g) butter
4 oz (113 g) all-purpose flour
10 fl oz (3 dl) milk
1 lb (0.5 kg) Chinese gooseberries
   or Kiwi fruit*
Freshly ground salt

Freshly ground white pepper
Nutmeg
2 fl oz (5.6 cl) dry white wine
1 oz (28 g) mild Cheddar cheese
Fish stock:
1 snapper head
Bouquet garni
10 fl oz (3 dl) water
1 onion

First prepare:

Fillet fish reserving head and tail. Peel and very finely slice Chinese gooseberries. Measure milk and dry white wine. Sift flour. Finely grate cheese. Preheat broiler. Prepare fish stock by simmering head, tail and bones with water, onion and herbs for 30 minutes and then strain.

Now cook!

1. Heat fish stock and milk in a pan. Add snapper fillets. Season with salt and pepper. Cover pan and allow to cook gently for 5 minutes.

2. Place butter in a saucepan and when melted stir in flour to form a roux and cook gently for 1 minute. Remove from heat and gradually stir in milk. Cook, stirring constantly until sauce thickens. Cook gently for 10 minutes, whisking all the time, forming a thick sauce. Season with salt, pepper and a dash of nutmeg.

3. When fillets are cooked, drain off poaching liquid into sauce, leaving a small quantity of liquid in pan with fillets. Keep fillets warm. Whisk sauce and beat in white wine.

4. On an oval serving dish, reconstruct fish (head and tail) and cover with sauce. Place slices of Chinese gooseberries over fish to simulate scales. Dust with cheese and place under broiler until cheese melts (approximately 1½ minutes).

A special hint:

At Step 4, you simply stack poached fillets to resemble a whole fish body and then lay head and tail on either end. Be sure to dust head and tail well with cheese.

FORELLE—FIRSCHEN KRAUTERN

For 2 servings, you will need:

2 small trout each 10 oz (283 g)
1 medium onion
1 clove garlic
8 fl oz (2 dl) dry white wine
2 fl oz (5.6 cl) heavy cream
Pinch tarragon
1 tsp lemon juice
1 tsp Worcestershire sauce
Parsley

Freshly ground salt
Freshly ground white pepper
Clarified butter*
Sauce:
2 tbs all-purpose flour
1 tbs butter
Garnish:
Tiny new potatoes boiled with
mint, parsley and butter

First prepare:

Take gutted trout (heads still on) and with a clean cloth dipped in salt, clean inside. Finely chop onion, smash garlic, measure wine and cream. Squeeze 1 tsp lemon juice, shake bottle of Worcestershire sauce and measure 1 tsp. Wash and chop parsley. Preheat a frypan, warm a serving dish.

Sauce: Sift flour, measure butter.

Now cook!

1. Scrape new potatoes and pop them into water with a pinch of salt and tarragon. Bring to a boil, reduce heat and cook covered gently for 17 minutes.

2. Pour clarified butter in a heated frypan to just cover bottom and add onion and garlic. Stir—fry evenly—season with salt and pepper.

3. Stir 6 fl oz (1.6 dl) of white wine and tarragon into poaching liquor and lower in trout. Increase heat, cover pan and cook gently for 6 minutes.

4. After 6 minutes poaching, the fish should be tested. If not quite cooked, reduce heat and cook for a further 2 minutes.

5. Gently remove fish with spatula and place on serving platter. Keep warm.

6. Meanwhile strain fish juices into another saucepan and add remaining 2 fl oz (5.6 cl) of white wine, heavy cream, Worcestershire sauce and lemon juice. Mix well and bring to boiling point.

7. To thicken this poaching liquid mix butter and flour. Stir the mixture (beurre manie) into sauce. Cook while stirring until thickened.

8. Remove as much skin as possible from trout and place on platter.

9. Add chopped parsley to bubbling thickened sauce and pour over fish, covering the whole fish head to tail. Garnish with a little fresh parsley.

10. Drain potatoes, return to heat to dry off any excess water and then cover with a cloth for a moment to make them slightly flaky. Place around trout and serve at once.

A special hint:

Refer to Step 4 above. To test degree of "doneness" in fish, just insert a small knife between the fish flakes and pull back from bone. It will come away cleanly when fish is done.

COLD SALMON AND WATERCRESS SAUCE

For 8 servings, you will need:

5 lb (2.3 kg) salmon
Court bouillon:
140 fl oz (4.0 l) water
4 fl oz (1 dl) vinegar
3 medium carrots
2 large onions
2 oz (56 g) parsley stalks*
1 bay leaf
Sprig thyme

1 tbs rock salt
Sauce:
10 fl oz (3 dl) mayonnaise
1 tbs chopped shallot
1 bunch watercress
1 tbs white wine vinegar
1 stiffly beaten egg white
1 egg yolk

First prepare:

Prepare court bouillon by combining bouillon ingredients in a saucepan. Bring to a boil, simmer 10 minutes, strain and allow to cool. Cut long length of muslin 2 inches (5 cm) wide to wrap around salmon.

Sauce: Finely chop watercress discarding thick stalks. Add finely chopped shallot and watercress to mayonnaise. Stir in vinegar and 1 egg yolk. Fold in stiffly beaten egg white.

Now cook!

1. Place salmon on the grid of a fish kettle on its belly to resemble a swimming fish. Wrap salmon with muslin around grid to hold fish in place. Cover with cold court bouillon. Bring liquid to a boil and skim. Turn heat to very low and allow fish to poach without boiling for 15 minutes. Cool in court bouillon.

2. Remove skin from salmon and place on serving platter. Serve sauce separately or spoon evenly over salmon.

SCALLOPS PORT LINCOLN

For 4 first course servings, you will need:

24 scallops
3 fl oz (8 cl) fish stock
3 fl oz (8 cl) dry white wine
2 tsp lemon juice
6 fl oz (1.6 dl) heavy cream
3 egg yolks

Freshly ground salt
Freshly ground white pepper
1 lb (0.5 kg) potatoes (mashed)
4 tbs clarified butter*
2 fl oz (5.6 cl) brandy
½ lb (227 g) grapes

First prepare:

Make fish stock. Cook potatoes and mash with cream, adding salt and pepper to taste. Peel and pit grapes.

Now cook!

1. Poach scallops in fish stock, white wine and lemon juice for 2 minutes.
2. Drain off cooking liquor into a saucepan and reduce to 2 tbs. Reserve.
3. Slice scallops in half.
4. Using a pastry bag with a star tip, pipe edge of 4 scallop shells with mashed potato.
5. Melt clarified butter in a pan, add scallops and toss in butter. Season with salt and pepper. Add warmed brandy and ignite.
6. Remove from heat and add cream beaten with egg yolks and reserved poaching liquid. Stir over low heat until liquid thickens.
7. Fill 4 scallop shells with mixture. Decorate with grapes and place under broiler until top is lightly browned.

SINGAPORE STEAMBOAT

For 8 to 10 servings, you will need:

½ lb (227 g) snapper fillets
1 chicken breast, skinned and boned
8 spring onions or scallions*
2 stalks celery
½ lb (227 g) scallops
2 eggs
½ lb (227 g) peeled raw jumbo
   shrimp, deveined
½ lb (227 g) pork fillets,
   thinly sliced
16 oz (453 g) can abalone
   (sliced thinly)
Fish balls
Shrimp balls
100 fl oz (2.8 l) chicken stock
Soya sauce
12 mussels
Chicken stock:
   1 oz (28 g) fresh ginger root*
   8 oz (227 g) chicken feet,
      bones, neck, etc.
   ½ lb (227 g) pork bones

1 oz (28 g) lard or 2 tbs
   clarified butter*
120 fl oz (3.4 l) water
Freshly ground salt
Freshly ground pepper
½ oz (14 g) celery
1 bay leaf
Parsley stalks*
5 water chestnuts
Fish balls:
   ½ lb (227 g) codfish fillets
   1 tsp freshly ground salt
   Freshly ground pepper
   ½ egg white
   2 tsp cold water
Shrimp balls:
   ½ lb (227 g) raw shrimp, shelled
      and deveined
   4 oz (113 g) lean pork
   Monosodium glutamate
   1 tsp lard
   1 to 2 tbs flour

First prepare:

Cut snapper into 1½-inch (3.8 cm) pieces. Cut chicken breast into quarters. Scrub mussel shells. Cut celery and spring onions into 3-inch (7.6 cm) pieces. Break eggs into small bowl and beat lightly. Cut pork fillets into pieces 2 inches x 1 inch (5 cm x 2.5 cm).

Chicken Stock: Place clarified butter or lard in a pan and add ginger and chestnuts, then add chicken and pork bones, celery, bay leaf, parsley stalks, seasoning and water. Bring to a boil and simmer for 1 hour. Strain.

Fish balls: Grind fish 3 to 4 times finely and add salt, pepper and egg white. Knead, add water and continue to knead until mixture is very smooth. Take a handful of mixture and squeeze a little of it out between the thumb and the forefinger and drop by ½-inch (1.2 cm) lengths into hot chicken stock. When balls float to surface, they will be cooked.

Shrimp balls: Grind shrimp and pork 3 to 4 times finely and add a touch of monosodium glutamate, lard and flour. Knead well, and continue to knead until very smooth. Take a handful of mixture and squeeze a little of it out between the thumb and forefinger and drop by ½-inch (1.2 cm) lengths into hot stock. When balls float to surface they will be cooked.

Now cook!

1. Heat chicken stock in a steamboat, or a large colorful casserole or fondue dish.

2. Place selected pieces of red snapper, chicken breast, scallops, shrimps, pork, abalone, celery, scallions, fish balls and shrimp balls into stock and allow to poach a few minutes. Remove with a slotted spoon or small ladle. Continue to add foods and after all the guests have eaten, spoon soup into bowls.

3. The hot poached food is dunked first into beaten egg to cool it and then into a bowl of soya sauce.

Singapore Steamboat

MOULES A LA DINARDAISE

For 2 servings, you will need:

12 mussels (in shell)
4 fl oz (1.2 dl) dry white wine
Freshly ground salt
Freshly ground black pepper
Thyme leaves
1 small onion
½ bay leaf

Sauce:

12 fl oz (3.2 dl) milk
3 tbs all-purpose flour
2 tbs butter
Freshly ground salt
Freshly ground white pepper
Nutmeg
4 oz (56 g) grated Cheddar cheese

First prepare:

Scrub mussels and remove beards. Slice onion finely. Make sauce. Grate cheese. Measure wine. Melt butter, stir in flour and cook gently 2 minutes. Gradually stir in heated milk and whisk until smooth. Season with salt, pepper and nutmeg and cook very gently for 20 minutes, stirring occasionally.

Now cook!

1. Place mussels in a pan with white wine, onion, bay leaf, salt, pepper and a light dusting of thyme leaves.
2. Place on high heat, cover with a lid, cook 2 minutes, then give saucepan a good shake. Allow to cook a further 2 minutes and give pan another shake.
3. Open shells and discard half the shell. Reserve cooking liquor.
4. Add half grated cheese and all cooking liquor, strained, to sauce and mix. (See hint below.)
5. Spoon sauce over each mussel, sprinkle mussels with rest of cheese. Slide under a hot broiler for 4 minutes.

A special hint:

I found by adding 2 fl oz (5.6 cl) dry white wine to sauce that dish was improved.

MOULES MARINIERE

For 2 servings, you will need:

24 mussels (in shell)
8 fl oz (2 dl) dry white wine
Freshly ground salt
Freshly ground black pepper

Thyme leaves
2 small onions
1 bay leaf
2 oz (56 g) butter

First prepare:

Scrub and "beard" mussels. Slice onions finely. Measure wine and butter.

Now cook!

1. Place mussels in a large saucepan with white wine, onion, bay leaf, salt, pepper and a light dusting of thyme leaves. Cover pan, cook on high heat 2 minutes, then give saucepan a good shake. Cook 2 minutes longer, then give pan another shake.
2. Place mussels into 2 dishes. Strain cooking liquor. Stir in butter and pour over mussels.

A special hint:

It is not always possible to "beard" mussels completely until they have been cooked.

LOUPE EN PAPILLOTES

For 2 servings, you will need:

1½ lb (680 g) loupe* or striped
   sea bass
2 tbs Pernod
1 medium onion
1 bay leaf
8 oz (227 g) long grain rice

2 fl oz (5.6 cl) dry sherry
2 oz (56 g) butter
Freshly ground salt
Freshly ground white pepper
Clarified butter*
2 oz (56 g) sultana raisins

First prepare:

Remove scales from fish by rubbing with back of a knife under water. Gut fish. Wash and rub cavity of fish with a piece of muslin dipped in salt. A length of aluminum cooking foil will be required. Thinly slice onion, measure sherry, preheat oven to 400°F (205°C). Heat a serving platter in a warm oven.

Now cook!

1. Boil rice for 5 minutes and sieve it. (Do not rinse it, just let it drain). Pop back into a dry pan, add butter and mix into rice.
2. Stir in sultanas and sherry. Keep pan over low heat until required.
3. Cut a piece of foil 4 inches (10 cm) longer than the length of the fish and brush on a little clarified butter.
4. Season buttered sheet of foil liberally with salt and pepper.
5. Pour Pernod on foil and blend seasoned butter and Pernod together with a brush.
6. Scatter sliced onion on foil to form a bed for fish.
7. Place fish on onions and pop bay leaf inside.
8. Spoon rice mixture over bass until it looks as though it is covered with a blanket.
9. Fold foil loosely over fish in order to allow for expansion. Seal in the shape of fish.
10. Place on a broiler rack set in a shallow pan and bake in a preheated oven 400°F (205°C) for 25 minutes.
11. Remove fish from oven and place on a serving dish.
12. Gently fold back foil to expose fish and pour on a little melted butter.

Service:

You can either serve the fish whole, in the foil, or try filleting it a couple of times before you get to the dining room "performance" stage. This is how to handle the fish:

Take off the head, push rice to one side, then remove top fillets. Lift off back bone exposing bottom fillets. Spoon rice onto platter and lay fillets on it. Quartered lemons can be added for garnish.

A special hint:

So often people loathe handling whole fish because of the "scale" problem. By using underwater scaling method described in this recipe, all your scale problems are over.

———————— ⟲G ————————
*The silence of gastronomic rapture
is a cook's symphony of praise.*

POMPANO EN PAPILLOTE

For 4 servings, you will need:

8 fillets Pompano (or sole) or 2 whole
    fish each 1¼ lb (566 g)
1 clove garlic
1½ oz (42 g) butter
3½ oz (99 g) all-purpose flour
8 fl oz (2 dl) white wine
6 oz (170 g) raw jumbo shrimp
6 oz (170 g) crab meat
2 large shallots

8 fl oz (2 dl) fish stock
2 egg yolks
2 fl oz (5.6 cl) heavy cream
Clarified butter*
Freshly ground salt
Freshly ground white pepper
4 sheets vegetable parchment
    paper each 23 x 12¾ inch
    (58 cm x 32 cm)

First prepare:

Finely slice onion. Smash garlic. Measure dry and liquid ingredients. Shell shrimp and cut down back to remove sand tract, chop flesh. Finely slice shallots. Mix egg yolks with heavy cream in a small bowl. Heat a serving platter in a warm oven. Preheat oven to 500°F (260°C).

Now cook!

1. Place butter in a saucepan on medium heat and when melted stir in 1½ oz (42 g) of flour.
2. Stir in onion and garlic and season with salt and white pepper.
3. Lower heat under saucepan and stir in dry white wine. Simmer.
4. Place remaining 2 oz (56 g) of flour onto a plate and season with salt and white pepper.
5. Dip fillets of fish into seasoned flour.
6. Pour enough clarified butter to just cover bottom of a large frypan on medium heat and cook fillets, skin side up for 4 minutes.
7. Into a small frypan on medium heat pour 2 tbs clarified butter and add shrimp and crab. Cook only until hot.
8. Sprinkle shallots over frying fish fillets. Turn them with pancake turner so that shallots fall underneath.
9. To the simmering sauce, add fish stock and continue to reduce.
10. Strain sauce through a sieve into a clean pan. Raise heat to high. When sauce boils, remove from heat and beat in blended egg yolks and heavy cream.
11. Now stir in shrimp and crab mixture. Season to taste with salt and pepper.
12. Place cooked fillets on a heated serving platter and keep warm until required.
13. Pour fish sauce into a bowl and place in refrigerator to set.
14. Cut a sheet of vegetable parchment paper into a heart shape and brush with clarified butter.
15. Take cooled sauce out of refrigerator and place 2 tbs on buttered paper and top with 2 fillets of fish.
16. Fold paper over and crimp edges to seal.
17. Allow enough breathing space inside so paper can swell.
18. Place on a baking dish, brush with clarified butter and heat in preheated oven at 500°F (260°C) for 5 minutes until paper is brown.
19. Remove from oven, slide packets on serving platter and serve.

1. EN PAPILLOTE. The filling for this dish (Scallopine Don Quixote) is described on page 461.

2. A heart shape is drawn on a half-folded sheet of vegetable parchment paper and then cut out.

3. Opened out, it is then basted with clarified butter.

4. The scallopine is placed upon one side of the "heart" and covered with prosciutto and cheese.

5. The vegetable filling is then heaped onto the cheese.

6. The heart is folded over.

7. Start sealing the edges.

8. You can secure this point here with a metal staple but a tight fold will hold it.

9. Brush with clarified butter and place in a hot oven.

PART V
PASTRY

PART V
PASTRY

Pies are convenient ways of serving less, without drawing attention to it. This apparently niggardly effort is held up as an example of great home-cooking ability. The golden, flaky crust, the warm, plump, sealed-in flavors all conspire to make the juices run, and even if the waistline does bulge . . . well, there's always tomorrow for good intentions!

This Part starts off with an Egyptian Five Minute Puff Pastry, then the Greek Philo or Fila, savory short crust, a Spanish sherry-flavored pastry, the traditional English suet, the American cracker crust and a worldwide favorite, sweet short crust. As you can see, the scope is literally worldwide, and with it comes the dreaded problem: What flour do you use? Dear reader, if I knew, I'd be lying on a beach somewhere and not flogging my floating kitchen around the world in search of this culinary Shangri-La.

In every case you use the best possible *pastry* flour available. If possible, it should contain about 20 percent stone-ground nonrefined wheat flour (see Introduction to Part X Natural Foods, page 637), but be careful how long you store this naturally good flour because it tends to go sour. Be sure that no self-raising ingredient has been added. Now work up to the recommended water content gradually. It may be that your flour will absorb less liquid. When the dough is pliable and just leaves the fingers cleanly, check the liquid left unused (or the extra needed). Note this quantity change in the margin next to the recipe. With the next pastry style you try, make a similar adjustment. I'm sorry not to be of more use but I detest food authors who waffle on about this simply because they can't or won't do their homework. In my case, I've suffered in twelve different areas from pastry recipe problems, and were it not for the occasional superb crusts I have made, I would long ago have given up the ghost and admitted not having the hands for it. All the recipes given in this section are, or have been, excellent. They were made with good-quality Canadian pastry flour.

FIVE MINUTE PUFF

Professional pastry cooks now have a sophisticated machine that works like a combined conveyor-belt and mangle. No doubt it can be a source of satisfaction to compete with machines, but it isn't much fun when you lose on time, cost and quality. I buy my puff pastry in frozen 1-lb (0.5 kg) packets, defrost it, roll it, cut it, cook it, serve it and . . . never take the praise. My moment comes when I make less easy-to-make pastry where the leaves can be evident yet chaotically arranged. In five minutes I produce a light, flaky pastry. Another five minutes of turning and it makes a superb puff pastry pie top. Another five minutes would be a waste of time!

PHILO OR FILA

This is an incredibly thin pastry made in Greece and in Greek pastry shops around the world. There is no alternative to the machine-made article, so I suggest you check the classified section of your telephone directory and phone some Greek shops. I have kept a couple of pounds under deep freeze for over a year without the slightest change in texture. It is well worth searching for.

SAVORY SHORT

A good standby for the famous quiche dishes. All short crusts need to be "relaxed" under refrigeration for a couple of hours after molding. I always roll the dough onto a sheet of greaseproof paper and invert the pastry onto the dish—it prevents the inevitable tearing you get with a good short crust.

WINE

Since I discovered this pastry I've used it dozens of times. It is short yet remarkably easy to handle, especially in the miniature empanada style (see page 280). I'm sure that it would work equally well on a wide range of pies and pastries. Why don't you experiment, use it over your favorite filling and let me know how you got on?

SUET

I suspect that pudding crusts made with suet represent Public Enemy Number One to weight watchers! Compound the tragedy with my Spotted Dick recipe, when the thick, suety rounds of sweet boiled pudding are fried gently in butter and served sprinkled with sugar. But it's so good and yet so utterly bad it makes up for all those diet days when you were impossibly self-controlled with such iron discipline.

CRACKER

For three years I was put off making a cracker crust largely because almost every recipe called for GRAHAM crackers and even at my worst I would never have gotten away with that on television! Then one day I experimented with a ginger cookie crushed with butter and dampened with a shot of rum. Since then you could say that my whole life-style has changed. Well, you could say it . . . but it would be a terrible exaggeration! Cracker crusts are useful and from my experience eliminate (when well-buttered) that unfortunate malady of deep cheese cakes—a soggy crust.

SWEET SHORT CRUST

A good recipe for a sweet short-crust pastry is as invaluable as a tin hat in the trenches, but real success lies in the handling, *not* the recipe. A good dessert pie filling has to be moist. How then to avoid the dreaded "sog"? As a matter of principle, I always prebake (called bake "blind") the crust for 10 minutes and then I brush the hot bottom and sides with either apricot jam or egg white. Both these mixtures provide a moisture-proofing that counteracts the effect of moist fillings. The pie is then filled and topped or whatever, and baked as specified.

Five Minute Puff Pastry (page 254)

FIVE MINUTE PUFF PASTRY

6 oz (170 g) butter
1 lb (0.5 kg) all-purpose flour

4 fl oz (1.2 dl) ice water
Pinch of freshly ground salt

First prepare:

Cut butter into small cubes and place in bowl with sifted flour. Shake to cover with flour. Add salt. Squeeze out each piece of butter into a thin sheet by pressing between forefinger and thumb. Do this lightly and quickly. Add water all at once and stir into dough. Turn out onto floured board, knead a few times and roll out and cut to size required. Can be wrapped and chilled until ready to use.

55

Now cook!

For normal pastry topping over precooked fillings, allow 25 minutes at 450°F (232°C). Otherwise see recipe directions. Makes 1 lb 10 oz pastry.

LANGOUSTE EN CROUSTADES

For 4 servings, you will need:

1 lb (0.5 kg) puff pastry*
  (see page 254)
2 lobsters, or Australian crayfish
  each 2 lb (1 kg)
2 fl oz (5.6 cl) brandy
20 fl oz (6 dl) heavy cream
2 oz (56 g) butter
2 oz (56 g) all-purpose flour

2 tbs clarified butter*
4 oz (113 g) button mushrooms
Juice of ½ lemon
Freshly ground salt
Freshly ground white pepper
8 fl oz (2 dl) heavy cream
  (This second amount of cream
  is insurance. See Step 5 below.)

First prepare:

Pastry Cases: Roll out the puff paste ¼ inch (7 mm) thick and cut out 4 oblong pieces slightly larger than a playing card. Mark top of each "card" with a sharp knife ½ inch (1.2 cm) in from the outside and ⅛ inch (3 mm) deep. Bake in an oven set at 450°F (232°C) for 20 minutes until browned and at least 3 inches (7.6 cm) high (good pastry will rise that high). Lift off pastry cap and gouge out doughy interior leaving a shell with a cap. Keep them dry.

Lobsters: Buy them live if possible and place them into tepid 98.6°F (37°C) water in the sink. They die at this temperature without apparent discomfort. When dead plunge them into boiling water and cook for 8 minutes. After 8 minutes remove and dump them directly into a pail of ice cold water (stops them from cooking in their shells). When cold remove all meat from tails and claws and set aside in a cool place. Keep shells and cut lobster into large chunky pieces.

Measure brandy, both amounts of cream (keep them separate), butter and flour. Juice lemon. Stem and slice mushrooms. If very small leave whole.

Now cook!

1. Place clarified butter in a large non-stick (if possible) saucepan to just cover bottom. Add empty lobster shells and fry them.

2. Pour brandy over shells and set afire. Let flames die down and then add 20 fl oz (6 dl) heavy cream.

3. Crush shells flat with a potato masher and allow to simmer in cream for 10 minutes.

4. Meanwhile melt butter in a medium-sized saucepan, stir in flour, and cook together to make a roux but don't allow it to color. Cook it gently for 3 minutes stirring all the time.

5. Simmer cream for full 10 minutes (you can allow more time; 10 minutes is the minimum. At Antibes they go a full hour but this is too long in my opinion, and you lose a great deal of cream by evaporation). Sieve hot cream and gradually stir it into roux base. Stir in fresh cream from "insurance" 5 fl oz (1.5 dl) if needed. The sauce should be thick, heavy and very rich.

6. Now place some clarified butter in a large skillet to just cover bottom and when hot add mushrooms, lemon juice, salt and pepper. Toss quickly and then add cubed lobster meat. Toss in with button mushrooms to heat through.

7. Drain surplus butter from pan and stir in cream sauce. Adjust seasoning with salt and pepper.

8. Spoon sauce into pastry cases. Serve at once.

1. FIVE MINUTE PUFF PASTRY. To compete with frozen pastry this recipe has to be simplicity itself.

2. Cut the firm butter into small, even-sized cubes.

3. Shake the cubes into the flour. Each should be individually coated.

4. Pinch the cubes lightly so that they go quite flat. Don't overdo this stage.

5. Have the water well iced.

6. Add the water all at once.

7. Mix lightly with a knife to cut in the water.

8. Turn the dough onto a floured board and work in flour until the fingers leave the dough without sticking.

9. Fold once, and let rest in a cool place wrapped in plastic bag. Fold and roll out again; fold, roll out.

CARRE D'AGNEAU EN CROUTE

For 8 servings, you will need:

1 whole saddle of lamb (cut
    between 3rd and 4th ribs
    at shoulder and just
    behind kidneys at haunch)
6 lamb kidneys
1 egg yolk
4 cloves garlic
Pinch rosemary
Pinch thyme
Pinch savory

4 slices white bread
1 lb (0.5 kg) puff pastry*
    (see page 254)
Freshly ground salt
Freshly ground black pepper
Clarified butter*
Garnish:
    Boiled halved tomatoes, French
      beans and watercress

First prepare:

Ask your butcher to bone saddle of lamb and cut sides fairly short on skirt or flank. Ask for bones to use for stock. Cut suet away from kidneys, wash them and remove outer membrane and white core. Cut them in half, wash again. Smash garlic, decrust bread and cut into small cubes. Add a pinch of salt to egg yolk. Make or buy pastry and set aside. Preheat oven to 450°F (232°C). A large serving platter will be required; place in a warm oven to heat.

Now cook!

1. Pour some clarified butter into a hot pan to just cover bottom. Cut into fat side of saddle to form diamond shapes all over surface. Season with salt and white pepper. Lower meat into hot butter and sprinkle with pinches of "Provencale" herbs. Cover.

2. Remove lid after a few moments and baste meat with pan juice to seal in all the succulent juices. Cover once again.

3. Now pop pan into preheated oven 450°F (232°C) and cook for 10 minutes.

4. In a second pan pour some clarified butter to just cover bottom and when hot add kidneys and garlic and sizzle gently.

5. Add cubed bread to the pan to soak up some of the kidney juices. Fry for 4 minutes. Cool.

6. Remove undercooked saddle of lamb from oven and set aside to cool.

7. Roll out pastry on a lightly floured board (or marble slab), large enough to wrap around lamb. Let pastry relax in rolled-out position.

8. Remove excess moisture from meat surface with absorbent paper.

9. Place lamb on pastry and lay kidney mixture down center.

10. Brush beaten egg yolk along outer edge of pastry and fold over to form a parcel firmly sealing edges. Trim edges.

11. With a spatula turn it over so that center sealing edge is now seam side down on the baking pan.

12. Roll out trimmings and cut a few pastry leaves with a sharp knife. Brush pastry with egg yolk, decorate with leaves and cover whole dish with aluminum foil. Pop onto middle shelf of hot oven at 450°F (232°C) for 30 minutes. Raise temperature to 475°F (246°C).

13. Remove foil and bake uncovered for another 5 minutes.

14. The pastry should be a rich golden brown. Slide out onto a serving platter and serve at once garnished with watercress.

CHICKEN YANKOVA

For 4 servings, you will need:

1 chicken, 3½ lb (1.6 kg)
2 cloves garlic
4 oz (113 g) butter
1 tsp rosemary
2 sprigs thyme
4 sage leaves
½ tsp cayenne pepper

1½ lbs (680 g) puff pastry*
  (see page 254)
1 egg white
1 egg yolk, to gild
Freshly ground salt
Freshly ground black pepper
Parsley

First prepare:

Remove wings from chicken. Make an incision down breastbone and pull away skin from entire chicken. Remove any excess fat from rear end. Smash garlic. Measure and soften butter. Finely chop herbs. Roll out pastry to ¼ inch (7 mm) thick. Preheat oven to 375°F (190°C).

Now cook!

1. Mix butter with garlic, sage, rosemary, thyme and cayenne and salt and pepper to taste. Place two-thirds of herb butter inside chicken. Tie chicken legs together and dry chicken well. Rub remaining butter over chicken breast.

2. Place chicken breast down on pastry and wrap up, molding pastry to chicken. Trim off excess pastry. Seal the edges of the pastry with egg white (trim off inside of each end flap and wrap over). Place on a greased shallow baking pan. With the back of a knife mark pastry in crisscross fashion.

3. Decorate breast with 3 pastry leaves cut from trimmings and gild all over with egg yolk. Bake 1 hour and 15 minutes.

4. Remove chicken. Slice crust down middle and pull away from chicken cutting away any soggy pastry. Remove string from legs. Carve chicken and place meat on a heated serving dish. Garnish chicken pieces with the two halves of the pastry crust and place some sprigs of parsley in center.

A special hint:

Step 2 above is hard to explain. I believe it is enough to say avoid overlaps and keep the sealed edge under the chicken.

STEAK, KIDNEY, MUSHROOM AND OYSTER PIE

For 4 large servings, you will need:

1 lb (0.5 kg) beef shoulder steak
  (boned)
½ lb (227 g) beef kidney
1 bay leaf
6 parsley stalks*
4 oz (113 g) mushrooms
4 oz (113 g) onions
4 oz (113 g) carrots

Freshly ground salt
Freshly ground black pepper
12 oysters
1 lb (0.5 kg) puff pastry*
  (see page 254)
1 egg yolk
1 tbs arrowroot

First prepare:

Cut steak in 1-inch (2.5 cm) cubes. Remove center core and cut kidney into 1-inch (2.5 cm) cubes. Slice mushrooms including stems. Cut onion and carrot into chunks. Roll out pastry ¼ inch (7 mm) thick. Cut a 9-inch (22 cm) round and a ¾-inch (2 cm) wide strip of pastry to fit around edge of a 9-inch pie pan. Preheat oven to 425°F (218°C).

Now cook!

1. Place steak, kidneys, onions, carrots, bay leaf, mushrooms and parsley stalks into an enamel or heat-resistant 1½-quart bowl and season well with salt and pepper. Put this bowl into a large deep saucepan and fill pan with sufficient water to a depth of 3 inches (7 cm). Place tight-fitting lid onto saucepan, covering bowl.

2. Place saucepan containing bowl on low heat and simmer for 8 hours. Do not allow to boil.

3. Remove bay leaf and parsley stalks. Pour off liquid into a saucepan and thicken with arrowroot mixed with a little water.

4. Place meat and vegetables into a pie plate and cover with sauce.

5. Place raw oysters in pie dish.

6. Place 9-inch round of pastry on pie dish. Brush edge with water and lay ¾-inch (2 cm) strip around edge of dish. An egg cup is often placed in center of pie to keep pastry from sinking in center and becoming soggy. Crimp edges of pastry together, decorate with flowers or leaves cut from leftover pastry. Brush pastry with beaten yolk and cut hole in center to let steam escape.

7. Place pie in oven for 30 minutes.

8. Serve with plain boiled potatoes heated in butter and sprinkled with chopped mint and parsley, and carrots glazed in butter, sugar and parsley.

PARRAMATTA PIE

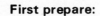

67

For 4 servings, you will need:

1 chicken, 3 lb (1.4 kg)
Juice of ½ lemon
4 oz (113 g) sliced smoked ham
8 oz (227 g) mushrooms
1 bay leaf
1 sprig thyme
6 parsley stalks*
4 oz (113 g) celery
½ medium onion
Freshly ground salt
Freshly ground white pepper

1 oz (28 g) butter
2 tbs all-purpose flour
5 fl oz (1.5 dl) chicken stock
2 fl oz (5.6 cl) white wine
4 fl oz (1.2 dl) heavy cream
1 egg yolk
Pastry:
6 oz (170 g) butter
16 oz (453 g) all-purpose flour
Freshly ground salt
4 fl oz (1.2 dl) water

First prepare:

Place chicken in pot with water to cover. Add bay leaf, thyme and parsley stalks. Cover and simmer 25 minutes. Remove chicken, cool and cut into 1-inch (2.5 cm) cubes. Finely slice onions and celery. Measure flour, butter, cream and wine. Make pastry by combining flour and salt. Cut in butter and mix into a dough with water. Knead lightly and form into a ball. Allow to rest in a cool place for 1 hour. Lightly fry mushrooms in a little clarified butter. Preheat oven to 375ºF (190ºC).

Now cook!

1. Melt butter and stir in flour. Gradually stir in chicken stock, cream and wine. Cook over low heat stirring constantly until sauce thickens. Season with salt and pepper. Whisk until smooth and allow to simmer for 5 minutes.

2. Place half the chicken into bottom of 9-inch pie dish, cover with onion and celery and then ham slices. Cover this surface entirely with whole mushrooms and add lemon juice. Add rest of chicken and pour sauce over top.

3. Place a ¾-inch-wide pastry band on outer edge of pie dish and dampen it with water, then cover with 9-inch round of pastry. Cut an air hole in top and decorate with flowers and leaves cut from pastry trimmings. Gild with egg yolk.

4. Place in oven and cook for 40 minutes.

A special hint:

When you roll out pastry let it rest fully rolled for 20 minutes, otherwise you can get shrinkage. Don't forget—long fingernails destroy pastry!

FILLET STEAK WELLINGTON

For 6 servings, you will need:

2 lbs (0.9 kg) trimmed beef tenderloin	1 lb (0.5 kg) puff pastry*
Freshly ground salt	1 egg yolk
Freshly ground black pepper	4 fl oz (1.2 dl) sour cream
2 tbs clarified butter*	2 tbs horseradish
10 oz (283 g) liverwurst	

First prepare:

Trim tenderloin: remove fat and periostium skin. Roll out puff pastry to ⅛ inch (3 mm) thickness. Separate egg. Soften liverwurst. Preheat oven to 480⁰F (248⁰C).

Now cook!

1. Place clarified butter in a heated pan and when hot add tenderloin (which has been seasoned with salt and black pepper) and sear on all sides.
2. Remove meat from pan and place in a baking dish. Put in oven for 20 minutes. Remove meat and refrigerate. When cool wipe meat dry.
3. Mark off size of tenderloin on pastry and spread this area thickly with liverwurst. Place the beef in the middle of the liverwurst and fold over all sides of the pastry, sealing the seams with water to form an envelope. Place in a shallow baking pan seam side down. Mark pastry with the back of a knife in crisscross fashion to form diamond pattern and brush with beaten egg yolk.
4. Bake in a 425⁰F (218⁰C) oven for 25 minutes.
5. Slice and serve with a mixture of sour cream and horseradish.

A special hint:

I suggest that you can prepare right up to and including Step 3 above. Then place directly into preheated oven ½ hour before it is required.

CORNISH HEN AND BEEF PIE

For 6 servings, you will need:

1 lb (0.5 kg) beef chuck
6 oz (170 g) shoulder bacon*
   (raw shoulder ham)
4 Cornish hens
4 fl oz (1.2 dl) beef stock
Bouquet garni of 2 sprigs of
   parsley, ½ tsp thyme, 1 bay
   leaf and 6 black peppercorns
4 tbs all-purpose flour
1 tbs tomato paste

2 cloves garlic
1 bottle red wine 26 fl oz (8 dl)
8 baby onions
8 oz (227 g) button mushrooms
3 fl oz (8 cl) brandy
2 packets 26 oz (736 g) puff
   pastry*(page 254)
1 egg
Clarified butter*
Freshly ground salt
Freshly ground black pepper

First prepare:

Cube beef and bacon into 1-inch (2.5 cm) cubes. Chop birds in half, detach thighs just behind ball and socket joints. Remove wings and keep for stock, cut off breasts and set aside. Smash garlic. Wash mushrooms. Measure brandy and open bottle of red wine. Make bouquet garni tying up bay leaf, black peppercorns, thyme and parsley in a piece of cheesecloth. Break egg into a bowl and sprinkle with salt for an egg wash for pastry. Preheat oven to 350°F (177°C). Measure tomato paste. Sift flour.

Now cook!

1. Into a heated 3-quart (3 l) shallow casserole over moderate heat, pour some clarified butter to just cover bottom.

2. To this add beef and bacon and fry together until meat is a good rich brown color. Coat cubed beef and bacon with flour and turn. Add garlic, tomato paste, beef stock and 16 fl oz (4 dl) of red wine. Cover pan and cook on very low heat for 90 minutes.

3. Place legs, thighs and breasts of Cornish hens into a hot frypan and gently fry over moderate heat.

4. Add onions and mushrooms to hen pieces. Add brandy and set alight. Add 8 fl oz (2 dl) dry red wine and bouquet garni. Stir all into beef mixture. Cook for 45 minutes.

5. Roll out pastry to form a lid for top of casserole.

6. Cut two 1-inch (2.5 cm) strips of pastry and place around edge of casserole. Brush with cold water.

7. Discard bouquet garni. Pour meat mixture into casserole.

8. Place pastry lid over casserole and crimp onto rim of pastry. Cut off excess pastry on sides with a sharp knife. Trim edges of pastry to give a fluted effect.

9. Make two steam holes.

10. Brush pastry with beaten egg and place on center shelf of preheated 350°F (177°C) oven for one hour.

11. After cooking period, remove pie from oven and serve at once.

A special hint:

Roll out the pastry at least 30 minutes before you lay it onto the pie and bake it. This lets the pastry "rest" and it will not shrink as much as it does when used immediately following a "roll out."

RAMEQUINS

For 10 servings, you will need:

12 oz (340 g) puff pastry*
  (see page 254)
2 eggs
8 fl oz (2 dl) heavy cream
16 oz (453 g) Emmenthal cheese
¼ tsp freshly ground salt

Pinch nutmeg
¼ tsp dry mustard
⅛ tsp cayenne pepper
2 tbs chives
Parsley

First prepare:

Roll out pastry thinly and line 2-inch (5 cm) ramequins (see below). Finely grate cheese. Chop chives. Measure cream. Preheat oven to 400ºF (205ºC).

Now cook!

1. Beat eggs with cream and season with mustard, salt, cayenne and nutmeg. Fold in grated cheese.

2. Place pinch of chopped chives in bottom of each ramequin and fill three-quarters with egg and cheese mixture. Bake for 15 minutes until puffed and golden brown.

3. Remove from pan and serve hot on a serving dish, covered with a paper doily or a bright purple serviette.

4. Garnish with the inevitable parsley!

Service:

You need special ramequin dishes. These are usually plain white, ribbed on the outside like miniature soufflé dishes.

A special hint:

The cheese must be very finely grated; otherwise it tends to sink to the bottom.

CRAB CAPTAIN COOK

For 4 small servings, you will need:

8 oz (227 g) king crab leg meat

4 fl oz (1.2 dl) dry white wine

8 sheets fila (Greek) pastry*

6 spring onions* or small white onions

1 lemon

4 oz (113 g) button mushrooms

2 fl oz (5.6 cl) heavy cream

Clarified butter*

Freshly ground salt

Freshly ground white pepper

First prepare:

Chop crab meat into rough pieces. Measure wine and cream. Clean and finely slice mushrooms. Wash and finely slice spring onions. Preheat oven to 400ºF (205ºC). Grease a cookie sheet. Heat a serving platter in warm oven. Squeeze 2 tsp of juice from lemon.

Now cook!

1. Pour a little clarified butter into a heated frypan (just a thin coating) and add onions—fry gently.

2. Add finely sliced mushrooms and sprinkle lemon juice over them. Stir constantly.

3. Add crab meat and white wine. Cook gently over low heat.

4. Pour in cream. Season with salt and white pepper. Allow mixture to reduce over moderate heat.

5. Remove from heat and place contents on a platter to cool.

6. Arrange 4 piles of pastry, 2 sheets thick, and brush top sheets with clarified butter. Divide crab mixture among them.

7. Fold ends over filling and roll up like a strudel-type package and place on greased cookie sheet. Brush them with clarified butter.

8. Place in preheated 400ºF (205ºC) oven for 15 minutes.

9. When crisp and golden brown, remove from oven and place on heated serving platter.

Crab Captain Cook

VEAL SWEETBREAD AND BACON PIE

67

For 4 servings, you will need:

10 oz (283 g) veal sweetbreads
8 bacon rashers*
1 lemon
3 medium tomatoes
Freshly ground black pepper
30 marjoram leaves
1 egg

Clarified butter*
Pastry:
6 oz (170 g) butter
8 oz (227 g) all-purpose flour
Freshly ground salt
3 fl oz (8 cl) water

First prepare:

Soak sweetbreads for 1 hour, then rinse, cover with cold water and bring slowly to a boil. Drain immediately after they come to a boil and plunge into a bowl of cold water. Remove skin and place sweetbreads on a dinner plate, cover with another dinner plate, press together tightly, wrap in a towel and place a heavy weight on top. Leave for 30 minutes. Cut sweetbreads into slices. Cut bacon into ½-inch (1.2 cm) cubes. Cut tomatoes into ½-inch (1.2 cm) slices. Make pastry. Preheat oven to 375°F (190°C). Lightly beat egg together.

Pastry: Make a well in center of sifted flour. Add salt and butter cut into ½-inch (1.2 cm) cubes. Mix quickly with water to form a smooth dough. Knead lightly on a floured surface, wrap and refrigerate for 30 minutes. Remove and roll out.

Now cook!

1. Place some clarified butter into a pan to just cover bottom and when hot fry bacon.

2. Line a 9-inch pie plate with half the bacon and cover with a layer of dried pressed sweetbreads. Add remaining bacon and rest of sweetbreads. Moisten with lemon juice and cover with tomatoes. Season with black pepper and marjoram leaves.

3. Cover with pastry by first placing a ¾-inch-wide strip of pastry on edge of dish, brushing with water and topping with a 9-inch round of pastry. Trim edges. Cut a chimney in center and paint with egg. Bake in a 375°F (190°C) oven for 45 minutes.

A special hint:

The technique used for veal sweetbreads in this recipe also applies to lamb sweetbreads and brains, except that brains are not pressed between plates.

1. VEAL SWEETBREAD AND BACON PIE. An Australian dish.

2. After soaking, put sweetbreads in cold water and bring to boil.

3. When blanched, place in cold water. Remove skin and glands.

4. Place sweetbreads between two or more plates.

5. Press them under a heavy weight.

6. Fry chopped bacon to release fat. Dump half into quiche dish.

7. The sweetbreads are now pressed.

8. They should be dried with a paper towel.

9. Place sweetbreads over bacon.

10. The remaining bacon goes over the sweetbreads.

11. Cover bacon with overlapped sliced tomatoes just touch fried.

12. Add marjoram leaves and pepper (for pastry see page 268).

1. PIE DECORATION doesn't take all that long and it really is worthwhile (see Veal Sweetbread and Bacon Pie page 266).

2. Roll the pastry onto a sheet of greased paper large enough to cover the pie. Allow the pastry to *rest* in fully rolled position for 10 minutes.

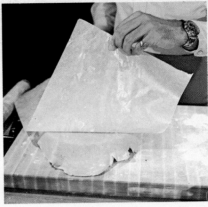

3. Swiftly invert pastry and peel off the paper "backing."

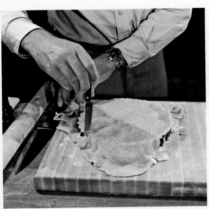

4. Cut around the sides. The paste will not "creep back" due to its rest in Step 2.

5. Roll out all the trim and using a rolling pin (in my case typically scorched!), mark out diagonal lines so that diamond shapes are formed.

6. Mark the diamond leaves with the back of a small knife to suggest veins.

7. Brush the pie with salted egg yolk and fix the leaves in place.

8. I always start on the outside and work in.

9. Finally brush the entire surface and set immediately in a hot oven.

Veal Sweetbread and Bacon Pie (page 266)

70

For 4 servings, you will need:

Pastry:
4 oz (113 g) butter
8 oz (227 g) all-purpose flour
2 fl oz (5.6 cl) ice water
4 scallop shells

Sauce:
1 oz (28 g) butter
2 oz (56 g) all-purpose flour
8 fl oz (2 dl) milk
4 oz (113 g) mushrooms

½ lemon
3 fl oz (8 cl) dry sherry
1 lb (0.5 kg) scallops
4 oz (113 g) can herring roe
1 tsp paprika
1 tbs parsley
Clarified butter*
Freshly ground salt
Freshly ground white pepper

First prepare:

Pastry: Preheat oven to 375ºF (190ºC). Measure butter for pastry, cube and chill. Place flour in a bowl and season with salt. Cut in cubed chilled butter. When particles are very fine, blend in ice water.

Sauce: Measure sherry, scallops and milk. Wash mushrooms and leave whole. Open can of roe. Chop parsley.

Now cook!

1. Roll out the pastry ¼ inch (7 mm) thick on a floured surface and mold it onto the outside of the scallop shells. Trim edges. Bake for 15 minutes at 375ºF (190ºC). Allow to cool slightly and then remove pastry "shells" from scallop "shells."

2. Melt 1 oz (28 g) butter in a saucepan and stir in flour. Cook for 3 minutes over moderate heat.

3. Gradually stir milk into the "roux," bring to a boil while stirring with a whisk. Simmer 5 minutes, stirring occasionally.

4. Season sauce with salt and white pepper.

5. Into another saucepan, pour enough clarified butter to cover bottom. Add mushrooms and sprinkle with lemon juice. Fry gently and then flame with 2 oz sherry.

6. Place scallops and natural juices in with mushrooms, simmer 1 minute.

7. Pour juice from roe into simmering scallops and mushrooms. Now add sauce to scallop mixture.

8. After 3 minutes, remove scallops with a slotted spoon (see hint). Increase heat under pan for 3 minutes to let sauce reduce to half its original volume.

9. Stir paprika and parsley into sauce.

10. Put herring roe and scallops in reduced sauce.

11. Moisten with 1 fl oz (2.8 cl) sherry.

12. Spoon into cooked pastry shells and serve at once.

Service:

It is vital to serve dish immediately, otherwise sauce can soften and destroy pastry shell.

A special hint:

See Step 8. Scallops are removed to prevent their overcooking. In my view scallops are almost always overcooked. At most they only need 3 to 4 minutes to poach.

SYDNEY ROCK OYSTER PASTY

For 2 servings, you will need:

2 dozen oysters
1 tbs all-purpose flour
Freshly ground salt
Freshly ground black pepper
4 bacon rashers*
1 tsp lemon juice
1 medium tomato
1 tbs parsley

1 egg white
1 egg
Pastry:
6 oz (170 g) butter
8 oz (227 g) all-purpose flour
Freshly ground salt
3 fl oz (8 cl) water

68

First prepare:

Pastry: Sift flour and salt. Place into a bowl, make a well in center and add butter cut into ½-inch (1.2 cm) cubes. Work together with fingertips and stir in water, mixing to form a smooth dough. Knead lightly on a floured surface and place wrapped in refrigerator for ½ hour.

Roll out pastry. Cut out a 10-inch (25 cm) circle. Drain oysters. Fry bacon until crisp (bacon cut into 2-inch (5 cm) pieces). Skin and seed tomato and slice finely. Finely chop parsley. Beat egg. Preheat oven to 400ºF (205ºC).

Now cook!

1. Place 10-inch round of pastry on a greased cookie sheet. Put flour in a bag, add oysters and shake to coat in flour. Place oysters on one half of 10-inch round of pastry. Season with salt and pepper.

2. Place crisp bacon on top of oysters. Sprinkle with lemon juice and cover with tomato slices. Season tomatoes with pepper, and add parsley.

3. Paint edges of pastry with egg white and fold one side over the filling securing edges together by crimping them with a fork. Paint with beaten egg. Cut a steam hole in center and bake for 35 minutes.

GRAHAM KERR SPINACH TART

For 8 servings, you will need:

Pastry:
1 lb (0.5 kg) all-purpose flour
8 oz (227 g) butter
1 egg
3 to 4 tbs ice water
Freshly ground salt
Filling:
2 medium onions
4 bacon rashers*
1 clove garlic

2 egg yolks
2 lb (0.9 kg) spinach
Freshly ground salt
Freshly ground black pepper
Nutmeg
5 fl oz (1.5 dl) heavy cream
12 oz (340 g) cottage cheese
   (or ricotta cheese)
8 back bacon rashers*
Clarified butter*

69

First prepare:

Finely chop onions and bacon. Sauté in a little clarified butter until golden. Wash spinach well, put in a large pot, season with salt and pepper and cook covered 4 minutes, shaking spinach from time to time. Drain, cool and press moisture out of spinach with hands. Chop spinach finely. Cut back bacon into small cubes and fry until crisp. Smash garlic.

Now cook!

1. Sift flour with salt, form a well in center and add softened butter and egg. Mix gently with fingertips. Stir in ice water until soft dough is formed. Knead dough a few times into a ball. Refrigerate ½ hour.

2. Roll out pastry to fit 13-inch (32 cm) tart tin and bake in a 375°F (190°C) oven for 20 minutes. Allow to cool thoroughly.

3. *Filling:* Spread onion and bacon mixture over bottom of tart.

4. Heat a little clarified butter to just cover bottom of pan and add garlic. Stir in chopped spinach, season with salt, pepper and nutmeg. Combine egg yolks with cream and stir into spinach. Cook gently over low heat for 1 minute. Do not boil.

5. Spoon creamed spinach over bacon and onion mixture and scatter cheese and back bacon over top of tart.

6. Bake in a 375°F (190°C) oven for 10 minutes.

QUICHE A LA LORRAINE

For 6 servings, you will need:

12 oz (340 g) short crust pastry*	12 fl oz (3.2 dl) milk
6 oz (170 g) bacon rashers*	Freshly ground salt
3 oz (85 g) Gruyère cheese	Freshly ground pepper
3 eggs	Nutmeg

First prepare:

Roll out short crust pastry to fit an 8-inch (20 cm) pie plate fluting a high edge on pastry shell. Prick bottom with a fork. Place a piece of cheesecloth over bottom and sides of pastry. Fill with dried peas and bake in a 425°F (218°C) oven for 20 minutes. Remove cheesecloth and dried peas and allow to cool. Remove rind from bacon rashers and cut into strips to fit pastry bottom. Cut cheese into thin slices. Mix eggs with milk and season with salt, pepper and nutmeg. Preheat oven to 400°F (205°C). Lightly sauté bacon.

Now cook!

1. Place bacon strips on bottom of pastry shell. Strew with thin slices of Gruyère cheese. Pour over ½ milk and egg mixture, leave for 2 minutes to set and then add remainder.

2. Bake for 25-30 minutes. Remove from oven, place on serving dish and serve hot or cold, cut into small wedges.

A special hint:

You can use bread crusts in lieu of peas. Allow a ¼-inch (7 mm) clearance between egg and cream mixture and the pastry shell lip.

TIDDY OGGY

For 1 Oggy, you will need:

4 oz (113 g) butter	2 oz (56 g) beef kidney
8 oz (227 g) all-purpose flour	2 oz (56 g) onion
1 tsp freshly ground salt	2 oz (56 g) white turnip
3 fl oz (8 cl) water	2 oz (56 g) potatoes
2 oz (56 g) lard	1 tbs parsley
Filling:	Freshly ground salt
5 oz (142 g) rump steak	Freshly ground black pepper

First prepare:

Pastry: Place sifted flour and salt in a bowl. Make a well in the center and add butter and lard cut into small pieces. Cut butter and lard into flour finely. Add water and stir to form a smooth dough. Knead pastry lightly and place in refrigerator to rest for 30 minutes before rolling out.

Roll out on a floured surface into 10-inch (25 cm) circle. Cut steak into ½-inch (1.2 cm) cubes. Cut kidney into ¼-inch (7 mm) cubes. Finely slice onion. Cut turnip and potato into ¼-inch (7 mm) cubes. Preheat oven to 375⁰F (190⁰C). Grease a cookie sheet. Finely chop parsley.

Now cook!

1. Place 10-inch pastry round on a greased cookie sheet. Lay onion on one side of pastry circle, cover with beef, kidney, potatoes, turnip and parsley. Season heavily with salt and pepper.

2. Brush edges of pastry with cold water, fold ½ of the pastry over filling and crimp two edges together carefully. Bake 1 hour. Remove and place on a heated serving dish and garnish with parsley.

PRIDDY OGGY

For 1 Oggy, you will need:

Cheese pastry:	*Filling:*
2 oz (56 g) butter	4 oz (113 g) pork tenderloin
2 oz (56 g) lard	3 thin slices of smoked loin of
8 oz (227 g) all-purpose flour	pork (raw)
2 oz (56 g) grated sharp	1 oz (28 g) sharp Cheddar cheese
Cheddar cheese	1 sage leaf
3 fl oz (8 cl) water	1 small sprig thyme
Pinch freshly ground salt	Freshly ground salt
	Freshly ground black pepper

First prepare:

Pastry: Place sifted flour and salt in a bowl. Make a well in center. Cut butter and lard into flour until small pieces. Add grated cheese. Add water and stir to form a smooth dough. Knead lightly on a floured board and place in refrigerator to rest for 30 minutes.

Make pastry. Roll out on a floured surface and cut an 8-inch (20 cm) circle. Measure pork tenderloin against pastry circle and cut so that tenderloin measures 1 inch (2.5 cm) shorter. Cut tenderloin almost in half and beat to flatten out. Preheat oven to 375⁰F (190⁰C). Lightly grease cookie sheet.

1. Place round of pastry on a greased cookie sheet. Lay flattened pork tenderloin in center of pastry. Cover with two slices of smoked pork loin and then a slice of Cheddar cheese. Lay the third slice of smoked pork loin on top and add crumbled sage leaf and thyme. Season with salt and pepper.

2. Paint edges of pastry with water and enclose filling by bringing edges to top and crimping together carefully in torpedo shape. Bake for 1 hour.

A special hint:

An Oggy is the West Country (England) name for a pasty. A Cornish pasty is torpedo-shaped: a Devon pasty is flat, made to fit in a back pocket!

For 8 servings, you will need:

4 oz (113 g) venison (or elk)
4 oz (113 g) beef rump
4 oz (113 g) pork loin
4 oz (113 g) veal
4 oz (113 g) goose meat
4 oz (113 g) rabbit
½ tsp cinnamon
½ tsp allspice
Freshly ground salt
Freshly ground black pepper

12 fl oz (3.2 dl) water
1 medium onion
1 lb (0.5 kg) peeled potatoes
Pastry:
2½ oz (70 g) butter
2½ oz (70 g) lard
8 oz (227 g) all-purpose flour
Pinch freshly ground salt
4 tbs ice water

First prepare:

Put meats through a fine grinder. Cut onion into paper-thin slices. Peel, cook and mash potatoes and allow to cool. Preheat oven to 400°F (205°C).

Pastry: Sift flour with salt, place in a bowl and make a well in center. Add lard and butter cut into small cubes. Mix lightly with the fingertips until particles are very fine. Stir in ice water and form a smooth dough. Knead a few times on a floured surface. Wrap and refrigerate for ½ hour. On floured surface roll out 2/3 of pastry large enough to line bottom and sides of a 10-inch pie plate.

Now cook!

1. Place onion in a dry frypan on heat. Add meat and allow to fry gently in its own fat. When juices start to form in the bottom of the pan, season with cinnamon, allspice, pepper and salt. Moisten meat with water, cover and cook very gently for 1 hour.

2. When meat is cooked stir in cold mashed potatoes. Season with more salt to taste.

3. Line pie plate with pastry and brush surface with egg white. Prick bottom and fill with meat mixture. Pack down tightly and smooth over. Paint rim with egg white. Roll out remaining pastry large enough to cover top of pie. Secure edges by crimping them together. Paint pie with egg yolk and bake for 40 minutes.

SPINATHWAHE

For 12 servings, you will need:

Pastry:
1 lb (0.5 kg) all-purpose flour
6¾ oz (190 g) butter
7½ fl oz (1.9 dl) ice water
Freshly ground salt
Filling:
13 oz (368 g) fresh spinach

6 fl oz (1.6 dl) heavy cream
1 tsp arrowroot
1½ eggs
8 oz (227 g) bacon
1 tsp nutmeg
Freshly ground salt
Freshly ground black pepper

First prepare:

Pastry: Cut butter into little cubes and chill in refrigerator. Sift flour. Place measured water in refrigerator (it should be ice cold). Place flour in a bowl and cut in butter (keep shaking bowl to keep large particles of butter rising to top) until butter is evenly distributed through flour and looks like fine bread crumbs. Add a good pinch of salt, then gently work in ice water using pastry blender or a fork. Finally use fingertips to roll dough around bowl to gather up all pastry. The texture should be firm. Knead a few times on a floured surface into a smooth ball. Wrap in a piece of waxed paper and put in refrigerator to rest until morning.

Filling: Finely chop fresh cleaned spinach and place in a bowl. Measure cream, crack open 1½ eggs (see hint) and finely cube bacon. Preheat oven to 375ºF (190ºC).

Now cook!

1. Remove pastry from refrigerator and roll out on a floured board to shape of a 10-inch flan tin.
2. To turn pastry simply roll it over the rolling pin and unroll in the opposite direction. Avoid picking it up in your hands as this causes the dough to stretch and then shrink when baked.
3. Roll out pastry ⅛-inch (3 mm) thick, roll onto rolling pin, unroll onto flan tin and line bottom and sides. Prick bottom of flan with a fork.
4. Set aside in a cool place.
5. Add arrowroot and cream to chopped spinach in bowl. Stir together, blend in eggs and continue to stir. Add finely chopped bacon, season and add nutmeg.
6. At this point it is easier to use one's hands to cream mixture evenly.
7. Brush a little egg white on pastry bottom to prevent it getting soggy and add remainder of egg white to spinach mixture.
8. Pour deep green "grass" looking mixture into flan tin and press down firmly.
9. Pop into preheated oven at 375ºF (190ºC) and cook for 40-50 minutes.
10. Cut into strips as soon as it comes out of oven and serve at once.

A special hint:

Only chop spinach with a knife. It should not be blended or ground. To do this hold tip of a large knife on the board with index finger, and chop by raising and dropping the handle. To measure ½ an egg, beat egg, measure and use half the amount.

TASTING ROOM PIE NO. 2

For 6 servings, you will need:

1 lb (0.5 kg) shoulder veal	1 lemon
1 lb (0.5 kg) shoulder pork	1 orange
8 oz (227 g) mushrooms	Clarified butter*
1 clove garlic	Freshly ground salt
1 medium onion	Freshly ground black pepper
1 stalk celery	*Pastry:*
1 medium carrot	2 eggs
25 fl oz (7.2 dl) red wine	12 oz (340 g) all-purpose flour
Bouquet garni: 1 inch (2.5 cm)	7 oz (198 g) butter
bay leaf, 3-inch (7.6 cm)	2 eggshells full of ice cold
stalk celery, ½ tsp thyme, 6	water
peppercorns, parsley	

First prepare:

Cut the veal and pork into 1-inch cubes. Slice onion, carrot and celery into large pieces. Place meat, sliced onion, carrot and celery into a bowl and season generously with salt and black pepper. Pour red wine over this, cover with plastic film and set in a cool place to marinate overnight at room temperature. Slice mushrooms. Bruise clove of garlic. Squeeze juice from lemon. Peel orange. Preheat oven to 375ºF (190ºC).

Pastry: Sift flour into a bowl. Cut chilled butter into cubes. With a pastry cutter cut the butter into flour. Stir until dough is formed. Add one egg and 2 eggshells full of water. Knead a few times. Set aside until required. Beat second egg adding a pinch of salt.

Now cook!

1. Strain marinade from meat and reserve. Dry meat with a linen towel (pick out vegetables and keep them on one side).

2. Place a frypan on the heat and add some clarified butter to just cover bottom.

3. Put pieces of meat into very hot butter to seal in juices and color meat.

4. Cover meat with marinated vegetables and allow this mixture to simmer over a low heat, stirring constantly for 10 minutes.

5. Pour some clarified butter in another pan and add garlic, mushrooms, orange peel and lemon juice. Add bouquet garni tied in cheesecloth and reserved wine marinade. Simmer 10 minutes.

6. Roll out pastry on a lightly floured board to fit top of a 2-quart casserole.

7. Pour meat mixture into casserole, add mushrooms and wine. Remove and discard bouquet garni, orange peel and garlic clove.

8. Cover with pastry, trim and crimp the edges.

9. Reroll trimmings and cut into pastry leaves (a strip of pastry cut into diamonds). Make a 1-inch steam hole in the center of pie. Place leaves around hole.

10. Brush pastry with beaten egg to which a pinch of salt has been added to give a high gloss.

11. Place in preheated 375ºF (190ºC) oven for 1½ hours.

12. After cooking period remove pie from oven and serve.

CHICKEN WITH GRAPES

For 4 servings, you will need:

1 chicken 3 lb (1.4 kg)
12 oz (340 g) seedless green grapes
8 oz (227 g) bacon slices
2½ fl oz (6.8 cl) sweet sherry
2½ fl oz (6.8 cl) dry sherry
Freshly ground salt
Freshly ground black pepper
2 sage leaves
1 tsp allspice
1 tsp paprika

1 tbs firmly packed brown sugar
1 tbs all-purpose flour
Pastry:
5 tbs butter
5 tbs lard
½ tsp salt
4 tbs ice water
1 lb (0.5 kg) all-purpose flour
1 egg yolk

First prepare:

Remove wings from chicken and cut into 4 pieces, removing backbone and breast bones. Remove rind from bacon. Measure sherry. Make pastry by cutting butter and lard into flour mixed with salt. Add water and mix to a dough. Knead a few times on a floured board. Form into a ball, wrap and refrigerate ½ hour. Preheat oven to 400°F (205°C).

Now cook!

1. Fry bacon in a pan until fat is released. Remove bacon to a dish and reserve. When cooled cut into 1-inch (2.5 cm) cubes.

2. Dry chicken pieces and brown both sides in bacon fat. Season with salt and pepper. Add allspice and paprika. Remove chicken and place in bottom of 10-inch pie dish. Place ½ sage leaf on each chicken piece.

3. Stir flour into bacon fat to form a roux and then stir in sweet and dry sherry until smooth. Pour over chicken pieces. Surround chicken pieces with grapes and sprinkle grapes with brown sugar. Cover with bacon cubes.

4. Roll out pastry on a floured surface. Cut a pastry round 1 inch (2.5 cm) larger than pie dish and then cut a 1-inch (2.5 cm) wide band of pastry. Dampen edge of pie dish with water and place band of pastry onto edge of pie dish, pressing down with fingers. Dampen pastry band with water and cover dish with pastry round. Crimp edges, cut an air hole in center and decorate with flowers and leaves cut from pastry trimmings. Paint pie with egg yolk and bake in oven for 30 minutes.

A special hint:

Step 1. If you get insufficient bacon fat add a little butter.

For 20 little pies, you will need:

4 oz (113 g) crab meat
4 oz (113 g) raw shrimp
　(shelled weight)
12 mussels
1 green pepper (capsicum)
2 pimentos (canned)
Freshly ground salt
Freshly ground black pepper
Sprig of lemon thyme*
½ medium onion
1 tbs clarified butter*
40 fl oz (1.2 l) olive oil

2 tbs dry white wine
Parmesan cheese
Egg white, slightly beaten
Pastry:
½ tsp baking powder
1½ tsp sugar
½ tsp freshly ground salt
1 egg
1½ tbs melted butter
2 fl oz (5.6 cl) dry sherry
3 oz (85 g) flour

First prepare:

Pastry: In a bowl mix flour with baking powder, sugar and salt. Make a well in the center of flour and add egg, sherry and melted butter. Mix quickly with a spatula to form a smooth dough. Knead lightly and then chill in refrigerator for 1 hour. Roll out to ⅛-inch thickness on a floured surface.

Pour olive oil into deep fryer and preheat to 370ºF (187ºC). Dice onions finely. Dice green pepper finely. Finely slice shrimp. Finely slice crab. Finely dice pimento. Put mussels in saucepan with wine, cover and place on heat, shaking from time to time. Cook for 2 minutes. Take mussels from shell, remove beard, finely slice mussels. Grate Parmesan.

Now cook!

1. Place clarified butter in a frypan and add green pepper and onion. Sauté gently and then add raw shrimp with pimento. Stir until shrimp is colored. Add crab and mussels. Season with salt, pepper and lemon thyme. Remove mixture from heat and allow to cool completely.

2. Cut pastry into 1½ inch x 3 inch (3.8 cm x 7.6 cm) pieces. Brush lightly with egg white and place 1 tsp of filling in the center of each. Fold pastry over with floured fingers and secure by pressing gently around edges. Drop empanadas into hot oil and cook for 3½ minutes or until puffed and golden. Turn them once. Drain on absorbent paper.

3. Place on a dish and dust with grated Parmesan cheese.

A special hint:

Don't overfill the pies—1 tsp is quite sufficient.

1. EMPANADA MARISCADA are small pastry cases made with a wine pastry; quite unique!

2. Every particle of the filling is chopped very fine. A grinder would be useful here.

3. Shallow fry the vegetables lightly; then add the shrimp.

4. Cut the pastry into ruler-wide lengths (1½ inches: 3.8 cm). Then cut into 3-inch (7.6 cm) widths.

5. Brush the surface with egg wash.

6. Place a very small quantity of the filling on each rectangle.

7. Fold the forward edge back over to seal on the back edge.

8. Tamp the edge to insure a good seal.

9. Deep fry at 370°F (187°C). Drain on kitchen paper before service and cover with grated Parmesan cheese. Serve hot.

68

For 4-6 servings, you will need:

1 lb (0.5 kg) all-purpose flour
9 oz (255 g) grated suet
1 heaped tsp baking powder
Freshly ground salt
10 fl oz (3 dl) water
Filling:
1 chicken, 3½ lb (1.5 kg)
8 oz (227 g) chicken livers

4 oz (113 g) celery
4 oz (113 g) onion
1 sprig fresh thyme
1 tbs parsley stalks*
2 fl oz (5.6 cl) dry white
 wine
4 fl oz (1.2 dl) water
1 oz (28 g) all-purpose flour

First prepare:

Make pastry by mixing flour, suet, baking powder, salt and water to form a smooth dough. Cut raw flesh from chicken into 1-inch (2.5 cm) pieces. Cut livers into 1-inch (2.5 cm) pieces. Slice onion and celery into ½-inch (1.2 cm) pieces. Roughly chop parsley stalks. Grease pudding basin holding 1½ quarts (1.5 l). Flour pudding cloth or double thickness muslin.

Now cook!

1. Roll out 2/3 of dough reserving 1/3 for lid. Sprinkle with a little flour and shape into a circle large enough to line basin. Mold pastry to fit bowl. Trim dough leaving top rim of basin covered with dough.

2. Mix chicken with livers, celery, onion, thyme and parsley stalks. Season highly with salt and pepper. Dust mixture with flour and mix well.

3. Place chicken mixture in suet crust, add water and white wine. Roll out reserved pastry large enough to fit top of basin. Brush edge of crust with water and cover with pastry lid. Trim off any excess dough. Place floured pudding cloth over top and secure with a piece of string. Tie up ends of cloth.

4. Place pudding in a deep kettle with water reaching ¾ up side of bowl and add 2 marbles (to warn you if the water boils away). Cover and allow to boil 3 hours.

5. Remove pudding and cloth. Place bowl on a decorative serving dish and serve direct from pudding basin.

A special hint:

Be quite sure that you like chicken livers before adding them to the dish. They tend to be an acquired taste. Just buy a few, roll them in seasoned flour, fry in butter for 4 minutes, squeeze on lemon juice. Taste them, then if you like them use them in chicken pudding.

For 4 servings, you will need:

Pastry:
  1 lb (0.5 kg) all-purpose flour
  1 heaped tsp baking powder
  Freshly ground salt
  9 oz (255 g) grated suet
  10 fl oz (3 dl) water
Filling:
  8 oz (227 g) beef kidney

1½ lbs (680 g) rump steak
4 oz (113 g) mushrooms
6 parsley stalks*
1 tsp fresh thyme
Flour
12 oysters plus their juice
2 fl oz (5.6 cl) red wine
Freshly ground salt
Freshly ground black pepper

First prepare:

Make suet pastry by mixing flour, suet, baking powder, salt and water to form a smooth dough. Cut kidney into 1-inch (2.5 cm) pieces. Cut steak into 1-inch (2.5 cm) cubes. Slice mushrooms into ½-inch (1.2 cm) slices. Reserve oyster juice. Measure wine. Cut parsley stalks into ¼-inch (7 mm) pieces.

Now cook!

1. Dust a board with flour and flatten out pastry with fingers to form a circle about ¼ inch (7 mm) thick. Place a pudding cloth into a 1½-quart (1.5 l) basin and mold suet pastry to shape of basin allowing pastry to overhang bowl long enough to fold over top after filling.

2. Place meat and kidney in a bowl, season very highly with salt and pepper. Add parsley stalks and thyme. Dust with a little flour.

3. Place half meat mixture into suet crust, add half the mushrooms, then remaining meat and finish with mushrooms. Add enough oyster juice to wine to make 4 fl oz (1.2 dl) and pour into pudding.

4. Brush edges of suet crust with water and lift pudding cloth so as to fold overhanging pastry over filling. Cut away portions that overlap. Secure pudding cloth with a string. Place basin in a large boiler or deep kettle with boiling water reaching to ¾ up the basin. Remove nob from saucepan lid and thread string through hole until cheese cloth is taut but pudding is still in basin. Secure string to handle. Boil pudding for 3½ hours.

5. Remove pudding from basin, carefully peel away pudding cloth and invert onto heated serving dish. Cut a hole in middle of crust and add oysters, mixing them in with a fork.

A special hint:

See Step 4. The incredible business of suspending pudding under saucepan lid to achieve proper heat circulation is only way of getting round baby's head finish!

Empanada Mariscada (page 280)

Spotted Dick and Whisky Butter (page 286)

SPOTTED DICK AND WHISKY BUTTER

For 12 servings, you will need:

1 lb (0.5 kg) self-rising flour
8 oz (227 g) suet
4 oz (113 g) castor sugar*
4 oz (113 g) currants
2 oz (56 g) sultana raisins
2 eggs
Pinch freshly ground salt
2 fl oz (5.6 cl) milk
1 oz (28 g) butter

Castor sugar to dust*
Whisky butter:
2 fl oz (5.6 cl) whisky
2 oz (56 g) butter
2 oz (56 g) confectioners' sugar
Peel of ½ orange
½ tsp ground coriander

First prepare:

Sift flour with salt. Finely grate suet. Wash currants and sultanas. Measure milk. Make whisky butter. Refrigerate. Lightly flour boiled pudding cloth or double thickness muslin. Fill large deep kettle or Dutch oven to ¾ with boiling water.

Whisky butter: Warm finely chopped orange rind in a saucepan in whisky and set alight. Mix softened butter with confectioners' sugar in a bowl and stir in coriander. Add whisky and orange rind residue. Stir until smooth. Refrigerate.

Now cook!

1. Rub suet into flour with fingertips until well blended. Stir in salt, sugar, currants and sultanas and then beat in eggs and milk to form a smooth thick dough. Place mixture in center of pudding cloth and roll in cloth, overlapping ends well to form a long sausage shape. Secure ends of cloth with string, place in boiling water to cover and allow to boil covered for 1½ hours. Add more boiling water as it boils away.

2. Remove from water, cut string and peel off pudding cloth. Cut spotted dick into 1 inch (2.5 cm) slices and fry in butter for 30 seconds on either side. Lay on a serving dish and sprinkle with castor sugar.

3. Serve with whisky butter.

A special hint:

Place two marbles in bottom of boiling container (I use a covered baking dish). When water level drops to a danger point marbles kick up quite a racket reminding you to add more water.

WACHAUER APRIKOSENKNODEL

For 6 servings, you will need:

1 lb (0.5 kg) cold cooked potatoes
30 oz (850 g) all-purpose flour
3 oz (85 g) butter
1 egg yolk
Pinch freshly ground salt
12 whole apricots (or 24 halves)
12 lumps sugar
10 oz (283 g) bread crumbs*
2 oz (56 g) castor sugar*

4 oz (113 g) butter
Cinnamon
3 tbs brandy
Sauce:
10 canned apricot halves
2 fl oz (5.6 cl) apricot juice
   (drained from apricots)
2 fl oz (5.6 cl) brandy

First prepare:

Peel and grate potatoes. Measure and sift flour. Measure butter. Soak sugar lumps in brandy. Halve and pit whole apricots. Measure bread crumbs, sugar and brandy. Measure ingredients for sauce.

Now cook!

1. Mix flour with grated potatoes and salt. Rub in butter until particles are very fine. Stir in egg yolk. Turn dough out onto a floured board and knead. Roll out dough to ¼-inch (7 mm) thick oblong 12 x 16 inches (30 x 40 cm).

2. Place a lump of brandied sugar in each half apricot, cover with another apricot half.

3. Cut dough into twelve 4-inch (10 cm) squares. Place apricot in center and wrap dough around, squeezing edges of dough together. Trim off outside. Roll dumpling between palms of hands to make as round as possible.

4. Drop dumplings into a large saucepan of salted boiling water. Boil gently for 12 minutes. Remove with slotted spoon and drain.

5. Fry bread crumbs with sugar and butter until crisp.

6. Roll dumplings in bread crumbs and sprinkle with cinnamon. Place on a heated serving dish. Coat with some of the apricot sauce. Serve remaining sauce separately.

7. *Sauce:* Puree apricot halves with brandy and apricot juice in a blender. Heat gently in a saucepan.

A special hint:

When you mold the paste around the apricot be sure that the seams are firmly sealed—they can come unstuck!

BANANA LIME CHEESE CAKE

71

For 6 servings, you will need:

9 oz (255 g) ginger snaps
6 oz (170 g) walnuts
9 oz (255 g) sugar
4 oz (113 g) butter
2 fl oz (5.6 cl) rum

1½ lbs (680 g) cream cheese
3 eggs
3 limes
2 fl oz (5.6 cl) brandy
2 bananas

First prepare:

Peel two of the limes, slice thinly and then cut in half. Marinate in 1 fl oz (2.8 cl) rum for an hour. Crush ginger snaps into fine crumbs and pour into a bowl. Add finely chopped walnuts, butter, 1 fl oz (2.8 cl) rum and mix well. Grease 8-inch (20 cm) spring-form pan with butter and place crumb mixture into it smoothing to form a biscuit crust halfway up the sides of the pan. Set aside. Juice 1 lime, measuring remaining dry and liquid ingredients. Preheat oven 325°F (163°C). Peel a banana, finely slice and coat with 2 tsp lime juice and mix with lime slices to marinate.

Now cook!

1. Mash together cream cheese with sugar until fluffy.
2. Add eggs one at a time beating thoroughly into creamed cheese mixture.
3. Stir in juice of one lime.
4. Flavor with 2 fl oz (5.6 cl) brandy and whip until smooth.
5. Spoon this fantastic filling into crumb base in pan. Smooth out and bake on middle shelf of preheated oven set at 325°F (163°C) for 30 minutes.
6. Remove cheese cake from oven when cooked, then cool.
7. When cool you can remove the "cake" from pan and refrigerate.
8. Garnish with marinated lime and banana slices.

Banana Lime Cheese Cake

JOHN BAILEY'S CHEESECAKE

66

For 8 servings, you will need:

3 eggs
4 oz (113 g) castor sugar*
1½ lb (680 g) cream cheese
2 tsp orange flower water*
Peel from 1 orange
1 tbs brandy

Crust:
6 oz (170 g) Nice biscuits*
2 oz (56 g) chopped walnuts
6 tbs butter

Toffee Walnuts:
4 oz (113 g) walnut halves
4 oz (113 g) sugar

First prepare:

Cut orange peel into matchstick pieces and place in boiling water for 5 minutes. Drain and place in a bowl with brandy. Leave for at least 2 hours. Crush biscuits. Roughly chop walnuts. Butter 8-inch (20 cm) spring form pan. Preheat oven to 325⁰F (163⁰C).

Now cook!

1. Combine crushed biscuits, walnuts and melted butter. Mix well and press into bottom of pan and 2 inches up sides.

2. Beat cream cheese until soft and stir in sugar. Add eggs one at a time, beating until mixture is very smooth. Fold in orange flower water with orange peel and brandy and pour into biscuit crust.

3. Bake cheesecake for 30 minutes in a 325⁰F (163⁰C) oven. Turn off heat and let cake cool in oven with door open.

4. *Toffee Walnuts:* Place sugar in pan and cook over low heat without stirring until golden brown. Watch carefully. When caramelized stir in walnut halves until coated with syrup. Pour onto greased board. When cold break into small pieces for garnishing.

5. Unmold cheesecake and decorate with toffee walnuts.

HERRKERRSTORTEN

70

For 7 servings, you will need:

3½ oz (100 g) butter
2 tbs sugar
Pinch of freshly ground salt
8 oz (227 g) plus 1 tbs all-purpose flour
10 fl oz (3 dl) sour cream
1 lb (0.5 kg) raspberries

1 tbs kirsch
5 fl oz (1.5 dl) heavy cream
8 toasted hazelnuts
4 oz (113 g) toasted blanched almonds
1 oz (28 g) toasted hazelnuts
Confectioners' sugar to dust

First prepare:

Grind 1 oz (28 g) hazelnuts and almonds finely. Beat cream stiffly. Measure flour and sift. Measure butter and sugar. Preheat oven to 375⁰F (190⁰C).

Now cook!

1. Add sugar to soft butter and beat until fluffy. Add sifted flour, salt, nuts and mix into a smooth dough. Refrigerate for 1 hour.

2. Line a shallow cookie sheet with buttered foil.

3. Remove pastry from refrigerator and cut in half. Press out each piece to form 2 circles 9 inches (22 cm) in diameter. Put one circle on foil and trim to a perfect circle, scraping away excess pastry with a teaspoon. Cut remaining circle into 7 wedges. Place both in oven for 8 minutes. Remove and allow to cool.

4. When cool place uncut layer on a serving dish. Mix raspberries with sour cream and spread mixture on pastry. Place 7 wedges of pastry on top, leaving a space in between each portion.

5. Pipe a whipped cream rosette onto each portion and one in center and place a toasted hazelnut on each. Sift confectioners' sugar over cake.

A special hint:

Allow ultra thin nut pastry to cool completely before attempting to lift it. It is extremely fragile.

BARBIES BAKED APPLE

For 4 servings, you will need:

1 lb (0.5 kg) all-purpose flour
8 oz (227 g) butter
4 egg yolks
4 oz (113 g) confectioners' sugar
1 tsp freshly ground salt

Filling:

4 oz (113 g) strawberry jam
2 oz (56 g) ground almonds
4 large baking apples

67

First prepare:

Remove core from apples and enlarge cavity with melon baller. Measure all ingredients. Preheat oven to 400°F (205°C).

Now cook!

1. Sift flour, confectioners' sugar and salt together.
2. Rub butter into flour until particles are very fine.
3. Add egg yolks and mix into a dough. Knead dough a few times on a floured surface.
4. Roll out pastry to a 12-inch (30 cm) square and cut into 4 large squares.
5. Place apple onto center and fill each with jam, almonds and jam and top with almonds.
6. Brush pastry with beaten egg and fold up edges to envelop apple. Trim off surplus and crimp edges.
7. Brush again with beaten egg and bake in 400°F (205°C) oven for 25 minutes.

FRUIT TART

63

For 10 servings, you will need:

Pastry:
12 oz (340 g) all-purpose flour
Pinch freshly ground salt
8 oz (227 g) butter
4 tbs fruit sugar*
2 eggs
Vanilla

Cream Cheese filling:
8 oz (227 g) cream cheese
2 egg yolks
4 tbs sour cream
1 tbs confectioners' sugar
2 tbs kirsch

Fruit for garnishing:
8 oz (227 g) dark sweet
 cherries (pitted)
8 oz (227 g) prunes (pitted)
1 lb (0.5 kg) canned apricot
 halves
2 lb (0.9 kg) canned peach
 halves

Glaze:
1 tbs cornstarch or arrowroot
8 fl oz (2 dl) fruit juice
2 tbs kirsch
2 tbs fruit juice

Now cook!

1. *Pastry:* Mix butter with flour and salt, add sugar, mix in eggs and when smooth add vanilla. Form pastry into a ball, allow to stand in a cool place ½ hour. Then roll out to fit 13½ inch (33 cm) flan tin (which has been lined on bottom with foil). Prick bottom with a fork. Bake for 25 minutes in a 375ºF (190ºC) oven. Allow to cool thoroughly. Remove shell from pan and place on a platter.

2. *Cream Cheese filling:* Beat cream cheese with egg yolks, sugar and sour cream until smooth, flavor with kirsch and spread on tart case.

3. *Garnish:* Arrange fruits on top of tart (peach halves, prunes, apricots, and cherries) in a decorative manner.

4. *Glaze:* Heat fruit juice until boiling. Mix cornstarch with 2 tbs extra fruit juice until smooth. Stir in fruit juice, bring to a boil, and stir until thickened. Stir in kirsch and allow to cool 1 minute. Pour over fruit and allow to set.

Fruit Tart

DUTCH GATEAU

For 8 servings, you will need:

Pastry:
4 oz (113 g) butter
4 oz (113 g) all-purpose flour
Pinch of freshly ground salt
1 tbs water
1 tsp castor sugar*
1 egg yolk

Filling:
4 oz (113 g) butter
4 oz (113 g) castor sugar*
1 lemon rind
2 eggs

4 oz (113 g) ground almonds
1¾ oz (49 g) all-purpose
flour
2 tbs cointreau

Icing:
1 egg white
2 oz (56 g) confectioners'
sugar
1 tbs cointreau
3 tbs apricot jam
Egg white to seal pastry

First prepare:

Make pastry. Roll out on a floured surface into circle 10 inches (25 cm) in diameter. Measure butter, sugar and almonds. Roughly grate lemon rind. Sift flour. Preheat oven to 375°F (190°C).

Pastry: Place sifted flour into a bowl, make a well in center, add butter cut into ½ inch (1.2 cm) cubes, sugar, salt, egg yolk and water and mix to form a smooth dough. Refrigerate.

Now cook!

1. Cream butter and sugar together and stir in lemon rind, eggs and almonds. Fold in flour. Flavor with cointreau.
2. Place pastry into an 8 inch (20 cm) fluted flan ring standing on a baking sheet. Trim off excess pastry and reserve. Fill flan with almond mixture.
3. Roll out pastry trimmings and cut into ½ inch (1.2 cm) wide bands. Lay over filling to form a lattice, securing at edges with a little egg white. Place cake in oven and bake for 30 minutes.
4. When cake is baked take it out and remove flan ring.
5. Heat apricot jam until melted.
6. Mix confectioners' sugar, egg white and cointreau to form a glaze.
7. Paint still warm cake with apricot jam and spoon glaze evenly over jam.

DEEP DISH APPLE AND BLACKBERRY PIE

For 10 servings, you will need:

Pastry:
4 oz (113 g) lard
6 oz (170 g) butter
1 lb (0.5 kg) all-purpose flour
Pinch freshly ground salt
2 tsp baking powder
Juice of ½ lemon
2 egg yolks
4 tbs water

Filling:
3 lbs (1.4 kg) Granny Smith
apples*
10 oz (283 g) blackberries
4 oz (113 g) butter
2 oz (56 g) castor sugar*
Juice of ½ lemon
Milk to glaze
Castor sugar to dust*

First prepare:

Make pastry and roll out ¾ of the pastry on a floured surface to a circle 2 inches (5 cm) larger than the top of a 3-quart (3 l) casserole and a 1-inch (2.5 cm) strip long enough to go around casserole. Peel and thickly slice apples. Measure butter and sugar. Preheat oven to 475⁰F (246⁰C).

Pastry: Place sifted flour into a bowl, make a well in center and add other ingredients. Stir quickly to a smooth dough, knead lightly on a floured surface and then refrigerate for ½ hour.

Now cook!

1. Place apples into a large pan with butter, sugar and lemon juice. Cover and allow to cook gently for 5 minutes. Allow to cool a little. Add blackberries.

2. Place a pastry strip 1 inch (2.5 cm) wide on rim of casserole, dampen with a little water. Fill casserole with apple and blackberry mixture and cover with pastry, securing edges. Crimp deeply at 1-inch (2.5 cm) intervals. Cut a steamhole in the center of pie and bake in oven for 35 minutes.

3. Remove pie and while still warm brush with a little milk and sprinkle with castor sugar.

4. Serve with whipped cream.

PUMPKIN PIE

For 8 servings, you will need:

1½ lbs (680 g) diced pumpkin
6 oz (170 g) sugar
14 fl oz (3.4 dl) milk
2 eggs
Freshly ground salt
½ tsp cinnamon
½ tsp ginger

¼ tsp nutmeg
¼ tsp cloves
Pastry:
10 oz (283 g) all-purpose flour
5 oz (142 g) butter
Pinch freshly ground salt
2 fl oz (5.6 cl) water

First prepare:

Cook pumpkin in salted water until soft (about 15 minutes). Measure sugar. Measure milk. Make pastry by combining sifted flour and salt. Cut in butter until particles are very fine. Mix to a smooth dough with water. Allow pastry to stand in a cool place for ½ hour. Roll out pastry to fit bottom and sides of a 9-inch (22 cm) pie plate, fluting a high edge. Preheat oven to 400⁰F (205⁰C).

Now cook!

1. Mash pumpkin with a potato masher. Add milk, sugar, eggs, cinnamon, ginger, nutmeg and cloves. Beat with a whisk and then pour into a pitcher.

2. Pour pumpkin filling over back of a large spoon into pastry shell. Fill pastry shell two-thirds full. Bake in oven for 50 minutes. Cool.

3. Decorate pie with whipped cream and pecans. Serve with vanilla ice cream.

TREACLE TART

For 10 servings, you will need:

Pastry to line tart:
  6 oz (170 g) self-rising flour
  3 oz (85 g) butter
  2 fl oz (5.6 cl) milk
  ½ egg
  Pinch of freshly ground salt
Filling:
  16 fl oz (4 dl) Tate & Lyle's
  golden syrup*

5 oz (142 g) fresh white
  bread crumbs*
Top pastry:
  4 oz (113 g) butter
  2 oz (56 g) castor sugar*
  ½ egg
  6 oz (170 g) self-rising flour
  1 egg
  2 tsp castor sugar*

First prepare:

Make pastry by mixing butter lightly into sifted flour and then stirring into a dough with milk, half an egg and salt. Knead lightly and refrigerate for ½ hour.

Make bread crumbs. Measure golden syrup.

Make top pastry by creaming butter with sugar, adding half-beaten egg and when thoroughly mixed folding in sifted flour. Refrigerate. Lightly beat egg. Preheat oven to 375°F (190°C).

Now cook!

1. Roll out bottom pastry on a floured surface to a 11-inch (27 cm) circle. Line a 9-inch (22 cm) flan ring standing on a greased tray. Trim off pastry and prick base with a fork.

2. Combine bread crumbs with golden syrup and fill pastry case.

3. Roll out top pastry to a 9-inch (22 cm) round on a well floured board or press out with hands. Roll lightly with rolling pin and then roll over pin.

4. Brush rim of tart with egg white and then place pastry top onto tart. Press edges together and trim off any excess pastry. Crimp edges and brush surface with beaten egg. Prick surface with a fork. Sprinkle with castor sugar and bake in oven for 20 minutes. Remove and allow to cool.

Service:

The tart must first cool for an hour and then can be reheated at 250°F (121°C) for 5 minutes. Whipped cream goes well on the side.

NORTHERN PECAN PIE

71

For 6 servings, you will need:

6 oz (170 g) sugar
8 fl oz (2 dl) 100% maple syrup
3 eggs
2 oz (56 g) butter
1 tsp vanilla extract
2 oz (56 g) whole pecans
8 fl oz (2 dl) heavy cream
2 bananas

½ oz (14 g) semi-sweet chocolate
Short crust pastry:
3 fl oz (8 cl) chilled water
8 oz (227 g) all-purpose flour
4 oz (113 g) butter
1 oz (28 g) sugar
Dusting flour
1 egg white

First prepare:

Pastry: Sift flour and sugar into a bowl, cube 4 oz (113 g) butter and with a pastry cutter cut into flour and sugar until it is the texture of fine bread crumbs. Gradually stir in chilled water until a dough is formed. Dust counter top with flour and roll out dough

⅛ inch (3 mm) thick, large enough to line bottom and sides of a 8-inch (20 cm) pie pan. Flute or decorate border of pastry.

Break eggs into a bowl and beat. Grate chocolate finely. Beat heavy cream (to be used for final decoration). Measure dry and liquid ingredients. Preheat oven to 450°F (232°C).

Now cook!

1. Into a preheated saucepan on medium heat pour maple syrup and then the 4 oz (113 g) granulated sugar. Stir to dissolve and cook until the mixture thickens (approximately 15 minutes).

2. Prick bottom of pastry with a fork (prevents it from rising) and brush with beaten egg.

3. Remove sugar mixture from heat and cool slightly.

4. Gradually beat syrup into beaten eggs.

5. Stir in 2 oz (56 g) melted butter and vanilla extract.

6. Sprinkle pecans over bottom of pie shell. Pour in syrup mixture.

7. Place in preheated oven at 450°F (232°C) and bake for 10 minutes on middle shelf.

8. Then reduce heat to 300°F (149°C) and continue baking for another 35 minutes.

9. Whisk 2 oz (56 g) granulated sugar into whipped cream.

10. Remove pie from oven and cool.

11. Peel bananas, cut through in halves and slice each half into three. Lay on top of cooled pie. Garnish with whipped cream and dust with grated chocolate.

LE TARTE AUX POIRES

For 6 servings, you will need:

3 large dessert pears

Frangipane:
4 oz (113 g) butter
4 oz (113 g) castor sugar*
2 eggs
4 oz (113 g) ground blanched almonds
1 oz (28 g) all-purpose flour
2 tbs kirsch

Pastry:
8 oz (227 g) all-purpose flour
4 oz (113 g) butter
1 oz (28 g) castor sugar*
1 egg

Apricot glaze:
4 tbs apricot jam
5 fl oz (1.5 dl) cold water
2 tsp lemon juice

First prepare:

Pastry: Measure butter, cut it into little cubes and refrigerate. Sift flour. Sift castor sugar. Grease and flour flan ring. Preheat oven to 350°F (177°C). Beat egg.

Frangipane: Sift sugar. Measure butter and sift flour. Weigh ground almonds.

Glaze: Measure jam and place in small pan. Squeeze lemon juice (2 tsp required). Measure cold water. A pastry brush will be required.

Pears: Use firm fruit. Cut off the top and bottom and with a vegetable scraper peel away the outer skin. Cut in half and remove tough inner core and soak prepared pears in lemon juice (prevents discoloring).

Now cook!

1. Commence with pastry base.

2. Place flour in a bowl and cut in butter. Mix in sugar. When texture is like fine bread crumbs, bind mixture together with beaten egg. This is now a rich sweet pastry and rather crumbly.

3. If you have a marble slab (keeps the pastry cool) roll pastry out on this sprinkled with flour into an 11-inch (27 cm) round. Roll pastry over rolling pin and unroll over 9-inch (22 cm) flan ring. Press pastry firmly around bottom and sides. Roll pin over top of flan and all unnecessary pastry will gently drop off sides. Set flan aside in a cool place.

4. *Frangipane:* Put butter in a bowl with sugar and mix until mixture is light and creamy.

5. Gradually beat in eggs, one at a time.

6. Whisk flour into this a little at a time. Fold in ground almonds.

7. One tbs of kirsch can be added to give flavor.

8. Beat ingredients well together and set aside for a moment.

9. Brush bottom of flan with a little apricot jam (prevents pastry from rising).

10. Pour frangipane into flan ring and arrange drained pears in circle cored side down. They will settle down into frangipane mixture.

11. Pop this into preheated oven at 350°F (177°C) on middle shelf for 30 minutes.

12. While flan is cooking make apricot glaze.

13. Place pan containing apricot jam on low heat. Add lemon juice and water. Stir together with a wooden spoon. Increase heat to boiling point and allow to reduce until a thickened glaze forms.

14. Remove baked flan from oven and brush top of pears with apricot glaze.

ENGADINE NUSSTORTE

For 6 servings, you will need:

Pastry:
  12 oz (340 g) all-purpose flour
  3 oz (85 g) lard
  5 oz (142 g) butter
  5 oz (142 g) sugar

  1 egg
Filling:
  8 oz (227 g) sugar
  8 fl oz (2 dl) heavy cream
  8 oz (227 g) walnuts

First prepare:

Pastry: Sift flour and sugar, chill butter and lard, break the egg into a bowl.
Filling: Sift sugar, chop walnuts, grease flan tin, preheat oven to 350ºF (177ºC).

Now cook!

1. Place flour into a bowl and cut butter and lard into it with a pastry cutter until it has texture of fine bread crumbs.
2. Add sugar.
3. Add egg and mix to a smooth dough with fingertips.
4. Turn out onto a lightly floured board. Divide dough into 2/3 and 1/3. Roll 2/3 of dough to a 10-inch (25 cm) round and use to line an 8-inch (20 cm) flan ring on a greased cookie sheet. Roll out 1/3 pastry to an 8-inch (20 cm) round for lid.
5. Roll pastry over rolling pin and unroll into flan tin pressing it firmly down around bottom and sides. Prick bottom with a fork. Chill flan and lid.
6. Sprinkle 8 oz (227 g) sugar into a heated skillet and stir until it caramelizes.
7. Heat cream, add to sugar and stir in thoroughly. Increase heat for a few moments until it bubbles.
8. Remove skillet from heat, add chopped walnuts and cool slightly.
9. Take flan pastry and lid from refrigerator. Pour walnut filling into flan. Top with lid and seal edges.
10. Make a steam hole.
11. Pop into preheated oven at 350ºF (177ºC) for 35 minutes.
12. When cooked, remove from oven, cool slightly and remove flan from ring. Serve at once or cool and serve cold.

SOUTH AUSTRALIAN STRAWBERRY PIE

67

For 8-10 servings, you will need:

Mincemeat:
- ½ lb (227 g) grated beef suet
- ¾ lb (340 g) raisins
- ½ lb (277 g) sultana raisins
- ¾ lb (340 g) Granny Smith apples*
- ¾ lb (340 g) dried currants
- ¾ lb (340 g) dark brown sugar
- ½ lb (227 g) mixed candied lemon and orange peel
- ¼ lb (113 g) blanched almonds
- Rind of 2 lemons
- Juice of 2 lemons
- 1 vanilla bean (grated)
- 5 fl oz (1.5 dl) brandy
- ½ tsp freshly ground nutmeg
- ½ tsp freshly ground allspice
- ½ tsp freshly ground cinnamon
- ½ tsp freshly ground coriander
- ½ tsp freshly ground ginger

Pastry:
- 1 lb (0.5 kg) all-purpose flour
- 12 oz (340 g) butter
- 1 tbs castor sugar*
- 1 egg yolk
- 8 tbs ice water
- 10 oz (283 g) hulled strawberries
- 10 fl oz (3 dl) heavy cream

First prepare:

Mix all ingredients for mincemeat together and moisten with brandy. Place in jars and seal. Make at least 1 month ahead.

Pastry: Cut butter into small cubes, measure flour and sift. Separate egg.

Now cook!

1. *Pastry:* Make well in sifted flour and place butter in well. Add egg yolk, sugar, salt and 2 tbs water. Mix all ingredients with fingertips, adding ice water as needed until all flour is moistened. Knead several times on a floured surface. Place pastry on plate and refrigerate for an hour.

2. Roll out 2/3 of the pastry to fit a 10-inch (25 cm) pastry ring placed on a cookie sheet. Prick with a fork and cut a 10-inch round of greaseproof paper, place in pastry shell, fill with dried peas or rice. Bake pastry in 400°F (205°C) oven for 15 minutes. Remove paper and rice and allow pastry shell to cool.

3. Fill cooled pastry shell with mincemeat. Roll out remaining 1/3 pastry to a 10-inch (25 cm) round. Place on top, crimp edges and glaze with beaten egg yolk. Place in 400°F (205°C) oven for 30 minutes until golden brown.

4. Remove pie from oven and cool. When cold spread with whipped cream and cover entire surface with strawberries.

A special hint:

Try a little freshly ground pepper on strawberries. Helps to bring out their flavor.

PART VI
THE MAIN COURSE

PART VI
THE MAIN COURSE

No matter how important the "sandwich" course may be, it's the meat in the middle that counts. *Inspire* with the first course, *revive* with the dessert—but *satisfy* with the main dish. Satisfaction should never be interpreted as a gut stretched as tight as a drum. Gustatory satisfaction is achieved by an infinitely cautious seduction of the senses. I firmly believe that it is possible to defeat hunger without completely filling all of the available stomach. To achieve intellectual hunger satisfaction, you need to "jangle the nerve ends."

Put a plate of roast beef, baked potato and a green salad in front of a man and what happens?

Sight On: He will look at it. It looks like roast beef with potato and a green salad. End of sensory interest. *Sight out.*

Smell On: He sniffs. It smells like roast beef with potato and salad. End of sensory interest. *Smell off.*

Taste On: He eats. It tastes like roast beef with potato and salad. End of sensory interest. *Taste off.*

Gut Stretch On: He fills his gut. This sensory interest remains as a primary satisfaction motive. It is the one outstanding *unknown*. Gut stretches, brain registers fact. *Gut stretch off.* Subject stops eating.

The same subject can be presented with a totally *new* dish. New to his senses. Now what happens?

Sight On: He savors the aroma. As taste relies almost entirely upon sense of smell, the interest really hits the roof. (Providing that the food is hot and the hot aroma keeps rising, then it remains sensorily active.) *Smell still on.*

Taste On: He bites. Texture and taste, juiciness, salt, acidity, all mingle and jingle his senses. *Taste still on.*

The brain is now receiving a constant flow of sensory perceptive messages. It is this flow of food-oriented messages that "block" or "scramble" the gut stretch reaction. The degree of intellectual hunger satisfaction depends almost completely on your dinner companions and the degree to which you pit your culinary wits against their senses of sight, smell, taste and touch. As I have implored you to eat only among friends, it remains for me to list some culinary "wits" that may help you to win in the battle of the senses.

SIGHT

• Dark foods look better on light-colored dishes and vice versa.

- Dark foods should have glossy sauces that catch the light and sparkle.

- All vegetables must be brilliant in color. I use two lots of vegetables in casseroles. The first are roughly cut and used as a flavor base. The second are carefully cut to an even size and replace the tired vegetables, which are thrown away.

- Light-colored dishes should contain pastel-colored ingredients such as pink shrimp and pale green asparagus, but they can also benefit from brilliant surface garnish like the red of paprika and the green of finely chopped parsley.

- Beware of false garnish. If it isn't edible, it really shouldn't be on the plate. There are of course, exceptions, such as shellfish shells and leaves, but these are natural. What I find offensive is the use of aluminum foil, chicken in inedible baskets and swatches of sterno-impregnated absorbent cotton blobs set alight to draw other people's attention to your own lack of taste! I especially detest sparklers jabbed in a Bombe Alaska. I usually cherish the thought that just possibly it could be a fuse and the dessert would disappear in a blast of soggy meringue.

- Within the scope of "natural" foods try to avoid the usual garnishes of lettuce and sliced tomatoes. Literally anything carefully and *unobtrusively* cut and cooked looks just fine, so experiment and innovate.

- Unobtrusiveness is an art. It is the reason why the great classic dishes have lasted. They are almost always *simple to look at* and elegant in their lack of confusion; and of even greater importance is the feeling that the food hasn't been *overhandled*. This is one reason why I don't enjoy those carefully "turned" mushrooms (the ones with grooves twirled into the caps). To perform this skillful operation means that the chef has to grasp and finger the mushroom for at least a minute and it doesn't, for me anyway, improve the taste one iota.

In the same way I rebel against the art of the *Garde Manger*. Although I spent hundreds of happy hours performing minute decorative tasks in the hotel business, I look back on it as self-gratification. As a diner and home cook I avoid intricate cold buffet work like the plague. Too much fiddling spoils the galantine!

- Serve, whenever possible, from the table. A dish in quantity always looks better than a lonely spoonful on the plate (see "The Dining Table" on page 34).

- Vegetables can be last-minute glossed with a little hot butter. No vegetable should, in fact, have a matte finish except for the old potato which, at best, should have a powdery flour-like surface.

- Carving is as big a visual plus as it is a minus. Done well it makes the juices run (which helps the digestion). Done badly and the meat would be better blown to pieces by a bomb in the kitchen. Obviously practice makes perfect and at every single roast meal the *man of the house* must carve at the table. At first the attempt will be like a massacre, then little by little the blade will begin to move with the precision of a violin bow. It does *not* help to practice standing up in the kitchen; such an act is as cowardly as requesting a blindfold after losing a military coup. -
To assist in carving you will need:
   —A wood-based carving platter at least 10 inches by 12 inches (25 cm x 30 cm).
   —A pair of holding tongs or a very good straight-pronged fork.
   —A longish (say 10 to 12 inches: 25 cm-30 cm) narrow (1 inch: 2.5 cm) flexible knife which can have a pronged tip. If you use the holding tongs you'll need the pronged knife for service.
   —A sharpening steel and a hand cloth.
   —Each time the blade is stropped it is covered with minute steel filings and while you won't come to harm they show up as a gray ridge against a snowy white slice of chicken breast.
   —Finally, please spare the garnish in volume. By the time you surround a roasted joint with stuffed tomatoes, peas, game chips and so on, it looks exactly like a

centerpage spread in a glossy food magazine. Super to look at but absolutely impossible to serve; like seven-a-side table tennis!

SMELL

• Both the plates and the food must be very hot (see "The Dining Table" page 34). The hotter the food the greater the upward rush of air and the stronger the impact of aroma.
• I have a personal preference for clarified butter (see page 54) rather than other fats and oils. This is, to a large extent, due to its aroma. Hot oils linger, especially in upstairs drapes.
• The use of both table and fortified wines considerably increases the aromatic appeal, especially when they are added at the last practical moment.
• Soups and casseroles are best kept tightly covered until they are served at the table. When you raise the lid a smoke signal arises and positively demands recognition and comment. Those of my readers in England will recall the "Bisto Kids" and know exactly what I mean.
• Of equal importance to good smells are the anti-smells. You should watch out for such things as:
   —Pungent flowers like gardenias and some roses. They look and smell heavenly but unless they're to be eaten they will almost certainly get in the way of the aroma of a good wine.
   —Lavender (and other scented) furniture waxes are also super on a piano or in a lounge but freshly applied to a dining table will give you the same problem as flowers.
   —The soap you provide for your guests to wash their hands is also disruptive. Can you recall the violent liquid soaps used in some of the best restaurants? Try raising a glass of 1924 claret to savor its bouquet with a hand so carefully decontaminated!
   —Heating fluids such as methylated spirits and paraffin are sometimes used to ignite flambé lamps or table heaters. Even worse, some restaurants heat brandy snifters over a methylated spirit burner. Such waiters themselves should be roasted on a spit.

IMPORTANT

It would be quite wrong to leave the sense of smell without stating the obvious. Roughly eighty percent of our sense called taste is in fact dependent upon our sense of smell. Work hard on that aroma factor—it will grab the attention and start the digestive juices flowing. You are now well over halfway to victory and the food hasn't even been tasted!

TASTE

This is what it's all about isn't it? The real crunch—how does it taste? There are more excuses made than there are errors. How often have you heard it said:
"That's the way it's done in Greece—very oily but classical, you know."
"Well it's actually an acquired taste."
"I love that earthy outdoor smoky taste."
"Just think, they ate the same dish a thousand years before Christ."
But the one that really takes the biscuit is:
"Everyone has a different set of tastebuds and so what appeals to one may be unpleasant to another."
What utter damn stupid downright CODSWALLOP! You can't even call them half truths. It is total deceit, an excuse for plain bad cooking! I shall agree that people develop *attitudes* towards certain foods. I disliked macaroni cheese because it was served to me three times a week when I was at school during the Second World War. I disliked it because of the association, not because of the actual *taste*.

When I last visited Rome I ate some pasta in a good cheese sauce and found it excellent. It isn't *taste*—it's *prejudice!* If a guest refuses to eat or finish a dish you have cooked, then you simply have not cooked it well enough to overcome his prejudice. I'll add right now that there are some things that cannot be defeated, such as religious or physical requirements. When you've had shellfish poisoning *twice* it's very hard to convince yourself that it was simply coincidence!

All I seek to suggest to you is that food left uneaten is more likely to have been badly cooked than *not to his or her taste* and that it is better never to allow oneself the luxury of such escapism.

• Always, always, taste as you cook. To sample is to judge and to remember.

• Never send a dish to the table without *correcting the seasoning*. By all means slightly *under season* but never (unless for salt-free diets) leave salt out altogether. The help that salt gives to that first all-important mouthful is enormous.

• Be very careful with monosodium glutamate (M.S.G.). This substance is used in many dried packaged foods as a tastebud stimulator (like salt). Unfortunately it can quickly overwhelm a dish if used in any other but minute quantities.

• The *art* of good cooking is to blend ingredients in such a way that the major star is outstanding. It can be as simple as a seasoned plain broiled steak with a salad, or as complex as a sauté of veal with cockscombs and truffles bathed in a superb velouté. Anything can be perfectly blended; no single piece of food should be tastelessly "dumped" onto a plate. BUT try to get *underneath* the actual food and support it with complementary flavors, not drown it with competitors.

• When you experiment, do your best to reduce any possible conflict. I have made mistakes with too much red currant jelly and have added lemon to offset the sweetness. Had I been less heavy-handed with the jelly, the acidity would have been unnecessary and the dish less complicated. Remember:

> Addition is easy
> Cancellation is undesirable
> Subtraction is impossible.

• The greater the list of ingredients the less chance there is for success by experiment. Only well-tested recipes carefully followed to the letter can come off with a *big cast of characters*.

• Finally taste is a question of "quiet control." You should practice the art of *creeping up on* your main ingredient. No matter how childish this may seem at first you must believe me that, given the essential appreciative audience, your best prop as a cook is to have an attitude to the major food item in every recipe. To develop this attitude to the degree that you endeavor to surprise IT, is about the highest level you can reach in the kitchen (or a padded cell if you've missed the meaning).

TOUCH (TEXTURE)

By now we have appealed to the eye, engaged the nostrils and caressed the tastebuds. All of this is to no avail if you can't get your teeth into the food! Touch is basically divisible into four headings: *tender, firm, smooth, moist.*

• *Tenderness* can almost be reduced to the purely materialistic business of buying good food. Care is needed, however, in preparation and the food should be cooked at low temperatures. The tender fillet steak or tenderloin, for example, is ruined if the silvery skin is not removed. A fillet of sole or a slice of abalone can resemble shoe leather if cooked at too high a heat.

• *Firmness* is more important to me than tenderness. I would choose *grass-fed* in preference to *artificially-fed* cattle any day. I hold the opinion that you have to accept a loss

Laberspiessli Zuri-Hegel (page 310)

in flavor as part of the price you pay for tenderness. While I have my own teeth I'll go with flavor.

• *Smoothness* relates more to soups, sauces and desserts. By *smooth* I mean absolute unctuous uniformity. NOTHING breaks into the absolute *roundness* of the sensation. Never a lump or blemish, a stray seed or pip, a strand of fruit fiber or an undissolved grain of sugar. That's smooth!

• I left *moist* until last because of its importance. Dry foods are generally less easily digested, less flavorsome, less aromatic, less attractive, less colorful and almost always overcooked! By moist I don't mean undercooked, for this is as great a crime of neglect as overcooking.

Moist is that pinnacle of culinary perfection when it's just right. Generally, this is held to mean when the dark meat fluids are still slightly pink and when the less mature or so-called white meat fluids are colorless.

I find that the now-perfected meat thermometer is helpful in achieving such perfection and frankly, at the price we must now pay for our meat, a thermometer is essential.

• Even the best—tender—firm—smooth—moist dishes can be ruined by the three other inedible "touch" sensation: *the knife, the plate, the glass.*

The knife must be easy to hold and *extremely* sharp.

The plate should respond with that *clink* of good china or enamel; a sound unable to reproduce on plastic.

The glass should be as thin as possible at the point of contact with the mouth yet (from a purely design point of view) as sturdy in the stem and base as practical.

SESAME SCALLOPS

For 6 servings, you will need:

2 oz (56 g) butter
1 tbs lemon juice
Freshly ground salt
Freshly ground black pepper

1 lb (0.5 kg) scallops
Bacon slices
1 oz (28 g) sesame seeds

First prepare:

Melt butter and mix with lemon juice. Season with salt and pepper. Place scallops in this mixture. Cut bacon into slices large enough to wrap around scallops. Place sesame seeds in dish. Preheat broiler.

Now cook!

1. Wrap bacon around scallops, secure with a toothpick and roll bacon in sesame seeds.
2. Place on greased broiler rack and broil about 5 inches (12 cm) away from heat until bacon is crisp (about 5 minutes). Turn so bacon becomes crisp on all sides.

66

LAMB KEBABS

For 6 servings, you will need:

1 leg of lamb, 3½ lb (1.6 kg)
  (shank removed)
Marinade:
3 thin slices fresh ginger root✻
4 cloves garlic
2 oz (56 g) onion

3 tbs soya sauce
Freshly ground salt
Freshly ground pepper
Juice of ½ lemon
3 tbs honey
1 large ripe pineapple

First prepare:

Trim off fell and a little of the heavy fat on leg of lamb. Cut meat away from bone in 2 large pieces. Slice meat lengthways into 1-inch (2.5 cm) strips and then cut into 1-inch (2.5 cm) cubes. Remove skin from ginger root and slice in paper-thin slices. Peel and smash garlic roughly. Finely slice onion. Preheat broiler.

65

Now cook!

1. Combine ginger, garlic, soya sauce, onion, lemon juice and honey. Season with salt and pepper. Place meat in marinade and refrigerate overnight.
2. Place cubes of marinated lamb on 6 skewers, lay on a broiler rack and broil 5 minutes on each side.
3. Remove flesh and core from a pineapple leaving whole pineapple shell. Cut flesh away from core and cut into 1-inch (2.5 cm) chunks. Refill pineapple and stick cooked kebabs into outer pineapple shell.

A special hint:

You can baste kebabs with marinade. If you do this, strain it and bring to a boil for one minute. Brush over meat 4 times during cooking. This is essential if you cook lamb on a barbecue.

You can give these kebabs a special lift by putting hickory sawdust on bottom of broiler tray. It smokes and gives a light "open air" flavor.

LABERSPIESSLI ZURI-HEGEL

For 2 servings, you will need:

1 lb (0.5 kg) calves liver
(cut one inch: 2.5 cm thick)
12 sage leaves
12 slices fat bacon*
10 oz (283 g) green beans

¼ lemon
Pinch nutmeg
Freshly ground salt
Freshly ground black pepper
Clarified butter*

First prepare:

Cut outer skin from liver and wash it thoroughly. Cut liver into 1 inch (2.5 cm) strips and then into 2-inch (5 cm) oblongs (you should have 12 pieces). Squeeze lemon. Trim and french green beans. Some metal skewers will be required.

Now cook!

1. Place a sage leaf on every oblong of liver. Season with salt and pepper. Wrap this in slice of bacon.

2. Make sure liver is completely covered with bacon.

3. Place six pieces on each skewer.

4. Put a pan on heat, pour in some clarified butter to just cover bottom and add filled skewers. Fry until bacon turns pink, 4 minutes on either side. Then place in warming oven on a plate.

5. Meanwhile cover bottom of another pan with clarified butter about ¼ inch (7 mm) deep. Season generously with salt and pepper and pinch of nutmeg.

6. Add green beans and lemon juice, cover and simmer on low heat and let them cook in their own juices until tender.

7. Remove liver from warming oven and place skewers on a serving platter. Drain beans and put them on a vegetable dish.

A special hint:

Cook bacon until just pink so liver won't be overcooked.

1. LABERSPIESSLI ZURI-HEGEL is the most difficult thing about this simple dish.

2. Calf's liver is first trimmed and then sliced into 1-inch thick slices.

3. All heavy skin or glands are removed. The meat is then cut into cubes.

4. Use fatty bacon strips with rind off. Lay liver on and top with a piece of sage.

5. Roll up each parcel.

6. Skewer carefully to hold bacon in place (6 per skewer).

7. Cook in a large frypan (or they can also be broiled).

8. Turn when only *just* done—liver is never good when overcooked.

9. Serve with green beans seasoned with nutmeg, lemon juice and tossed in butter.

LA BROCHETTE DES CORSAIRES

For 4 servings, you will need:

1 lb (0.5 kg) halibut
  (or large close grained fish)
12 scallops
12 raw shrimp (medium size)
4 fl oz (1.2 dl) light oil
¼ tsp thyme
¼ tsp rosemary
¼ tsp marjoram
Freshly ground salt
Freshly ground white pepper
Savory rice:
Clarified butter*

1 medium onion
1 medium red pepper (capsicum)
1 medium green pepper
  (capsicum)
2 oz (56 g) peas
8 oz (227 g) long grain rice
12 fl oz (3.2 dl) fish stock
1 eggplant
1 zucchini
2 tomatoes

First prepare:

Stock: Pour 16 fl oz (4 dl) of salted water into a pan and heat. Wash peppers, slice off tops and bottoms, seed and add to water. Wash eggplant, slice it in half and remove seedy center and add this to water. Wash halibut and remove bones. Add these to pan. The shells from fresh shrimp will also enhance stock. Bring these "throw aways" to a boil and then let them bubble away for 15 minutes. Strain through a sieve and there you have a simple fish stock made up from pieces normally thrown away.

Rice: Slice onion, finely dice peppers, zucchini, tomatoes and eggplant. Preheat oven to 400ºF (205ºC).

Fish: Cut halibut into large cubes, leave shrimp and scallops whole. Pour oil into a small pan and add herbs, place on low heat and allow these Provençale herbs to infuse for 10 minutes. Preheat broiler, warm a serving platter.

Now cook!

1. To strained stock in a pan add shrimp and scallops and allow to poach gently.
2. Bring to boiling point, strain stock from poached seafood and reserve stock.
3. Place cubes of raw fish on skewers. Then cooked shrimp and scallops. Repeat three times on each skewer.
4. Strain herbs from oil and keep oil.
5. Having arranged fish, cover it and keep ready for use. You can now go ahead with rice.
6. Pour some clarified butter to just cover bottom in a large heated casserole and add eggplant, onion, red and green peppers and rice. Stir all ingredients together, increase heat and shallow fry for one minute.
7. Pour into rice 12 fl oz (3.2 dl) of the prepared fish stock and add zucchini, tomatoes and peas. Place in an oven preheated to 400ºF (205ºC) for 20 minutes.
8. Brush broiler rack with "herbed" oil.
9. Place individual skewers on broiler rack and paint them with seasoned oil.
10. Pop rack under broiler for 3 minutes approximately 3 inches (7.6 cm) from heat. Turn skewers and cook on other side for a further 3 minutes.
11. Remove cooked rice from oven and arrange broiled fish over top. Serve at once.

PORK TEKO TEKO

For 4 servings, you will need:

4 slices pork tenderloin each
    6 oz (170 g)
8 bacon slices
2 fl oz (5.6 cl) olive oil
Freshly ground white pepper
10 fl oz (3 dl) mushroom sauce
Sauce:
1 small onion
1 tbs clarified butter*
2 fl oz (5.6 cl) dry white wine

Juice ½ lemon
4 oz (113 g) mushrooms
Sprig parsley
2 tbs arrowroot
10 fl oz (3 dl) water
Meat concentrate to season
Lemon
Parsley
Cayenne pepper

64

First prepare:

Trim excess fat from pork fillets. Finely dice onion. Finely chop mushroom stalks. Slice mushroom caps finely. Squeeze lemon juice. Preheat broiler.

Now cook!

1. Place a skewer down center of pork fillets from thick end. Season meat with white pepper and wrap with strips of bacon like a papoose. Brush bacon with oil and place under broiler. Cook about 8 minutes on either side. Turn once.

2. *Sauce:* Melt butter in saucepan and fry onion over low heat until tender. Add mushroom stalks to onion.

3. Mix arrowroot with white wine. Stir mixture and hot water and meat concentrate into saucepan. Bring to a boil and stir until thickened. Add sliced mushrooms, squeeze of lemon juice and cayenne pepper all at last moment.

4. Dust with parsley and serve.

A special hint:

The Teko Teko can be slid from skewer, sliced into medallions and served in sauce.

*Refined sugar and refined flour are,
in my opinion, the greatest
food threat to the health of mankind.*

SATEH

For 4 servings, you will need:

5 oz (142 g) chicken breast
5 oz (142 g) veal tenderloin
5 oz (142 g) pork tenderloin
2 cloves garlic
2 tsp djawa (curry powder)*
1 tsp ketoembar (coriander)*
2 tsp ketjap (spiced soya bean
    sauce)*
1 lemon
1 small onion
Freshly ground salt
Freshly ground black pepper

Clarified butter*
Katjaug sauce:
2 cloves garlic
1 medium onion
1 tsp kentjoer (ground spices)*
½ tsp trassie (shrimp sauce)*
1 tsp goela djawa (brown sugar)*
4 oz (113 g) peanut butter
2 fl oz (5.6 cl) coconut milk
4 fl oz (1.2 dl) water
Freshly ground salt
Sambal oelek (very hot chili pickle)*

First prepare:

Meats: Cut all meat into ½-inch (1.2 cm) cubes. Leave skin on chicken. Place in a large bowl. Smash garlic, measure dry ingredients, squeeze juice from ½ lemon, finely slice onions.

Sauce: Measure dry ingredients. Break coconut and drain off milk. Measure peanut butter, finely slice onion. Preheat broiler. Thin wooden skewers will be required.

Now cook!

1. Into a bowl place garlic, djawa, ketoembar, juice of lemon, ketjap and stir together thoroughly. Season with salt and pepper. Add onion. Pour this marinade over meats and allow to soak for 1 hour.

2. After this period, drain pieces of meat and chicken and dry with a paper towel. Place each meat type on wooden skewers alternately and brush with clarified butter to keep them moist.

3. Place skewers on pan 4 inches (10 cm) away from preheated broiler and broil for 6 minutes on one side.

4. Quickly make sauce.

5. Pour some clarified butter to just cover bottom in a heated saucepan and shallow fry onion and garlic.

6. To this add kentjoer, trassie and goela djawa. Season with salt and sambal oelek, increase heat and add peanut butter. Stir briskly and remove sauce from heat.

7. Turn meat on skewers and broil another 4 minutes.

8. Return sauce to low heat, stir in coconut milk and water. Reheat until bubbly. Remove from heat.

9. Take skewered meat from broiler, drain off juice and add to sauce in pan. Pour sauce into sauceboat and serve at once piping hot.

A special hint:

The peanut sauce has to be made at the very last moment. It can, with ease, separate if kept on a low heat.

Sateh

67

SEAFOOD CREPES WATSONS BAY

For 4 large servings, you will need:

4 crepes 10 inch (25 cm)
40 fl oz (1.2 l) white sauce made
    with 50% fish stock
4 fl oz (1.2 dl) dry white wine
1 lb (0.5 kg) peeled raw shrimp
2 dozen oysters
2 fl oz (5.6 cl) Pernod
4 tbs clarified butter*
2 oz (56 g) sharp Cheddar cheese
2 lemons
Parsley
Cayenne pepper
Freshly ground salt
Freshly ground pepper
Crepes:
8 oz (227 g) all-purpose flour
1 pinch freshly ground salt

Freshly ground white pepper
1 egg
1 egg yolk
5 fl oz (1.5 dl) milk
5 fl oz (1.5 dl) fish stock
2 oz (56 g) butter
Sauce:
16 fl oz (4 dl) fish stock
16 fl oz (4 dl) milk
4 oz (113 g) butter
5 oz (142 g) all-purpose flour
Freshly ground white pepper
Freshly ground salt
Bouquet garni (1 clove, 1 tbs
    chopped onion, 1 bay leaf,
    2 parsley stalks*)

First prepare:

Grate cheese. Cut lemon into wedges. Finely chop parsley. Warm Pernod. Heat broiler.

Crepes: Sift dry ingredients together. Place in a bowl, make well in center and add eggs and milk and fish stock. Beat with a whisk until smooth. Whisk in cooled melted butter. Cover and leave for 4 hours.

Sauce: Place butter in saucepan and when melted stir in flour. Stir over low heat for 2 minutes. Gradually add milk and fish stock. Whisk over low heat until sauce is smooth and thick. Season with salt and pepper. Add bouquet garni. Cook over a very low heat for 30 minutes stirring occasionally. Remove herbs and season again to taste with salt and pepper.

Now cook!

1. Heat sauce gently and stir in white wine.

2. Melt clarified butter in frypan and add raw shrimp. Toss until colored pink. Season with salt and pepper. Add Pernod and set alight. Add enough sauce to bind shrimp.

3. Heat a small quantity of butter in 10-inch (25 cm) omelet pan, turn pan around to grease surface and pour off surplus butter. Add a small amount of batter and revolve pan until batter covers bottom. Cook until waxy bubbles form on surface and then loosen crepe and remove from pan. Repeat, oiling surface of omelet pan before making each crepe.

4. Lay crepes on a warmed serving dish, place shrimp in center of crepe with 6 oysters. Fold over either side and turn the whole crepe upside down so as to conceal the join. Lay crepes on dish with ¼ inch (7 mm) in between each. Cover crepes with remaining sauce. Dust surface with cheese and place under a broiler to brown lightly.

5. Dust with cayenne pepper and chopped parsley.

CREPES FRUITS DE MER

For 4 large servings, you will need:

4 crepes (10 inches: 25 cm) in
   diameter
30 fl oz (9 dl) white sauce
4 fl oz (1.2 dl) dry white wine
1½ lb (680 g) flounder or sole
   (filleted and skinned)
4 tbs clarified butter*
12 oysters
1 small lobster about 1½ lbs
2 fl oz (5.6 cl) brandy
6 oz (170 g) all-purpose flour

1 lb (0.5 kg) mushrooms
1 lb (0.5 kg) tomatoes
8 oz (227 g) cooked, shelled
   and deveined shrimp
2 tbs Parmesan cheese
2 lemons
Freshly ground salt
Freshly ground pepper
Parsley
Cayenne pepper
Clarified butter*

First prepare:

Make white sauce. Make crepes. Measure and warm white wine. Cut flounder into 2 inches x 1 inch (5 cm x 2.5 cm) fingers. Cut oysters in half. Shell lobster. Cut lobster into 1-inch (2.5 cm) pieces. Finely chop parsley. Warm brandy. Season flour with salt and pepper. Slice mushrooms finely. Skin, peel, seed and chop tomatoes. Grate cheese.

Now cook!

1. Heat white sauce and stir in wine. Flour flounder fingers and shake off excess flour.

2. Heat clarified butter in large pan, add floured fish, then add lobster, tomatoes and oysters. Toss gently in butter, moving foods to one side of pan. Pour over warmed brandy and light. Stir seafood into flames. Pour over white sauce to douse flames. Add shrimp.

3. In a separate pan heat some clarified butter to just cover bottom and cook mushrooms with lemon juice and pinch of cayenne until wilted. Stir into seafood in sauce.

4. Lay crepes on warmed heatproof serving dish, place a large tablespoonful of seafood mixture in center. Fold over either side and turn whole filled crepes upside down. Continue in this manner until all crepes are filled.

5. Add 1 tbs of cheese to remaining sauce, spoon sauce over crepes, dust surface with remaining cheese and place under broiler to brown. Serve dusted with cayenne pepper and finely chopped parsley. Serve accompanied by lemon wedges.

A special hint:

You can prepare crepes up to their filled and folded stage (Step 4). Cover them with buttered paper and keep 12 hours maximum under refrigeration. Reheat in oven set at 350°F (177°C) for 15 minutes. Cover with hot sauce (Step 5) and brown under broiler.

LES CREPES D'OR

For 2 servings, you will need:

2 large chicken breasts
3 tsp caviar**
4 slices prosciutto ham*
1 tsp dried tarragon
3 oz (85 g) Parmesan cheese
16 fl oz (4 dl) chicken stock
1½ oz (42 g) butter
1½ oz (42 g) all-purpose flour
2 tsp chives

Batter:
1 egg
1 egg yolk
10 fl oz (3 dl) milk
1 oz (28 g) butter
1 oz (28 g) all-purpose flour
Clarified butter*
Freshly ground salt
Freshly ground white pepper

**Best caviar buy for the money is USSR Malassol, about $5 per 1 oz (28 g) jar!! If this is too high, then leave it out; the dish is still excellent.

First prepare:

The batter: Sift flour and measure milk. Combine all dry ingredients. Add eggs and milk gradually, beating all the time. Season with salt and white pepper. Set aside in a cool place for 4 hours.

Remove chicken breasts carefully from bone (keep bones for chicken stock). Measure caviar, tarragon, chicken stock, butter, flour, chives and finely grate cheese. Heat a serving platter in warm oven. Preheat broiler.

Now cook!

1. Put butter into a heated saucepan and melt over moderate heat. Stir in flour and cook for 3 minutes, stirring constantly.

2. To butter and flour base gradually stir in chicken stock. Stir and bring to a boil. Cook for 3 minutes, reducing heat to a gentle simmer. A delicious velouté sauce!

3. Pour a little clarified butter into a frypan to just cover bottom over a moderate heat and lay two breasts of chicken into it. Sprinkle dried tarragon leaves over them (after rubbing herb between palms of hands).

4. Season generously with salt and white pepper.

5. Turn breasts over and reduce heat.

6. Place 1 oz (28 g) butter into an omelet pan and melt, stirring melted butter into prepared crepe batter.

7. Make a fairly heavy crepe and scatter ½ oz (14 g) grated cheese over uncooked side, place under broiler for a moment to brown top. Repeat and prepare a second crepe.

8. Stir sauce. Cook breasts thoroughly; it takes about 4 minutes each side.

9. Slide 2 cooked crepes onto warmed serving platter.

10. Lay breast of chicken on cheese side of each crepe, cover with 2 slices prosciutto ham and fold to form a semicircle. Repeat with the other portion of chicken and prosciutto and place them side by side.

11. Stir 1 oz (28 g) cheese into sauce and pour over stuffed crepes. Sprinkle remaining 1 oz (28 g) cheese over top and place under broiler for 2 minutes.

12. Sprinkle with chives and garnish with caviar.

1. LES CREPES D'OR can be garnished with caviar.

2. Add rubbed herbs to chicken breasts; cover and cook slowly.

3. Butter omelet pan and add butter to pancake batter.

4. Wipe the pan to distribute the butter evenly.

5. Beat batter to mix butter evenly for *self-buttering* pancakes.

6. Roll the batter around but not up the pan sides.

7. For thin pancakes turn with spatula. A quick twist does it!

8. Grate cheese on uncooked side; slide onto a shallow dish.

9. Broil cheese until light brown. Make one per person.

10. Place chicken covered with proscuitto on pancake and fold it.

11. Cover the filled pancakes with a good coating of sauce.

12. Grate cheese over sauce, broil until light gold. Garnish.

LE BLINET DE SAUMON FUMEE

For 2 servings, you will need:

Batter:
4 oz (113 g) all-purpose flour
1 egg
1 egg yolk
10 fl oz (3 dl) milk
2 oz (56 g) butter
Pinch freshly ground salt

Filling:
Freshly ground white pepper
¼ lemon
4 fl oz (1.2 dl) heavy cream
Chopped parsley
4 oz (113 g) smoked salmon

First prepare:

Batter: Sift flour into a bowl and make a well in center. Add whole egg, plus yolk and blend thoroughly. Add milk. Cover and allow to stand for 4 hours. Place serving dish in oven to warm. Heat oven to 400°F (205°C).

Now cook!

1. Melt butter in a heated 10-inch (25 cm) omelet pan and stir butter into batter mixture.
2. Return pan to heat and add batter rotating pan to cover bottom evenly.
3. Cook until waxen in appearance.
4. Loosen from side of pan with spatula, flip over and cook on other side.
5. Remove serving dish from oven and butter well to prevent crepes from sticking.
6. Slip crepe onto dish.
7. Make second crepe and set aside.
8. Cover first crepe with thinly sliced smoked salmon and pop second crepe on top.
9. Pour cream over crepes and squeeze lemon over top.
10. Sprinkle with white pepper and a pinch of salt. Shake dish so that seasoned cream covers crepe "sandwich."
11. Put dish in a heated oven for 3 minutes.
12. Garnish with chopped parsley liberally sprinkled over top and serve at once.

CREPE NONATS

70

For 4 servings, you will need:

Batter:
Ingredients as above recipe
Filling:
8 oz (227 g) whitebait or canned
   tuna fish
1½ oz (42 g) butter
1½ oz (42 g) all-purpose flour
4 oz (113 g) mushrooms
½ lemon

1 medium tomato
6 fl oz (1.6 dl) heavy cream
2 oz (56 g) Parmesan cheese
1 fl oz (2.8 cl) dry sherry
10 fl oz (3 dl) fish stock
Flour
Clarified butter*
Freshly ground white pepper
Deep fat

First prepare:

Make crepe batter as above recipe. Measure fish stock, heavy cream and sherry. Squeeze juice from half lemon. Skin, core and seed tomato, roughly chop flesh. Grate cheese. Finely slice mushrooms. A deep fat fryer will be required, set at 400°F (205°C). Preheat broiler. Heat a serving platter.

Now cook!

1. Make 4 crepes as in recipe above and keep them warm.
2. Melt butter in a heated pan and stir in flour. Cook for 3 minutes but don't allow it to color.

3. Slowly stir in 5 fl oz (1.5 dl) fish stock and continue cooking over moderate heat. Gradually stir in remaining 5 fl oz (1.5 dl) of fish stock and bring to boil. Reduce heat and allow sauce to simmer gently. Season generously with salt and pepper. Stir occasionally.

4. Stir in heavy cream and cheese. Stir thoroughly to melt cheese. Stir in sherry.

5. Pour enough clarified butter to just cover bottom into a frypan and allow mushrooms to fry gently. Pour lemon juice over and season with salt and white pepper.

6. Add tomato to mushrooms and simmer gently.

7. Stir tomato and mushrooms into sauce.

8. Cover whitebait or tuna fish with about 4 fl oz (1.2 dl) of hot sauce.

9. Place a crepe on a serving dish. Arrange 2 oz (56 g) of the sauced whitebait in center and roll up. Repeat with other three crepes.

10. Spoon remaining sauce over them.

11. Place under broiler for 2 minutes 6 inches (15 cm) away from heat.

12. Serve at once when browned.

CREPES ANTONIN CAREME

For 8 servings, you will need:

1 chicken, 3½ lb (1.6 kg)
   (or boiling fowl)
1 onion
1 medium carrot
Clarified butter*
8 oz (227 g) celery
4 oz (113 g) all-purpose flour
20 fl oz (6 dl) milk
Freshly ground salt
Freshly ground white pepper
Nutmeg
4 fl oz (1.2 dl) dry white wine

4 oz (113 g) butter
20 fl oz (6 dl) reduced
   chicken stock
4 tbs grated Parmesan cheese
Cayenne pepper
Parsley

Crepe batter:
4 oz (113 g) all-purpose flour
1 whole egg plus 1 egg yolk
10 fl oz (3 dl) milk
Freshly ground salt
½ oz (14 g) butter

First prepare:

Make crepe batter by placing flour in a bowl, make a well in center and add egg and yolk, salt and milk. Whisk to form a smooth batter. Allow to stand 4 hours. Chop onion and carrot roughly. Measure butter, flour, milk and wine. Preheat broiler. Cut celery finely and place in salted boiling water. Poach 5 minutes and drain.

Now cook!

1. Place clarified butter to just cover bottom into a casserole dish on heat and add carrot and onion. Allow to fry until golden and then add chicken. Cover and allow to steam 10 minutes. Then add cold water to cover, bring to a boil and simmer covered 1¼ hours or until tender. Remove chicken, skin and bone and cut into small pieces. Reduce chicken stock to 20 fl oz (6 dl). Strain and reserve.

2. Make crepes by placing 1 tbs of butter in 8-inch (20 cm) crepe pan and when melted stir into crepe batter. Place a small ladle of batter into pan and roll it around so that it covers bottom evenly. Cook until waxy bubbles appear on surface and then turn pancake with a spatula and cook on other side. Remove to a plate and continue until 8 crepes are made.

3. Melt butter in a pan and stir in flour to form a roux. Whisk in milk gradually to make a thick sauce. Season with salt, pepper and nutmeg. Stir in wine and allow sauce to simmer 10 minutes. Stir in chicken stock and simmer sauce 5 minutes longer.

4. Add poached celery to diced chicken and mix with 16 fl oz (4 dl) of the sauce.

5. Stir 3 tbs of cheese into remaining sauce.

6. Lay crepes on an ovenproof dish, place a heaped tbs of the celery and chicken mixture in center of each crepe. Fold and turn over. Spoon cheese sauce over crepes. Sprinkle with remaining cheese and slide under broiler to brown (5 minutes).

7. Serve sprinkled with cayenne pepper and garnished with finely chopped parsley.

Service:

I use this dish more than any other when I give informal parties. I make the dish up to Step 6 and stop when crepes are filled. I then cover the crepes with plastic film and set entire platter in refrigerator. When times comes to serve, platter goes into oven 300°F (149°C) for 15 minutes. The sauce is heated and then poured over heated pancakes and finished under broiler as before. Twenty minutes and you are ready to eat!

Crepes Antonin Carême

DIMITRI'S CREPINETTES WOLLAHRA

For 4 servings, you will need:

1½ lbs (680 g) spinach
2 oz (56 g) parsley
2 oz (56 g) dill
4 spring onions*
20 fl oz (6 dl) béchamel sauce
1 tbs dry sherry
24 oysters
1 small onion
8 oz (227 g) feta cheese
2 eggs
Freshly ground salt
Freshly ground white pepper
Parmesan cheese
4 crepes
Juice of 1 lemon

Clarified butter*
Crepes:
8 oz (227 g) all-purpose flour
1 egg plus 1 egg yolk
14 fl oz (3.4 dl) milk
1 tsp freshly ground salt
1 tbs butter
Béchamel sauce:
2 oz (56 g) butter
20 fl oz (6 dl) milk
2 tbs all-purpose flour
Freshly ground salt
Freshly ground white pepper
Nutmeg

First prepare:

Slice spinach (after discarding root ends and stalks) into 1-inch (2.5 cm) strips and season with salt and pepper. Finely chop onion. Finely chop spring onions, parsley and dill. Juice lemon. Roughly break up cheese. Make béchamel sauce and add sherry. Pre-heat broiler.

Béchamel sauce: Heat butter until melted, stir in flour to form a roux. Heat milk and gradually stir into roux. Cook while stirring over low heat until sauce thickens. Season with salt, pepper and nutmeg. Cook gently for 12 minutes, stirring from time to time.

Now cook!

1. *Crepes:* Place flour into a bowl with salt, make a well in center and add egg and yolk and milk, whisking until smooth. Allow to stand 2 hours.

2. Heat butter in 10-inch (25 cm) crepe pan and when just melted, stir into crepe batter. Place a ladleful of mixture into pan on high heat and roll around pan to cover bottom thinly. Place back on heat and cook until tiny bubbles appear on surface. Flip over with spatula and cook on other side. Remove to a dish and continue as before until all batter is used.

3. *Filling:* Place clarified butter to just cover bottom into a deep casserole dish and when hot add onion. Sauté until golden and then add spinach, dill, spring onions and parsley. Season with salt and pepper. Cover and allow to cook for 2 minutes. Drain spinach and press out surplus water.

4. Stir pressed spinach into 8 fl oz (2 dl) béchamel sauce. Allow to cool for a few minutes. Beat crumbled feta cheese with eggs and stir into spinach mixture along with lemon juice.

5. Place crepes on a large ovenproof dish and put 6 oysters on each. Add a large spoonful of spinach mixture and roll crepes. Cover crepes with remaining béchamel sauce and sprinkle with Parmesan cheese. Brown under broiler.

PANNEQUETS

For 2 servings, you will need:

Beer Batter:
2 eggs
2 oz (56 g) all-purpose flour
2 fl oz (5.6 cl) beer

White Sauce:
1 oz (28 g) butter
1 oz (28 g) all-purpose flour
6 fl oz (1.6 dl) milk
½ oz (14 g) onion
2 parsley stalks❋
1 bay leaf
Pinch of mace

Filling:
7 oz (198 g) Camembert cheese
1 tsp dry mustard

Pancake Batter:
4 oz (113 g) all-purpose flour
1 egg yolk
1 whole egg
10 fl oz (3 dl) milk
1 oz (28 g) butter
Freshly ground salt
Freshly ground white pepper

First prepare:

The Batter: Pour measured beer into a bowl and allow to flatten. Sift flour into another bowl.

White Sauce: Measure milk. Sift flour, weigh butter, finely chop onion, wash parsley.

Filling: Measure mustard, cube and chill cheese.

Pancakes: Sift flour, measure milk, melt butter and cool slightly. Set aside yolk and whole egg.

Now cook!

1. *Commence with Beer Batter:* Beat two eggs until light and frothy. Add a pinch of salt. Sprinkle in flour, add beer and beat until no lumps show. Set aside mixture for 2 hours. (Helps to break down the raw "flour" taste and allows air bubbles to rise to surface.)

2. *The Pancake Batter:* Combine dry ingredients in a bowl and make a well in the center. Add egg, egg yolk and milk gradually, beating all the time. Beat well and set aside in a cool place for 2 hours.

3. Make white sauce by melting butter in pot. Remove from heat and stir in flour. Return to low heat to cook for 5 minutes without browning. Again remove from heat and gradually stir in milk. Add bay leaf, onion, mace and parsley stalks. Increase heat and stir sauce until it thickens. Boil for 3 minutes stirring constantly. Cool. Remove herbs when sauce is used.

4. Put 1 oz (28 g) butter into a 7-inch omelet pan and melt. Add this to prepared pancake batter and beat well. Return pan to heat and lightly cover greased surface with a thin layer of batter. Loosen from sides of the pan with a palette knife. When underside is brown, flip over and cook other side. Continue making pancakes until you have 4 ready. Cool.

5. Add 3 fl oz (8 cl) of the white sauce to half the beer and egg batter. Add all cubed chilled Camembert and mustard. Cream well together.

6. Take ¼ of this mixture and place on a chilled pancake, fold in the sides and then roll up like a small package.

7. Heat oil in a deep fryer to 375⁰F (190⁰C).

8. Place little packages one at a time in a wire basket and lower into hot oil. Cook until golden brown—about 4 minutes.

9. Lift out, drain on a paper towel and place on serving platter. Serve at once.

CREPES FARCI COLONY

For 4 servings, you will need:

Curry sauce:
1 medium onion
1 tbs clarified butter*
3 tsp curry powder (hot Madras)
1 large clove garlic
2 tsp flour
8 fl oz (2 dl) coconut stock

Mustard sauce:
2 oz (56 g) butter
1½ oz (42 g) all-purpose flour
10 fl oz (3 dl) chicken stock
4 tsp dry mustard

1 tbs milk
Filling:
8 oz (227 g) raw, shelled and
    deveined shrimp
2 tbs clarified butter*
1 tsp lemon juice
6 oz (170 g) Alaskan king crab
8 crepes (see page 322)
1 fl oz (2.8 cl) milk
Freshly ground white pepper
Freshly ground salt

First prepare:

Curry sauce: Finely slice onion, lightly bruise garlic (keep it in one piece), measure curry powder, make coconut stock.
Mustard sauce: Measure butter and flour, make chicken stock. Mix mustard and milk.
Filling: Weigh shrimp and chop them finely, squeeze lemon, weigh crab. Make crepes. Measure milk.

Now cook!

1. *Curry sauce:* Into a hot frypan add clarified butter, onion and curry powder. Stir and allow to cook gently over low heat.

2. Stir garlic and 2 tsp flour into curry mixture. Let cook for 4 minutes over low heat.

3. Stir coconut stock into curry mixture. Let "sauce" cook away for 5 minutes at low heat.

4. *Mustard sauce:* Mix 2 oz (56 g) butter with 1½ oz (42 g) flour in a small saucepan over moderate heat to form a roux. Cook this for 4 minutes. Stir all the time, do not brown.

5. Stir chicken stock into mustard sauce roux until "lumpless." Gradually stir in mustard and milk mixture. Stir for 5 minutes over low heat.

6. *Filling:* Place clarified butter into a small frypan and add chopped shrimp. Season with salt and white pepper and lemon juice. Fry at medium heat for 3 minutes.

7. After 3 minutes, flake crab over shrimp and let it heat through. Do not overcook.

8. Stir butter and juices from shrimp and crab into curry sauce. Strain curry sauce through a fine wire sieve pressing through onion pulp. Keep it warm.

9. Stir half the mustard sauce into shrimp and crab to bind. Place 2 tbs of mixture on each crepe and roll up.

10. Serve two crepes side-by-side per portion. Cover crepes with alternating "bands" of remaining mustard and curry sauce.

A special hint:

Step 7. Never (or very seldom) allow cooked (as is the crab) shellfish to do anything other than warm up. Too much heat and shellfish toughens.

Lamb in Coconut Milk (Kuzhambu) (page 329)

CRAB KOFTA CURRY

For 4 servings, you will need:

1 lb (0.5 kg) canned crabmeat
3 tbs parsley
4 cloves garlic
¼ oz (7 g) fresh ginger root*
2 red chilis
1 egg
1 tsp turmeric
½ tsp garam marsala*
All-purpose flour

Sauce:
2 tbs clarified butter*
6 cloves garlic

¼ oz (7 g) fresh ginger root*
½ small onion
1 tbs ground coriander
2 tsp cumin
1 tsp turmeric
16 fl oz (4 dl) chicken stock
1 chili
Freshly ground salt
1 oz (28 g) coconut cream
Juice ½ lemon
Oil to deep fry

First prepare:

Finely chop parsley, green ginger and chilis. Smash garlic. Place crabmeat with parsley, ginger, chilis and garlic through fine blade of a grinder. Stir in beaten egg, turmeric, garam marsala. Mix thoroughly and shape into 12 balls. Lightly flour balls. Preheat oil to 350ºF (177ºC). To prepare coconut cream, grate a fresh coconut (with rind removed). Place grated coconut into cheesecloth and squeeze out all liquid.

Sauce: Smash garlic, finely slice and chop ginger. Finely dice onion. Measure chicken stock and juice lemon.

Now cook!

1. Place clarified butter into a frypan and add 6 cloves of garlic and ginger. Allow to fry very gently, do not allow to brown. Add onions, coriander, cumin and turmeric and allow spices to fry for 1 minute. Add chicken stock, chili and salt. Cover pan and cook very gently for 20 minutes.

2. Stir lemon juice and coconut cream into curry sauce.

3. Place crab balls into a frying basket and deep fry for 3 minutes. Shake basket from time to time to prevent sticking. Remove and drain on absorbent paper.

4. Place crab balls into a shallow serving dish and cover with sauce.

A special hint:

The sauce is very strong on coconut. I suggest you add half the quantity, taste and then add the rest according to your personal liking.

LAMB IN COCONUT MILK (KUZHAMBU)

For 6 servings, you will need:

1 tbs clarified butter*
1 medium onion
1 tsp paprika
2 tsp ground coriander
1 tsp ground cumin
½ tsp ground fenugreek*
½ tsp freshly ground black pepper
1 tbs ground poppy seed
2 lbs (0.9 kg) lamb (shoulder
   meat is best, all fat cut off)
4 fl oz (1.2 dl) coconut cream

16 fl oz (4 dl) coconut stock
2 oz (56 g) chopped parsley
1 tsp ground cardamon
2 fl oz (5.6 cl) lemon juice
9 oz (255 g) coconut meat or
   dried unsweetened coconut
10 fl oz (3 dl) water (for cream)
20 fl oz (6 dl) water (for stock)
2 feet (60 cm) of muslin or
   cheesecloth

First prepare:

Measure spices. Finely slice onion. Finely chop parsley. Squeeze lemon juice. Cut lamb into 1-inch (2.5 cm) cubes and dry well. If using fresh coconut, grate meat finely, or measure dried. Measure water for cream and stock, measure muslin.

Coconut cream: Boil 10 fl oz (3 dl) water and pour over coconut. Cover tightly and allow to infuse (like tea) for 30 minutes. Pour entire contents into muslin and squeeze out moisture. This is cream.

Stock: Boil 20 fl oz (6 dl) of water and pour over squeezed coconut used to make the cream. Cover tightly and infuse again for 30 minutes. Strain and squeeze through muslin. This makes stock.

Now cook!

1. Place clarified butter into a pan on heat and fry onions until softened. Then remove three-quarters of onion. Allow onion remaining in pan to fry until crisp. Stir in paprika, coriander, cumin, fenugreek, pepper and poppy seeds. Allow onions and spices to fry gently for 4 minutes.

2. Add lamb to pan and brown all over. Pour over coconut stock and reduce heat. Cover and allow meat to simmer for 30 minutes.

3. Stir in coconut cream and simmer uncovered for 30 minutes more. Remove from heat and stir in parsley, cardamon and lemon juice.

Service:

Serve with following side dishes: pappadums,* cashew nuts, finely cubed cucumber with sliced garlic in yogurt. Bananas with lemon juice and dried coconut. Mango chutney or various Indian pickles, sliced tomatoes and onion slices.

A special hint:

If you have time make curry a day before you plan to serve it. Refrigerate. Flavors blend in this time and are more mellow on reheating.

GORDON'S SEAFOOD CURRY

For 4 servings, you will need:

12 oz (340 g) raw, shelled and deveined
    jumbo shrimp
6 oz (170 g) crab meat
5 medium onions
2 tomatoes
4 cloves garlic
1 cucumber
4 oz (113 g) preserved ginger
8 tbs clarified butter*
24 fl oz (7 dl) coconut milk
1 tbs lemon juice
2 tbs all-purpose flour

Curry paste:
1 tbs curry powder
2 tsp ground ginger
1 tbs turmeric
2 tsp ground cumin
2 tsp ground coriander
2 tsp ground fennel
2 tsp freshly ground salt
4 fl oz (1.2 dl) peanut oil
Coconut milk:
8 oz (227 g) dried unsweetened
    coconut
24 fl oz (7 dl) water

First prepare:

Cut shrimp and crab meat into cubes. Cut onions finely. Skin and chop tomatoes. Peel and smash garlic. Cut cucumber into ¼-inch (7 mm) cubes with seeds removed. Cut preserved ginger into ¼-inch (7 mm) cubes. Squeeze lemon. Measure flour. Prepare curry paste by mixing all ingredients together with peanut oil. Make coconut milk by pouring the 24 fl oz (7 dl) boiling water over coconut. Allow to infuse for 20 minutes and then strain through muslin squeezing out all liquid.

Now cook!

1. Heat butter and sauté onions, cucumber, tomatoes, ginger and garlic for approximately ten minutes.
2. Stir in curry paste. Cook for ten minutes more, covered.
3. Stir in flour. Gradually stir in coconut milk and lemon juice. Stir over low heat until thickened.
4. Stir in seafood and cook gently for five minutes.

Service:

Serve with boiled rice, mango chutney and pappadums.*

MALAY CUCUMBER CURRY

For 4 servings, you will need:

4 tbs clarified butter*
1 medium onion
4 cloves garlic
4 cucumbers
2 tsp turmeric
1 tsp hot chili powder
2 cinnamon sticks 1 inch each (2.5 cm)
½ tsp cardamon
6 cloves
½ tsp ground ginger

Freshly ground salt
2 lbs (0.9 kg) shelled and deveined
 raw jumbo shrimp
12 inch (30 cm) lemon grass*
16 fl oz (4 dl) coconut stock
3 tsp arrowroot
Coconut stock:
4 oz (113 g) dried unsweetened
 coconut
20 fl oz (6 dl) water

First prepare:

Finely dice onion. Smash garlic. Peel cucumbers and cut into ½-inch (1.2 cm) slices. Soak in cold water for 1 hour and drain. Remove sand tract from shrimp. Smash cloves.

Coconut stock: Place coconut in a bowl, add boiling water, cover and allow coconut and water to infuse. Allow to stand for 30 minutes. Strain through muslin squeezing out all liquid.

Now cook!

1. Place clarified butter into a large frypan and fry onion and garlic until soft but not colored. When onions are soft stir in turmeric, cinnamon sticks, cardamon, cloves, chili powder, ginger and salt. Allow spices to fry for 1 minute and then add shrimp. Toss shrimp in butter and allow to fry gently until they turn pink.

2. Stir in cucumber, lemon grass and coconut stock. Cover and allow to simmer for 5 minutes. Remove lid from frypan and allow curry to simmer for 15 minutes longer, stirring occasionally.

3. Remove cucumber and shrimp to a heated serving dish and keep warm. Remove lemon grass and cinnamon sticks and discard. Bring heat up under frypan and allow sauce to reduce for 10 minutes. Mix arrowroot with a little water and stir it into sauce, thickening it immediately. Put shrimp and cucumber back into curry sauce, allow to heat through and then place on serving dish.

Home is a place for friends you have no need to impress.
For the rest—there's always a restaurant.

65

GARNALEN AU CURRY

For 4 servings, you will need:

14 oz (396 g) fresh or frozen
   raw shrimp
3 tsp curry powder (Madras hot)
1 fl oz (2.8 cl) dry sherry
4 fl oz (1.2 dl) heavy cream
1 medium onion
1 fl oz (2.8 cl) brandy
1 tsp Worcestershire sauce
Clarified butter*
Curry rice salad:
12 oz (340 g) long grain rice

4 tbs mayonnaise
1 tbs heavy cream
3 tbs piccalilli (mustard pickles)
1 tsp Worcestershire sauce
5 cocktail gherkins
1 red pepper (capsicum)
1 green pepper (capsicum)
1 tsp curry powder (Madras hot)
64 fl oz (1.8 l) cold water
Freshly ground salt
Freshly ground white pepper

First prepare:

Rinse rice under running cold water. Boil cold water and add a pinch of salt. Slice onion very thinly. Measure curry powder, sherry, brandy, heavy cream, Worcestershire sauce, piccalilli. Chop gherkins into small pieces. Seed and finely dice half green pepper and half red pepper. Cut remaining halves of peppers into long thin strips for decoration. Heat a serving platter in warm oven. Long matches will be needed.

Now cook!

1. Pour rinsed rice into boiling salted water and cook for 10 minutes.
2. Pour a little clarified butter to just cover bottom into a heated frypan and add onion. Cook slowly until transparent (not brown). Stir in 3 tsp curry powder.
3. Cook shrimp gently with curry and onion in hot butter over low heat for 5 minutes.
4. Pour on brandy and light. Allow flame to die down. Add sherry and flame again (using long matches).
5. Stir in the heavy cream.
6. Stir in Worcestershire sauce and let shrimp mixture continue to simmer gently over low heat until ready to serve, about 5 minutes.
7. Drain rice and place in a sieve over hot water. Cover rice with a lid and allow to steam for 8 minutes.
8. Put fluffy white rice into a bowl, stir in piccalilli, gherkins, diced red and green pepper, mayonnaise, 1 tbs heavy cream, 1 tsp curry powder and Worcestershire sauce. Season with salt and white pepper. Stir well.
9. Spoon savory rice salad onto serving dish to form border.
10. Pour hot curried shrimp into center of dish and decorate rice border with the strips of red and green peppers and serve.

A special hint:

No matter what is written on the package you must pre-rinse all rice before it is boiled. Rinse until the water is absolutely clear.

KARE POAKA NO. 1

For 4 servings, you will need:

2 lbs (0.9 kg) pork (blade steak)
Freshly ground salt
Freshly ground black pepper
4 tbs clarified butter*
1 medium onion
1 tbs curry powder (mild)
4 oz (113 g) green pepper (capsicum)
1 bay leaf
1 clove garlic
1 tsp mustard seeds
Juice ½ lemon

1 tbs red currant jelly
10 fl oz (3 dl) coconut stock
2 fl oz (5.6 cl) ketchup
8 fl oz (2 dl) coconut cream
1 heaped tsp chili powder
Coconut stock and cream:
8 oz (227 g) dried unsweetened
    coconut
10 fl oz (3 dl) water (for cream)
20 fl oz (6 dl) water (for stock)
Muslin or cheesecloth

First prepare:

Remove fat from pork and cut into 1-inch (2.5 cm) cubes. Season with salt and pepper. Slice onion into 1-inch-wide (2.5 cm) rings. Cut pepper into 1-inch (2.5 cm) squares. Smash garlic. Squeeze lemon. Make coconut stock and cream. Combine tomato sauce with stock.

Coconut cream: Boil 10 fl oz (3 dl) of water. Pour over coconut in bowl. Cover and allow to infuse for 30 minutes. Place mixture in a piece of muslin and squeeze out all moisture; this is coconut cream.

Coconut stock: Boil 20 fl oz (6 dl) of water, pour over squeezed coconut. Place lid on top and infuse for 30 minutes. Squeeze out coconut stock through muslin.

Now cook!

1. Heat clarified butter in large saucepan, add meat and fry gently. Add onion and curry powder. Then add mustard seeds, green pepper (capsicum), bay leaf and garlic and continue to fry gently, stirring.

2. Pour in lemon juice, red currant jelly, tomato sauce and coconut stock. Simmer in open pot for 1½ hours. This is better made day before.

3. Skim off all fat and add 5 fl oz (1.5 dl) of coconut cream, reheat and pour off 2 fl oz (5.6 cl) of the sauce. Blend this sauce with chili powder and pour into small sauceboat. This extra hot sauce can be added by those who prefer "undemocratic curry."

A special hint:

Coconut cream can be purchased in cans (frozen) at good markets.

BEEF VINDALOO

For 4 servings, you will need:

2 lbs (0.9 kg) beef (chuck steak)
14 cloves garlic
4 fl oz (1.2 dl) red wine vinegar
4 hot chilies (small)
¼ tsp cumin seeds
¾ tsp turmeric
1 tsp English mustard
1 lemon
1 level tsp ground ginger
1¼ tsp freshly ground salt

2 oz (56 g) sugar
3 tbs poppy seeds
1 small onion
4 fl oz (1.2 dl) tomato paste
Clarified butter*
Freshly ground salt
Freshly ground black pepper
1 bay leaf
4 whole cloves

First prepare:

Cut beef into 1-inch (2.5 cm) cubes. Make a vinegar marinade: place garlic and red wine vinegar in a blender. Blend to a smooth paste. Cut off tops and bottoms from chilies and remove seeds (do not put your fingers near your eyes or they will become inflamed). Add peppers to blended paste. Add cumin seeds, turmeric, mustard, ginger, salt and sugar to blender. Remove peel from lemon, squeeze juice, discard seeds and chop inner pulp. Add lemon juice and seedless pulp to blender. Whirl until smooth. Place cubed beef in a bowl and pour blended mixture over it. Stir in poppy seeds and marinate for 2 hours. Finely slice onion. Measure tomato paste.

Now cook!

1. Pour enough clarified butter to cover bottom into a heated pan and add onions. Cook until translucent. Add bay leaf and cloves.
2. With a slotted spoon, lift meat from marinade and add to frying onions. Increase heat to brown meat quickly.
3. Pour in marinade.
4. Cover tightly, reduce heat and simmer for 1 hour.
5. After 1 hour stir in tomato paste and cook covered for another 30 minutes.
6. When meat is tender season and serve at once piping hot with sauce poured over.

A special hint:

When using very hot chilies it is a help to remove the seeds and the placenta (the inside fleshy membrane). This contains capsaicin—an ether—a soluble reddish oil that can cause inflammation if you eat too much.

Rijstaffel dishes from bottom left counterclockwise: Roedjak Manis (page 338), Sambal Goreng Beans (page 337), Indonesian Rice (page 340).

RIJSTAFFEL—ATJAR TJAMPOER

For 6 servings, you will need:

1 cucumber
20 fl oz (6 dl) tarragon vinegar
1 clove garlic
6 fl oz (1.6 dl) cold water
1 tsp koenjit (turmeric)*
1 lombok (green or red pepper)*
1 tsp ground ginger
½ tsp sugar

1 tsp goela djawa*
3 medium carrots
1 medium onion
2 oz (56 g) cauliflower
4 oz (113 g) green beans
1 bay leaf
1 tsp arrowroot
Freshly ground salt

First prepare:

Smash garlic, slice cucumber lengthways and remove center seeds, chop flesh. Measure dry ingredients. Slice carrots into long strips, slice onion, break cauliflower into little flowerettes. Blend arrowroot with a little water in a small bowl. Finely slice pepper. Cut green beans into 1-inch (2.5 cm) pieces.

Now cook!

1. Pour into a heated pan tarragon vinegar, garlic and cold water. Raise heat.
2. Season with salt.
3. Mix in koenjit and finely sliced green or red pepper. Add ginger and dark sugar.
4. Stir mixture and boil.
5. Remove vinegar mixture from heat and set aside for a moment.
6. Place onions in a dry pan, dribble in a few drops of oil and allow them to gently sweat. Season with salt.
7. Add prepared vegetables, sugar and bay leaf to onions, pour on vinegar liquid. Stir in arrowroot and boil until thickened.
8. Pour everything from pan into a bowl and allow to cool. When cold it can be bottled.

RIJSTAFFEL NO. 2—SAMBAL GORENG BEANS

For 2 servings, you will need:

9 oz (255 g) green beans
1 medium onion
1 clove garlic
12 oz (340 g) ground beef sirloin
¼-inch (7 mm) slice trassie*
   (shrimp paste)
1 tsp sambal oelek*(spiced
   peppery relish)
½ tsp laos*

2 salam leaves* or 1 bay leaf
16 fl oz (4 dl) beef stock
8 fl oz (2 dl) santen
   (coconut stock)
1 tsp arrowroot
Clarified butter*
Freshly ground salt
Freshly ground black pepper

First prepare:

Dice onion, chop garlic. Pinch meat into small lumps. Slice trassie. Measure remaining dry ingredients. Measure beef stock, wash and trim beans. Heat a platter in warm oven.

Now cook!

1. Heat some clarified butter to just cover bottom in a skillet. Add diced onion and garlic and pop beef into this. Increase heat to brown meat.

2. Stir in trassie, sambal oelek, laos and bay leaf. Fry everything together stirring constantly over low heat.

3. Add santen (coconut stock) to bubbling, fried meat mixture and simmer until the meat is tender.

4. Cut beans in half, place in a saucepan and cover with boiling beef stock. Season with salt and pepper, bring to a boil and simmer until half cooked (about 4 minutes).

5. Strain beans and stir into meat. Remove bay leaf. Increase heat and allow liquid to reduce.

6. Stir in blended arrowroot and cook until stock has thickened. Serve at once.

RIJSTAFFEL— SAJOER LODEH TJAMPOER

For 6 servings, you will need:

16 fl oz (4 dl) beef stock
2 medium carrots
4 oz (113 g) green beans
2 small onions
4 oz (113 g) cauliflower
1 tsp laos*(ginger)
1 slice trassie*(shrimp paste)
Pinch of koenjit*(turmeric)
1 small salam leaf*(bay leaf)

1 clove garlic
2 tsp sambal oelek (peppery relish)*
1 lb 3½ oz (552 g) green cabbage
24 fl oz (7 dl) coconut stock (see page 51)
Clarified butter*

First prepare:

Finely slice onions, cut carrots into round slices, break beans in two. Cut cauliflower into small "flowers." Measure herbs and spices. Make and/or measure coconut stock. Finely slice cabbage. Smash garlic.

Now cook!

1. Pour clarified butter to just cover bottom into a large skillet.
2. Add beans, onions, carrots and cauliflower.
3. Stir in laos, trassie and koenjit.
4. Add 1 salam leaf and garlic.
5. Moisten with beef stock.
6. Simmer for 15 minutes until vegetables are half cooked.
7. Add finely sliced cabbage and coconut stock. Simmer until cabbage is just cooked.
8. Stir in sambal oelek, a little at a time (it is *very* hot). Taste and add more if you wish. Remove salam leaf.
9. The soup is now ready to serve as a starter.

RIJSTAFFEL—ROEDJAK MANIS

For 6 servings, you will need:

1 fl oz (2.8 cl) cold water
¾ oz (21 g) goela djawa*
¼ inch (7 mm) thick slice trassie*
2 tsp sambal oelek*
1 medium cucumber
2 crisp eating apples

2 firm pears
4 oz (113 g) strawberries
4 oz (113 g) cherries
Freshly ground salt
Freshly ground black pepper

First prepare:

Measure water, herbs and spices. Shave goela djawa. Cut ends from cucumber but do not peel. Cut it in quarters, removing seed section, then dice. Wash, core and dice remaining fruit.

Now assemble!

1. Dissolve goela djawa in water.
2. When dissolved add trassie and sambal oelek.
3. Season freshly chopped fruit with salt and pepper and stir in prepared sugar-spiced sauce.
4. Marinate this mixture for 2 hours in refrigerator.
5. Serve ice cold.

Rijstaffel dishes from bottom left counterclockwise: Seroendeng (page 340), Sajoer Lodeh Tjampoer (page 338), Bottled Atjar Tjampoer (page 336) served with Kroepock Oedang Baroe (shrimp crackers).

RIJSTAFFEL—SEROENDENG

For 4 servings, you will need:

2 oz (56 g) dried unsweetened coconut

1 oz (28 g) butter

2 oz (56 g) shelled unsalted peanuts

1 tbs goela djawa (raw natural sugar)*

½ tsp djahé (ginger)*

½ tsp koenjit (turmeric)*

2 cloves garlic

First prepare:

Weigh dry ingredients, chop garlic.

Now cook!

1. Melt butter in heated frypan, stir in peanuts and add goela djawa.
2. Blend in djahé and koenjit.
3. Add garlic and fry everything together. Stir in coconut, place in a bowl and serve.

RIJSTAFFEL—INDONESIAN RICE

For 6 servings, you will need:

12 oz (340 g) long grain rice

32 fl oz (1 l) water

Freshly ground salt

Now cook!

1. Bring water to a vigorous boil.
2. Add sufficient salt so that it is just noticeable to taste (about 2 tsp).
3. Rain rice into water so that water continues to boil.
4. Boil for exactly 10 minutes.
5. Drain rice through a colander or sieve.
6. Place a little water (1½ inches: 3.8 cm) back in saucepan and place colander on saucepan. Let water boil underneath. Put a slightly smaller saucepan lid over rice (this contains the steam).
7. Steam rice until soft and separate (8 minutes maximum).

A special hint:

In this way you get perfect rice in only 18 minutes—almost half the time it takes for normally recommended techniques.

CHICKEN IN ALMOND SAUCE

For 4 servings, you will need:

6 tbs clarified butter*
4 oz (113 g) blanched almonds
2 chicken breasts each 2 lbs (0.9 kg)
40 fl oz (1.2 l) chicken stock
4 fl oz (1.2 dl) dry sherry
½ tsp chili powder or finely chopped fresh serrano chilies*
1 lb (0.5 kg) tomatoes

Freshly ground salt
Freshly ground white pepper
Garnish:
1 lb (0.5 kg) fresh leaf spinach
2 oz (56 g) butter
Freshly ground salt
Freshly ground white pepper

First prepare:

Measure clarified butter and almonds. Cut major backbone from breast meat area leaving breast meat on its breastbone. Use the backbone for making chicken stock; you will want 40 fl oz (1.2 l). Wash and thinly slice tomatoes. Measure sherry. Wash spinach at least 3 times and remove heavy stalks. Measure butter used for spinach.

Now cook!

1. Pour 4 tbs of the clarified butter into a heated frypan and add blanched almonds. Allow them to cook gently until they "pop"—about 7 minutes.

2. When the almonds "pop" pour them plus butter and a further 2 tbs clarified butter into a blender and whirl them until they form a paste. Set aside.

3. Drop two "backless" breasts of chicken into the prepared chicken stock.

4. Cook breasts at a slow boil for 30 minutes. Remove them and allow to cool slightly. Then detach each breast from bone (4 half breasts in all) and strip away skin.

5. Keep stripped breast covered with a little stock in a warm place. (In a shallow casserole over a saucepan of boiling water is fine.) Reserve chicken stock.

6. Place a teaspoonful of clarified butter into a large frypan and add tomatoes. Season with salt and pepper and fry.

7. Add 3 fl oz (8 cl) dry sherry and 10 fl oz (3 dl) of reserved chicken stock.

8. Allow tomato "base" to boil rapidly.

9. Now sieve "tomatoed stock" to remove all seeds and skin and pour it over drained warm breasts in a saucepan. Bring sauce to a boil to heat chicken. Stir in last remaining 1 fl oz (2.8 cl) of sherry.

10. Stir almond paste *into* hot chicken and tomato sauce. Add chili powder and serve immediately. (Cook spinach in butter. Season with salt and pepper.) Serve spinach with chicken in sauce.

A special hint:

Refer to Step 10. Have everything ready to go at time you add almond paste to tomato sauce. Keep sauce on low heat and add half the almond paste and then taste. Don't overdo the almonds, it's an acquired taste.

QUEENSLAND DUCKLING

67

For 4 servings, you will need:

1 duck, 3 lb (1.4 kg)
  (preferably Muscovy)
1 tbs salt
4 fl oz (1.2 dl) peanut oil
30 oz (850 g) can pineapple tidbits
2 green peppers (capsicum)

2 tsp fresh ginger root*
8 fl oz (2 dl) pineapple juice
  (from can)
2 tbs soya sauce
1 tsp black peppercorns
2 tbs arrowroot

First prepare:

Grate ginger. Drain pineapple and reserve liquid. Dice green pepper to same size as pineapple pieces. Mix pineapple juice, soya sauce, peppercorns and arrowroot until arrowroot is dissolved. Cut duck into 4 even-sized pieces. Place in a large saucepan with 120 fl oz (3.4 l) of water and salt. Bring to a boil, then simmer covered for 2 to 2½ hours or until duck is tender. Remove duck and strip flesh with skin from bones and dry with cloth. Strain cooking liquid. Allow to cool and remove fat.

Now cook!

1. Place oil in frypan and when hot add pieces of duck meat and shallow fry for 15 minutes until crisp golden brown on all sides.

2. Place duck back into large saucepan, add 10 fl oz (3 dl) of reserved cooking liquid, pineapple tidbits, green pepper and ginger. Cover and simmer another 15 minutes. Remove duck, put into serving dish and place in warm oven.

3. Skim any fat from surface of cooking liquid and bring to a boil. Stir in pineapple juice and arrowroot mixture until mixture thickens and clears. Pour sauce over duck.

A special hint:

Leave skin on duck. When fried this crisps and is the most delicious part of dish.

ROLPENS MET HATEBLIKSEM

For 4 servings, you will need:

12 oz (340 g) beef tenderloin
8 oz (227 g) pork tenderloin
6 oz (170 g) tripe (stomach)
    cooked for 2 hours in milk
    with 2 oz (56 g) onion
1 clove garlic
½ tsp mace
¼ tsp thyme
¼ tsp nutmeg
¼ tsp sage
½ tsp coriander

Freshly ground salt
Freshly ground black pepper
3 feet (90 cm) pig's casing*
Hatebliksem:
2 lbs (0.9 kg) potatoes
4 sour apples
2 sweet apples
4 oz (113 g) butter
32 fl oz (1 l) cold water
Freshly ground salt
Freshly ground white pepper

First prepare:

Grind beef and pork twice and tripe once. Put into a bowl and add smashed garlic and spices. Cover with a clean cloth and allow to stand at room temperature overnight. Soak pig's casing in cold water, cover and let stand overnight. Next day, peel potatoes. Peel and cover apples with water and soak until required. Measure butter and cold water. Heat a serving platter in warm oven.

Now cook!

1. Season cold water with 1 tsp salt and slice potatoes and apples in ¼-inch (7 mm) slices. Place slices in pan over heat and cook covered for 30 minutes.

2. Drain pig's casing and pass warm water through it by placing one end onto faucet.

3. Attach casing to end of a sausage funnel on a grinder and put seasoned sausage meat into scoop. Gently force ground mixture through funnel into casing and your sausage is being made.

4. When 12 inches (30 cm) long, cut and tie ends of casing together to form a circle. Repeat and place them in a pan. Cover with water and cook for 7 minutes. Drain and cool.

5. Drain juice off cooked potatoes and apples and mix with a potato masher. Stir in butter. Season with salt and white pepper.

6. Return to heat and allow to dry out slightly.

7. Prick sausages, place them in a frypan with some clarified butter and cook for 5 minutes, turning once.

8. Place potatoes on warmed serving platter.

9. Lift out sausage rings and place them on top of potatoes.

10. Serve piping hot.

A special hint:

Make each sausage ring slightly (1 inch: 2.5 cm) less in diameter so they will fit into each other in frypan.

BOULETTES AND PIG'S HOCKS

For 4 servings, you will need:

Boulettes:
3 lbs (1.4 kg) ground pork meat
6 oz (170 g) onion
2 tbs parsley
2 tbs chives
1 tsp powdered thyme
1 tsp tarragon
Freshly ground salt
Freshly ground white pepper
All-purpose flour
Clarified butter*
1 large onion
Juice ½ lemon
Small bunch parsley
Sprig thyme

2 bay leaves
Sprig tarragon
Pig's hocks:
2 fresh pig's hocks
1 large onion
Bouquet garni (2 bay leaves, 3
    sprigs thyme, 3-inch (7.6 cm)
    piece celery, 6 parsley stalks*)
3 tbs all-purpose flour
½ tsp mace
¼ tsp allspice
¼ tsp cinnamon
4 cloves
4 tbs sour cream
Parsley to garnish

First prepare:

Place 3 tbs flour to brown in 450°F (232°C) oven for 10 minutes. Roughly chop 6 oz (170 g) onion. Finely chop parsley and chives. Remove bottom and top from one 16-oz (453 g) can. Slice large onion roughly. Place pig's hocks into boiling water to cover, add onion cut finely and bouquet garni, and when water comes to a boil cover and cook very slowly for 4 hours.

Now cook!

1. In a bowl, mix ground pork meat with 6 oz (170 g) onion, parsley, chives, thyme and tarragon. Season with salt and pepper. Work mixture together thoroughly. Flatten meat on a board with hands to form a square ¾ inch (1.8 cm) thick. Take can and cut out patties, flour lightly and then form into a ball.

2. Place some clarified butter to just cover bottom into a pan and when hot add boulettes and brown on all sides.

3. Into a large saucepan of boiling salted water place large onion, lemon juice, parsley, thyme, tarragon and bay leaves. Place boulettes into boiling water and simmer 30 minutes. Remove and drain.

4. Remove pig's hocks when they have cooked for 4 hours. Add to cooking liquor the mace, allspice, cinnamon and crushed cloves. Mix browned flour with a little cold water and whisk into spiced liquor. Add salt if necessary. Bring to a boil, return hocks to sauce and then simmer covered for a further 30 minutes.

5. Add the boulettes to cooked pig's hocks and heat through. Stir in sour cream. Remove boulettes and pig's hocks to a deep serving dish, cover with sauce and dust with finely chopped parsley.

A special hint:

Please be absolutely certain that pig's hocks are fresh and not pickled. Also the larger the hock the better.

HAND OF PICKLED PORK WITH MUSTARD SAUCE

For 6-8 servings, you will need:

1 hand of pickled pork 4 lbs (1.8 kg)*

Mustard sauce:

2 oz (56 g) butter
1½ oz (42 g) all-purpose flour
2 level tbs dry mustard
20 fl oz (6 dl) veal stock

Freshly ground salt
Freshly ground white pepper
1 tbs lemon juice
2 egg yolks
10 carrots
Parsley

First prepare:

Leave pork in cold water to stand for 4 hours. Drain off water, place pork into cold water to cover, bring to a boil and cook 1 hour 20 minutes. Allow to cool in its liquid. Half an hour before end of cooking time add carrots split into quarters. Measure butter, flour, veal stock, mustard and lemon juice. Separate eggs.

Now cook!

1. Place butter in a saucepan and when melted stir in flour to form a roux. Allow to cook on low heat for 1 minute. Gradually stir in hot stock, whisking to form a smooth sauce. Stir in mustard and lemon juice and cook 12 minutes. Season with salt and pepper.

2. Mix egg yolks with a little of the hot sauce and return mixture to saucepan, whisking over low heat.

3. Remove outside skin from pork and carve into thick slices. Place overlapping slices in serving dish and cover with sauce. Sprinkle with parsley and surround with carrots.

4. Serve with Bennet potatoes (for recipe see page 534).

For 6 servings, you will need:

1 oxtail
1 lb 12 oz (793 g) fresh beef brisket
1 lb 8 oz (680 g) lean salt pork
3 oz (85 g) fat bacon, in one piece*
1 lb 9 oz (708 g) cooked tongue
1 lb 12 oz (793 g) cooked smoked ham
28 oz (793 g) can sauerkraut**
2 medium onions

2 medium potatoes
10 juniper berries
8 fl oz (2 dl) white wine
8 fl oz (2 dl) beef bouillon
Freshly ground salt
Freshly ground black pepper
2 tbs clarified butter*
2 bay leaves

**You can, of course, make your own but you have to wait at least two months for a good result!

First prepare:

Soak salt pork in water, chop oxtail and brisket, remove rind from fat bacon and cut latter into ¼-inch (7 mm) strips. Chop onions, measure wine and stock. Grate potatoes, open can of sauerkraut and drain. Heat a large meat platter.

Now cook!

1. Into a large pot of cold water, place oxtail, beef brisket and crumbled bay leaves. Add salt.
2. Cover and cook this for 1½ hours over moderate heat.
3. In a second pot place salt pork and cover with fresh water. Skim while cooking (again over moderate heat).
4. Preheat a frypan, add fat bacon and fry gently to release liquid fat. Pop in onions and shallow fry. Add clarified butter and continue to fry.
5. Skim fat from cooking meats and stir frying onions.
6. Pour sauerkraut onto a board and tease it out (to make it very loose). Add to bacon and onions. Stir in juniper berries, white wine and beef bouillon. Bring to a boil.
7. Reduce heat and stir in grated potato. Cover and simmer for 35 minutes.
8. Place cooked tongue and cooked smoked ham into a pan, cover with water and cook gently for 15 minutes.
9. Remove meat platter from warm oven and cover it with sauerkraut. Top with drained oxtail, brisket, pieces of salt pork, tongue and ham.

A special hint:

The addition of grated potato to sauerkraut reduces "tart" quality and greatly improves dish in my opinion. It also thickens liquid cooking with sauerkraut.

BOILED BEEF AND CARROTS

For 8 servings, you will need:

5 lbs (2.3 kg) corned beef
6 medium carrots
1 medium onion
1 clove
2 large Spanish onions
2 small white turnips
Bouquet garni (1 bay leaf, 1 sprig thyme
   6 black peppercorns, 8 parsley stalks*,
   3-inch piece [7.6 cm] celery)

Freshly ground salt
Freshly ground black pepper
Dumplings:
4 oz (113 g) grated suet
8 oz (227 g) all-purpose flour
2 tbs parsley
6 fl oz (1.6 dl) cold water
Freshly ground salt
Freshly ground black pepper

First prepare:

Meat: Soak meat in cold water completely covered for one hour. Tie bouquet garni in a piece of cloth. Stick clove into medium onion. Cut carrots into quarters. Roughly slice turnips. Finely slice Spanish onions. Warm a large serving dish.

Dumplings: Grate suet, sift flour. Wash parsley, dry and chop roughly into little pieces. Measure cold water.

Now cook!

1. Pour off water in which meat has been soaking as this will be rather salty.

2. Place meat in a large pot and cover with cold water and bring it to boiling point. Pour off this water and cover once again with fresh cold water. Pop in bouquet garni.

3. When stock has come to a boil reduce heat and allow to simmer covered for 1¼ hours. Skim fat frequently.

4. After this period of cooking remove bouquet garni and add roughly cut vegetables and onion containing clove. Bring to a boil, skim and continue to simmer.

5. The vegetables are always added ½ hour before end of cooking time required.

6. *Dumplings:* Add grated suet to flour and rub together with the fingertips. Season with salt and pepper and bind together with cold water. Add parsley. Knead dough in the bowl until it holds together.

7. Tip dough onto a floured board.

8. Divide dumpling mixture into 16 even pieces and roll them into little balls with floured hands.

9. Check that the meat is tender and then pop dumplings into stock 15 minutes before end of cooking time. Cover tightly. Cook gently along with meat and vegetables for 15 minutes.

10. When dumplings are cooked, remove meat from stock and place on a warmed serving platter. Slice meat and surround with drained vegetables and dumplings. Skim stock and if it is not too salty serve it in a sauceboat.

POT AU FEU

For 6 huge servings, you will need:

3 lbs (1.5 kg) stewing beef (cut in
    strips 2 inches x 1 inch x 1 inch
    [5 cm x 2.5 cm x 2.5 cm])
2 lbs (1 kg) soup bones
3 lbs (1.5 kg) marrowbones (only
    bone and marrow, not outer fat
    of meat)
128 fl oz (3.8 l) cold water
1 lb (0.5 kg) yellow turnip (blanched)
2 cloves
2 medium onions
4 carrots

8 oz (117 g) leeks
½ tsp ground coriander
½ small green cabbage head,
    12 oz (340 g)
1 lb (0.5 kg) potatoes
1 oz (28 g) freshly ground salt
Freshly ground black pepper
1 clove garlic
Bouquet garni (1 bay leaf,
    4 stalks parsley, 3-inch
    [7.6 cm] piece celery)

Now cook!

1. Bring water to boiling point in a very large pot. Place the washed bones in this liquid, cover and simmer for three hours. Skim frequently.

2. 4 fl oz (1.2 dl) of ice water can be added occasionally to check stock from boiling to make it easier to skim unnecessary fat and foam from top.

3. After 3rd hour, add beef, bouquet garni and coriander and continue to simmer for another hour.

4. Now remove bones (keeping marrow bones for later use) and bring stock to boiling point. Add turnip, carrots, leeks, potatoes, all roughly sliced.

5. Stick cloves into whole onions and add them.

6. Skewer garlic with a metal or wooden pick or needle (so you can find it) and add to stock. Simmer 10 minutes.

7. Add cabbage sliced into wedges (one piece per guest) and simmer 20 minutes.

8. Add salt and pepper when vegetables are tender. Remove garlic.

Service:

Pour stock, meat, vegetables and marrow bones into a serving pot or large casserole with lid and keep covered until required. Pot au Feu is usually served in 20 fl oz (6 dl) capacity earthenware pots called marmites, but large soup plates can be used. However you must always serve little gherkins (sour type), coarse table salt and hot mustard on side.

A special hint:

Absolutely vital you use the 4 fl oz (1.2 dl) ice water technique (Step 2). It clears stock as you go and stops "bone taint"—the stewed taste of bones.

*Memory, like good red wine,
improves with age.*

BEER AND RUMP POT ROAST

For 6 servings, you will need:

3 lbs (1.4 kg) rump roast
1 medium onion
4 bacon slices
All-purpose flour
Clarified butter*
Freshly ground salt
Freshly ground black pepper
1 tbs brown sugar

1 bay leaf
15 fl oz (3.6 dl) water
15 fl oz (3.6 dl) beer (flat and bitter)
2 tbs white wine vinegar
3 cloves
2 tsp arrowroot
12 oysters
4 oz (113 g) mushrooms

65

First prepare:

Lard meat with strips of pork fat. Finely slice onion. Cut bacon into ½-inch (1.2 cm) pieces. Measure water and beer. Finely slice mushrooms. Fry mushrooms in a little clarified butter. Reserve.

Now cook!

1. Dry and lightly flour meat and season with salt and pepper.
2. Place a little clarified butter to just cover bottom into a large casserole on heat and add onion and bacon. Allow to fry gently until browned. Remove bacon and onion to a dish and brown meat on all sides. Remove meat. Place onion and bacon back into pan. Place meat on onion and bacon bed and reduce heat.
3. Mix brown sugar, water, beer, wine vinegar, bay leaf and cloves. Pour over meat. Cover and allow to simmer 2½ hours. Skim fat from surface and remove meat to a carving board.
4. Strain liquid and then place back on heat. Skim any remaining fat. Mix arrowroot with a little beer and stir into boiling liquid to thicken. Add oysters and sautéed mushrooms. Reheat slightly.
5. Carve meat into thick slices. Lay on a serving dish and cover with beer, oyster and mushroom sauce.

SMOKED LOIN OF PORK AND RED WINE SAUCE

For 6 servings, you will need:

3½ lbs (1.6 kg) smoked loin of
    pork
2 tbs French mustard

2 tbs white sugar
8 fl oz (2 dl) red wine

67

First prepare:

Cook smoked pork and then remove thin portion of fat surrounding loin. Measure wine. Set oven temperature at 400ºF (205ºC).

Now cook!

1. Smear fat side of pork with mustard and sprinkle with sugar.
2. Place pork in a baking pan and place high in oven to brown for 15 minutes.
3. Lower heat of oven to 375ºF (190ºC) and add red wine to pan. Baste pork occasionally. Cook for 15 minutes.
4. Remove bones from meat and carve in slanting slices. Spoon a little of red wine sauce over meat.
5. Serve accompanied by sugar browned potatoes (see page 531) and creamed spinach (see page 518).

RUM AND PORK POT ROAST

For 4 servings, you will need:

2¼ lbs (1 kg) pork (cross-cut
   leg 2 inches: 5 cm thick)
1 clove garlic
3 bulbs cardamon or 1 tsp
   powdered cardamon
¼ tsp ginger root*
20 fl oz (6 dl) canned pineapple
   juice, unsweetened
2 large bay leaves

2 lbs (0.9 kg) fresh pineapple
   (medium size, slightly green)
1 tbs clarified butter*
2 fl oz (5.6 cl) rum
1 tsp (level) arrowroot
1 fl oz (2.8 cl) rum
Freshly ground salt
Freshly ground black pepper

First prepare:

Dry meat with a towel. Smash garlic and chop finely. Break open cardamon, and collect small black seeds (or measure powdered kind). Have ginger ready. Measure pineapple juice. Cut pineapple husk away, then cut flesh in half and remove center core with a small V-shaped cut. Slice halves into 8 inches x ½ inch (20 cm x 1.2 cm) thick spears. Combine rum with arrowroot.

Now cook!

1. Spread garlic onto top of pork. With a sharp knife make shallow incisions in meat, about ⅛ inch (3 mm) apart.

2. Mash garlic pulp down into cuts. Add ginger and cardamon and spread this in too.

3. Finally season with salt and black pepper and press this also into cuts.

4. Pour unsweetened pineapple juice into a casserole just large enough to hold meat (see special hint). Add piece of pork seasoned side up. Add bay leaves.

5. Cover, turn heat to low and simmer gently for 20 minutes.

6. After 20 minutes, turn pork. Remove cover and place in oven at 350°F (177°C) for 2 hours 15 minutes (one hour per lb: 0.5 kg).

7. Set timer for one hour and turn pork once at halftime.

8. When pork is tender heat clarified butter in a frypan over medium heat and add pineapple spears. Pour in 2 fl oz (5.6 cl) rum and flame.

9. Remove pork, skim fats from juices, bring them to boil and stir in rum mixed with arrowroot. Boil until it thickens. Taste and adjust seasoning with salt and pepper.

10. Place pork on a platter surrounded with flamed pineapple. Coat with the brilliantly clear sauce.

A special hint:

For best results you should have a large 200 fl oz (6 l) and a medium-sized 100 fl oz (3 l) casserole. Always choose the one that just contains cut of meat or poultry.

Rum and Pork Pot Roast

CHICKEN ALI BABA

For 4 servings, you will need:

1 chicken, 3½ lbs (1.6 kg)
Bouquet garni (2 sprigs thyme, rosemary, sage, 1 bay leaf, 2 parsley stalks* and a small piece of celery)
40 cloves garlic, unpeeled
7 fl oz (1.8 dl) olive oil

Freshly ground black pepper
Parsley
1½ tbs butter
Flour and water dough:
16 oz (453 g) all-purpose flour
Water
1 tbs salt

First prepare:

Cut wings off chicken at breastbone and dry chicken thoroughly. Tie herbs together with a long length of string. Preheat oven to 350°F (177°C). Make flour and water dough by mixing flour with salt and adding enough cold water to make soft dough. Cut parsley finely.

Now cook!

1. Cover base of a frypan with some of the olive oil and when hot add garlic and bouquet garni. Toss in oil and allow cloves to sweat gently for 2 minutes. Remove garlic cloves to an ovenproof casserole with a lid large enough to hold whole chicken and place bouquet garni inside chicken.

2. In oil remaining in frypan, place chicken and turn to brown lightly all over. Season chicken and place it on top of bed of garlic. Add remaining olive oil. Place lid on casserole and seal with flour and water dough by placing a ring of dough around casserole lid, and pressing down lid to secure. Bake in 350°F (177°C) oven for 1½ hours.

3. When cooked, remove lid and dough. Cut off chicken legs and then the backbone in one slice. Next remove bones from breast and cut breast in two. Remove all outer skin from each "quarter." Cover with finely chopped parsley. Heat butter until foaming and pour over "parsleyed" chicken.

CHICKEN GLORIA

For 2 servings, you will need:

1 large chicken breast (from a 5 lb: 2.3 kg capon)
Clarified butter*
½ medium onion
Cayenne pepper
Freshly ground salt
Sprig rosemary
12 juniper berries

8 oz (227 g) button mushrooms
Lemon juice
2 slices smoked ham each ¼ inch (7 mm) thick
4 whole brandied apricots
1 tsp brown sugar
2 tbs brandy
2 fl oz (5.6 cl) chicken stock

First prepare:

Remove breast from rib cage. Finely slice onion. Crush juniper berries. Measure chicken stock. Heat brandy.

Now cook!

1. Place some clarified butter to just cover bottom into a pan on heat and add chicken breast, skin side down. Fry gently and add onion, rosemary, juniper berries and season with salt and cayenne. Turn chicken, reduce heat, cover pan and allow to cook for 6 minutes.

2. Place some clarified butter to just cover bottom into another pan on heat. Add mushrooms, some lemon juice and season with salt and cayenne. Fry for 2 minutes.

3. Place smoked ham slices over chicken breast, cover, and allow to heat through (approximately 2 minutes).

4. Remove ham slices and place them on a warmed serving dish. Cover with chicken breast. Keep warm. Remove rosemary and juniper berries from sauce and add apricots with brown sugar. Raise heat under pan and add cooked drained mushrooms. Pour over brandy and set alight. Stir until flames die down and add chicken stock.

5. Remove apricots and mushrooms and place around chicken breast. Bring sauce to boil and reduce until thick. Strain over chicken.

6. Serve with a bowl of black currant jelly.

TANDOORI CHICKEN

For 4 servings, you will need:
1 chicken, 3 lb (1.4 kg)
First spice paste:
2 onions
6 cloves garlic
1½ tsp cayenne pepper
1 tsp garam marsala*
2 tsp ground ginger
2 tsp freshly ground salt
Second spice paste:
1 tsp garam marsala*

½ tsp ground cardamon
½ tsp cayenne pepper
1 tsp cumin
Juice of 1 lemon
½ tsp powdered saffron
8 tbs clarified butter*
Garnish:
Juice of ½ lemon
Parsley
1 tsp cumin

First prepare:

Preheat oven to 350°F (177°C). Cut onions into quarters. Peel cloves of garlic. Place garlic, onion, 1½ tsp cayenne, 1 tsp garam marsala, ginger and salt into a blender and blend until reduced to a paste. Cut wings off chicken. Make second paste by mixing 1 tsp garam marsala, cardamon, cayenne, cumin, lemon juice and saffron.

Now cook!

1. Paint chicken with blender mixture and place half the mixture inside chicken. Put chicken in a steamer and steam covered for 15 minutes. Remove chicken and allow to cool.

2. Scrape off paste mixture and then remove skin from chicken. Cut 2 neat incisions in each breast. Make 3 deep incisions in each thigh and rub second paste into all the incisions.

3. Place chicken in a small roasting pan. Brush thoroughly with clarified butter and place in a 350°F (177°C) oven for 35 minutes. Baste the chicken frequently with clarified butter.

4. Remove chicken from oven. Place on a heated serving dish surrounded by boiled rice. Sprinkle with cumin and squeeze juice of ½ a lemon over chicken. Place sprigs of parsley between thighs and breasts.

A special hint:

Take your time when adding second paste. It must go right into each incision.

GOOSE WITH PRUNE AND APPLE STUFFING

For 4 servings, you will need:

1 gosling, 5 lb (2.3 kg)*
Clarified butter*
½ medium onion
1 tsp dried rosemary
1 tsp ground cloves
3 tsp caraway seeds
1 tbs white wine vinegar
Freshly ground salt
Freshly ground black pepper
12 fl oz (3.2 dl) dry red wine

2½ oz (70 g) brown sugar
3 Granny Smith apples*
3 tbs sugar
2 tsp lemon peel
3 oz (85 g) fresh bread crumbs*
2½ fl oz (7 cl) prune juice
Whole blanched almonds
6 oz (170 g) prunes
Juice of ½ lemon

First prepare:

Remove wings close to breast and dry inside of gosling. Cook prunes with juice of lemon and 1 tbs sugar for 5 minutes. Allow to cool and remove pits from prunes. Replace prune pits with 2 blanched almonds. Peel and core apples. Slice into ¼-inch (7 mm) slices. Measure bread crumbs, red wine and prune juice. Finely slice onion. Measure brown sugar. Roughly grate lemon peel. Preheat oven to 450°F (232°C).

Now cook!

1. *Basting sauce:* Heat clarified butter in saucepan and when hot add onion and stir over low heat. Add rosemary, cloves, 2 tsp of the caraway seeds (rubbed between the palms of the hands), vinegar, red wine, brown sugar. Season with salt and pepper. Bring mixture to a boil and simmer for 5 minutes. Cool.

2. In a separate pan pour enough clarified butter to cover bottom ¼ inch deep. Add sliced apples with 2 tbs sugar. Dust with cloves and 1 tsp crushed caraway seeds. Stir apples to cover them with butter and allow to cook for 2 minutes.

3. Place bread crumbs in a bowl, add roughly grated lemon peel, apples and prune juice, mix and season to taste with salt and pepper.

4. Prick gosling with fork and season with salt and pepper. Place 4 prunes inside gosling, then a handful of the bread crumb mixture, and so on until the bird is completely full. Close opening with poultry pins.

5. Place gosling in oven and cook for 30 minutes. Baste with basting sauce. Lower heat of oven to 300°F (149°C) and cook for 2¾ hours, basting from time to time. Allow gosling to stand 10 minutes prior to carving.

6. Remove excess fat from pan gravy and serve separately in a sauceboat.

Service:

Serve accompanied by spiced red cabbage (see page 518) and oven roasted potatoes.

A special hint:

When you prick the skin do it with a sharp fork. The more it is pricked the less fatty it will be.

1. GOOSE WITH PRUNE AND APPLE STUFFING.

2. This implement slices and cores an apple in one stroke.

3. The apples are seasoned and fried gently.

4. Add the bread crumbs to the apples.

5. Place peeled whole almonds into pitted prunes. Takes time but it's worth it!

6. Say Ahh! Divide prunes one to each spoonful of dressing.

7. Palmed herbs bring out flavor. This is the "baste."

8. Prick the skin to release the oil. A short time in a hot oven then sweats out the excess.

9. After the degreasing, brush with the baste. Set the bird on a rack over baking dish.

GG
69

ROAST TURKEY WITH CHESTNUT STUFFING

For 8 servings, you will need:

1 turkey 10 lb (5 kg)
Freshly ground salt
Freshly ground white pepper
Ground pork dressing:
1 medium onion
Clarified butter*
2 oz (56 g) lean bacon
3 tbs parsley
2 lb (0.9 kg) ground pork
Freshly ground salt
Freshly ground black pepper
1 egg
Chestnut stuffing:
1 lb (0.5 kg) natural chestnut puree

1 tbs veal jelly
Freshly ground salt
Freshly ground black pepper
1 oz (28 g) butter
Giblet stock:
Turkey neck (½ lb: 227 g
   meat)
1 medium onion
Clarified butter*
30 fl oz (9 dl) water
2 bay leaves
Sprig thyme
2 fl oz (5.6 cl) port

First prepare:

Remove neck from turkey and finely chop. Finely slice onion for giblet stock. Finely dice 1 onion for ground pork dressing. Cut bacon into fine strips. Finely chop parsley. Dry turkey well inside and out. Make veal jelly (see page 52). Preheat oven to 325⁰F (163⁰C). Paint broiler rack with clarified butter.

Now cook!

1. *Ground pork dressing:* Place 3 tbs clarified butter into a frypan and add diced onion. Allow to fry for 2 minutes. Add bacon and fry for 1 minute. Remove from heat and place into a bowl with chopped parsley and ground pork. (Season with salt and pepper.) Mix ingredients with an egg.

2. *Chestnut stuffing:* Mix chestnut puree with veal jelly and blend, season with salt and pepper and stir in softened butter.

3. Place chestnut dressing in neck opening, pressing it in firmly. Place ground pork dressing in rear end. Truss turkey. Lightly flour breast. Place turkey on its side on broiler rack in baking dish and roast for 1 hour. After this time turn bird onto other side and roast for 1 hour. Then turn bird breast side uppermost. Paint with clarified butter, season with salt and white pepper and roast for a further 2½ hours basting every 30 minutes with clarified butter.

4. *Giblet stock:* Place finely sliced onion into 2 tbs clarified butter and fry. Add chopped turkey neck and brown onions and neck. Add water, bay leaves and thyme and allow stock to simmer uncovered for 1 hour. After this time add port and simmer 5 minutes more. Strain.

5. *Gravy:* Remove fat from roasting pan and stir in strained giblet stock. Boil, scraping up all particles. Serve gravy separately in a sauceboat.

ROAST TURKEY WITH PARSNIP DRESSING

GG
64

For 8 servings, you will need:

1 turkey 10½ lb (5 kg)
10 oz (283 g) onions
1 lb (0.5 kg) parsnips
4 tbs clarified butter*
14 oz (396 g) bulk sausage meat
3½ oz (100 g) turkey liver
1 clove garlic
1 tsp sesame seeds
1 apple
2 tsp lemon thyme leaves*

1 tbs parsley stalks*
6 oz (170 g) bread crumbs*
2 eggs
Freshly ground salt
Freshly ground black pepper
Turkey giblets
10 fl oz (3 dl) water
2 bay leaves
1 parsley stalk*
4 bacon slices

First prepare:

Peel and finely slice onion and parsnips. Melt butter in pan. Finely dice liver, smash garlic, peel and cube apple. Chop thyme leaves and parsley stalks. Preheat oven to 325°F (163°C).

Now cook!

1. Fry onion and parsnip in clarified butter over low heat for 15 minutes until soft. Remove and set aside. Add sausage meat, garlic, sesame seeds and liver to pan and fry for 5 minutes. Stir from time to time.

2. Crush parsnips with a potato masher and add sausage meat mixture to parsnips. Beat well and stir in apple, eggs, bread crumbs, parsley and thyme.

3. Season inside of turkey with salt. Stuff neck area only. Skewer neck skin and tie legs. Brush with melted butter. Season with salt and pepper. Cover breast and top of thighs with bacon. Cook for 3 hours basting occasionally during cooking. Remove bacon when crisp. (If turkey browns too much cover with brown paper dampened with water.)

4. Allow turkey to stand for 20 minutes before carving. Make gravy with liquid obtained by simmering giblets in 10 fl oz (3 dl) of water with bay leaves. Stir liquid into roasting pan drippings, bring to a boil and scrape up all particles. Thicken with a mixture of flour and water.

ROAST DUCK WITH SOUR CREAM SAUCE

For 2 servings, you will need:

1 duckling 2½ lb (1.2 kg) (Long Island, Brome Lake or Aylesbury)	2 tsp grated orange peel
6 tbs clarified butter*	1 tbs sweet sherry or spätlese wine*
6 juniper berries	1 medium onion
Freshly ground black pepper	8 fl oz (2 dl) sour cream
Freshly ground salt	2 tbs dill
2 tsp vinegar	1 tbs black currant jelly
1 tsp paprika	1 egg yolk
Stuffing:	2 tbs heavy cream
1½ oz (42 g) bread crumbs*	1 tsp arrowroot
4 oz (113 g) ground hazelnuts	2 fl oz (5.6 cl) sweet sherry
12 juniper berries	or spätlese wine*

First prepare:

Crush 6 juniper berries. Grate orange peel. Measure sherry. Remove neck from duck. Dry well. Finely chop onion. Measure sour cream. Mix arrowroot with a little water. Blend hazelnuts and 12 juniper berries together. Preheat oven to 350°F (177°C). Chop dill.

Now cook!

1. In a pan place crushed juniper berries and clarified butter. Add vinegar and season with salt and pepper. Heat gently and allow to infuse. Remove from heat and stir in paprika. Set aside for glaze for duck.

2. Mix bread crumbs, hazelnut and juniper berry mixture with orange peel and 1 tbs sweet sherry. Season with black pepper. Stuff duck with mixture. Tie duck with string. (Loop string around legs, bringing together—turn duck and pass string under front of wings bringing wings together—tie and place neck flap under string.)

3. Paint broiler rack with additional clarified butter and then paint duck with butter glaze. Place in oven and allow to roast 1 hour 10 minutes.

4. Remove duck—pour fat from pan. Add onion to pan juices and allow to fry gently for 1 minute. Add 2 fl oz (5.6 cl) sweet sherry. Pour into blender and puree. Sieve blended mixture into a saucepan. Stir in sour cream, dill and black currant jelly. Mix yolk with cream and arrowroot and stir into sauce. Stir until thickened. Do not boil. Serve in sauceboat.

1. TO TRUSS POULTRY. Tie legs straight with center of string.

2. Turn bird on breast, cross and tie in middle of the back.

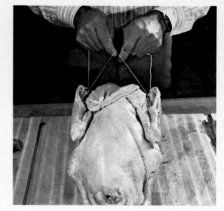

3. Loop the string around the wings and tie once.

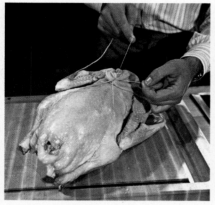

4. To contain neck dressing catch neck flap in a simple noose.

5. To contain body dressing place toothpicks in sides every inch.

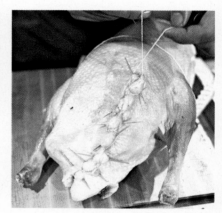

6. Finally lace it up like a ski boot.

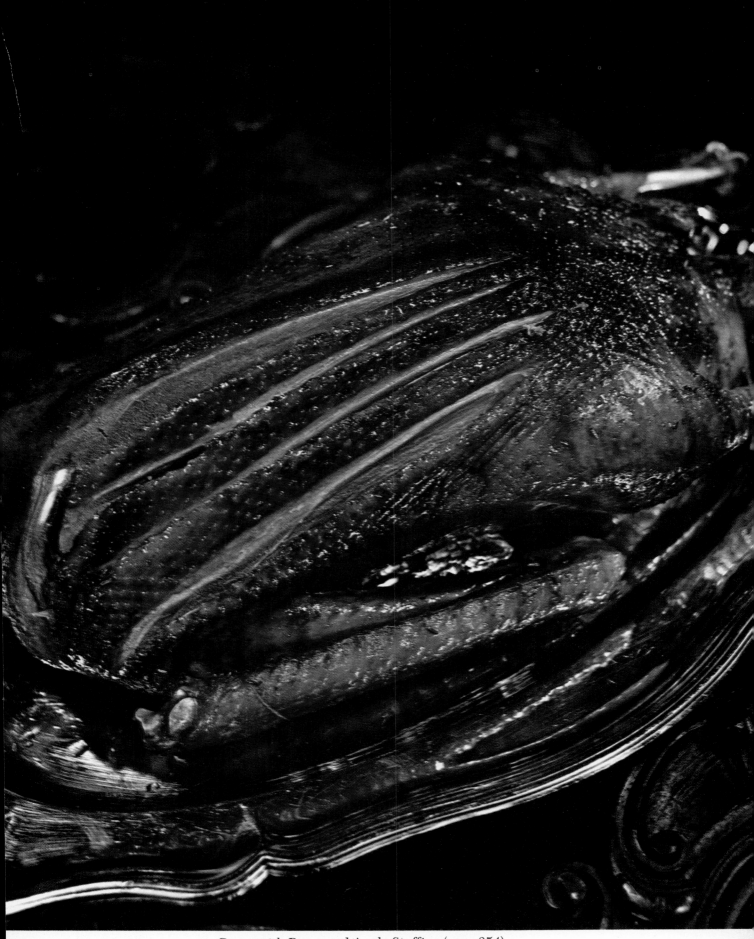

Goose with Prune and Apple Stuffing (page 354)

DUCK A LA NORMANDE

For 4 servings, you will need:

1 duck, 4½ lbs (2 kg) (Aylesbury, Long Island or Brome Lake)	2 green apples
5 oz (142 g) seedless raisins	3 oz (85 g) onion
9 fl oz (2.5 dl) cider	2 tsp arrowroot
2 fl oz (5.6 cl) port wine	Freshly ground salt
4 fl oz (1.2 dl) heavy cream	Freshly ground black pepper
	Clarified butter*

First prepare:

With a fork prick duck all over, especially around back so that fat will be released during cooking. Slice onion thinly, measure port. Remove giblets from bird. Set aside raisins in a bowl and pour 5 fl oz (1.5 dl) of cider over them. Allow these to marinate for at least one hour. Measure remaining 4 fl oz (1.2 dl) of cider. Wash and core apples. Place a serving dish in a warm oven. Preheat the oven to 400°F (205°C). A little string will also be required.

Now cook!

1. Truss duck with string and place in a casserole. Do not add any grease or seasoning.

2. Place bird uncovered into preheated oven, 400°F (205°C), for 20 minutes.

3. After 20 minutes remove duck, pour off fatty juices and discard. Season the bird very well with salt and pepper and coat it with clarified butter.

4. Return to oven (now reduced to 350°F: 177°C) and continue cooking for about 1¾ hours. No basting is required.

5. Into a hot skillet add some clarified butter to just cover bottom and fry onion gently. Add neck and giblets and cook to extract their natural juices. Season with salt and pepper.

6. Strain juice from marinated raisins into onion mixture. Allow to bubble gently.

7. Reduce heat under sauce and occasionally add a little more cider from measured amount.

8. Pour port wine over strained raisins.

9. Cut cored apples into 10 thick slices.

10. Pour a little cold clarified butter into an unheated pan, just enough to coat the bottom, pop in slices of apple and set heat at medium.

11. Turn apples after 2 minutes. They will have softened but not browned. Turn heat off and drain off fat.

12. Sieve onion "sauce" pressing through pulp and pour it over apple slices. Add raisins and port and shake gently together.

13. Gradually pour in cream and return pan to low heat increasing it slowly to boiling point.

14. Blend arrowroot with remaining 2 fl oz (5.6 cl) of cider and stir into sauce.

15. You will find sauce thickens instantly. Keep warm on low heat. Do not overcook or apples will fall apart.

16. Remove duck when browned and tender. Cut away string, place bird on heated serving dish. Arrange apple slices around duck.

17. Cover duck with sauce. Garnish platter with chopped parsley.

A special hint:

Refer to Step 1 & 2 above: "Pricking" the duck or goose is an excellent idea especially if you let it "run" for 20 minutes at 400°F (205°C). This releases the fluid fatty tissues and drains surplus "greasiness" from duck leaving a perfectly colored, crisp, juicy skin without basting ever!

PATITO CON MARMALADA DE NARANJA

For 2 servings, you will need:

3¼ lbs (1.5 kg) duckling (Brome Lake,
    Long Island or Aylesbury)✱✱
Freshly ground salt
Freshly ground black pepper
1 orange
8 oz (227 g) Seville orange marmalade

4 oz (113 g) honey
1 tsp cinnamon
1 tsp ground clove
2 tsp dried rosemary
1 fl oz (2.8 cl) port

✱✱3¼ lbs (1.5 kg) is rather specific, don't worry if it's 3½ lbs (1.6 kg). Also it serves 2 gluttons or 4 dieters.

First prepare:

Remove wings as close to breast as possible. Remove neck and half of long neck flap. Prick duck breast. Preheat oven to 450⁰F (232⁰C). Measure marmalade and honey. Peel orange.

Now cook!

1. Season duck inside and out with salt and pepper. Stuff with orange slices. Place in a small baking dish and put in oven for 20 minutes to allow some of excess fat to escape.
2. Place marmalade in a bowl and add honey, cinnamon, clove and rosemary. Mix together to form basting sauce.
3. Remove duck from oven and lower oven temperature to 300⁰F (149⁰C). Pour fat from duck.
4. Heavily cover duck with one half of basting sauce. Place the duck (in its pan) into another pan containing 1 inch (2.5 cm) hot water and roast in oven for 1½ hours. Baste duck again after ½ hour reserving 2 tbs of basting sauce.
5. Remove duck, allow to stand in warm oven for 10 minutes to set and then cut in half, slicing meat away from carcass. Arrange on a serving platter.
6. Skim fat from pan juices, add rest of basting sauce and the port and allow sauce to reduce and thicken.
7. Cover duck with sauce and serve.

A special hint:

The trick of high initial heat rids the duck of its fatty overtones and the "dish within a dish" idea at Step 4 prevents the basting sauce from caramelizing.

MARCO POLO DUCK

For 4 servings, you will need:

1 duckling, 5½ lb (2.5 kg)
Freshly ground salt
Freshly ground black pepper
Peel ½ lemon
2 tbs green peppercorns**
1 fl oz (2.8 cl) white wine
2 red peppers (capsicum)
Clarified butter*
1 fl oz (2.8 cl) cognac
Duck and veal jelly:
1 veal knuckle

1 onion
40 fl oz (1.2 l) water
White sauce:
1 oz (28 g) all-purpose flour
1 oz (28 g) butter
10 fl oz (3 dl) milk
Freshly ground salt
Freshly ground white pepper
Nutmeg

** Hard to obtain but suggest you order from "Aphrodisia," 28 Carmine Street, New York, N.Y. 10014. Phone 212 989-6440

First prepare:

Remove neck from duckling and cut off wings at second joint. Dry duck thoroughly and truss with string. Prick skin with a fork. Season with salt and pepper. Paint a broiler rack with clarified butter. Drain peppercorns and reserve juice. Remove lemon peel using a potato parer, place peel into boiling water and blanch 1 minute. Remove and cut into fine strips. Finely dice red peppers. Preheat oven to 375°F (190°C).

Duck and veal jelly: Chop duck wings and neck finely. Place some clarified butter to just cover bottom into a saucepan and when hot add duck meat and brown. Add veal knuckle and onion. Cover with water and allow to simmer 3 hours. Season with salt and pepper. Strain and refrigerate.

White sauce: Place butter into a saucepan and when melted stir in flour to form a roux and allow to cook on low heat 1 minute. Gradually whisk in milk to make a smooth sauce. Season with salt, pepper and nutmeg. Bring to a boil and then allow to simmer 12 minutes, stirring occasionally.

Now cook!

1. Place duck on broiler rack in a baking dish and roast for 1 hour 10 minutes.

2. Place green peppercorn juice into a small saucepan, add blanched lemon rind, white wine and cognac. Allow to reduce to half. Add green peppercorns and veal and duck jelly. Allow to simmer gently 5 minutes.

3. Place some clarified butter to just cover bottom into a frypan and add red peppers. Allow to soften in butter and then stir into white sauce. Stir in peppercorn reduction. Simmer sauce on low heat.

4. Drain juices from roasted duck, skim off fat and add 3 fl oz (8 cl) of duck juice to white sauce.

5. Carve duck into quarters and lay on a heated serving platter. Serve sauce separately in a sauceboat.

ROAST PHEASANT TRIDENT VILLAS

For 2 servings, you will need:

2½ lbs (1.2 kg) pheasant
   (dressed weight)
2 lb (0.9 kg) fresh pineapple
Clarified butter*
8 fl oz (2 dl) pineapple juice
   (canned, unsweetened)
2 tsp arrowroot

12 fl oz (3.2 dl) dry red wine
Freshly ground salt
Freshly ground white pepper
Pommes Gaufrettes (thin "crisp"
   potatoes cut on a special
   "Mandolin" slicer)
Watercress

First prepare:

Cut off top and bottom of a fresh pineapple and remove outer skin and hard center core. Slice flesh into ½-inch (1.2 cm) slices. Rinse neck and giblets of pheasant. Measure pineapple juice and red wine. Heat a serving platter. Preheat oven to 350°F (177°C). Chop wings off pheasant. Wash inside and dry very thoroughly with a paper towel. In a bowl, blend arrowroot and 4 fl oz (1.2 dl) red wine.

Now cook!

1. Pour a little clarified butter to just cover bottom into a casserole over high heat. Cover bottom of pan with rings of pineapple.

2. Place neck, giblets and chopped wings over pineapple slices.

3. Turn pineapple slices, keeping heat high so they get a good color on both sides.

4. Season inside of bird with salt and pepper. Repeat on outside.

5. To keep the bird's shape while cooking, wrap string around the drumsticks. Turn the bird over and tie the neck flap back in middle of back bone.

6. Place bird on bed of pineapple, giblets, neck and wings. Cover and let cook for 5 minutes by "steam bursting method" (see hint).

7. Remove lid and see how bird has increased in bulk. Check to see pineapple rings are not sticking. Pour over unsweetened pineapple juice.

8. Brush bird with clarified butter and place uncovered in preheated oven set at 350°F (177°C) for 1 hour.

9. Baste during cooking to keep bird moist.

10. After 1 hour, cover with brown paper and let cook for another 20 minutes.

11. Remove casserole from oven, lift out bird and strain off the fat keeping the dark residue. Sieve the residue to remove the pineapple and giblets.

12. Bring sieved residue to a boil. Stir in arrowroot mixture and remaining 8 fl oz (2 dl) wine. Let bubble away until arrowroot thickens and clears.

13. Cut off string from pheasant.

14. Carve legs from pheasant, then cut off back portion. Split breast in two—beautifully tender!

15. Take bones out of breast so that they are completely filleted. Arrange on heated serving platter, with legs.

16. Cover pieces with sauce and garnish with gaufrettes potatoes and watercress.

A special hint:

"Steam bursting" is a simple matter of letting a fowl pot steam over a bed of vegetables (or fruits) with lid on pot. After 5 minutes at high heat flesh swells and the sinews are stretched. Later, by reducing heat they relax and become tender.

ROAST PHEASANT AND CUMBERLAND SAUCE

For 2 servings, you will need:

1 pheasant
4 bacon slices
2 fl oz (5.6 cl) port
Clarified butter*
Freshly ground salt
Freshly ground black pepper
2 fl oz (5.6 cl) brandy
Cumberland sauce:
2 oz (56 g) glacé cherries*
4 fl oz (1.2 dl) chicken stock
Arrowroot
Peel of ½ orange

Peel and juice of 1 lemon
1 tbs castor sugar*
1 medium onion
12 fl oz (3.2 dl) cold water
2 tbs red currant jelly
3 fl oz (8 cl) tawny port
1 fl oz (2.8 cl) red wine vinegar
1½ tsp English mustard
Dash cayenne pepper
1½ bay leaves
Clarified butter*

First prepare:

The pheasant: Remove and chop liver, kidney, heart, neck, tips of wings and set a-side in a bowl. Measure port and brandy. Preheat oven to 350°F (177°C). Have a ball of string at hand, and some matches. A small casserole will also be required.

Cumberland sauce: Pare peel of ½ orange and 1 lemon with a vegetable peeler. Squeeze juice of lemon. Finely slice medium onion, wash glacé cherries, measure chicken stock, cold water, port and red wine vinegar. Open jar of red currant jelly and English mustard. Warm serving dish in oven. In a smaller pot put some water and pop in peel of orange and lemon to "blanch" (to "blanch" means to bring food to the boil starting with cold water); this removes bitterness from skins and also softens them. It takes only a couple of minutes. Strain and set aside peels to cool, then slice into fine strips.

Now cook!

1. Dry bird thoroughly inside and out and season inside of bird with freshly ground salt and black pepper.

2. Wrap bacon around pheasant, covering breast and legs to keep them moist and well basted.

3. With a long piece of string, truss legs together and then over the neck, forming a little package to hold bacon securely around bird.

4. Into your casserole pour port and add trussed bird.

5. Cover tightly.

6. Place casserole in preheated oven 350°F (177°C) for 1½ hours. No basting is required (see hint).

7. *Cumberland sauce:* Into a saucepan pour some clarified butter.

8. To this add the finely sliced onion and allow to fry gently.

9. Add the chopped giblets (liver, kidney, heart, neck and ends of wings) and continue to fry.

10. To browning onions, stir in sugar. (This will not sweeten the mixture but it will caramelize and darken it).

11. Pour in cold water and bring almost to a boil. Add bay leaves and reduce heat.

12. In a frypan place cooled peels of orange and lemon which have been finely sliced.

13. To this add port, red wine vinegar, juice of lemon and orange and red currant jelly.

14. To add further pep, stir in mustard and a dash of cayenne and allow the bubbling aromatic sauce to come to the boil and reduce gently.

15. At this point chicken stock may be added, to further enhance sauce.

16. 1 tsp arrowroot blended with a little water can be added to thicken mixture.

17. Pop in glacé cherries and continue to allow Cumberland sauce to simmer gently.

18. Remove bird from oven and turn on broiler unit.

19. Drain juices from casserole in a bowl and skim off the grease. Add residue to sauce.

20. Remove string from pheasant and peel away bacon. The bird should be beautifully tender. Place it in a broiler pan.

21. Baste bird with clarified butter and then add brandy and set alight. When flames die, slide bird under broiler to give it better color (takes about 3 minutes). Add juices from broiler pan to sauce.

22. Remove lightly broiled bird, place on a cutting board and split into two, then place on a heated serving platter.

23. Pour a little of the sauce over pheasant, just enough to cover it and serve at once piping hot. The remainder of sauce should be served in a sauceboat.

24. Garnish with potato chips and fresh watercress and serve with spinach.

A special hint:

Seal casserole completely with a flour and water dough if necessary; otherwise port will lose its effect on pheasant.

REBHUHN MIT ANANAS

For 4 servings, you will need:

1 chicken, 3 lb (1.4 kg)	4 fl oz (1.2 dl) pineapple juice
Freshly ground salt	Peel ½ orange
Freshly ground black pepper	4 tbs slivovitz
1 tsp rosemary	2 tsp juniper berries
5 tbs slivovitz	2 tsp cider vinegar
Pinch cinnamon	1 tbs honey
Pinch mace	2 tsp arrowroot
16 oz (453 g) pineapple chunks	4 fl oz (1.2 dl) chicken stock

First prepare:

Cut wings off chicken and dry thoroughly. Measure slivovitz. Measure pineapple and juice. Finely grate orange peel. Measure juniper berries and crush. Measure chicken stock. Preheat oven to 350°F (177°C).

Now cook!

1. Season inside of chicken with salt, pepper and rosemary.

2. Sprinkle pineapple with cinnamon and mace and then add slivovitz. Allow to marinate a few minutes. Drain and reserve juice. Spoon pineapple inside chicken and pack tightly. Spoon a little juice into cavity. Tie chicken, passing string around legs and behind parson's nose and then tie legs down tight onto the parson's nose. Put chicken into a small baking dish, placed in another pan of water.

3. Basting mixture: Add pineapple juice to juices remaining from marinated pineapple, together with orange peel and 4 tbs of slivovitz. Season with salt and pepper and add juniper berries, vinegar and honey. Place mixture into a saucepan, bring to a boil, lower heat and simmer 2 minutes.

4. Paint chicken with some of the basting mixture and then pour a little more mixture over chicken. Place into oven for 1 hour 10 minutes. Turn the bird over 20 minutes before end of cooking. Baste chicken from time to time.

5. Remove chicken to a dish and keep warm.

6. Place remaining basting sauce into pan juices. Heat slowly, strain through a sieve. Add chicken stock mixed with arrowroot. Stir until thickened.

7. Carve chicken and cover with sauce.

A special hint:

Use good fresh pineapples. Unless they're very good it's better to use canned.

POULET FARCI TRUFFIERE

For 4 servings, you will need:

1 chicken 3 lb (1.4 kg)
5 oz (142 g) Pâté de Foie Gras
   Strasbourg
3 truffles and their juice*
2 slices fresh bread
2 fl oz (5.6 cl) madeira
½ tsp thyme

Freshly ground salt
Freshly ground white pepper
4 slices bacon
Garnish:
  Broiled halved tomatoes
  Fresh green beans
  Tiny new boiled potatoes

First prepare:

To marinate bird (for one day) remove giblets and ends of wings and keep for stock. Dry chicken and place two truffles inside. Slice another truffle very, very thinly, pull up skin of chicken breast and insert truffle slices under skin (it looks like black blotches). Cover bird with wax paper and place in refrigerator for one day.

The following day. Sprinkle wine over chopped crustless fresh bread and set aside until required. Preheat oven to 350°F (177°C). Place a serving dish in warm oven. Put liver pâté into a bowl. A long piece of string for trussing will be required.

Now cook!

1. To pâté add thyme, salt, pepper and wine-soaked bread; mix until smooth.
2. Remove truffles from cavity of chicken, slice thinly and add to blended pâté mixture. Stuff bird with mixture.
3. Either sew bird, or use poultry pins to hold meat together.
4. Take a long piece of string and place it over and around legs—secure tightly—turn bird over and crisscross string over back and then around wings. Tie firmly in center.
5. Sprinkle salt and pepper over breast and place bacon over bird to keep it moist.
6. Place trussed bird on a baking dish and roast in preheated oven 350°F (177°C) for 1¼ hours.
7. 20 minutes before end of cooking remove bacon and set aside to use as a garnish.
8. Cut string from browned bird and place bird on a heated serving platter. Arrange vegetables around chicken, sprinkle with bacon and serve at once.

Poulet Farci Truffière

CHICKEN APRICOT

For 4 servings, you will need:

4 lbs 4 oz (1.9 kg) chicken
8 oz (227 g) dried apricots
20 fl oz (6 dl) chicken stock
1 medium onion
4 cloves
4 oz (113 g) apricot jam
2 limes

2 fl oz (5.6 cl) apricot liqueur
Clarified butter*
1 tsp ginger root*(or ground
  ginger)
Freshly ground salt
Freshly ground white pepper
All-purpose flour

First prepare:

Remove all giblets from inside chicken. Detach neck but don't cut off neck skin flaps. Dry chicken thoroughly both inside and out. Prepare chicken stock. Peel onion and leave whole. Press the 4 cloves into onion. Weigh apricot jam. Juice 2 limes. Measure apricot liqueur.

Now cook!

1. Place apricots into a medium saucepan with sieved chicken stock. Cook over low heat for about 15 minutes until plump.

2. Take "dried" chicken and cut off wings at first joint (from the wing end). Place the wing tips with apricots. Press down onto the breast bone to compress the shape of chicken.

3. Place onion, stuck with cloves, into chicken cavity. Now "truss" (tie up) chicken by taking a piece of string about 2 feet (60 cm) long. Find middle point and loop this around both the leg ends pulling tight so that the legs stay close together. Now turn the chicken on its breast and tie string into a knot in the center part of the back. Pull neck flap back over knot and tie string tightly to flap. Cut off extra string. This keeps the bird in good shape during roasting.

4. Grate fresh ginger over chicken (1 tsp should be enough). Rub this into skin (see end of this step if using dried ginger). Now season a little flour with pepper and salt and dust bird with it liberally, but don't let it pile up between legs and breast or it will get soggy. Brush bird with clarified butter and set it on a wire cake rack over a roasting pan. (If you are using dried ginger add it at this time after bird is buttered).

5. Roast at 375°F (190°C) for 18 minutes per pound (0.5 kg). After first 30 minutes, cover bird with a well dampened brown paper bag. This keeps flesh juicy and not burnt.

6. Carve roasted bird into 2 breasts, 2 thighs and 2 drumsticks. Keep warm. Deglaze roast pan (having first poured off fats) by straining reduced "apricot chicken stock" off apricots and into roasting pan. Scrape to loosen all particles and then pour back over apricots.

7. Add jam and lime juice. Let jam melt, then at last moment add apricot liqueur. Heat through and pour over chicken.

A special hint:

See Step 2. Press down on chicken breast. This keeps bird flatter and as a result breast doesn't dry out as much.

ROCK CORNISH HEN CHINEEMAN

For 4 servings, you will need:

4 Rock Cornish hens—usually about
    1 lb (0.5 kg) each
12 tbs clarified butter＊
4 oz (113 g) onion
7 oz (198 g) cucumber
2 tbs firmly packed brown sugar
3 fl oz (8 cl) tarragon wine
    vinegar
4 fl oz (1.2 dl) chicken stock
2 fl oz (5.6 cl) rum
1 tsp soya sauce
1 oz (28 g) crystallized ginger
4 medium bananas (firm, but
    not green)

1 medium fresh pineapple
4 large mango pieces (usually
    canned, but better fresh)
6 oz (170 g) dark sweet
    cherries
1 tsp granulated sugar
3 fl oz (8 cl) brandy
1 level tsp arrowroot
1 fl oz (2.8 cl) tarragon
    wine vinegar
Freshly ground salt
Freshly ground white pepper

71

First prepare:

Wash inside of hens and dry very thoroughly. Cut off wings and chop and then cut through back on either side of backbone, removing backbone (keep bones for stock). Measure clarified butter. Peel and thinly slice onion. Slice unpeeled cucumber. Measure sugar and vinegars. Make chicken stock. Measure rum. Have soya sauce handy. Weigh crystallized ginger and slice. Cut pineapple into equal quarters and remove core. Cut mangoes into thin wedges. De-stalk or drain cherries. Measure brandy. Mix arrowroot with tarragon wine vinegar.

Now cook!

1. Place all four trussed hens into a baking dish, season with pepper and salt and baste with clarified butter.

2. Roast basted hens in an oven set at 350°F (177°C) for 35 minutes. During this time, cover wing tips and backbone with water in a pan and cook for 30 minutes for stock. Strain and reserve.

3. Into a pan pour 4 tbs warmed clarified butter and add sliced onions, cucumber and season with salt and pepper. Add brown sugar and wine vinegar.

4. Reduce heat to low. Pour 4 fl oz (1.2 dl) chicken stock into a bowl, stir in rum and soya sauce. Pour this over vegetables. Add slices of ginger and cook over low heat.

5. Pour 2 tbs clarified butter into another pan, lay in 4 firm peeled bananas on high heat. Add slices of mango and black cherries. Sprinkle with sugar.

6. Pour brandy onto frying fruit and flame. Turn heat to low.

7. Strain juices from cucumber and onion and remove grease. Add this juice to fruits (also save ginger from vegetables and add this).

8. Remove cooked hens and remove strings.

9. Surround hens with fruits. Bring fruit juices to a boil and thicken with arrowroot mixed with vinegar. Pour sauce over chicken and fruit. Garnish with pineapple quarters.

PIGEONNEAUX PARADIS

For 4 servings, you will need:

4 Rock Cornish hens 1¼ lbs
   each (566 g)
Clarified butter*
4 oz (113 g) carrots
4 oz (113 g) onion
4 oz (113 g) celery
2 fl oz (5.6 cl) dry sherry
3 tbs clarified butter*
1½ oz (42 g) all-purpose flour
1 oz (28 g) truffle*

4 fl oz (1.2 dl) madeira
16 fl oz (4 dl) veal stock
2 tbs red currant jelly
4 fl oz (1.2 dl) red wine
1 tbs lemon juice
8 oz (227 g) seedless green
   grapes
Parsley
Freshly ground salt
Freshly ground white pepper

First prepare:

Wash inside of hens and dry very thoroughly. Cut off wings and chop and then cut through back on either side of backbone to remove it. (Keep bones for stock.) Cut hens into halves. Slice carrot, celery and onion. Finely slice truffles. Halve grapes. Wash, dry and finely chop parsley. Squeeze juice of lemon. Measure dry and liquid ingredients. Preheat oven to 400ºF (205ºC).

Now cook!

1. Pour 4 tbs clarified butter into a baking dish and place over high heat. Put wings and backbone in and fry.

2. Stir in carrots, onion, and celery and continue to fry.

3. Place hen halves on bed of vegetables and pour on sherry. Season generously with salt and white pepper and baste with a little clarified butter. Roast in preheated oven set at 400ºF (205ºC) on middle shelf for 45 minutes.

4. Make a roux of 3 tbs clarified butter and flour by melting butter in a pan, stirring in flour until it browns. Gradually stir in madeira and veal stock. Stir in red currant jelly and juice of truffle, bring to a boil and simmer over low heat for 40 minutes (until hens are cooked) stirring occasionally.

5. Stir in red wine and lemon juice.

6. Remove Cornish hens from oven after 45 minutes, check if cooked.

7. Lift hens onto a serving platter and keep warm. Stir sauce into bed of vegetables. Bring to a boil, skim fat and sieve into a clean pan. Discard vegetables.

8. Sprinkle hens with halved green grapes and sliced truffles.

9. Dust with chopped parsley and serve.

ROAST SADDLE OF MUTTON—CUMBERLAND SAUCE

For 8 servings, you will need:

1 boned saddle of mutton (with kidneys)
    12 lb (5.4 kg)
Clarified butter*
Freshly ground salt
Freshly ground black pepper
Flour
Dried rosemary
Cumberland sauce:
Peel and juice of 1 lemon

Peel and juice of 1 orange
4 fl oz (1.2 dl) port
2 tbs red currant jelly
1½ tsp English mustard
2 tbs vinegar
Cayenne pepper
Freshly ground salt
2 oz (56 g) glacé cherries*
1 tsp arrowroot

First prepare:

Remove kidneys from mutton. Trim and cut into ½-inch slices. Score fat diagonally and rub rosemary leaves into cuts. Tie up saddle tightly, flour and season with salt and pepper. Preheat oven to 325°F (163°C). Place two long skewers through the eye meat down the entire length of the saddle.

Cumberland sauce: Cut lemon and orange peel into very fine slivers. Blanch in boiling water 5 minutes. Drain. Measure mustard. Juice lemon and orange. Roughly chop cherries.

Now cook!

1. *Meat:* Place saddle on rack in shallow pan in oven. Pour a little clarified butter over it. Roast for 20 minutes per lb (0.5 kg). Fifteen minutes before the end of cooking place slices of kidneys down back of saddle securing them with toothpicks and return to oven for remainder of cooking time.

2. Carve joint. Pour a little sauce over meat and accompany with braised celery heart and salamanca potatoes (see page 545).

3. *Cumberland sauce:* Place blanched orange and lemon peel in saucepan, add all but 1 tbs port, red currant jelly, mustard, cayenne, salt, orange and lemon juice and vinegar. Boil 2 minutes.

4. Stir in arrowroot mixed with 1 tbs port until thickened. Allow to cool. Add cherries to cooled sauce and serve in sauceboat.

A special hint:

It is most important to put long metal skewers through the saddle. They help to transmit heat to the center and they stop a natural tendency the saddle has to bunch up at the ends.

LAMB APOLLO

For 6-8 servings, you will need:

1 saddle of lamb 14 lb (6.4 kg)
  bone-in weight
3 lambs kidneys
1 medium onion
2 sticks celery
1 medium carrot
2 cloves garlic
2 shallots

1 dozen oysters
4 oz (113 g) mushrooms
2 eggs
Juice ½ lemon
Clarified butter*
Freshly ground salt
Freshly ground black pepper
Flour

First prepare:

Debone saddle of lamb. If courage fails you coax your butcher. Wash and scrape carrots then slice very finely. Wash and finely chop celery, peel and finely dice onion. Smash garlic, finely slice shallots. Wash and slice mushrooms, squeeze lemon juice. Trim fat off kidneys, remove core and outer skin and then cut in halves. Break two eggs, pour juice from oysters. Two skewers and some string will be required. Preheat oven to 325°F (163°C) and place a large serving platter into warm oven.

Now cook!

1. Pour some of clarified butter into a frypan to just cover bottom and when heated add finely cut vegetables—onion, celery, garlic, shallots and carrots—allow to shallow fry. Season thoroughly with salt and pepper.

2. Add mushrooms sprinkled with lemon juice, reduce heat and allow to simmer.

3. To this mixture add kidneys and continue cooking for 15 minutes.

4. Pour mixture into a bowl and allow to cool.

5. Add two eggs to cooled mixture.

6. Open saddle and pour mixture into center allowing 2 inches (5 cm) free at either end and side.

7. The oysters can be added at this point and laid over ingredients. Again season thoroughly with salt and pepper.

8. Close the two flaps so that they just overlap and secure with two skewers.

9. Then with a piece of string bind the whole saddle firmly together like a long roll.

10. Pop stuffed lamb into a roasting pan.

11. Sprinkle a little flour over top, season generously with salt and pepper. Pour 8 tbs clarified butter over roast and place in preheated oven 325°F (163°C) for 3 hours. Do not baste at all as there should be enough natural fat covering the lamb to self-baste.

12. When lamb is tender remove from oven, cut off string, place on a serving dish and serve at once.

13. The juices from lamb should be made into a gravy and served in a sauceboat with lamb.

Lamb Apollo

LAMBCARRE PROVENCALE

For 6 servings, you will need:

2 racks of lamb**2 lb (0.9 kg) each
   (English loin)
1 lb (0.5 kg) potatoes (large)
1 oz (28 g) white bread crumbs*
4 tsp dry mustard
½ tsp rosemary
½ tsp basil

½ tsp thyme
1 clove garlic
Clarified butter*
All-purpose flour
Freshly ground salt
Freshly ground white pepper

**Cut between 3rd and 4th rib at shoulder (5 ribs long).

First prepare:

Peel potatoes and place whole in cold water. Measure herbs and mustard. Score outer skin of the lamb in diagonal strips. Cut down and up between ribs to form diamonds. Preheat oven to 400°F (205°C). Heat a serving platter in warm oven.

Now cook!

1. Rub herbs between your hands and add to mustard powder.
2. Spread outer scored skin of lamb with herbed mustard, pressing it well down into cracks.
3. Dust lightly with flour.
4. Push fine slivers of garlic into pockets cut into meat. (Remove before serving; they can be located more easily if marked with toothpicks).
5. Season with salt and white pepper and set aside for moment.
6. Cut potatoes in ½ inch (1.2 cm) slices and place in a heated frypan lightly coated with clarified butter. Fry until golden brown—about 9 minutes.
7. Place prepared lamb onto potatoes (no basting will be required as meat has its own natural fat).
8. Roast in preheated oven set at 400°F (205°C), for 1 hour.
9. After 30 minutes dust roasting lamb with bread crumbs and continue roasting for another 30 minutes.
10. When cooked, remove meat from oven, drain off fat and place it on a heated serving platter. Put potatoes under broiler for 2 minutes to give a crusty golden brown surface. Arrange these around meat.

ROAST LEG OF LAMB NELSON

65

For 4-6 servings, you will need:

1 leg of lamb, 4 lb (1.8 kg)
1 tbs seasoned flour
Freshly ground salt
Freshly ground white pepper

6 parsley stalks*
16 fl oz (4 dl) apple and orange juice
Roasting vegetables: diced potatoes,
onions, carrots, turnips

First prepare:

Rub lamb with seasoned flour, shake off excess. Make several even and decorative shallow incisions in heavy outer fat layers and pack into these some well-washed pieces of parsley. Preheat oven to 325°F (163°C). Open fruit juice can. Prepare roasting vegetables of your choice.

Now cook!

1. Place leg fat side uppermost on oven rack. Place drip pan on the next rack down underneath lamb.

2. After 10 minutes cooking, draw out your oven racks so that the lamb is exposed and place lamb over another roasting pan. Remove first drip pan. Add roasting vegetables to pan and replace in oven. Baste lamb with apple and orange juice. The drippings from the lamb will collect in the pan and keep the roasting vegetables from drying. Allow 30 minutes per 1 lb (0.5 kg) lamb and baste with juice at least 4 times during cooking.

3. When lamb is cooked, remove from oven. Set aside and remove vegetables from pan drippings. Place pan over heat and boil drippings until reduced and thickened. Raise oven temperature to 500°F (260°C). Replace lamb over a pan as before and spoon thickened juices over lamb. Roast for 5 minutes to form a crisp golden orange and apple glaze. Place lamb on a platter. Skim fat from pan juices and use juices as a gravy over slices of lamb.

A special hint:

The lamb can be cooked on a rotisserie if you have enough space to insert a pan between the leg and the baking pan.

71

LAMB ANDREW

For 6 servings, you will need:

5 lb (2.3 kg) leg of lamb
4 oz (113 g) bread crumbs*
2 medium onions
1 medium carrot
1 leek
22 fl oz (6.5 dl) cold water
1 tsp crystal salt
2 oranges
2 oz (56 g) sugar

5 fl oz (1.5 dl) Grand Marnier
1 tbs plus 1 sprig parsley
2 bay leaves
2 tsp arrowroot
2 fl oz (5.6 cl) water
8 tbs clarified butter*
All-purpose flour
Freshly ground salt
Freshly ground white pepper

First prepare:

Carefully remove bones from leg of lamb, leaving last shin bone. Roughly chop onions, carrot and leek. Peel rind from oranges, remove whiteskin (pith) and cut into slivers. Measure water and Grand Marnier. Finely chop parsley. Combine 2 tbs flour with salt and pepper for dusting. Preheat oven to 350°F (177°C). Heat a serving dish in warm oven. Blend arrowroot and water in a small bowl.

Now cook!

1. Place bread crumbs into a heated frypan and pour over them 4 tbs clarified butter and let cook gently until golden.

2. Pour remaining clarified butter into a hot saucepan, add onions, carrots and leek, stir and add lamb bone and 16 fl oz (4 dl) cold water. Raise heat, bring to a boil and simmer until reduced to half.

3. Season stock with a sprig of parsley, bay leaves and crystal salt.

4. Place orange rind into a small pan with 6 fl oz (1.6 dl) cold water and bring to a boil.

5. Add granulated sugar to boiling orange rind and reduce on low heat to form an orange glaze.

6. With a sharp knife detach segments of oranges, leaving skinless portions.

7. Add segments to frying bread crumbs.

8. Place bread crumbs and orange segments into a bowl and add 1 fl oz (2.8 cl) Grand Marnier.

9. Season stuffing with salt and white pepper and 1 tbs chopped parsley.

10. Fill pouch in leg of lamb with stuffing. Close pouch with 5 skewers and crisscross string in between.

11. Make shallow diagonal slashes over top of lamb. Dust with seasoned flour.

12. Place roast in a roasting pan and put into preheated 350°F (177°C) oven for one hour and forty minutes.

13. After this period, remove lamb from oven and place roasting pan in another pan of water (baste lamb with orange glaze) and return to oven. Increase heat to 500°F (260°C) and cook for another 15 minutes.

14. Pour juices from first roasting pan and strain them into a saucepan. There should be 6 fl oz (1.6 dl). Strain reduced stock and add 8 fl oz (2 dl) to pan drippings.

15. Add drippings from a small pan in which lamb was glazed. Stir in arrowroot mixture. Cook until mixture is thickened. Stir in remaining 4 fl oz (1.2 dl) Grand Marnier.

16. Remove skewers and string from lamb and let roast "set" in warm oven for 15 minutes.

17. Place lamb on a platter and spoon over sauce. This roast is easily carved because it is boned.

Lamb Andrew

67

ROAST LEG OF PORK WITH SPICED PEACHES

For 8-12 servings, you will need:

1 fresh ham, 8 lb (3.6 kg)

Seasoned oil:
½ tsp thyme
½ tsp caraway seed
2 cloves garlic
4 fl oz (1.2 dl) olive oil
Freshly ground salt

Apple Wine gravy:
1 tart apple
Black peppercorns
Cloves

4 fl oz (1.2 dl) dry white wine

Spiced peaches:
8 cling peach halves (canned)
10 fl oz (3 dl) wine vinegar
½ tsp cloves
1 small cinnamon stick
½ tsp whole allspice
Large bunch watercress

First prepare:

Get ham without skin removed. Score outer skin of ham, simmer oil ingredients together on low heat for 30 minutes. Strain, bottle for use. Peel, core and finely slice apple, grind pepper, strain off juice from canned peaches. Wash watercress well. Set oven at 350°F (177°C). Place drip pan under oven rack.

Now cook!

1. Puncture ham in deepest muscle areas with steel skewer, sprinkle well with salt.

2. Brush joint with seasoned oil allowing oil to penetrate punctures.

3. Stand for 1 hour before roasting. Place joint directly on oven rack with drip pan on shelf below. Roast 30 minutes per lb (0.5 kg) (185°F: 85°C).

4. Simmer wine vinegar, cloves, cinnamon and allspice in a covered saucepan for 30 minutes. Pour over peach halves. When cold, lift out halves and place them around roasted ham. Strain and bottle spicy vinegar for later use.

5. Keep roast warm. Pour fat from drip pan and scrape meat residue into small frypan. Add clove, peppercorns, wine and apple. Simmer until soft. Bring to a boil, sieve, reheat and serve with sliced meat.

A special hint:

Don't leave peach halves in spiced vinegar longer than 15 minutes. You can strain vinegar and use it again and again for spicing fruit—it gets better!

CARRE DE PORC FARCI

For 15 servings, you will need:

10 lbs (4.5 kg) saddle of pork
  (6 ribs) cut short on flap or skirt
3 pork kidneys
Pinch thyme

Freshly ground salt
Freshly ground white pepper
Clarified butter*

First prepare:

Get pork without skin removed. Coax your butcher to debone saddle of pork for you. Wash kidneys thoroughly and slice them in half lengthwise. Preheat oven to 375°F (190°C). Heat a meat platter in warming oven. Butchers' twine will be required.

Now cook!

1. Remove rind from lower flaps (or breast).
2. Score remaining top rind with a sharp knife in long diagonal strokes both ways to form diamonds.
3. Place saddle flat on board inside up and season generously with salt and white pepper and thyme. Place kidneys onto this and roll up firmly.
4. Tie securely with string every 2 inches (5 cm).
5. Place saddle on a roasting pan and season outside with salt and pepper.
6. Drizzle clarified butter across meat.
7. Pop into preheated oven 375°F (190°C) for 3 hours and 20 minutes (20 minutes to the lb: 0.5 kg).
8. No basting is required. The meat has its own fat to keep it moist.
9. After cooking period remove saddle (which will be crisp and golden brown) from oven and cut off string.
10. Place on a meat platter and cut down center. Run carving knife under crisp rind to loosen it—superb crackling!

ROAST SUCKLING PIG (COCHINILLO)

For 8 servings, you will need:

1 suckling pig, 17 lb (7.7 kg)
2½ oz (70 g) dark brown sugar
6 cloves garlic
Freshly ground black pepper
Freshly ground salt
2 fl oz (5.6 cl) olive oil

2 fl oz (5.6 cl) white wine
    vinegar
Basting sauce:
Remaining garlic marinade
12 fl oz (3.2 dl) dry white wine
1 tbs thyme

First prepare:

Cut length of foil 5 inches (12.7 cm) larger around than grill rack. Fold edges to form a tray. Cut off head behind shoulder of pig. Split down inside of back, opening it out, but don't completely sever. Turn pig skin side up and place a skewer through rump. Place another skewer through front of pig. Measure oil and vinegar. Measure sugar. Measure white wine. Preheat oven to 375°F (190°C).

Now cook!

1. Mix brown sugar, garlic, vinegar and olive oil together. Season with salt and black pepper.

2. Make cuts on underside of pig to release fat when cooking. Place pig on tray and spoon half of the marinade mixture into breast cage. Allow to stand for 1 hour.

3. To remaining marinade stir in white wine and thyme to form a basting sauce.

4. Brush inside of pig with basting mixture and then place in foil tray on oven rack and roast for 2 hours. Place an oven pan on a lower oven shelf under pig. Baste pig from time to time with basting sauce.

5. Raise heat to 450°F (232°C), turn pig and cook for 25 minutes longer, or until skin (crackling) is crisp.

6. Strain 10 fl oz (3 dl) of drippings from foil pan and add 2 fl oz (5.6 cl) of basting sauce remaining. Bring sauce to a boil and reduce. Skim fat and serve in a sauceboat with sliced roasted pork.

Method to turn pig:

1. Puncture foil dish to release 10 fl oz (6 dl) drippings into a pan.

2. Add 2 fl oz (5.6 cl) basting liquor.

3. Withdraw entire oven rack and pig. Sandwich pig between two oven racks over a large roasting pan to catch drippings and turn upside down.

4. Remove foil pan being careful not to tear skin. Place whole rack into oven and then raise oven heat to 450°F (232°C). Keep roasting pan underneath.

A special hint:

Use heavy duty foil for special "roasting dish." This dish fits into a 28 inch (72 cm) inside-width oven.

Roast Suckling Pig (Cochinillo)

PORK SPARERIBS

70

For 4 servings, you will need:

4 pieces pork spareribs, 14 oz
(396 g) each
Freshly ground salt
Freshly ground black pepper
Sauce:
2 fl oz (5.6 cl) oil
1 medium onion
2 cloves garlic

1 green pepper (capsicum)
1½ tbs firmly packed brown sugar
Juice and peel of 1 lemon
4 fl oz (1.2 dl) tomato sauce
4 fl oz (1.2 dl) malt vinegar
1 tsp cayenne pepper
1 tsp dried tarragon
1 tbs Worcestershire sauce

First prepare:

Paint broiler rack with oil. Puncture spareribs with a knife. Finely slice onion. Smash garlic. Finely dice green pepper. Remove peel from lemon and juice. Measure tomato sauce and malt vinegar. Preheat oven to 350°F (177°C). Finely slice lemon peel.

Now cook!

1. Place oil into a saucepan and when hot fry onions, garlic and green pepper for 2 minutes. Stir in brown sugar and when dissolved stir in lemon peel and juice, tomato sauce, vinegar, Worcestershire sauce, cayenne and tarragon. Reduce heat and allow sauce to simmer for 5 minutes.

2. Place spareribs onto broiler rack standing in a roasting pan, season with salt and pepper and paint with a little of the sauce. Allow spareribs to roast for 1½ hours basting every 15 minutes with sauce.

3. Remove and cut spareribs into sections.

A special hint:

This is a pleasant mild tasting rib dish. To enforce its flavor add an additional 4 fl oz (1.2 dl) malt vinegar and marinate ribs in sauce overnight. Drain ribs and then proceed as at Step 2 above.

GEVULDE KALFSFILET

For 4 servings, you will need:

4 oz (113 g) pork tenderloin
1½ lbs (680 g) veal tenderloin
5 oz (142 g) fat bacon*
1 bay leaf
1 tsp rosemary
1 tsp thyme
1 tsp basil
4 oz (113 g) mushrooms
2 fl oz (5.6 cl) cognac

5 fl oz (1.5 dl) red wine
½ lemon
1 tsp arrowroot
4 tbs clarified butter*
Freshly ground salt
Freshly ground black pepper
Freshly ground white pepper
Garnish:
Broiled tomato halves and spinach

First prepare:

Put bacon, mushrooms, pork tenderloin and 4 oz (113 g) only of veal tenderloin (use the trimmings and the thin end of the tenderloin) through a grinder. Set aside in a bowl. Measure herbs, cognac and red wine. Squeeze juice of lemon. String and toothpicks will be required. Heat a serving platter in warm oven. Trim silver skin off remaining veal fillet, slit lengthwise almost in two. Open it up and beat slightly flat. Blend arrowroot with 1 fl oz (2.8 cl) red wine.

Now cook!

1. Heat a pan and pour in cognac. Add bay leaf and other herbs. Bring to a boil and then reduce to 1 tsp. Keep pan covered.
2. Season ground meat with salt and white pepper.
3. Sieve cognac and flavored herbs and place herbs into a clean pan containing 4 tbs clarified butter. Heat through over a low heat. Reserve liquid.
4. Add strained liquid to ground meat mixture.
5. Place savory meat filling down center of opened and beaten fillet of veal. Wrap veal around filling.
6. Lace together with toothpicks, then secure with string tied in a crisscross fashion like a ski boot.
7. Place stuffed fillet in a cast iron casserole and strain herb flavored butter over fillet. Season with salt, black pepper and lemon juice. Roast in a preheated 350°F (177°C) oven for 45 minutes.
8. Place strained herbs back into a pan and add 4 fl oz (1.2 dl) of wine.
9. When cooked, remove stuffed veal fillet from oven, cut off string and remove toothpicks. Place on a heated serving platter and keep hot in warm oven.
10. Skim excess fat from pan drippings. Add drippings to herb flavored wine.
11. Stir in blended wine and arrowroot until sauce thickens.
12. Pour sauce over stuffed fillet and serve at once. Garnish with broiled tomato halves and spinach.

A special hint:

Refer Step 11. When adding arrowroot it is vital to stir it completely before pouring it into cooking liquid. Be sure to have liquid at a boil and stir as you make addition. Add only a little at a time to avoid "overthickening," which makes sauce repulsive.

FEINSCHMECKERROLE

For 4 servings, you will need:

4 slices leg of veal
Clarified butter*
4 large flat mushrooms
4 slices smoked ham
8 sage leaves

Freshly ground black pepper
Freshly ground salt
2 tbs ground hazelnuts
1 tbs paprika
Juice ½ lemon

First prepare:

Beat veal slices until thin. Finely slice sage leaves. Squeeze lemon. Preheat oven to 400°F (205°C).

Now cook!

1. Place 1 slice of smoked ham on each veal slice, season with pepper and sprinkle each with sage leaves and ground hazelnuts.

2. Fry whole mushrooms in a little clarified butter and place 1 mushroom on each veal slice.

3. Roll up veal and tie with string. Season with salt and pepper.

4. Place veal rolls in an ovenproof dish, brush with clarified butter and dust generously with paprika. Brush once more with clarified butter. Place in oven and bake uncovered for 20 minutes, basting from time to time.

5. Remove veal from oven and slice each roll in half lengthways with a very sharp knife. Arrange on a serving dish.

6. Heat pan juices and add lemon juice. Stir well to scrape up all particles and spoon over veal rolls.

7. Accompany with Broccoli with French Dressing (see page 516).

A special hint:

The mushrooms must be large and have heavy veins.

ROAST SPICED PRIME RIBS OF BEEF AND YORKSHIRE PUDDING

For 8 servings, you will need:

1 standing beef rib roast
(prime ribs), 8 lb (3.6 kg)
Clarified butter*

Spice mixture:
2 cloves garlic
Freshly ground salt
1 tsp ground ginger
½ tsp nutmeg
½ tsp cinnamon

½ tsp cardamon
1 tsp freshly ground black
pepper

Yorkshire pudding:
8 oz (227 g) all-purpose flour
4 eggs
20 fl oz (6 dl) milk
Freshly ground salt

First prepare:

Spice mixture: Mix smashed garlic with salt, ground ginger, nutmeg, cardamon, cinnamon and black pepper.

Meat: Make incision in between bones, open pockets out and fill with spice mixture. Preheat oven to 350°F (177°C).

Yorkshire pudding: Sift flour and salt into a bowl, make a well in center, add eggs and milk and whisk into a smooth batter. Cover and leave for 1 hour.

Now cook!

1. Place meat into a small roasting pan. Paint with clarified butter and allow to roast for 1 hour and 35 minutes in 350°F (177°C) oven (medium rare).

2. Raise oven heat to 400°F (205°C). Remove beef and place in the center of a shallow ovenproof serving dish. Pour drippings from roasting pan around meat (¼ inch: 7 mm deep). Pour pudding batter around meat and bake for a further 40 minutes.

3. Serve beef surrounded by Yorkshire pudding.

A special hint:

The fat must be smoking before batter is added; to achieve this set serving dish on top of range while oven temperature is increased.

DAUBE NEW ORLEANS

For 4 servings, you will need:

5 lbs (2.3 kg) beef round
   (boneless "silverside")
12 oz (340 g) onion
3 cloves garlic
2 tbs fresh parsley stalks*
4 cloves
1 tsp thyme
16 fl oz (4 dl) red wine
1 fl oz (2.8 cl) olive oil
4 oz (113 g) pork fat (purchase in
   a strip at least 6 inches: 15 cm
   long, rind off)

½ tsp cayenne pepper
1 tsp Tabasco sauce
2 fl oz (5.6 cl) brandy
7 fl oz (1.8 dl) sherry
2 bay leaves
6 fl oz (1.6 dl) beef stock
1 tsp arrowroot
Clarified butter*
Freshly ground salt
Freshly ground black pepper

First prepare:

Thickly slice 8 oz (227 g) onion and place as a bed in a bowl. Smash garlic cloves and spread them on surface of meat, wipe off and repeat on other side of meat. (Scrape off surplus.) Add scraped-off garlic to onions. Chop parsley stalks and add together with cloves and ½ tsp powdered thyme to onions. Pour on red wine. Add meat and sprinkle with olive oil. Season generously with salt and black pepper. Cover bowl with a piece of muslin and marinate in a cool place (not refrigerator) for three days! Turn meat every day. Slice pork fat into ½-inch (1.2 cm) thick shoelaces and place in a small bowl, sprinkle with ½ tsp thyme, cayenne pepper and six shakes of Tabasco sauce. Moisten with brandy and 2 fl oz (5.6 cl) sherry. Add bay leaves, cover and also marinate for three days! Slice 4 oz (113 g) onion. Measure remaining dry and liquid ingredients. Preheat oven to 350°F (177°C).

Now cook!

1. Three days later.
2. Pour off marinade into a pan on high heat and bring to a boil. Skim completely.
3. Place meat and fat on a board and place strips of pork fat into a larding needle and thrust through boneless beef (this assists the fattiness of meat and improves the flavor and juiciness considerably).
4. After wine marinade has boiled and been skimmed clear, strain it through a sieve and discard vegetables.
5. Dry meat thoroughly and place in a deep casserole. Cover with 2 fl oz (5.6 cl) clarified butter.
6. Sprinkle 4 oz (113 g) onion over meat. Moisten with beef stock and 4 fl oz (1.2 dl) of strained marinade (liquid should come halfway up pan).
7. Place in preheated oven 350°F (177°C) for three hours, but keep an eye on it to check liquid level. Add more straight red wine if necessary.
8. After three hours cooking take casserole from oven and remove meat. Skim fat from pan juices.
9. Increase heat to high and bring liquid in casserole to boiling point.
10. Add another 4 fl oz (1.2 dl) sherry and 6 fl oz (1.6 dl) remaining wine marinade.
11. Blend arrowroot in a small bowl with 1 fl oz (2.8 cl) sherry. Stir into bubbling liquid in casserole until sauce thickens.
12. Pour slightly thickened sauce over "daube" and serve.

Daube New Orleans

CHICKEN LA BRESSE

For 4 servings, you will need:

1 chicken, 2½ lb (1.2 kg)
8 oz (227 g) button mushrooms
1 medium onion
Clarified butter*
12 raw jumbo shrimp
1 medium carrot
2 celery stalks
Juice of ¼ lemon
Freshly ground salt
Freshly ground white pepper
5 fl oz (1.5 dl) water

50 fl oz (1.5 l) chicken stock
2 tsp basil
6 parsley stalks*
1 bay leaf
1 tbs butter
1 tbs all-purpose flour
1 egg yolk
1 tbs heavy cream
1 truffle*
1 tbs brandy

First prepare:

Cook shrimp in boiling salted water for 2 minutes. Drain, shell and devein and cut into round slices. Slice onion and carrot into ¼-inch (7 mm) slices. Finely slice celery. Remove wings from chicken. Measure water and chicken stock. Measure butter and flour. Sift flour. Slice truffle thinly.

Now cook!

1. Place some clarified butter to just cover bottom in a casserole dish on heat. Add onion, carrot and celery. Place chicken on bed of vegetables. Cover and allow to steam for 1 minute.

2. Cover chicken with stock and add basil, parsley stalks and bay leaf. Bring to a boil and allow chicken to poach covered for 30 minutes.

3. In another pan on heat place some clarified butter to just cover bottom. Add mushrooms (vein side uppermost), lemon juice, water and season with salt and pepper. Allow to cook gently for 4 minutes.

4. Melt butter in another saucepan and stir in flour, forming a roux. Drain mushrooms and add liquid gradually to roux. Strain off 8 fl oz (2 dl) of the chicken stock in which chicken is cooking and stir into roux. Whisk until smooth and thickened. Season with salt and pepper. Bring to boil, lower heat and simmer for 10 minutes, whisking from time to time. Beat egg yolk into sauce until thick. Then beat cream into sauce. Whisk to mix. Add shrimp and drained mushrooms to sauce with brandy.

5. Remove chicken from pot. Slice off thighs at ball-and-socket joint and remove skin. Trim off first leg joint. Detach whole breast at wishbone. Press down and then lift meat off rib cage. Cut whole breast in half. Remove skin.

6. Lay chicken on serving dish and cover with sauce. Decorate with slices of truffle.

A special hint:

Normally sauces thickened with egg yolk and cream are made by mixing the egg and cream and then adding. In this case I add yolk first — beat until thick and then add cream.

POULET FREDERIC

For 4 servings, you will need:

4 chicken legs (drumstick and thigh)
2 oz (56 g) leek
4 oz (113 g) liver pâté
4 oz (113 g) prosciutto ham (cured
   and smoked sliced raw ham)*
8 fl oz (2 dl) red wine
6 oz (170 g) carrot
8 oz (227 g) peas
6 oz (170 g) parsnips
6 oz (170 g) green beans

6 oz (170 g) mushrooms
6 oz (170 g) white turnip
Bouquet garni—3 inch (7.6
   cm) pieces celery, 4 parsley
   stalks,*1 bay leaf, 6 peppercorns
24 fl oz (7 dl) cold water
2 tsp arrowroot
Clarified butter*
Freshly ground salt
Freshly ground white pepper

70

First prepare:

Wash and peel all vegetables. Chop leek roughly. Finely slice turnip, mushrooms, parsnips. Leave beans whole. Cook peas briefly (3 minutes). Blend arrowroot with a little red wine. Measure wine. Prepare chicken legs by cutting each in two (4 thighs and 4 drumsticks). Remove bones from thighs and from drumsticks. To do this, carefully scrape the skin away from bone starting at the ball-and-socket joint, ending approximately 1 inch (2.5 cm) away from "ankle." These bones may then be chopped off (keep bones for a good chicken stock).

For stock, pour a little clarified butter into a frypan to just cover bottom, brown leek, then add chicken bones and cold water. Season with salt and white pepper. Simmer for one hour (should reduce to 16 fl oz (4 dl) stock). Preheat oven to 350°F (177°C).

Now cook!

1. Into a hot frypan add a little clarified butter to just cover bottom and fry parsnips and turnip.
2. Add mushrooms to frying parsnip and turnip and continue to cook over moderate heat.
3. Place one tsp of pâté into each thigh and drumstick cavity and then roll a little ham around each portion. Fasten with a toothpick.
4. Pour vegetables into a casserole.
5. Add chicken stock, red wine and bouquet garni to vegetables.
6. Lightly cover frypan again with clarified butter and put in chicken packages and fry gently on both sides.
7. Transfer fried chicken to casserole containing vegetables.
8. Place uncovered in preheated 350°F (177°C) oven for 60 minutes.
9. Cook beans in a pot of boiling water for 7 minutes.
10. Remove chicken from oven, place chicken pieces on a platter and keep warm. Remove bouquet garni from pan juices. Reduce juice in pan and thicken with blended arrowroot. Bring to a boil. Add cooked peas and beans, reheat and spoon over chicken portions.
11. Serve at once piping hot.

A special hint:

The prosciutto ham should be ordered in good, even, very thin whole slices with a sheet of greased paper between each slice. This will make a more even wrapping.

BREADCRUMBED BREAST OF LAMB WITH CANTERBURY SAUCE

For 4 servings, you will need:

2 breasts of lamb
1 carrot
1 onion
4 tbs clarified butter*
1 tsp sugar
30 fl oz (9 dl) veal stock
1 oz (38 g) celery
Bay leaf
4 black peppercorns
1 tsp thyme
2 cloves garlic (tied in muslin bag)
2 tsp dry mustard
1 tsp cayenne pepper
Milk
2 egg yolks

2 tsp oil
3 oz (85 g) bread crumbs*
Parsley
1 lemon
Flour
Deep fat or oil
Canterbury sauce:
6 fl oz (1.6 dl) lamb breast
  braising liquid
2 tbs ketchup
2 tbs dry white wine
1 tbs red currant jelly
1 heaped tsp capers
2 tbs arrowroot

First prepare:

Slice carrot and onion, measure stock, measure bread crumbs. Mix egg yolks with oil. Preheat oven to 350°F (177°C).

Now cook!

1. Melt butter in large 4-quart oval casserole. Add carrot and onion and shallow fry with sugar until golden.

2. Add lamb breasts and brown slowly on both sides.

3. Add stock, celery, herbs, garlic and place in oven for 1 hour covered. Remove lamb breasts from casserole and take out bones.

4. Place boned lamb in an 8-inch square pan, pour over a little cooking liquid to cover lamb and place another pan on top with a heavy weight. Put in refrigerator to cool. Reserve remaining cooking liquid.

5. Remove from refrigerator when meat is cold and slice into finger lengths. Mix mustard and cayenne pepper to a paste with a little milk. Paint lamb pieces with this and dip them into the flour, beaten egg yolks and then bread crumbs.

6. Fill deep frypan with oil and fry pieces of lamb until golden—about 2 minutes.

7. *Canterbury sauce:* Place 6 fl oz reserved cooking liquid in pan and bring to a boil. Add ketchup, wine, red currant jelly and capers.

8. Mix arrowroot with a little braising liquid and stir into sauce until thickened.

9. Serve garnished with parsley sprigs and lemon wedges. Cover with Canterbury sauce.

BROILED LONGREACH OXTAIL

For 4 servings, you will need:

2 oxtails
Flour (seasoned)
2 tbs clarified butter*
2 onions
2 large carrots
3 small beef bones
2 beef stock or bouillon cubes
1 tbs tomato puree
2 fl oz (5.6 cl) red wine
1 bouquet garni
Freshly ground salt
Freshly ground black pepper

French mustard
1½ oz (42 g) bread crumbs*
Sauce:
2 tbs clarified butter*
1 medium onion
Chili powder
1 tbs flour
10 fl oz (3 dl) oxtail stock
1 tbs tomato puree
Freshly ground salt
Freshly ground black pepper

62

67

First prepare:

Cut oxtail into 3-inch (7.6 cm) pieces. Peel onions. Make stock. Measure wine. Fry bread crumbs gently in a little clarified butter until golden and crisp. Cut carrots in half crosswise.

Now cook!

1. Cover oxtail pieces with seasoned flour. Brown on all sides in clarified butter. Add onions and carrots and then cover with stock made from bouillon cubes. Add beef bones, tomato puree, wine, bouquet garni and season with salt and pepper. Bring to a boil and simmer covered for 4 hours. After 3 hours remove smaller pieces of oxtail and reserve.

2. Place oxtail in bowl and strain stock over meat. Chill and then remove fat.

3. *Sauce:* Fry onion in butter. Stir in chili powder and flour. Add tomato puree and 10 fl oz (3 dl) oxtail stock. Season with salt and pepper. Stir until sauce thickens.

4. Place oxtail pieces under a hot broiler to heat through. Remove and cover thinly with mustard. Breadcrumb oxtail pieces and then place back under hot broiler for 1 minute.

5. Place on serving dish with sauce.

MASTERTON CHICKEN

For 2 servings, you will need:

1 roasting chicken, 1½ lb (680 g)
3 oz (85 g) all-purpose flour
  (seasoned)
4 tbs clarified butter*
2 fl oz (5.6 cl) olive oil
2 fl oz (5.6 cl) brandy
20 fl oz (6 dl) dry red wine
4 oz (113 g) small mushrooms
2 oz (56 g) cooked ham ¼ inch
  (7 mm) thick

Freshly ground salt
Freshly ground black pepper
4 parsley stalks*
¼ tsp thyme
1 bay leaf
6 peppercorns
6 small onions
2 tbs arrowroot
2 tbs water or wine
1 tbs parsley

62

First prepare:

Cut chicken into halves, cut away backbones. Place in plastic bag with seasoned flour and shake well. Melt butter with oil. Warm brandy. Peel onions. Place parsley stalks, thyme, bay leaf, peppercorns in muslin bag. Mix arrowroot with water. Chop parsley for garnish. Preheat oven to 350°F (177°C).

Now cook!

1. Heat oil and butter in a casserole and fry chicken pieces till golden. Add onion and ham and fry until onion is just colored.

2. Pour over warmed brandy and set alight. Add wine, mushrooms and herbs. Mix flour, salt and water into a paste similar in consistency to soft clay. Use to seal edge of casserole and prevent moisture from escaping. Place in oven and bake for 45 minutes.

3. Test chicken, remove from sauce and thicken sauce with arrowroot and water. Remove herbs. Place chicken on serving dish and cover with sauce. Sprinkle with parsley.

A special hint:

To test chicken for "doneness," drive a small skewer into thick part of thigh. If the juice that issues forth is colorless, then it is cooked.

POULET SAUTE MAISON

For 2 servings, you will need:

2½ lb (1.2 kg) chicken
5 oz (142 g) shoulder bacon*
6 small mushrooms
1 medium onion
24 olives
4 tsp capers
2 tsp shallots
6 fl oz (1.6 dl) dry white wine

16 fl oz (4 dl) brown sauce
1 tsp clarified butter*
Parsley
Freshly ground black pepper
Freshly ground salt
All-purpose flour
1 tbs oil

First prepare:

Cut chicken into halves. Sprinkle with salt and pepper and coat with flour. Cut bacon into ½-inch (1.2 cm) cubes. Slice onion thinly. Cut mushrooms into quarters. Finely chop shallots. Measure wine. Preheat oven to 375°F (190°C). To make brown sauce see page 494.

Now cook!

1. Heat oil in pan and add bacon. When bacon is browned, add chicken, placing chicken in pan breast first.
2. Turn chicken when golden, add mushrooms and onion. Cover pan and simmer for 10 minutes.
3. Remove chicken, ham, mushrooms and onions. Add shallots to pan and then wine. Allow wine to reduce until 2 fl oz (5.6 cl) remains, stirring to scrape crust from bottom of pan.
4. Replace chicken, ham, mushrooms and onion in the pan and stir in brown sauce and olives.
5. Cover pan and place in oven for 45 minutes.
6. Serve garnished with capers and finely chopped parsley.

BLUFF BOLAR

62

For 4 servings, you will need:

4 rump or round steaks 6 oz (170 g)
2 oz (56 g) all-purpose flour
2 oz (56 g) carrot
1 bay leaf
2 parsley stalks*
1 sprig thyme
Clarified butter*
Freshly ground salt
Freshly ground black pepper

1 clove garlic
20 fl oz (6 dl) beef stock
  or bouillon
4 oz (113 g) mushrooms
2 dozen oysters
2 oz (56 g) onion
Parsley
Cornstarch

First prepare:

Dry steaks well. Flour and season them. Melt butter. Slice onion and carrot. Tie up herbs. Measure stock. Smash garlic. Peel mushrooms. Heat frypan to 400°F (205°C).

Now cook!

1. Heat clarified butter to just cover bottom of a skillet. Brown steaks thoroughly on both sides.
2. Remove from pan. Add onions and carrots to pan and brown.
3. Add garlic and steak, stock and herbs.
4. Stir well to scrape off meat residues. Replace lid and simmer slowly over low heat for 2½ hours. Add mushrooms 20 minutes before serving.
5. Skim fat from surface. Take out herbs, thicken with cornstarch mixed with water. Add oysters, reheat slightly and serve dusted with parsley.

HAWKE'S BAY LAMB

For 4 servings, you will need:

1 lb (0.5 kg) cold roast lamb
Onion Sauce:
2 medium onions
4 tbs clarified butter*
2 oz (56 g) all-purpose flour
20 fl oz (6 dl) cold milk
4 fl oz (1.2 dl) dry white wine

Freshly ground salt
Freshly ground white pepper
1 lb (0.5 kg) potatoes
Butter
1 tbs parsley
Paprika
Nutmeg

61

First prepare:

Cut lamb into ½-inch (1.2 cm) cubes. Slice onions finely. Measure flour, butter, milk and wine. Boil potatoes and mash them with butter, salt and nutmeg until very smooth.

Now cook!

1. Over low heat, shallow fry onion in clarified butter; don't color. When onion begins to soften, stir in flour.

2. Gradually whisk in milk slowly to form a smooth sauce. Cook sauce over low heat for 10 minutes and stir in lamb. Heat through, stir in wine and season to taste with salt and pepper.

3. Place mashed potatoes in a large pastry bag with star-shaped tip. Pipe a ring of potato onto each plate, building up a nest about 3 inches (7.6 cm) high with a cavity large enough to hold all of the finished dish. Fill center with lamb in onion sauce, garnish with chopped parsley and dusting of paprika.

LAMB THERESA

For 4 servings, you will need:

1 lb (0.5 kg) cold roast lamb
4 tbs clarified butter*
2 cloves garlic
10 fl oz (3 dl) tomato juice
4 medium tomatoes
2 tbs ketchup

1 tbs sugar
1 tbs parsley stalks*
Paprika
Freshly ground salt
3 tbs beurre manie

62

First prepare:

Cut meat into ½-inch (1.2 cm) cubes. Peel and smash garlic. Measure tomato juice. Skin, seed and chop tomatoes. Make beurre manie by mixing 1 oz (28 g) butter with 1 oz (28 g) all-purpose flour until it resembles bread crumbs. Chop parsley stalks.

Now cook!

1. Melt butter in a heavy bottom saucepan and add lamb. Toss gently over medium heat. Stir in smashed garlic. Pour over tomato juice, ketchup and sugar. Allow to simmer 10 minutes in an open pot.

2. Now stir in tomato, parsley stalks and beurre manie. Do not allow sauce to boil after adding beurre manie, it should just gently simmer until thick. Season to taste with paprika and salt.

LAMB SHANKS

For 12 servings, you will need:

12 lamb shanks	3 cloves garlic
Seasoned flour	8 oz (227 g) onion
16 fl oz (4 dl) dry white wine	Bouquet garni
16 fl oz (4 dl) beef stock	Freshly ground salt
8 tbs clarified butter*	Freshly ground black pepper

65

Now cook!

1. Mix flour with salt and pepper and flour shanks. Place 4 tbs clarified butter in a pan and when hot brown shanks on all sides.

2. Place 4 tbs clarified butter in large casserole. Add sliced onion and smashed garlic and cook slowly until golden (3 minutes).

3. Add wine and simmer 10 minutes. Add lamb shanks, stock and bouquet garni and cover. Simmer for 1½ hours. Remove bouquet garni.

4. Remove meat from bones and divide into 3 equal portions. Place in containers with enough cooking liquid to cover. Freeze covered.

A special hint:

This basic mixture can be served in a variety of ways; for example, Lamb Shanks Paprika, Chili Lamb Shanks and Lamb Shanks in Apple and Horseradish Sauce.

LAMB SHANKS PAPRIKA

For 12 servings, you will need:

Diced, cooked lamb from 6 lamb shanks	1 tsp paprika
	2 fl oz (5.6 cl) water
1 can condensed tomato soup, 10 ¾ oz (297 g)	2 tbs sour cream

First prepare:

Measure cream. Dilute soup with water.

68

Now cook!

1. Place frozen meat into 6 oz (170 g) undiluted tomato soup. Heat gently to allow meat to thaw. Stir in paprika and sour cream. Reheat but do not boil.

2. Serve with boiled potatoes.

CHILI LAMB SHANKS

For 12 servings, you will need:

Diced, cooked lamb from
  6 lamb shanks
4 fl oz (1.2 dl) dry white wine
1 can (16 oz: 453 g) red kidney
  beans, drained

2 oz (56 g) bacon
8 fl oz (2 dl) tomato puree
2 fresh chilis
Parsley

First prepare:

Finely chop bacon, sauté until crisp. Chop chilis finely. Measure puree and white wine. Place lamb shanks in wine and let meat slowly thaw over low heat.

Now cook!

1. Stir kidney beans and crisp bacon into pan with meat.
2. Stir in fresh chilis and tomato puree and bring to a boil.
3. Serve sprinkled with chopped parsley.

68

LAMB SHANKS IN APPLE AND HORSERADISH SAUCE

For 12 servings, you will need:

Diced, cooked lamb from
  6 lamb shanks
12 fl oz (3.2 dl) thick white
  sauce
2 tbs apple sauce

2 tsp horseradish
1 medium tomato
2 fl oz (5.6 cl) dry white
  wine
4 oz (113 g) frozen peas

First prepare:

Skin and chop tomato, measure wine, measure peas and cook until tender.

Now cook!

1. Place frozen lamb shanks into heated white sauce. Simmer over low heat. When thawed stir in wine and apple sauce. Cover and simmer until hot and bubbly.
2. Stir in horseradish, green peas and chopped tomato. Heat through. Season if necessary with salt and pepper and serve.

68

LANCASHIRE HOT POT

For 4 servings, you will need:

1½ lbs (680 g) lean lamb shoulder
    meat
Clarified butter*
4 medium onions
1 oz (28 g) butter
16 fl oz (4 dl) beef stock
Freshly ground salt
Freshly ground black pepper
1 tbs Worcestershire sauce

1 tbs sugar
2 bay leaves
2 oz (56 g) all-purpose flour
4 lamb kidneys
4 dozen oysters
4 potatoes
4 oz (113 g) mushrooms
Parsley

First prepare:

Cut lamb into 2-inch (5 cm) squares. Cut each kidney into 4 slices after removing core. Slice onions thickly. Sift flour. Slice potatoes into ¼-inch (7 mm) thick slices. Preheat oven to 350ºF (177ºC). Dry meat well.

Now cook!

1. Heat 2 tbs clarified butter in a casserole and add lamb a little at a time so that each piece browns thoroughly on all sides.

2. In a separate pan heat a little clarified butter to just cover bottom and lightly brown onion slices. Add 1 oz (28 g) butter to onions and stir in flour. Cook until lightly browned.

3. Add onions to meat and mix together. Gradually stir in beef stock until sauce thickens. Stir in Worcestershire sauce, sugar and bay leaves. Season with salt and pepper. Lay kidney slices on top and spoon off 4 fl oz (1.2 dl) of gravy and reserve.

4. Lay mushrooms in a layer on top of kidneys and then add oysters. Season with salt and pepper. Cover with overlapping potato slices. Season again and pour over 4 fl oz (1.2 dl) of gravy. Place in oven for 1 hour uncovered.

5. Remove hot pot, heat broiler unit and brown hot pot under broiler (2½ minutes). Remove bay leaves.

6. Serve garnished with chopped parsley.

A special hint:

The meat must be thoroughly dried with a paper towel before browning.

POULET BASQUAISE

For 4 servings, you will need:

1 chicken, 3½ lb (1.6 kg)
2 fl oz (5.6 cl) plus 2 tbs
   olive oil
Freshly ground black pepper
Freshly ground salt
1 large clove garlic
2 green peppers (capsicum)

1 red pepper (capsicum)
4 large tomatoes
2 oz (56 g) mushrooms
5 oz (142 g) Csabai sausage*
6 fl oz (1.6 dl) dry white wine
1 tbs parsley
8 oz (227 g) long grain rice

First prepare:

Remove wings from chicken, cut chicken into 4 pieces: 2 legs and 2 half breasts. Dry meat thoroughly. Smash garlic and then finely chop. Cut peppers into strips. Finely dice mushrooms. Skin, seed and chop tomatoes. Cut sausage into ¼-inch (7 mm) slices. Measure wine. Roughly chop parsley. Wash rice well. Season chicken with salt and pepper. Boil rice.

Now cook!

1. Place 2 fl oz (5.6 cl) olive oil into a pan on heat, add chicken skin side down and brown on both sides.

2. In a separate pan place 2 tbs olive oil, add garlic, peppers and tomatoes and allow vegetables to sweat together for 5 minutes on medium heat.

3. Stir mushrooms and sausage into chicken. Moisten with 4 fl oz (1.2 dl) dry white wine and then stir in vegetable mixture. Simmer 25 minutes.

4. Remove chicken pieces to a heated serving dish and keep warm.

5. Add 2 tomatoes to sauce, raise heat under pan, bring to a boil and reduce sauce. Stir in parsley and 2 fl oz (5.6 cl) white wine. (Reduce for 2 minutes.)

6. Cover chicken with half of sauce.

7. Place boiled rice on a separate dish, make a well in center and fill with rest of sauce.

A special hint:

The vegetables are cooked in a separate pan in order to keep their color and crispness. Please don't overcook them!

MAPLE SYRUP CHICKEN

For 4 servings, you will need:

1 chicken, 3½ lb (1.6 kg)
8 fl oz (2 dl) maple syrup
1 tbs oil
2 fl oz (5.6 cl) white wine
   vinegar
14 fl oz (4.2 dl) tomato puree
4 fl oz (1.2 dl) dry sherry
Freshly ground salt
Freshly ground pepper
2 tsp hot curry powder

1 tsp powdered marjoram
1 tbs soya sauce
4 cloves
1 medium onion
1 oz (28 g) mushrooms
2 tbs sultana raisins
2 oz (56 g) blanched almonds
1 green pepper (capsicum)
2 celery stalks

First prepare:

Cut chicken into 4 pieces (2 legs and 2 breasts, first removing wings). Measure maple syrup, vinegar, tomato puree, and sherry. Smash garlic. Finely dice onion, finely slice mushrooms, including stalks. Cut green pepper into fine dice and cut celery finely.

Now cook!

1. Place chicken pieces into a casserole dish and cover with a mixture of maple syrup, oil, vinegar, tomato puree, sherry, soya sauce, curry powder, marjoram and cloves. Season with salt and pepper. Mix all ingredients and allow chicken to marinate for 4 hours at room temperature.

2. Place chicken and marinade in casserole on low heat and allow to simmer for 1 hour.

3. Thirty minutes before end of cooking add onion, mushrooms, sultanas, almonds, green pepper and celery. Cover and cook for 30 minutes.

4. Serve with wild rice.

⅁⅁

If a dinner guest is happier asleep, let him sleep.
He does you a compliment by relaxing.

Maple Syrup Chicken with Wild Rice and Spinach Pilaf

EMINCE DE VEAU ZURICHOISE

For 4 servings, you will need:

2 lbs (0.9 kg) veal rump steak
4 oz (113 g) baby mushrooms
2 oz (56 g) shallots
8 fl oz (2 dl) heavy cream
Freshly ground salt

Freshly ground black pepper
12 tbs clarified butter*
6 fl oz (1.6 dl) dry white wine
12 fl oz (3.2 dl) brown sauce
Paprika
Oil

First prepare:

Slice veal into ¼-inch (7 mm) pieces. Measure wine and cream. Chop shallots finely. Slice mushrooms finely. Measure butter. Dry meat well.

Now cook!

1. Place oil to just cover bottom in a pan and when hot sauté veal gently until browned (3 minutes). Remove meat from pan and place on a hot dish.

2. Place butter in pan and when melted stir in shallots and mushrooms. Cook gently 1 minute.

3. Stir in wine, allow to reduce a little and then stir in cream. Bring sauce to a boil, simmer 3 to 5 minutes. Stir in brown sauce and season with salt, pepper and paprika. Cook 5 minutes more. Pour over veal. Test veal for tenderness, cook for 4 more minutes if necessary.

A special hint:

For Brown Sauce, see page 494.

VORESSEN MIT ROESTI

For 6 servings, you will need:

1½ lbs (680 g) lean leg of veal
1½ lbs (680 g) lean leg of pork
2 oz (56 g) all-purpose flour
1 large onion
1 clove garlic
2 fl oz (5.6 cl) tomato paste
8 fl oz (2 dl) dry red wine
16 fl oz (4 dl) veal stock
1 tsp powdered thyme

1 bay leaf
4 oz (113 g) button mushrooms
2 tbs fresh parsley
4 fl oz (1.2 dl) heavy cream
Clarified butter*
Freshly ground salt
Freshly ground white pepper
1 oz (28 g) all-purpose flour

First prepare:

Cut meat into 1-inch (2.5 cm) cubes. Put the 1 oz (28 g) flour into a plastic bag with salt and white pepper. Shake meat cubes in bag to cover evenly with seasoned flour. Measure butter, flour, tomato paste, veal stock, red wine, thyme and cream. Clean mushrooms. Finely chop parsley. Put onion and garlic through a grinder.

Now cook!

1. Place 4 tbs clarified butter into a heated pan. Remove from heat and stir in flour to form a roux. Cook for 3 minutes.

2. Pour more clarified butter into a large heated flameproof casserole to just cover bottom.

3. Add ground onion and garlic and allow to sweat gently in hot butter on medium heat for 1 minute.

4. Pour cooked onion and garlic into roux.

5. Pour more clarified butter into casserole, add floured meat cubes and brown on all sides.

6. Stir tomato paste into roux.

7. Blend wine and veal stock into roux whisking until smooth.

8. Add thyme and bay leaf to sauce.

9. Stir frying meat cubes frequently.

10. Pour sauce over meat and add mushrooms. Cook slowly covered for 1 hour and 45 minutes.

11. Uncover and cook sauce and meat until smooth and thick. Remove bay leaf.

12. Sprinkle with chopped parsley and stir through mixture.

13. Stir in cream.

A special hint:

When you pour onions and garlic from large casserole (see Step 4) be careful to remove every speck of fried onion. If you leave any it will burn badly and spoil the dish.

VEAL BUCCO

For 4 servings, you will need:

1½ lbs (680 g) veal shin bones
   (bone removed and meat cut
   into 1 inch: 2.5 cm cubes)
4 oz (170 g) carrots
4 oz (170 g) celery
2 cloves garlic
2 tbs clarified butter*
Freshly ground salt
Freshly ground pepper

10 fl oz (3 dl) tomato puree
4 fl oz (1.2 dl) white wine
10 fl oz (3 dl) veal stock
Thyme
Bay leaf
6 parsley stalks*
Sliced lemon peel
Chopped parsley
1 tbs arrowroot

First prepare:

Dry meat well. Cut carrot and celery into very fine dice. Peel and smash garlic. Measure puree, wine and stock. Chop lemon peel finely.

Now cook!

1. Place clarified butter in pan and when hot add carrot, celery and garlic. Fry gently for 4 minutes.

2. Add veal cubes, raise heat and lightly brown meat. Season with salt and pepper.

3. Stir in tomato puree, 2 fl oz (5.6 cl) white wine and sufficient veal stock to cover meat. Add bouquet garni of thyme, bay leaf and parsley stalks. Cover pan and allow to simmer for 1½ hours.

4. Remove meat, place on platter and keep warm. Strain cooking liquid into a saucepan and bring to a boil. Stir in remaining wine. Mix arrowroot with a little cold water and stir into hot liquid until thick.

5. Pour sauce over veal. Sprinkle top with chopped parsley and finely chopped lemon peel.

A special hint:

The lemon peel must be very finely shredded. Add only a little, then taste before adding more.

RABBIT CACCIATORA

For 4 servings, you will need:

1 rabbit, 3½ lbs (1.6 kg)
2 tbs freshly ground salt
1 tbs vinegar
½ tsp ground cloves
Clarified butter*
2 tbs olive oil
2 cloves garlic
Freshly ground salt
Freshly ground black pepper
4 oz (113 g) spring onions or
 scallions*
1 green bell pepper (capsicum)
1 small celery heart

1 tbs parsley
¼ tsp ground cloves
1 bay leaf
1 tsp dried basil
1½ tbs tomato paste
4 fl oz (1.2 dl) dry red wine
2 fl oz (5.6 cl) dry sherry
Parsley to garnish
1 lb (0.5 kg) baby carrots,
 cooked and drained
1 tbs sugar
1 tbs butter

First prepare:

Place rabbit in a bowl with enough water to cover. Add vinegar, salt and ½ teaspoon cloves. Allow to stand for 2 hours. Drain and dry rabbit thoroughly. Cut into 6 pieces (2 haunches, saddle cut in two and 2 shoulders). Smash garlic. Cut spring onions into ½-inch (1.2 cm) pieces, cut green pepper into ½-inch (1.2 cm) cubes. Finely slice celery heart. Measure tomato paste and mix with red wine. Measure sherry. Roughly chop parsley for garnish and finely chop 1 tbs parsley.

Now cook!

1. Add enough clarified butter to a hot frypan to cover surface and then add olive oil. Fry garlic. Add rabbit pieces and brown. Season with salt and pepper.

2. Add spring onions, green pepper and celery, stirring to combine all ingredients. Stir in finely chopped parsley, ¼ tsp cloves, basil and bay leaf. Add tomato paste mixed with wine and sherry. Stir all ingredients together. Season with salt and pepper. Cover pan and allow to simmer for 1¼ hours.

3. Remove bay leaf and correct seasoning.

4. Cook carrots with sugar and butter until caramelized and add to rabbit.

5. Place rabbit into a decorative casserole dish and garnish with chopped parsley.

HARE OR RABBIT AND PORTED PRUNES

For 4 servings, you will need:

1 hare
4 beef chipolatas*
4 tbs clarified butter*
2 onions
4 cloves garlic
1 green and 1 red pepper (capsicum)
10 fl oz (3 dl) red wine
1 tbs wine vinegar
8 pitted prunes
2 fl oz (5.6 cl) port
1 lb (0.5 kg) small new potatoes, peeled

Bouquet garni
Freshly ground salt
Freshly ground black pepper
30 fl oz (9 dl) beef stock
 (beef bouillon cubes
 and hare trimmings)
All-purpose flour
8 stuffed olives
1 tbs capers
Parsley
3 heaped tsp cornstarch

First prepare:

Soak prunes in port for 2 hours. Drain and reserve liquid. Cut hare into 5 pieces: saddle, shoulders and legs. Slice peppers finely, peel garlic, slice onions. Cut chipolatas into 2-inch (5 cm) pieces. Make stock from hare trimmings and bouillon cubes.

Now cook!

1. Flour, season and fry pieces of hare in butter till well browned. Place hare in casserole.
2. Sauté onion, garlic and peppers in butter. Add beef stock, wine, wine vinegar and bouquet garni. Pour over hare in casserole.
3. Cover casserole very tightly with a heavy lid. Place in a 325°F (163°C) oven for 2½ hours.
4. Remove casserole from the oven, uncover and add new potatoes. Cover and bake another 30 minutes.
5. Shallow fry chipolatas in butter till crisp and golden.
6. Remove hare to clean casserole dish. Thicken casserole juices with the cornstarch which has been mixed with the liquid drained from prunes.
7. Pour sauce over hare and add olives, prunes, capers and chipolatas. Dust with chopped parsley.

SPRING SUNSHINE

For 4 servings, you will need:

2 lb (0.9 kg) fresh Boston butt
    shoulder of pork
All-purpose flour
4 oz (113 g) onion
2 parsley stalks*
1 bay leaf
1 sprig thyme
4 tbs clarified butter*

Freshly ground salt
Freshly ground black pepper
1 clove garlic
20 fl oz (6 dl) beef stock
6 oz (170 g) green pepper
    (capsicum)
5 oz (142 g) Granny Smith apples*
1 oz (28 g) sultana raisins
2 tsp arrowroot

65

First prepare:

Remove skin from pork and cut meat into 2 inch x ½ inch (5 cm x 1.2 cm) pieces. Season and flour. Slice onion thickly, cut green peppers into 2 inch (5 cm) strips. Soak sultanas. Measure stock. Ten minutes before serving, slice, core and dice apple. Blend arrowroot with a little water. Peel and smash garlic.

Now cook!

1. Melt clarified butter in frypan and brown meat thoroughly. Remove meat.
2. Add onion to pan and brown, replace meat with garlic. Stir in stock and herbs. Cover and simmer 1¾ hours.
3. Thirty minutes before end of cooking add green peppers. Continue cooking covered.
4. Skim fat from surface, remove herbs and stir in apple ten minutes before serving. Immediately before serving stir in drained sultanas. Stir blended arrowroot into sauce until thickened.

A special hint:

It is essential that you clear all fat from surface before you thicken this dish.

PISTO MANCHEGO

For 4 large servings, you will need:

2 lb (0.9 kg) pork neck bones
8 oz (227 g) onions
2 tbs clarified butter*
Freshly ground black pepper
Freshly ground salt
1 lb (0.5 kg) tomatoes
10 oz (283 g) peppers (capsicum)
20 fl oz (6 dl) veal stock

1 bay leaf
1½ lb (680 g) potatoes
4 fl oz (1.2 dl) dry white wine
2 tbs parsley
2 large tomatoes
2 hard-boiled eggs
1 clove garlic
40 ½-inch (1.2 cm) cubes of
bread fried crisp in lard

First prepare:

Cut pork meat into 2 inch (5 cm) pieces and season with salt and pepper. Slice onions finely. Cut tomatoes into quarters (reserve two tomatoes for garnish). Remove seeds and finely slice peppers, measure stock. Peel and cut potatoes into ¼-inch (7 mm) cubes. Measure wine. Finely chop parsley. Cut the two tomatoes for garnish into ¼-inch (7 mm) cubes.

Now cook!

1. Place clarified butter in large saucepan and when hot add onions and seasoned meat. Brown lightly, add tomato quarters and peppers. Shallow fry for 3 minutes. Add stock to just cover ingredients and add bay leaf.

2. Cook gently in an open pot for 1 hour. Skim top from time to time. After 1 hour add potatoes and a little more stock, if necessary. Raise the heat but don't allow meat to boil. Cook for 15 minutes more. Season to taste with salt and pepper.

3. Remove bay leaf, stir in cubed tomato and parsley garnish, together with white wine. Place in serving dish.

4. Slice eggs roughly. Mix with parsley and croutons. Sprinkle over pork.

A special hint:

You should always taste a dish before you serve it but in this case it is vital. The potato tends to soak up salt so you will need to add more.

VENISON CASSEROLE

For 6 servings, you will need:

1 cross cut saddle of venison,
   5 lb (2.3 kg)
1 lb (0.5 kg) onions
2 lbs (0.9 kg) carrots
2 bay leaves
1½ oz (42 g) all-purpose flour
Freshly ground salt
Freshly ground pepper
Clarified butter*
4 fl oz (1.2 dl) tomato puree

6 fl oz (1.6 dl) red wine
2 tbs red currant jelly
1 tsp arrowroot
Juice of ½ lemon
Pulp of 1 lemon
2 tbs red currant jelly
4 fl oz (1.2 dl) heavy cream
6 fl oz (1.6 dl) white wine
   vinegar
Parsley

First prepare:

Cut venison into 2-inch (5 cm) cubes. Thickly slice onions. Cut carrots in ½-inch (1.2 cm) cubes. Place onions, carrots, bay leaves and vinegar into a saucepan. Bring to a boil and pour over meat. Allow to stand at room temperature overnight. Drain and dry meat and vegetables. Measure wine. Measure tomato puree. Whip cream. Cut lemon pulp into thin slices. Finely chop parsley.

Now cook!

1. Mix dried meat and vegetables with flour and then season with salt and pepper.
2. Heat some clarified butter to just cover bottom of a large saucepan and when hot add venison and brown on all sides. When meat has browned add onions and carrots and brown. Add bay leaves.
3. Place tomato puree in a small saucepan and cook until it browns. Add to meat with red wine and red currant jelly. Reduce heat under saucepan, cover and allow to simmer for 1 hour or until meat is tender.
4. Remove cooked meat and vegetables to a heated serving dish. Mix arrowroot with a little red wine and stir into boiling gravy, thickening it instantly. Stir in juice of ½ lemon.
5. Cover meat and vegetables with gravy, garnish with lemon slices and place spoonfuls of whipped cream over surface. Top cream with a little red currant jelly. Dust with finely chopped parsley.

BEEFGULYAS "VIENNA STYLE"

For 4 servings, you will need:

2 lb (0.9 kg) beef (chuck)
1½ lb (680 g) onions
1½ tbs paprika
1½ tbs tomato puree
4 fl oz (1.2 dl) oil
1 tsp vinegar
1 sprig (pinch) marjoram
Freshly ground salt
6 tbs water or veal stock

Topping:

4 oz (113 g) 1-inch (2.5 cm) square
  pieces of broken egg noodles
4 oz (113 g) cottage cheese
1 tbs chopped parsley
A little blanched lemon peel
4 bacon slices
Fried cracklings

First prepare:

Slice onions. Cut meat into 2-inch (5 cm) pieces. Measure oil and tomato puree. Fry bacon until crisp.

Now cook!

1. In a saucepan fry onions in hot oil till golden. Stir in paprika.
2. Add meat, cover and allow to simmer 5 minutes. Stir in water or stock, tomato puree, salt, vinegar and majoram.
3. Cover and simmer on low heat for 3 to 3½ hours, adding more water only if it becomes necessary to prevent sticking. Pour into serving dish.
4. Serve with boiled potatoes or dumplings.
5. *Topping:* Boil egg noodles for 5 minutes in salted water. Drain.
6. Place onto Gulyas and cover with cottage cheese, chopped parsley, finely sliced lemon peel, crisp bacon and fried cracklings.
7. Serve immediately.

A special hint:

The finished dish should be quite soupy.

BEEF STROGANOV

For 2 large servings, you will need:

1 lb (0.5 kg) beef tenderloin
2 medium onions
1 tbs all-purpose flour
Clarified butter*
2 fl oz (5.6 cl) tomato ketchup

1 fl oz (2.8 cl) Worcestershire
  sauce
6 fl oz (1.6 dl) sour cream
Freshly ground salt
Freshly ground black pepper

First prepare:

Slice beef into fine strips 5 inches x ¼ inch (12 cm x 7 mm). Finely slice onions. Measure sour cream. Combine tomato ketchup with Worcestershire sauce.

Now cook!

1. Place some clarified butter to just cover bottom of a pan on high heat. Add onions and fry for 2 minutes until golden brown. Add meat, season with salt and pepper and fry gently for 5 minutes.
2. Stir in flour and allow flour to cook for 1 minute. Stir in ketchup mixed with Worcestershire sauce and sour cream. Simmer stroganov for 4 minutes.
3. Serve with French fried potatoes.

LA CONCHA BEEF TIPS

For 4 servings, you will need:

1½ lbs (680 g) fillet of beef tips
(thin end of beef tenderloin)
4 oz (113 g) peeled potatoes
Clarified butter*
1 tbs all-purpose flour
4 Serrano chili peppers*(canned)
3 medium tomatoes
3 fl oz (8 cl) red wine
8 oz (227 g) dried red beans
(frijoles)
48 fl oz (1.4 l) cold water

4 oz (113 g) frozen peas
1 tsp chili powder
1 egg yolk (hard-boiled)
2 tbs cilantro*(fresh coriander
leaves)
2 oz (56 g) butter
Dusting flour
Freshly ground salt
Freshly ground black pepper
1 lime
2 fl oz (5.6 cl) Serrano chili juice

First prepare:

Place frijoles (rinsed) into a large pan and cover with 40 fl oz (1.2 l) cold water. Bring to a boil and simmer for 2½ hours. Peel potato, slice and cut into small cubes. Squeeze lime juice over potato and season with salt. Remove silver skin from tenderloin. Very carefully remove and discard seeds from Serrano chilis and finely chop them. Blanch tomatoes in boiling water for 2 minutes. Remove with a slotted spoon and cool. Peel and discard seeds. Measure dry and liquid ingredients. Wash, dry, and finely chop cilantro. Cube meat into 1-inch (2.5 cm) cubes. Chop egg yolk into crumbs. Heat serving platter.

Now cook!

1. Stir simmering beans and when tender add 8 fl oz (2 dl) cold water. Set aside.
2. Place a large frypan on high heat and add 1 tbs of clarified butter. One by one drop cubes of meat into it. Season generously with salt and black pepper. Fry until brown on all sides.
3. Sprinkle 1 tbs of flour over top of meat and stir.
4. Pour 2 fl oz (5.6 cl) of chili juice from can of Serrano chilis into meat. Add finely chopped peppers.
5. Quickly cut two of the tomatoes into wedges and add to meat. Moisten with 2 fl oz (5.6 cl) red wine.
6. Stir meat once again (still on high heat).
7. Dry marinated potato strips on a paper towel and add to meat mixture. Add peas. Moisten again with 1 fl oz (2.8 cl) red wine and reduce heat to low. Cook meat only until just cooked; overcooking will toughen tenderloin.
8. Drain beans and mash. Beat in butter and season with chili powder. Cut remaining tomato into small pieces and stir into beans.
9. Pour meat onto a serving platter and arrange beans along the side. Sprinkle top with chopped egg yolk and cilantro and serve.

A special hint:

The potato will be undercooked and quite crunchy—this is fine and should be so. It's different and the idea may grow on you for other dishes.

BOEUF BOURGUIGNONNE

For 6 servings, you will need:

3 lb (1.4 kg) beef chuck
6 oz (170 g) shoulder bacon*
20 small onions
8 oz (227 g) small mushrooms
16 fl oz (4 dl) beef stock
1 tsp tomato paste
16 fl oz (4 dl) red wine

2 tbs flour
2 cloves garlic
Freshly ground salt
Freshly ground pepper
Bouquet garni
1 large carrot
2 tbs clarified butter*
2 tbs brandy

First prepare:

Cut meat into 2-inch (5 cm) pieces. Cut bacon into ½-inch (1.2 cm) cubes. Peel onions. Make beef stock. Peel and smash garlic. Peel and dice carrot. Warm brandy.

Now cook!

1. Place clarified butter into a casserole dish. When hot add onion and brown, add bacon and brown. Remove both onion and bacon and reserve.
2. Add meat and brown on all sides. Flame with brandy. Stir in flour, cook for 1 minute and stir in red wine, stock, tomato paste, garlic, carrot and bouquet garni. Season with salt and pepper. Cover and simmer 1½ hours.
3. Add onions and bacon and cook for ¾ hour longer.
4. Add mushrooms which have been lightly fried in butter and cook a further 15 minutes. Serve dusted with chopped parsley.

A special hint:

You must try to get oldest (in years) beef. A 4 to 5 year old animal will do fine. In this way you get sufficient connective tissue.

Blanquette Ris D'Agneau en Croustade (page 410)

66

BLANQUETTE RIS D'AGNEAU EN CROUSTADE

For 4 servings, you will need:

1 lb (0.5 kg) lamb sweetbreads
Juice ½ lemon
Sauce:
1 oz (28 g) butter
1 oz (28 g) all-purpose flour
16 fl oz (4 dl) veal stock
Freshly ground salt
Freshly ground pepper
1 fl oz (2.8 cl) heavy cream
2 egg yolks
2 fl oz (5.6 cl) heavy cream

4 oz (113 g) button mushrooms
Clarified butter*
15 small white onions
Freshly ground salt
Freshly ground black pepper
2 bay leaves
Squeeze of lemon juice
1 unsliced loaf, sandwich bread
  10 inch (25 cm) long
Egg white
Finely chopped parsley
Paprika

First prepare:

Soak sweetbreads in a bowl of cold water. After 1 hour drain and place into cold water in a saucepan and bring slowly to a boil. Drain and place into a bowl of cold water. Drain and skin. Slice in half. Parboil small onions for 15 minutes. Make veal stock and measure. Cut crusts from bread and cut bread into four 2-inch (5 cm) slices. Make a cut ½ inch (1.2 cm) from edge around slice and scoop out bread crumbs leaving a ½ inch (1.2 cm) layer on bottom to make a shell of bread. Paint all over with clarified butter. Place croustades into a 400ºF (205ºC) oven for 15 minutes. Finely chop parsley. Mix 2 tbs cream with egg yolks.

Now cook!

1. Place butter into a saucepan and when melted stir in flour to form a roux. Allow to cook for 1 minute over low heat. Gradually stir in veal stock and whisk until thickened. Season with salt and pepper. Add bay leaves and simmer for 5 minutes.

2. Place some clarified butter to just cover bottom of a frypan and when hot add mushrooms and onions. Fry gently for 2 minutes. Season with salt, pepper and a squeeze of lemon juice. Remove from heat and stir into sauce. Add sweetbreads to sauce and allow to simmer 5 minutes.

3. Remove croustades from oven, paint edges with egg white and dip into finely chopped parsley. Keep warm.

4. Stir a little of hot sauce into egg and cream mixture and then stir into remaining sauce. Remove bay leaves. Stir remaining 2 fl oz (5.6 cl) cream into sauce.

5. Fill croustades with sweetbread mixture, sprinkle with a little chopped parsley and garnish with dash of paprika.

A special hint:

Preferably use fresh mushrooms, but they must be very small (½-inch: 1.2 cm diameter caps). If not available then use canned variety.

SHOULDER OF LAMB WELLINGTON

For 4 servings, you will need:

2 lbs (0.9 kg) lamb shoulder meat
12 fl oz (3.2 dl) veal stock
2 medium carrots
2 medium onions
1 sprig parsley
1 oz (28 g) celery stalk
1 leek
¼ tsp or 1 sprig thyme
1 bay leaf
White peppercorns

2 fl oz (5.6 cl) dry white wine
8 small onions
8 cooked asparagus spears
6 tbs butter
7 oz (198 g) all-purpose flour
Paprika
10 fl oz (3 dl) milk
2 egg yolks
2 tbs heavy cream
4 fl oz (1.2 dl) dry white wine

First prepare:

Cut meat into 1-inch (2.5 cm) cubes and place in cold water for 1 hour. Slice carrots and onions thickly, tie parsley, celery, leek, thyme, peppercorns and bay leaf into a muslin bag. Peel small onions and lightly cook in water. Measure butter, flour, milk and wine. Blend yolks with cream. Cut asparagus into ½-inch (1.2 cm) pieces.

Now cook!

1. Drain water from lamb. Cover with stock and add sliced vegetables, herbs in bag, seasoning and wine.
2. Bring to a boil, skim and lower heat to simmer. Cover and cook for 1 hour.
3. Strain off cooking liquid (10 fl oz: 3 dl) into a bowl. Add an equal quantity of milk.
4. Melt butter and stir in flour to form a roux. Gradually whisk in stock and milk and cook to a thick creamy sauce.
5. Remove herbs and vegetables from meat. Pour sauce over meat, add wine, cooked onions, and asparagus and bring to serving temperature. Quickly stir in eggs and cream but don't allow to boil. Stir until slightly thickened. Garnish with paprika and parsley.
6. Serve with creamed potatoes and peas cooked in butter with ½-inch (1.2 cm) cubes of smoked ham.

A special hint:

It may seem a waste to remove vegetables but their flavor remains and after 1 hour of cooking they are pretty soft and pappy.

---

*When a chef is senior enough to select the utensils for his kitchen,
you can bet he never has to clean them.*

FRICASSEE DE POULET ET CEPES

For 4 servings, you will need:

    1 frying chicken, 3 lb (1.4 kg)

    Clarified butter*

    Freshly ground salt

    Freshly ground white pepper

    2 cloves garlic

Sauce:

    2 oz (56 g) all-purpose flour

2 oz (56 g) butter

10 fl oz (3 dl) chicken stock

6 fl oz (1.6 dl) dry white wine

4 fl oz (1.2 dl) heavy cream

1 14 oz (396 g) can cepes*

1 truffle*

First prepare:

Cut chicken into portions. Begin by removing legs and chop in half by cutting at center joint, giving you a drumstick and a thigh. Cut off neck and slice into little pieces and put this, together with wings, into chicken stock. Chop through breast and put back part of chicken into simmering stock. Cut breast into 3 pieces and remove tiny bones. Gently bruise garlic.

Sauce: Measure butter, sift flour, open and measure wine. Open can of cepes and bottle of truffles, reserve juice from both. Wash and chop parsley, measure cream. Heat serving dish in warm oven. Slice truffle finely.

Now cook!

1. Dry pieces of chicken with paper towel and season with salt and pepper.

2. Heat some clarified butter to just cover bottom of a frypan and when hot fry legs and thighs (these pieces take longest to cook).

3. After a couple of minutes turn chicken. You will see that it is now a crisp, golden color. Continue to keep pan on high heat.

4. Now add chicken breasts and allow all pieces to continue cooking. Turn breast pieces until evenly colored.

5. Heat another pan and put butter into it for sauce. Melt butter, remove pan from heat and stir in flour. Return to heat and stir roux briskly to cook flour.

6. Turn chicken pieces once again and reduce to medium heat.

7. Remove roux from heat and gradually stir in 10 fl oz (3 dl) of chicken stock. Stir over low heat and bring sauce to a boil. Boil for 3 minutes and then reduce heat to a low simmer.

8. Add juice from tin of cepes (4 fl oz: 1.2 dl), dry white wine and cream to simmering sauce and bring it to a boil stirring constantly.

9. Turn chicken once again, add garlic and allow it to give up its flavor for 2 minutes, then discard.

10. Whisk sauce until smooth and creamy.

11. Pour off butter and chicken juices into a dish (save for future use in a sauce or gravy) and fry cepes with chicken in frypan.

12. Pour sauce over chicken and cepes, add some truffle juice and chopped parsley. Reheat but do not boil. Place in a heated dish and sprinkle truffle over top.

Fricassée de Poulet et Cepes

SALZA A CALZADOR WITH PORK FILLETS

For 4 servings, you will need:

2 pork tenderloins
2 tsp caraway seeds
Freshly ground salt
Freshly ground black pepper
Clarified butter*

Sauce:
8 oz (227 g) dried apricots
1 lemon
2 fl oz (5.6 cl) dry sherry
Peel of ½ orange
4 oz (113 g) sugar

¼ tsp ground ginger
Freshly ground salt
1½ oz (42 g) toasted pine nuts
2 tbs brandy

Buttered Spring Onions:
8 oz (227 g) spring onions* or small whole white onions
12 toasted almonds, chopped
2 oz (56 g) butter
1 lemon

First prepare:

Place a skewer through each pork tenderloin. Cover apricots with water and soak overnight. Measure sherry. Remove peel from orange and blanch in boiling water for 1 minute. Remove and reserve. Measure sugar. Squeeze lemon and reserve halves. Measure brandy. Preheat broiler unit.

Now cook!

1. Make 4 shallow incisions around each pork tenderloin. Roll pork in caraway seeds. Brush broiler rack and pork tenderloins with clarified butter. Season with salt and pepper and place under broiler (2 inches: 5 cm away from heat) and broil for 8 minutes one side. Brush uncooked side with clarified butter, season with salt and pepper and broil for 5 minutes.

2. Place apricots with water in which they have soaked into a saucepan. Add lemon juice, salt, sherry, sugar, ginger and orange peel. Boil for 1 minute and then place in blender. Blend until smooth. Return sauce to pan and add brandy and toasted pine nuts. Keep hot.

3. Remove skewers from pork tenderloins and carve into ½-inch (1.2 cm) medallions. Place on a heated serving dish. Cover with apricot sauce.

4. Place ½ inch (1.2 cm) water into a saucepan, add butter, salt and reserved lemon halves. Bring to a boil and drop in spring onions and chopped toasted almonds. Cover saucepan and allow to steam 10 minutes or until onions are tender.

5. Remove onions and almonds with a slotted spoon. Reduce cooking liquid at a fast boil to one half. After removing lemon halves, return onions and almonds to saucepan to heat through. Place onto separate dish with sauce.

A special hint:

The trick of putting a metal skewer down the full length of the fillet is a good one. It keeps the fillet from curling up and helps to cook it more quickly by conducting heat to center of fillet, thereby retaining more natural juices.

PORK TENDERLOIN WITH GLAZED PEARS

For 4 servings, you will need:

2 pork tenderloins, 8 oz (227 g)
    each
Freshly ground salt
Freshly ground black pepper
4 sage leaves
2 bacon slices
Clarified butter*
2 pears (preferably fresh)
Syrup:
8 fl oz (2 dl) water

4 oz (113 g) sugar
1 tsp saffron
3 tbs sugar
1 tbs honey
10 fl oz (3 dl) white wine
    vinegar
½ tsp cloves
1 small cinnamon stick
½ tsp whole allspice berries

First prepare:

Preheat broiler unit. Peel pears, place into syrup (water, 4 oz sugar and saffron) and cook for 20 minutes. Remove pears, cut in half and remove core. Place wine vinegar, cloves, cinnamon stick and allspice berries into a saucepan. Cover and simmer for 30 minutes. Pour this spiced mixture hot over pear halves. Strain off spiced liquid when cold.

Now cook!

1. Make an incision along pork tenderloin cutting not quite all the way through and then open out. Beat until tenderloin is ½ inch (1.2 cm) thick. Season with salt and pepper.

2. Paint broiler rack with clarified butter. Place meat on broiler rack, paint with clarified butter and cover each tenderloin with bacon. Place under broiler for 8 minutes. Turn the pork, paint again with clarified butter, season with salt and pepper and place 2 sage leaves on each tenderloin. Place under broiler for 6 minutes longer.

3. Place sugar and honey in a pan on high heat, stir until mixed and then add spiced pears. Spoon sugar and honey mixture over pears until they caramelize.

4. Place pork tenderloins on a heated serving dish. Remove sage leaves and garnish with glazed pears.

A special hint:

It is vital to remove pears from spice liquid when liquid is cold. If they are immersed too long they sour badly. Spice liquid can be strained, bottled and kept for next spice job.

COTE DE PORC EDEN

For 2 servings, you will need:

2 double rib pork chops
   (about 10 oz: 283 g each)
1 small leek (about 1 oz: 28 g)
1 medium onion
1 red pepper (capsicum)
1 lb (0.5 kg) ripe tomatoes
6 fl oz (1.6 dl) dry white wine
¼ tsp dried sweet basil
1½ oz (42 g) butter
1½ oz (42 g) all-purpose flour

8 fl oz (2 dl) chicken stock
6 oz (170 g) Emmenthal cheese
1 black truffle*
1 large mushroom
1 oz (56 g) cooked ham
Clarified butter*
Freshly ground salt
Freshly ground white pepper
½ lb (227 g) potatoes

71

First prepare:

Ask butcher to remove bones and, starting at the fatty edge, cut chops into 2 slices but not all the way through, so that they can be flattened into a butterfly shape. Boil and mash potatoes and beat in cream and seasoning. Set in a warm place until required. A pastry bag with a large rosette tip will be required. Finely slice onion. Chop red pepper. Measure wine and chicken stock. Finely slice truffle, ham, mushroom and leek; the leek is cut into match sticks 1 inch (2.5 cm) long and 1/16 inch (2 mm) thick. Heat serving platter in warming oven. Preheat broiler. Roughly slice tomatoes. Cube Emmenthal cheese.

Now cook!

1. *Tomato Sauce:* Pour enough clarified butter to just cover bottom into a frypan and place finely sliced onion into it. Allow to fry gently. Add chopped red pepper, tomatoes and moisten with wine. Season generously with salt and pepper and add basil.

2. Put butter in a small saucepan and melt. Add flour and cook over a moderate heat for a few moments. (This is a roux base for the sauce.)

3. Blend in chicken stock gradually and bring to a boil, stirring constantly. Reduce heat and add cubed Emmenthal cheese a handful at a time, stirring until sauce is smooth and thick.

4. Add finely sliced leek, truffle and ham to cheese sauce.

5. Season pork chops on one side and place on broiler rack. Season the other side with salt and pepper, brush with clarified butter.

6. Broil for 8 minutes on each side (pork must *never* be undercooked).

7. Place mushrooms into simmering tomato sauce and allow to poach gently.

8. Strain tomato mixture into the cheese but don't force vegetables through.

9. Remove broiled pork chops and place in the center of a heatproof serving dish. Surround them with vegetables from tomato mixture.

10. Spoon "cheese" sauce over the chops. Return dish to the broiler to brown. Serve at once. Garnish with rosettes of whipped potatoes.

KALFHAAS AMSTERDAM

For 4 servings, you will need:

2 veal tenderloins, 1 lb (0.5 kg)
  each
2 fl oz (5.6 cl) dry sherry
8 fl oz (2 dl) red wine
2 fl oz (5.6 cl) Scotch whisky
4 oz (113 g) mushrooms
1 tbs parsley
2 oz (56 g) prosciutto ham*
¼ tsp Worcestershire sauce

4 oz (113 g) onion
4 oz (113 g) leek
4 oz (113 g) smoked tongue
4 fl oz (1.2 dl) heavy cream
1 medium clove garlic
Clarified butter*
Freshly ground salt
Freshly ground white pepper

First prepare:

Trim off silver outer skin from veal fillets. Measure sherry, red wine and Scotch whisky. Wash, dry and chop parsley. Slice onion and leek. Smash garlic. Measure cream. Weigh meat. Heat a serving platter in warm oven. Heat broiler. Finely slice tongue and ham. Wash mushrooms.

Now cook!

1. Season veal fillets with salt and pepper.
2. Pour some clarified butter to just cover bottom into a heated frypan and fry fillets on all sides.
3. When the veal is crusty and golden brown, remove from heat and place in a casserole with pan juices.
4. Place tenderloins under preheated broiler for 12 minutes.
5. Put the onion and leek into the pan used to cook tenderloins and add more clarified butter. Add garlic and cook over moderate heat.
6. Add sherry to vegetables and flame. When flame has died (see hint) pour on whisky and flame again.
7. Add red wine, Worcestershire sauce, mushrooms, prosciutto and tongue. Boil down rapidly until almost dry.
8. Turn veal fillets over and broil another 5 minutes.
9. Stir vegetable sauce and gradually stir in heavy cream.
10. Place this mixture into serving dish.
11. Remove meat from broiler and cut lengthwise. Place pieces, crusty side up, on top of vegetables. Put in 400ºF (204ºC) oven for 5 minutes to heat through. Sprinkle with freshly chopped parsley and serve at once.

A special hint:

When adding (as in Step 6) two lots of alcohol, be sure that the first flames are out before adding the second. You can get a "flash-back" in the bottle and it can explode causing serious injury.

APPLE GAMMON

For 4 servings, you will need:

4 ½-inch thick gammon steaks,
  8 oz (227 g) each (center cut
  Smithfield ham steaks)
Freshly ground black pepper
Clarified butter*
2 sliced apples
6 tbs demerara sugar*

Lemon Parsley Butter:
  8 tbs butter
  2 tbs parsley
  ½ tsp cayenne pepper
  2 tbs lemon juice
  1 clove garlic

62

First prepare:

Soak ½-inch (1.2 cm) thick gammon steaks for 12 hours in cold water. Drain and snip rind every 1 inch (2.5 cm). Dry and season with pepper. Slice apple, measure sugar. Preheat broiler.

Lemon Parsley Butter: Add all ingredients to softened butter. Roll in greaseproof paper to form long roll 1 inch (2.5 cm) in diameter. Refrigerate until firm. Cut into thin slices and place on steaks just before serving.

Now cook!

1. Brush steaks with clarified butter.
2. Place under medium broiler and broil for 5 minutes. Turn and broil for 3 minutes.
3. Remove from heat, cover with thick sliced apples and dust with brown sugar.
4. Replace under hot broiler for 2 to 3 minutes to glaze.
5. Serve topped with a large pat of lemon parsley butter.

SAUSAGES WITH OYSTERS

For 3 dozen sausages, you will need:

4 lbs (1.8 kg) chuck steak
4 oz (113 g) mutton fat
6 oz (170 g) all-purpose flour
2 tsp mace
1 tsp powdered thyme
1 tsp nutmeg
1 tsp powdered sage

2 tsp coriander
1 tsp freshly ground black pepper
4 tsp freshly ground salt
4 yds (4 m) pig's gut (intestine
  casing)*
Clarified butter*
6 dozen oysters

70

First prepare:

Mix flour and spices together. Put meat and fat through fine blade of grinder twice. Soak pig's gut in cold water overnight. Run cold water through gut to cleanse. Fit rinsed gut over end of sausage filler attachment for grinder, place ground meat in top of grinder and using both hands pull out 3 inches (7.6 cm) of skin. Grind meat pulling skin out slowly to allow to fill with meat. When completely full, knot both ends leaving 1 inch (2.5 cm) of space for expansion. Measure off 3 inch (7.6 cm) lengths and twist to form sausage. Twist every second sausage the other way to prevent sausages from untwining. Place sausages in refrigerator to firm for 4 hours before cooking.

Now cook!

1. Place sausages onto a broiler rack, prick skins with a fork, brush with a little clarified butter and broil for 5 minutes each side. Remove from broiler, make a slit in sausages and drizzle a little of the oyster juice over each one. Put back under broiler for 3 minutes.
2. Remove and place 2 oysters into slit in each sausage.

LAMB CUTLET IMPERIAL

For 4 servings, you will need:

8 French trimmed loin lamb chops
4 oz (113 g) carrots
4 oz (113 g) onions
2 shallots
1 leek
4 oz (113 g) celery
1 large clove garlic
6 stems parsley
1 tsp thyme
2 bay leaves
2 cloves
12 black peppercorns

6 juniper berries
Freshly ground salt
Freshly ground black pepper
24 fl oz (7 dl) dry red wine
8 fl oz (2 dl) red wine vinegar
8 fl oz (2 dl) salad oil
1 oz (28 g) all-purpose flour
Sauce:
2 tbs red currant jelly
4 fl oz (1.2 dl) heavy cream
2-3 tsp arrowroot

First prepare:

The Marinade: Finely chop carrots, onions, shallots, leek, celery, and garlic. Place parsley, thyme, bay leaves, cloves, peppercorns and juniper berries into a square of muslin (cheesecloth) and tie up tightly. Add dry red wine, red wine vinegar and oil. Place lamb chops into this mixture. Season with salt and black pepper. Marinate for 48 hours.

Measure red currant jelly, cream, flour and arrowroot.

Now cook!

1. Remove chops from marinade and dry them thoroughly. Refrigerate.

2. Strain vegetables and discard bag of herbs. Place liquid into a saucepan and bring to a boil. Reduce volume by half.

3. Place vegetables in a baking tray, dust them with flour and set in a 450°F (232°C) oven until nut brown, about 10 minutes.

4. When vegetables are browned (not burnt) add to reduced marinade liquid.

5. Reduce heat and simmer covered for 2 hours.

6. Pass contents of pan through a sieve. Test seasoning and stir in red currant jelly and cream.

7. Bring to a boil and thicken (if necessary) with arrowroot blended to a thin cream with some water.

8. The sauce being made, brush dried chops with clarified butter and broil them for 6 minutes on each side. Spoon sauce over chops.

TENDERLOIN TIPS JIMMY

For 4 servings, you will need:

2 lbs (0.9 kg) tenderloin tips
(ask for 4 equal sized tips from
the very end of the tenderloin)
3 tbs olive oil
1 clove garlic
4 shallots
3 serrano chilis*
6 fl oz (1.6 dl) dry sherry
4 fl oz (1.2 dl) port wine
Freshly ground salt

8-10 oz (227-283 g) dried
mushrooms (bolito)
8 fl oz (2 dl) beef stock
2 small onions
1 avocado
2 oz (56 g) butter
2 fl oz (5.6 cl) heavy cream
1 tsp butter
1 tsp flour
1 tsp paprika
2 tbs parsley

First prepare:

Trim meat. Chop garlic and shallots roughly. Cut up serrano chilis. Soak dried mushrooms in 4 fl oz (1.2 dl) warm water for 10 minutes. Very finely slice onion. Mix 1 tsp butter with flour. Slice beef tips down the center, not quite all the way through, open and flatten them with the back of a knife. Heat a serving platter in warming oven. Preheat broiler.

Now cook!

1. Pour 1 tbs olive oil into a large frypan on high heat and add garlic, shallots, serrano chilis and half the sliced onion.

2. Blend in 4 fl oz (1.2 dl) dry sherry and port wine and 3 fl oz (8 cl) of the liquid from soaked mushrooms (this is the marinade for the meat). Bring it to a boil.

3. Lay fillets in a shallow dish, season with salt and strain boiling marinade over fillets.

4. To strained vegetables add beef stock and return to a high heat to reduce.

5. Take the fillets out of the marinade and dry lightly with a paper towel. Reserve marinade. Place fillets in a broiler pan, brush with olive oil and broil 2-3 inches (5-7.6 cm) away from heat for 4 minutes on one side.

6. The beef stock should be almost a thick syrup now.

7. Strain vegetables once again. You should have approximately 2 fl oz (5.6 cl) of beef stock flavored with garlic and pepper. Rinse out the pan, pour in 1 tbs olive oil and add remaining onion.

8. Turn tenderloin tips to broil for a further 4 minutes on the other side (medium rare).

9. Add reduced stock to frying onions, then pour reserved marinade liquid over top and add soaking mushrooms. Let reduce.

10. Cut avocado pear in quarters, removing seed. Peel off skin, brush with lemon juice and reserve for garnish. Prick avocado with a fork and place under broiler with tenderloin.

11. Stir 2 oz (56 g) butter and cream into mushrooms and onions, then slightly thicken with blended butter and flour mixture.

12. Take off heat and add paprika. Return to heat and bring to a boil. Sprinkle with parsley.

13. Remove avocados from broiler and place on warmed serving platter.

14. Place a piece of tenderloin on each quarter of avocado.

15. Pour 2 fl oz (5.6 cl) dry sherry into the broiler pan to scrape up the meat drippings, add mushroom and onion mixture and then spoon over meat and avocado. Decorate outer edge of platter with avocado peel cut in eighths.

LONDON BROIL

For 2 servings, you will need:

2 lamb loin chops, each 1 inch
   (2.5 cm) thick
2 beef sausages*
2 lambs' kidneys
4 bacon rashers*
8 oz (227 g) sirloin steak
2 medium tomatoes
4 large mushrooms
Freshly ground salt
Freshly ground pepper
Ground cardamon

Basil leaves
2 small cloves garlic
Clarified butter*
Juice of ½ lemon
Cayenne pepper
Shoestring potatoes:
Deep fat or oil
1 lb (0.5 kg) potatoes
Parsley
Freshly ground salt

First prepare:

Remove fell (outer skin) and a little of the fat from chops. Remove sinew from the steak. Cut tomatoes in half and make a cross in the center of each half with a knife. Remove outside membrane from kidneys. Slice almost in half, remove their core and flatten out. Trim rind from bacon. Prick sausages with a fork. Make a light incision along the length of each sausage. Remove stems from mushrooms. Peel and smash garlic cloves. Preheat broiler. Finely chop parsley. Grate potatoes on coarse grater into a bowl of cold water.

Now cook!

1. Paint broiler rack with a little clarified butter. Season chops with salt and pepper, paint with a little clarified butter and place on broiler pan.

2. Season sausages with salt and pepper and place a dash of cardamon in the incision made in each sausage. Brush with a little clarified butter and place with chops.

3. Season steak with salt and pepper. Rub with 1 clove of garlic, paint with a little clarified butter and place under broiler.

4. Place a skewer through each end of the lamb kidneys so that they won't buckle during cooking (see hint), season with salt and pepper, paint with a little clarified butter and put with other meats under broiler.

5. Season tomato halves with salt, pepper and a little basil. Rub with smashed clove of garlic.

6. Broil meats for 8 minutes and then turn over. Cover chops with bacon rashers. Add tomatoes. Place once more under broiler for 8 minutes.

7. Place a little clarified butter into a frypan and add mushrooms vein side uppermost. Season with salt, pepper and cayenne and add juice of ½ lemon. Fry gently for 2 minutes.

8. Remove meats and tomatoes and place onto 2 serving dishes. Sprinkle with chopped parsley and garnish with shoestring potatoes sprinkled with parsley and mushrooms.

9. *Shoestring potatoes:* Drain potatoes and dry on a towel. Place potatoes in a layer on bottom and one inch up on the sides of the basket of a deep fryer and lower into preheated 380°F (193.3°C) oil. Cook for 1 minute and remove.

10. Raise heat of oil to 500°F (260°C) and then place potatoes once more into oil and allow to become golden (about 2 minutes). Remove from deep fryer. The potatoes will now look a little like a bird's nest. Drain well and remove from basket. Cut in half, season with salt and sprinkle with parsley.

A special hint:

To keep kidneys open, take almost-severed kidney and lay it cut side down on a board. Slip a long, narrow skewer through plump upper side of kidney lobes.

CHATEAUBRIAND HENRI IV

For 2 servings, you will need:

1 lb (0.5 kg) center cut beef
 tenderloin
1 large mushroom
4 slices cooked beef marrow
4 spring onions*
2 tbs dry red wine
1 tsp rosemary

Freshly ground salt
Freshly ground black pepper
Clarified butter*
Anchovy butter:
 3 tbs butter
 1 tsp anchovy paste
 1 tbs parsley

First prepare:

Commencing ½ inch (1.2 cm) from one end of meat cut a pocket in the side ending ½ inch (1.2 cm) from other end. Finely slice spring onions. Preheat broiler unit. Finely chop parsley. Finely slice mushroom.

Now cook!

1. Place marrow slices into a hot pan, add spring onions and mushrooms slices and fry gently. Add wine, rosemary and season with salt and pepper. Scrape mixture to one side of pan and allow it to melt away from heat.

2. Fill pocket in châteaubriand with mixture, pressing with a spoon to release some of the extra fat. Tie meat at each end to secure filling. Season with salt and pepper.

3. Brush broiler rack with clarified butter, place meat on broiler rack and brush with clarified butter. Broil 2 inches (5 cm) from heat, 5 minutes on each side for rare.

4. *Anchovy butter:* Place butter, anchovy paste and parsley on a board and work together with a knife until smooth. Place into a bowl.

5. Remove châteaubriand. Cut string and slice into ½-inch (1.2 cm) thick slices and top with anchovy butter.

A special hint:

Keep beef well brushed with clarified butter. Baste at least four times to keep moisture from evaporating.

64

WINEBURGER

For 4 servings, you will need:

12 oz (340 g) ground beef
Garlic salt
Freshly ground black pepper
1 loaf French bread
2 tbs butter
4 stuffed olives

Sauce:
1 medium carrot
1 medium onion

2 tbs clarified butter*
2 cloves garlic
3 tbs parsley stalks*
2 oz (56 g) ground beef
7 fl oz (1.8 dl) dry red wine
2 tsp arrowroot
1 tsp tomato puree
5 fl oz (1.5 dl) beef stock
Freshly ground salt
Freshly ground black pepper

First prepare:

Freeze olives in water in ball-shaped ice cube tray. Finely chop parsley stalks. Slice bread diagonally into eight ½-inch (1.2 cm) thick slices. Dice carrot and onion finely. Peel and smash garlic. Measure wine, stock and arrowroot.

Now cook!

1. *Sauce:* Fry ground beef in butter until brown. Stir in onion and garlic. Fry for a minute, then stir in carrot and cook on gentle heat for 4 minutes.

2. Add red wine, beef stock, tomato puree and parsley stalks. Allow to simmer until onion and carrot are tender.

3. Mix arrowroot with a little red wine, pour into hot sauce and stir until sauce thickens. Season to taste with salt and pepper. Keep warm.

4. Butter both sides of bread slices.

5. Divide ground beef into four 3 oz (85 g) patties. Season each with a little garlic salt and black pepper.

6. Remove frozen olives in ice and place 1 onto each patty. Mold meat quickly around olive and flatten, keeping edges smooth and unbroken.

7. Set electric frypan at 380°F (193°C) and place patties in pan. Fry for 2 minutes each side (rare) or 4 minutes each side (well done).

8. Place bread slices in pan and fry both sides or until brown. Place wineburger on one slice, top with another slice of bread and cover with sauce. Dust with parsley and serve.

A special hint:

By freezing stuffed olives in a ball-shaped mold and placing these in meat you keep burger juicy.

BREAST OF CHICKEN SUMMIT

For 2 servings, you will need:

2 chicken breast halves
Flour
Egg yolk
1 tbs oil
White bread crumbs*
Clarified butter*
Freshly ground salt
Freshly ground white pepper
Summit Sauce:
10 fl oz (3 dl) chicken stock

1 oz (28 g) hazelnuts roasted
whole and ground
1 oz (28 g) butter
Juice ¼ lemon
3 fl oz (8 cl) heavy cream
Freshly ground salt
Freshly ground white pepper
1 fl oz (2.8 cl) brandy
2 heaped tsp arrowroot

First prepare:

Season and lightly flour chicken breasts, paint with egg yolk mixed with oil and coat with bread crumbs. Measure ingredients for sauce.

Now cook!

1. Melt some clarified butter to just cover bottom of a frypan and gently fry chicken breasts on both sides until cooked and browned (about 30 minutes).

2. *Sauce:* Reduce chicken stock to two-thirds. Mix arrowroot with a little additional chicken stock. Melt the butter in a saucepan and slowly add stock while stirring. Stir in arrowroot mixture until thick. Stir in cream slowly, then hazelnuts and brandy. Season with salt, pepper and lemon juice.

3. Place chicken breasts on heated serving dish and cover with sauce.

CHICKEN POLESE

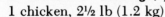

For 2 "romantic" servings, you will need:

1 chicken, 2½ lb (1.2 kg)
2 tomatoes
1 oz (28 g) onion
2 oz (56 g) green pepper
(capsicum)
Freshly ground salt
Freshly ground black pepper

2 oz (56 g) anchovy fillets (flat)
2 tbs clarified butter*
2 tsp capers
1 clove garlic
3 oz (85 g) Mozzarella cheese
2 tsp Worcestershire sauce
Parsley

First prepare:

Cut chicken in half, discarding wings and backbone. Peel garlic. Seed, skin and chop tomatoes. Slice onion finely. Cut pepper into strips. Cut cheese into thin slices. Soak anchovies in a little milk. Drain and cut lengthwise.

Now cook!

1. Heat clarified butter in frypan. Add chicken and when golden add garlic, pepper and tomatoes. Season with salt and pepper. Cover and allow chicken to simmer 30 minutes.

2. Remove lid and place several slices of cheese on back of chicken halves and then a few strips of anchovy. Stir Worcestershire sauce into pan drippings. Cover and simmer gently until cheese melts, forming a coating over chicken. Place on heated serving dish and keep warm.

3. Reduce vegetable pulp and juices until thick. Pour over chicken. Sprinkle with capers and parsley.

GROUND CHICKEN EDEN

For 2 servings, you will need:

1 lb (0.5 kg) breast of chicken
1 medium onion
Clarified butter*
Sauce:
　2 fl oz (5.6 cl) tarragon vinegar
　1 tsp dried tarragon

2 egg yolks
4 oz (113 g) butter
Freshly ground salt
Freshly ground white pepper
2 tbs parsley
Garnish:
　Buttered noodles

First prepare:

Slice meat away from breast bone and cut each breast into long thin strips. Cut onion into small dice.

Sauce: Chop parsley, measure vinegar, slightly soften butter. Heat a serving dish in warming oven.

Now cook!

1. Pour some clarified butter into a heated frypan to just cover bottom and add slices of chicken. Fry gently.

2. Reduce heat, add diced onion and stir over low heat.

3. Into another smaller frypan pour tarragon vinegar, add dried tarragon and season with salt and pepper. Bring this to a boil and keep your eye on it until liquid has almost completely reduced (you need only 1 tablespoonful).

4. In top of a double boiler over simmering water stir tarragon liquid and egg yolks. Whisk in butter gradually. Season and whisk briskly so that all ingredients are blended well together and texture is light and creamy (see hint).

5. Season simmering chicken, pour off juices. Lower heat and stir in sauce. The pan must not be too hot otherwise sauce will curdle.

6. Pour this mixture onto the heated serving platter and sprinkle freshly chopped parsley over the top. Serve at once with wide noodles.

A special hint:

Refer to Step 4 above. If pan heat is too high and sauce curdles, all you have to do is add one ice cube and whisk it around pan with sauce. The ice has the effect of making butter harden thus allowing sauce to smooth out once more.

CHICKEN GISMONDA

For 2 servings, you will need:

2 oz (56 g) butter
1 lb (0.5 kg) leaf spinach,
   fresh trimmed weight
6 oz (170 g) mushrooms
6 tbs clarified butter*
2 tsp lemon juice
2 roasting chickens, 3½ lbs
   (1.6 kg) each**
3 oz (85 g) bread crumbs*

1 oz (28 g) Parmesan cheese
2 eggs
4 tbs oil
3 oz (85 g) all-purpose flour
2 fl oz (5.6 cl) sherry
Freshly ground salt
Freshly ground black pepper
½ tsp nutmeg

** You actually need whole breasts only but I find that it is less expensive to buy whole birds instead of the parts.

First prepare:

Measure butter. Remove heavy stalks from spinach and wash leaves very well (at least 3 times). Rinse mushrooms in cold water and dry with a towel. Squeeze lemon juice. Make bread crumbs. Grate Parmesan and mix with bread crumbs. Break eggs into a soup plate, add oil and beat together. Measure flour onto a plate. Measure sherry.

Now cook!

1. Cut back bone off chicken breast piece. (If you purchased whole chickens you must also remove wings at point where they join wishbone, and legs and thighs where they join central carcass.)

2. Place breast skin side up and press down firmly in order to break breast bones and spread the double breast out flat.

3. Beat flattened breasts with a flat, heavy object. This loosens the fine breast bones and makes them easier to remove. Now remove the fine breast bones and all sinews.

4. Lay breasts skin side up, and make light diagonal cuts through skin (this stops skin from "bunching" and pulling flattened breasts out of shape). Now beat very thin but don't tear.

5. Flour breasts thoroughly and coat both sides in oil and egg mixture, then breadcrumb in cheese-flavored crumbs. Pat firmly and keep ready to cook (see hint) on waxed paper.

6. Slice mushrooms in half and cook over low heat in a frypan with 2 tbs clarified butter, lemon juice, salt and pepper. They take about 7 minutes to cook.

7. Meanwhile add butter to a large saucepan and add washed (but not too well drained—you need the moisture) spinach leaves. Season each layer as you add it with salt, pepper and nutmeg. Cook over medium heat for 6 minutes. Drain spinach immediately and keep it warm.

8. Meanwhile, (the dish takes only 9 minutes to cook) place 4 tbs clarified butter in a large frypan (you may need two pans to fit these very large slices of poultry) and fry breasts over medium heat for 4½ minutes either side (see hint).

9. Take heated dinner plates, place hot spinach on plate and shape it to form same size as chicken breast. Cover it with cooked chicken.

10. Drain butter from mushrooms and add sherry to mushrooms in their hot pan. Shake to heat sherry and then spoon both over chicken.

A special hint:

Refer to Step 5. You can prepare ahead of time up to this point. Refer to Step 8. Avoid turning chicken too often; each time you turn it you lose crumbs and they burn black in the pan.

DEVILED CHICKEN DRUMSTICKS

For 4 servings, you will need:

4 drumsticks and thighs of
 chicken
4 oz (113 g) onion
4 cloves garlic
1 green pepper (capsicum)
1 Jamaican pepper*
½ tsp ginger
¼ tsp thyme
2 limes

6 fl oz (1.6 dl) dry white wine
Clarified butter*
2 oz (56 g) tomato paste
4 oz (113 g) red pimento
Parsley
Tabasco sauce
Freshly ground salt
Freshly ground white pepper

71

First prepare:

Dry legs and cut into thighs and drumsticks. Roughly slice onion. Smash garlic. Slice top from green pepper, remove seeds and cut flesh into ¼ inch (7 mm) strips. Remove seeds from Jamaican pepper, slice flesh very finely and then chop. Juice limes, chop parsley. Measure herbs, white wine, tomato paste and pimento. Heat a serving platter.

Now cook!

1. Pour some clarified butter to just cover bottom of a large frypan over medium heat.
2. Season drumsticks and thighs with salt and pepper and place in hot butter.
3. Add onion, garlic and green pepper strips and fry.
4. Add finely sliced Jamaican pepper.
5. After 5 minutes turn drumsticks over.
6. Stir ginger and thyme into mixture.
7. Moisten with fresh lime juice.
8. Remove chicken pieces from pan.
9. Place vegetables and juices into a blender or pass them through a sieve. Stir in tomato paste and pimento.
10. Return chicken to frypan and let cook with 2 fl oz (5.6 cl) white wine. Spoon pureed vegetables over chicken pieces.
11. Pour 2 fl oz (5.6 cl) white wine into blender to rinse and pour into pan.
12. Turn chicken again.
13. Cook over low heat for 15 to 20 minutes adding remaining 2 fl oz (5.6 cl) white wine. Taste and add Tabasco if necessary.
14. Remove cooked chicken onto heated serving platter, cover with sauce and dust with parsley.

SALTIMBOCCA ALLA ROMANA

For 2 servings, you will need:

2 thin scallopini of veal
2 fresh sage leaves
4 thin slices of prosciutto*
1 lemon

Freshly ground salt
Freshly ground black pepper
Clarified butter*

First prepare:

Beat veal scallops until very thin. Cut lemon into quarters.

Now cook!

1. Season one side of veal scallops with salt and pepper. Heat some clarified butter in a skillet and when hot add veal, seasoned side down. Season other side with pepper only. Cook for 1 minute and then turn.

2. Place 1 sage leaf on each veal scallop and then cover with prosciutto. Turn veal scallop over so that prosciutto is next to heat and cook for 30 seconds. Squeeze lemon juice over veal.

3. Remove meat to a serving dish add butter to pan drippings and scrape to loosen pan particles. Spoon over veal. Squeeze more lemon juice over veal.

FRIED STEAK WITH BRUSSELS SPROUTS

For 3 servings, you will need:

½ lb (227 g) beef tenderloin
1 tsp soya sauce
¼ lb (113 g) brussels sprouts (small)
2 oz (56 g) carrots
Freshly ground salt
2 tsp arrowroot

1 tsp dry sherry
1 clove garlic
5 fl oz (1.5 dl) water
¼ tsp monosodium glutamate
2 tbs clarified butter*
¼ tsp sesame seed oil*

First prepare:

Peel garlic clove and smash. Trim brussels sprouts and cut into quarters. Slice carrots diagonally into ¼-inch (7 mm) thick slices, the same size as brussels sprouts. Measure sherry, soya sauce, water. Mix arrowroot with 1 tbs water. Slice beef thinly. Parboil carrots in a little water and rinse in cold water.

Now cook!

1. Mix sliced beef with soya sauce, sherry and monosodium glutamate.

2. Mix clarified butter and oil. Place 1 tbs into frypan. When hot add brussels sprouts, season with salt. Stir quickly and then add carrots and water. Cover tightly. Simmer until tender (about 3 minutes). Remove vegetables and liquid from pan and reserve. Wash pan.

3. In clean pan add rest of butter and oil mixture. When hot, add garlic and beef. Stir over highest heat until cooked. Add brussels sprouts, carrots and their juice. Stir in arrowroot mixture. Cook while stirring until sauce bubbles and thickens.

VEAL CUTLET YEREX

66

For 4 servings, you will need:

4 veal loin chops
Freshly ground salt
Freshly ground white pepper
2 tbs clarified butter*
5 fl oz (1.5 dl) heavy cream
2 egg yolks
3 Chinese gooseberries (Kiwi
    fruit)*
1 small cauliflower

1 bunch broccoli
2 fl oz (5.6 cl) dry white wine
Finely sliced lemon peel
20 black grapes
Juice 1 lemon
2 tbs butter
Mint
Paprika

First prepare:

Trim chops, mix cream with egg yolks, peel and slice Chinese gooseberries ¼-inch (7 mm) thick. Chop mint, finely slice lemon peel into slivers. Break up cauliflower and cut broccoli into small pieces. Preheat broiler.

Now cook!

1. Place broccoli and cauliflower into boiling salted water. Cook for 10 minutes. Drain, place vegetables in ovenproof dish, dot with pieces of butter and a squeeze of lemon juice and slide under broiler until lightly browned.

2. Season chops with salt and pepper and gently fry in clarified butter for about 6 minutes on each side. Remove chops and keep warm.

3. Place Chinese gooseberries in a small saucepan, add squeeze of lemon, 20 unpeeled black grapes, lemon peel, cream and egg yolks. Stir over low heat until thickened.

4. Deglaze pan in which veal chops were cooked with wine and stir half of pan juices into fruit cream.

5. Pour sauce over chops and serve garnished with very finely chopped mint and dusting of paprika. Pour remaining pan juices over broiled vegetables and spoon around meat.

6. Serve with small new potatoes garnished with chopped mint.

---
*You win more friends by trying
than you lose by failing.*

KALBSFILET MIT ZITRONEN SAUCE

For 4 servings, you will need:

1½ lb (680 g) veal fillet
8 oz (227 g) long grain rice
1 tsp whole dried tarragon leaves
   (or 6 fresh leaves)
1 lemon
4 oz (113 g) butter
1 oz (28 g) all-purpose flour

10 fl oz (3 dl) heavy cream
Parsley
Bunch watercress
Freshly ground salt
Freshly ground white pepper
Clarified butter*

First prepare:

Remove surplus fat and very fine silver skin from veal fillet. Blend flour and 1 oz (28 g) butter together in a small bowl (beurre manie). Wash rice and cut two thin slices of peel from lemon. Squeeze juice from ½ lemon. Measure cream. Wash and finely chop parsley. Wash and trim watercress. Put a pan of water on to boil for cooking rice. Heat a serving platter in warm oven.

Now cook!

1. Heat enough clarified butter to just cover bottom of skillet. Season fillet with salt and pepper and place in hot butter. Cover and cook for 25 minutes over a medium heat, turning occasionally.

2. Dip whole dry tarragon leaves into pan of boiling rice water, season with salt and pepper. Remove the now sparkling green tarragon. Add rice and lemon rind and simmer.

3. After veal has cooked 25 minutes remove from skillet and set aside covered in warm oven until required. Skim fat from pan juices.

4. Stir in lemon juice and cream and simmer gently.

5. Add parsley and tarragon to cream sauce and stir thoroughly. Gradually blend in beurre manie, stirring until sauce is thickened. Season and set aside to keep warm.

6. Drain water from cooked rice and remove lemon rind. Add 1 oz (28 g) butter, cover and return to a low heat to steam gently.

7. Season rice with salt and white pepper.

8. Remove veal from warm oven and place on a cutting board. Slice into small ¼-inch (7 mm) thick diagonal slices and arrange on a serving platter.

9. Place rice down one side of dish and watercress down the other.

10. Beat 2 oz (56 g) softened butter into sauce and pour it over sliced fillet. Serve at once.

A special hint:

Refer to Step 5. When you add beurre manie to thicken a mixture be careful to add it just at the last moment and only bring the mixture to a boil to thicken. Take it directly off heat afterward, otherwise flour "breaks out" and you get a "raw" flour taste in sauce.

VEAL PIZZAIOLA

For 2 servings, you will need:

2 thin slices of veal (leg cut)
Freshly ground salt
Freshly ground black pepper
2 fl oz (5.6 cl) olive oil
3 cloves garlic
1½ lbs (680 g) tomatoes

2 thin slices Mozzarella cheese
Sprig oregano (or ½ tsp dried)
1 tbs parsley
Parmesan cheese
2 tsp Worcestershire sauce

First prepare:

Beat veal slices until very thin and remove sinew from side of meat. Smash and finely chop garlic. Skin tomatoes and chop roughly. Finely slice Mozzarella cheese. Finely chop parsley.

Now cook!

1. Place 2 tbs olive oil into a heated frypan, add veal slices seasoned with salt and pepper, lower heat under pan and lightly fry veal on both sides.

2. Place 2 tbs olive oil into a separate pan on heat and fry garlic gently. Add tomatoes and oregano. Season with salt and pepper. Reduce heat and cook slowly a few minutes.

3. Add meat juices from frypan to tomatoes. Add Worcestershire sauce.

4. Place a slice of Mozzarella cheese on each veal slice and using a slotted spoon put tomato pulp and some of sauce over veal. Cover and allow to simmer for 5 minutes.

5. Press remaining sauce through a sieve and add parsley.

6. Place veal and tomatoes on a serving dish, powder heavily with Parmesan cheese and brown under broiler for 2 minutes.

7. Serve sauce separately in a sauceboat.

A special hint:

Although definitely not classical, you may add the Worcestershire sauce if you find the sauce too bland. In Italy, where this dish originates, they use partially dried tomatoes which have a gret deal more flavor than our ripe tomatoes.

VEAL BOWEN

For 6 servings, you will need:

8 slices veal scalloppini
  each 2 oz (56 g)
2 green apples
1 medium onion
2 tbs shredded coconut
2 tsp curry powder
1 red pepper (capsicum)
1 green pepper (capsicum)
5 fl oz (1.5 dl) pineapple juice

10 fl oz (3 dl) dry white wine
2 tbs mango chutney
1 ripe (firm) mango
2 tbs all-purpose flour
5 fl oz (1.5 dl) heavy cream
Clarified butter*
Freshly ground salt
Freshly ground white pepper

First prepare:

Remove skin from mango and cut into 8 segments. Finely slice onion. Core and slice apples. Slice top from peppers, remove seeds and slice lengthwise. Parboil for 4 minutes in boiling salted water and then drain. Measure cream, wine, pineapple juice, coconut and flour. Heat a serving platter in a warm oven. Flatten veal until paper thin with a mallet or empty wine bottle.

Now cook!

1. Pour enough clarified butter to just cover bottom into a frypan and heat over moderate temperature.

2. Wrap each piece of veal around a segment of mango. Secure with a toothpick. Dust with flour.

3. Place veal packages into hot clarified butter and season with salt and pepper. Fry gently until golden brown.

4. Carefully turn veal packages.

5. Turn veal packages once again to make sure they are evenly cooked. Continue to simmer gently.

6. Into a heated saucepan pour some clarified butter to just cover bottom and bring to moderate heat. Add apples.

7. Stir onion, curry powder and coconut into apples. Stir in flour. Gradually add pineapple juice and 5 fl oz (1.5 dl) dry white wine. Stir over low heat until it thickens (approximately 20 minutes).

8. Remove sauce from heat and sieve into a clean pan. Return to heat, add parboiled peppers and 5 fl oz (1.5 dl) dry white wine and simmer.

9. Place veal packages on a heated serving platter. Remove toothpicks. Pour off fat from frypan and add meat residue to simmering sauce. Stir in cream and mango chutney.

10. Gently pour sauce over veal and mango roll-ups and serve immediately.

A special hint:

It is possible that sauce may reduce too much and become very thick. In this case add more wine or some clear apple or pineapple juice.

VEAL SAVOYARDE

For 2 servings, you will need:

2 veal steaks (10 oz: 283 g)
  (cross cut leg includes bone piece)
4 oz (113 g) liver pâté
4 tbs clarified butter*
Freshly ground salt
Freshly ground white pepper
Sauce:
3 medium onions
1½ oz (42 g) flour
4 tbs clarified butter*

6 fl oz (1.6 dl) chicken stock
8 fl oz (2 dl) heavy cream
Freshly ground salt
Freshly ground pepper
Garnish:
Parsley
Paprika
¼ lb (113 g) button mushrooms
Butter
Lemon juice and cayenne pepper

First prepare:

Place veal steaks on a board and beat them with a wet milk bottle or meat mallet until thin. Slice pâté. Trim outside skin from steaks. Sift flour. Measure chicken stock and heavy cream. Thinly slice onions. Heat a serving dish in warming oven.

Now cook!

1. Prepare sauce by pouring 4 tbs clarified butter into a frypan on medium heat.
2. Add onions and stir them around so they are evenly coated with the butter.
3. Let them sizzle very gently—do not allow to brown—they will become translucent in 15 minutes.
4. Season cooked onions with salt and pepper.
5. Pour 4 tbs clarified butter into a large pan and add veal steaks. With a pair of tongs turn them immediately to coat with butter and seal in succulent juices.
6. While veal steaks are cooking gently, add flour to softened onions and stir to prevent them sticking to the bottom of the pan.
7. After 5 minutes onion mixture will become a light golden color and smell superb, and flour will be thoroughly cooked.
8. Turn veal steaks once again. The marrow bone should be intact.
9. Gradually stir chicken stock into onion mixture and blend in very thoroughly. Stir in 6 fl oz (1.6 dl) of the cream and allow to simmer gently on low heat while stirring.
10. Remove sauce from heat. Press through a sieve into a clean pan.
11. Add remaining 2 fl oz (5.6 cl) cream. Stir in very thoroughly. Simmer gently on low heat.
12. The steaks should now be completely cooked—lightly browned on both sides.
13. Preheat broiler.
14. Place steaks on heated serving platter.
15. Onto each half of steak place sliced pâté and fold over with eye (or marrow bone) looking at you!
16. Pour heavy cream sauce over the steaks, covering them evenly.
17. Slide platter under broiler for 2 minutes or until lightly browned.
18. Remove, sprinkle with parsley and dust with a little paprika.
19. Serve piping hot.
20. Serve veal with button mushrooms cooked in butter with a touch of lemon juice and cayenne pepper. Sautéed small whole potatoes add a crisp colorful touch.

ROLLITOS DE FILLETE DE TERNERA

For 4 servings, you will need:

2¼ lbs (1 kg) veal
2 hard-boiled eggs
4 slices cooked smoked ham
4 tsp Dijon mustard
8 asparagus tips
4 eggs
4 oz (113 g) Parmesan cheese

2 oz (56 g) all-purpose flour
2 oz (56 g) butter
2 tbs Worcestershire sauce
2 tbs parsley
4 tbs clarified butter*
Freshly ground salt
Freshly ground white pepper

First prepare:

Place piece of veal leg into a deep freeze for about 3 hours until partially frozen (this makes it easier to cut). Slice into thin strips about 4 inches (10 cm) long and 2 inches (5 cm) wide. Trim off all fat or skin and beat until very thin. You will need 12 slices. Hard-boil 2 eggs. Have ham slices ready. It is preferable to use freshly cooked asparagus but if not available use jumbo frozen. Break eggs into a bowl and mix with Parmesan cheese. Chop parsley finely. Melt clarified butter.

Now cook!

1. Lay veal slices out on a large board or table. Place half a hard-boiled egg, suitably seasoned with salt and pepper, on 4 slices of veal. Roll up and secure with a toothpick trimmed so that it is just long enough to go through roll. (See hint).

2. Lay slices of cooked ham on 4 slices of veal and spread 1 tsp of Dijon mustard over them. Roll up and secure as before.

3. Lay two fat tips of cooked asparagus (cut to fit) on 4 slices of veal, season with salt and pepper. Roll up and secure.

4. Season 2 oz (56 g) flour quite heavily with salt and pepper, and gently roll veal "rollitos" in flour.

5. Drop rollitos one by one into beaten egg and cheese mixture, turn until coated and place in a pan on medium heat in hot clarified butter.

6. Cook gently turning each rollito four times. Allow to cook for about 2 minutes on each side but no longer or they may burn.

7. When cooked place them on a serving platter. Remove toothpicks and keep rollitos warm.

8. Remove any surplus fat from pan and shake in 2 tbs of Worcestershire sauce. Scrape to loosen all particles. Stir in remaining egg and cheese mixture, parsley and 2 oz (56 g) butter. Blend together and place a spoonful of this herb butter on each rollito.

9. Serve three rollitos as a portion: one egg, one ham and one asparagus. A green salad tossed in a good light dressing goes well with this.

A special hint:

Be very careful when using toothpicks. First, they must come out before meat is served and second, they should be trimmed to size with scissors so that the wood does not extend on either side of meat as this would keep that side from browning properly.

Rollitos de Fillete de Ternera

GRILLARD

For 4 servings, you will need:

1½ lbs (680 g) veal tenderloin	1 fl oz (2.8 cl) brandy
1 green pepper (capsicum)	1 level tsp arrowroot
8 oz (227 g) tomatoes	3 fl oz (8 cl) sherry
4 oz (113 g) onion	2 tbs parsley
2 cloves garlic	4 fl oz (1.2 dl) chicken stock
1½ oz (42 g) celery	1 oz (28 g) butter
2 bay leaves	8 tbs clarified butter*
2 tbs flour	Freshly ground salt
1 tsp lemon juice	Freshly ground white pepper

First prepare:

Trim skin from veal and slice veal into ½-inch (1.2 cm) slices. Place pepper on a fork and hold over heat. Pull off skin. Cut open and remove seeds. Dice pepper. Remove core from tomatoes and blanch them in boiling water for 2 minutes. Cool, remove outer skin, cut into quarters and remove seeds. Chop tomato finely. Very finely slice onion. Smash cloves of garlic into a pulp. Finely dice celery. Squeeze juice of lemon (only 1 tsp needed). Put flour in a plastic bag. Wash, dry and finely chop parsley. Measure dry and liquid ingredients. Heat a serving platter in warming oven.

Now cook!

1. Into a large frypan over medium heat pour 4 tbs clarified butter and add green pepper. Stir in onion and garlic. Reduce to low heat.

2. Add celery and bay leaves.

3. Season flour in plastic bag with salt and white pepper; then add veal slices and shake until veal is evenly coated. Shake out of the bag into a colander and toss to remove excess flour.

4. Place another large frypan on high heat and pour in remaining clarified butter. To this add veal and let fry, turning slices often to get a good color.

5. Add tomatoes to frying vegetables and blend in lemon juice.

6. Blend 1 tsp of arrowroot with 1 fl oz (2.8 cl) brandy in a small bowl.

7. Pour off fat from veal until the pan is almost dry. Pour in 3 fl oz (8 cl) sherry and flame. Then reduce. Sprinkle parsley over this.

8. Remove bay leaves from frying vegetables and pour in chicken stock. Bring mixture to a boil and add blended arrowroot (careful here because the sauce must be "thin"). Stir until slightly thickened.

9. Place veal pieces on heated serving platter and clear pan of residue with 1 oz (28 g) butter. When melted, pour over veal. Pour vegetable sauce over top.

Service:

I serve long grain rice plain boiled, then steamed and finally buttered.

ADEMAS DOS SAUTE GOURMANDISE

For 4 servings, you will need:

½ lb (227 g) medium egg noodles
48 fl oz (1.4 l) boiling water
12 oz (340 g) beef tenderloin
12 oz (340 g) veal tenderloin
Clarified butter*
4 Serrano chilis*
2 cloves garlic
1 tsp oregano
1 bay leaf
12 oz (340 g) pork tenderloin

24 fl oz (7 dl) ice water
4 oz (113 g) mushrooms
2 fl oz (5.6 cl) brandy
2 oz (56 g) butter
10 fl oz (3 dl) sour cream
1 tbs parsley
Freshly ground salt
Freshly ground black pepper
Freshly ground white pepper

First prepare:

Trim "white skin" from beef, pork and veal tenderloins. Cut beef into ¼-inch (7 mm) slices and pork and veal into ¾-inch (2 cm) slices. Remove seeds from chili peppers and roughly chop flesh into ¼-inch (7 mm) slices. Wash, dry and finely chop parsley. Measure remaining dry and liquid ingredients. Heat a serving platter in a warm oven.

Now cook!

1. Boil water seasoned with salt over high heat. Add noodles and cook uncovered for 6 minutes constantly stirring to prevent them sticking.

2. After 6 minutes take noodles off heat and pour in ice water which immediately arrests boiling process. Strain but do not rinse them. Cover and let stand.

3. Into a large frypan over low heat pour 6 tbs clarified butter and add the Serrano chili and garlic. Sprinkle with oregano, add bay leaf and gently fry.

4. Place another frypan over medium heat and strain half of the seasoned clarified butter from first frypan into it. Add veal and pork medallions to one pan, season with salt and black pepper and let simmer.

5. Place beef into other frypan, increase heat to high and season with salt and black pepper.

6. Turn veal and pork.

7. Turn beef also and pour in 2 fl oz (5.6 cl) brandy. Flame and shake pan. Add beef to veal and pork.

8. Place mushrooms in empty beef pan, reduce to medium heat and stir in 1 oz (28 g) butter. Season with salt and white pepper.

9. Gently mix drained noodles with frying mushrooms. Stir in another 1 oz (28 g) butter and stir again.

10. With a slotted spoon place meat on heated serving platter, arranging slices down one side. Pour off surplus fats from pan into noodles and mushrooms. Add sour cream and toss gently to mix. Reheat and arrange alongside meat.

11. Dust with freshly chopped parsley and serve.

VEAL ELMWOOD

For 4 servings, you will need:

1 lb (0.5 kg) veal tenderloin
2½ lbs (1.2 kg) potatoes
5 fl oz (1.5 dl) olive oil
1 tsp oregano
½ tsp rosemary
4 fl oz (1.2 dl) cold water
4 tbs clarified butter✻
4 oz (113 g) onion
1 green pepper (capsicum)

1 clove garlic
2 oz (56 g) mushrooms
¼ tsp oregano
½ lemon
4 fl oz (1.2 dl) dry white wine
1 tsp arrowroot
1½ fl oz (4.2 cl) dry sherry
Freshly ground salt
Freshly ground black pepper

First prepare:

Peel potatoes and slice in half lengthwise. Soak until needed in cold lemon-flavored water to prevent discoloring. Remove silver skin from veal and cut meat into ¼-inch (7 mm) slices. Cut onion into rough cubes. Slice top from green pepper, remove seeds and also cut into rough squares. Smash garlic and finely slice it. Measure liquid and dry ingredients. Preheat oven to 375°F (190°C). Warm a serving platter. Now drain and dry potatoes. Cut mushrooms into rough slices.

Now cook!

1. Place a casserole or baking dish over high heat and pour in 4 fl oz (1.2 dl) olive oil. Arrange potatoes in it round side up. Season with salt and black pepper. Sprinkle oregano and rosemary around potatoes.

2. Slowly pour cold water into casserole and bring to a boil. Remove from heat and shake pan gently to prevent potatoes from sticking to bottom. Cover with foil, dull side up, and place in preheated oven set at 375°F (190°C) for 40 minutes.

3. Pour 2 tbs clarified butter into a frypan and add 1 fl oz (2.8 cl) olive oil. Place over moderate heat and fry onions to extract their natural juices. Stir in peppers and garlic. Don't overcook, 2 minutes frying is enough.

4. Remove vegetables from pan and put in a bowl. Put meat in hot pan and fry for 2 minutes.

5. After sautéing meat for 2 minutes add mushrooms, season with ¼ tsp oregano and lemon juice. Season generously with salt and black pepper.

6. Return vegetables to simmering meat and moisten with white wine. Cover and reduce heat to medium.

7. Blend arrowroot with sherry in a small bowl and pour into bubbling meat juices. Stir until thickened and adjust seasoning.

8. After 40 minutes remove potatoes from oven. Heat broiler.

9. Remove foil, brush potatoes with clarified butter and remove herbs from top of potatoes (to prevent them from burning while under broiler). Season well with salt, and broil 3 inches (7.6 cm) away from heat until brown.

10. Pour meat and vegetables onto serving platter and add ½ fl oz (1.4 cl) sherry to pan to loosen residue and pour over meat.

11. Remove potatoes from under broiler when they are golden brown and crusty. Serve with meat.

Veal Elmwood

PORK CHOPS NGAURUHOE

For 4 servings, you will need:

4 thick pork rib chops, each 1½ inch (4 cm) thick	Whole cloves
48 sultana raisins (1 oz: 28 g)	White peppercorns
1 apple	Freshly ground salt
¼ oz (7 g) root ginger (fresh)*	16 toothpicks
1 orange	6 tbs clarified butter*

63

First prepare:

Cut a pocket in pork chops by cutting along fatty edges into meat to the bone. Peel, core and finely slice apple. Peel and cut ginger into fine slivers. Cut off thin slices of orange peel and cut into very fine strips. Grind cloves and peppercorns. Heat frypan to 300°F (149°C).

Now cook!

1. Use 12 raisins, ½ of sliced apple, 1 sliver ginger, ¼ tsp sliced orange peel per chop. Mix and stuff into pocket.
2. Spear fat edges with toothpicks. Lace with string and tie up.
3. Melt butter in frypan, season chops with salt, cloves and pepper. Shallow fry for 20 minutes for 1½-inch (4 cm) chops, 35 minutes for 2-inch (5 cm) chops. Turn from time to time.

A special hint:

Use a lowish heat otherwise outside will burn.

DEVON PORKERS

For 4 servings, you will need:

4 pork loin chops	Clarified butter*
2 Granny Smith apples (or Golden Delicious)*	Freshly ground salt
1 tbs all-purpose flour	Freshly ground black pepper
1½ tsp dry mustard	16 fl oz (4 dl) sour cider (see hint)
2 tsp sugar	All-purpose flour to dust

First prepare:

Peel and cut apples into thick slices. Measure cider. Preheat oven to 375°F (193°C).

Now cook!

1. Lightly flour chops and season with salt, pepper, mustard and sugar.
2. Place enough clarified butter to just cover bottom into a frypan and when hot add chops and brown. Remove chops to a small baking dish.
3. To butter in frypan stir in flour. Gradually stir in cider. Whisk to form a smooth roux and allow to cook for 2 minutes.
4. Pour sauce over chops, cover with apple slices and bake in oven for 1½ hours.

A special hint:

The cider is important. First, it is necessary to get a dry cider. Then it is good to let it go flat and slightly sour. This is achieved in two ways.

1. To 16 fl oz (4 dl) cider, add 1 fl oz (2.8 cl) white vinegar.
2. Leave mixture in a bowl in refrigerator for 4 days.

STEAK DIANE

For 2 servings, you will need:

1 lb (0.5 kg) center cut beef
   tenderloin
2 oz (56 g) butter
1 tbs Worcestershire sauce
1 tbs brandy
1 tbs dry sherry
Freshly ground salt
Freshly ground black pepper
4 tbs parsley
1 clove garlic

Deep fried beans:
1 lb (0.5 kg) green beans
2 egg yolks
Flour
1 oz (28 g) fresh bread crumbs*
Freshly ground salt
Nutmeg
Juice ½ lemon
Deep oil

First prepare:

Measure butter. Measure brandy and sherry and warm. Finely chop parsley, trim green beans, beat egg yolks together and place on dish. Place flour and bread crumbs on separate dishes. Trim meat. Dry meat. Finely smash garlic. Cut a 1 inch (2.5 cm) steak from tenderloin and flatten out to a thickness of ¹⁄₁₆ of an inch (1.7 mm).

Now cook!

1. Place butter in a hot pan and when foaming add Worcestershire sauce and stir. Add steak and brown on one side. Turn and brown on other side. Add garlic, brandy and sherry and set alight.

2. Season with salt and pepper, dust with parsley and place on a serving dish. Cover with foaming sauce.

3. Lightly flour beans. Place into beaten egg and then into bread crumbs. Fry in hot oil at 380⁰F (193⁰C) for 2 minutes. Place on a serving dish covered with a paper doily. Dust with salt and nutmeg. Add a squeeze of lemon juice.

A special hint:

At Step 1 put butter into pan when the pan is hot but add Worcestershire sauce before butter browns.

STEAK A LA BOITE

For 2 servings, you will need:

2 slices beef tenderloin,
  12 oz (340 g) each
6 fl oz (1.6 dl) heavy cream
2 fl oz (5.6 cl) dry white wine
2 fl oz (5.6 cl) brandy
Clarified butter*
Freshly ground salt

Freshly ground black pepper
1 clove garlic
5 sage leaves
1 sprig rosemary
Dash Worcestershire sauce
3 tsp French mustard

First prepare:

Measure cream, mustard and white wine. Finely chop 2 sage leaves. Peel and mash garlic.

Now cook!

1. Put enough clarified butter to just cover bottom in a pan on heat. Season steak with garlic, salt and pepper. Add 3 sage leaves and rosemary sprig to butter in pan and then add steaks. Sear and cook each side.

2. Mix mustard with 2 fl oz (5.6 cl) cream. Mix 4 fl oz (1.2 dl) cream with white wine and Worcestershire sauce.

3. Pour off surplus fat from steak, add brandy and set alight. Lower heat a little and remove herbs.

4. Add the two cream mixtures to steak, bring to a boil and allow cream to reduce. Add two chopped sage leaves to sauce.

5. Place steaks on a warmed serving dish and cover with sauce.

A special hint:

Make sure that silvery skin is stripped from fillet. It will tighten and toughen steak if left.

FILLET OF BEEF MEURICE

68

For 4 servings, you will need:

2 lb (0.9 kg) beef tenderloin
8 oz (227 g) chicken liver pâté
Clarified butter*
10 oz (283 g) can sliced mushrooms
1 clove garlic
Freshly ground salt

Freshly ground black pepper
2 fl oz (5.6 cl) brandy
Squeeze lemon juice
5 fl oz (1.5 dl) heavy cream
1 tbs horseradish

First prepare:

Cut four 8-oz (227 g) steaks. Peel garlic. Measure brandy and warm. Open mushrooms and drain. Measure cream.

Now cook!

1. Season steaks with salt and pepper and squeeze garlic over them.

2. Put clarified butter in a frypan to just cover bottom and when hot add steaks and sear both sides. Remove to a dish. Add mushrooms, pour over brandy and set alight. Add squeeze lemon juice to mushrooms and then remove to a dish.

3. Add pâté to frypan. Stir until smooth and melted. Stir in cream and horseradish.

4. Place steaks on a serving dish, pour sauce over and decorate with mushrooms. Serve with green beans and stuffed tomatoes.

A special hint:

Always trim all sinew from tenderloin. Cut each steak into two ½-inch (1.2 cm) thick slices — 2 per serving. I think it improves appearance.

KAREWAI TENDERLOIN STEAK

For 4 servings, you will need:
2 lb (0.5 kg) beef tenderloin
Freshly ground salt
Freshly ground black pepper
1 clove garlic
2 tbs clarified butter*
4 oz (113 g) mushrooms
6 fl oz (1.6 dl) ketchup

6 fl oz (1.6 dl) dry white wine
1 tbs parsley stalks*
4 slices white bread
2 oz (56 g) butter
¼ lb (113 g) liverwurst sausage
Chopped parsley

64

First prepare:

Trim tenderloin and cut into 4 steaks. Peel and smash garlic. Finely slice mushrooms. Measure ketchup and wine. Finely chop parsley stalks. Cut bread into rounds. Mash liverwurst. Finely chop parsley for garnish.

Now cook!

1. Place clarified butter in frypan and when hot rub bottom of pan with garlic. Season steaks with salt and pepper and sear on both sides.
2. Place garlic into saucepan, add 1 oz (28 g) butter and fry gently. Add mushrooms and toss in butter. Stir in ketchup, cook for 2 minutes and stir in wine and parsley stalks. Simmer sauce for 5 minutes.
3. Remove steaks and keep warm. Add 1 oz (28 g) butter to pan and fry bread brown on both sides. Spread fried bread with liverwurst and place on serving dish. Place steaks on the bread and cover with sauce.
4. Garnish with parsley and serve.

STEAK AU POIVRE MA FACON

For 2 servings, you will need:

1 large sirloin steak (or 2 sirloin
    steaks each 8 oz: 227 g)
3 tbs clarified butter*
1 tsp rosemary leaves
1 tsp sage leaves
Rock salt
2 fl oz (5.6 cl) cognac
3 fl oz (8 cl) heavy cream

3 squares jellied veal stock
    each 1½ inches (4 cm) (page 52)
1 tsp Dijon mustard
1 tsp sour mustard*
Coarsely ground white pepper
Coarsely ground black pepper

First prepare:

Remove fat and gristle from meat and cut into 2 steaks. Warm cognac. Roughly crush peppercorns. Measure cream. Cut veal stock into squares.

Now cook!

1. Beat steaks to flatten a little, season with salt and press roughly crushed white pepper into each side.

2. Heat butter in frypan and when hot add rosemary and sage. Remove herbs after 1 minute otherwise they will burn. Add steaks and brown quickly on each side. Pour over warmed cognac and light.

3. Remove steaks from pan, place on serving dish and keep warm. Into cooking pan add veal jelly and when melted stir in cream to deglaze. Stir mustards into sauce and crushed black pepper to taste. Bring to a boil, pour sauce over steak and serve.

A special hint:

Always cut out heavy sinew that lies between fat and lean meat at broad end of steak.

To crush peppercorns: Place in an envelope and roll them with a bottle or rolling pin.

ENTRECOTE BORDELAISE

For 2 servings, you will need:

2 porterhouse steaks each
1½-inches (4 cm) thick
Freshly ground salt
Freshly ground black pepper
Clarified butter*
2 medium tomatoes
4 medium mushrooms
Cayenne pepper
Lemon juice
Sauce:
2 shallots or spring onions*

Clarified butter*
8 fl oz (2 dl) dry red wine
1 bay leaf
1 sprig thyme
Freshly ground white pepper
8 fl oz (2 dl) beef stock
2 oz (56 g) beef marrow (see hint)
2 oz (56 g) butter
1 tbs parsley stalks*
1 tsp soft brown sugar (if
necessary)

First prepare:

Remove sinew lying just under fat of steak. Dry meat and season with salt and black pepper. Finely dice shallots. Measure wine and beef stock. Finely cut parsley stalks. Measure butter. Cut beef marrow into 6 pieces, place in boiling water and poach gently for 2 minutes. Drain. Cut tomatoes in half and make a small crosswise incision in center. Preheat broiler.

Now cook!

1. Place a little clarified butter to just cover bottom into a saucepan and when hot add shallots and fry for 1 minute. Add wine, bay leaf, thyme and white pepper. Place over high heat and reduce to 4 fl oz (1.2 dl). Add beef stock, bring to a boil and leave on high heat for 8 minutes.

2. Place some clarified butter to just cover bottom in a large frypan and when hot add steaks. Turn once in butter and then allow to fry for 4 minutes each side. Remove to a warm dish.

3. Discard fat from pan in which steaks were cooked. Sieve sauce into this pan and stir to loosen meat residue. Add poached beef marrow. Remove from heat and whisk in butter. Stir in parsley stalks. Taste and if bitter add 1 tsp or more of soft brown sugar until bitter taste is gone.

4. Place tomatoes on a broiler rack, season with salt and pepper and drizzle a little clarified butter over top. Broil for 6 minutes.

5. Place some clarified butter to just cover bottom of a small frypan and add mushrooms. Season with salt and cayenne pepper and add squeeze of lemon juice. Allow to fry gently for 2 minutes.

6. Garnish steaks with broiled tomatoes, place 1 mushroom on each tomato half and cover steaks with sauce.

7. Serve with bowl of chilled watercress.

A special hint:

Beef marrow is obtained by asking at your meat market for shin beef bones sawed into 2-inch (5 cm) thick pieces. The marrow is in center of bone and can be poked out with your finger.

Addition of sugar is not classical but some dry red wines are very acid. Add only enough sugar to counteract acidity. Don't add enough to make it sweet.

CHATEAU SOLOGNOT

For 4 servings, you will need:

2 lb (0.9 kg) Châteaubriand
  (8 inch: 20 cm centercut
  tenderloin)
1 shallot (or spring onion)*
3 fl oz (8 cl) brandy
1 tsp Dijon mustard

½ tsp fresh lemon juice
1 oz (28 g) butter
1 fl oz (2.8 cl) heavy cream
Clarified butter*
Freshly ground salt
Freshly ground black pepper

First prepare:

Cut all silvery skin and fat from meat. Finely slice shallot. Place a serving dish in oven to warm. Season meat by rolling it around in salt and pepper very thoroughly. Measure all ingredients.

Now cook!

1. Heat your skillet to 400°F (205°C) and add just enough clarified butter to cover bottom of pan.
2. Place well seasoned piece of steak in butter and turn several times to seal in succulent juices. Use tongs for this purpose—never forks: they break seal and allow juices to drain from meat.
3. Into a second pot pour 1 tbs of clarified butter and heat. Fry sliced shallot gently.
4. Turn steak once again.
5. Continue stirring shallot. Stir in brandy and cream.
6. Lower heat under sauce.
7. Stir mustard and lemon juice into sauce and gradually allow liquid to reduce for 5 minutes.
8. Stir in butter. Sieve sauce into a clean pan on heat.
9. The steak should now be ready—5 minutes each side—medium rare. Remove from skillet and slice it in thick ½-inch (1.2 cm) diagonal steaks.
10. Pour off excess fat. Add sauce to pan and scrape to loosen all particles. Pour sauce over steak.

A special hint:

Be absolutely sure that all the silvery skin is taken off your piece of tenderloin (fillet) steak. If any remains the piece will curl up as the sinew contracts quicker than the meat and it becomes too tough to chew.

CHEESE STEAK

For 4 servings, you will need:

2 lbs (0.9 kg) beef tenderloin
3 oz (85 g) blue cheese
1 oz (28 g) butter
4 oz (113 g) Gruyère cheese
4 oz (113 g) jar red pimento
8 anchovy fillets

1 tbs chopped parsley
¼ tsp cayenne pepper
Clarified butter*
Freshly ground salt
Freshly ground black pepper

First prepare:

Trim skin from tenderloin, cut in half lengthwise and beat to flatten (about ½ inch: 1.2 cm thick). Cream blue cheese. Cut Gruyère cheese into thin slices. Slice pimento in long strips. Soak anchovy fillets in a little milk to make them less salty. Measure butter. Preheat broiler. String and paper towels will be required.

Now cook!

1. Cream blue cheese, butter and cayenne pepper and set aside.
2. Place some clarified butter into a medium hot frypan to just cover bottom. When butter is hot, add two halves of beef tenderloin well seasoned with salt and black pepper. Sear.
3. With a pair of tongs turn steak and sear other side.
4. Remove meat from pan. Dry steaks with a paper towel.
5. Place cheese mixture on cut half of tenderloin and cover with other half.
6. Tie meat "parcel" together with string.
7. Return steak to frypan and cook for following times:
    Cook for 1½ minutes on either side for rare.
    Cook for 3 minutes on either side for medium.
    Cook for 4 minutes on either side for well done.
8. Remove meat from pan and cut off string.
9. Cover tenderloin with sliced cheese, anchovy fillets and pimentos.
10. Place under broiler for 5 minutes (at least 4 inches: 10 cm from top of steak to heat source) until cheese is melted and lightly browned.
11. Remove from broiler and lift out onto a wooden meat platter. Sprinkle with chopped parsley and decorate with a few pieces of pimento. Serve.

A special hint:

When frying the steak in Step 7 be careful about blue cheese filling. If too much spills out into pan it can burn and form a bitter coating on steak. I prefer my steak medium rare and find that only 1 minute on each side is sufficient when additional 5 minutes broiling is taken into consideration.

TOURNEDOS EXCELLENCE

For 4 servings, you will need:

1 lb 12 oz (793 g) beef tenderloin	2 fl oz (5.6 cl) cognac
4 beef marrow bones, 1-inch	1 tbs paprika
(2.5 cm) thick	1 bunch watercress
12 fl oz (3.2 dl) beef stock	12 fl oz (3.2 dl) heavy cream
4 slices white bread	8 tbs clarified butter*
12 oz (340 g) chicken livers	Freshly ground salt
8 oz (227 g) button mushrooms	Freshly ground black pepper
1 oz (28 g) butter	1 tsp arrowroot
2 fl oz (5.6 cl) port wine	

First prepare:

Trim crusts from white bread and cut into rounds and then into crescent shapes. Wash chicken livers, remove white tissue, rinse and dry. Wash mushrooms and watercress and dry. Measure dry and liquid ingredients. Heat a serving platter. Cut meat into 4 equal pieces. Mix arrowroot with cold water to form a thin paste. Peel every vestige of skin from around marrow bones.

Now cook!

1. Into a saucepan on medium heat place marrow bones. Cover with beef stock and cook for 14 minutes.

2. Pour 4 tbs clarified butter into a frypan on high heat and fry crescent-shaped pieces of bread. Turn after 3 minutes — they should be crisp and golden brown. Drain on absorbent paper.

3. Into another frypan on high heat pour 2 tbs clarified butter, add steaks and fry for 3 minutes.

4. Turn steaks and season with salt and pepper.

5. Finely chop chicken livers and pour 2 tbs clarified butter into another frypan on medium heat.

6. Add mushrooms to the livers and stir in the 1 oz (28 g) butter.

7. Turn steaks again and reduce heat to medium.

8. Moisten chicken livers with port wine and cognac. Season with paprika and raise to high heat. When boiling, stir in cream.

9. Turn steaks once again and place on a warmed platter. Pour off fatty juices and spoon mushrooms and chicken livers into dry pan stirring in meat residue. Let reduce on medium heat or thicken with 1 tsp arrowroot mixed with water.

10. Lift marrow bones out of beef stock and arrange on serving platter. Place a piece of steak on each bone. Arrange croutons around. Pour some of hot sauce over each steak and pour rest around bottom.

11. Garnish with chilled watercress.

FILETE CORDON ROUGE

For 4 servings, you will need:

2½ lbs (1.2 kg) beef tenderloin
12 oz (340 g) chicken livers
1 tsp oregano
1 fl oz (2.8 cl) brandy
2 oz (56 g) butter
3 oz (85 g) onion
4 oz can (113 g) pimento
16 slices prosciutto ham*
6 tbs clarified butter*
4 fl oz (1.2 dl) red wine
1 tbs parsley

10 fl oz (3 dl) white sauce
White sauce:
1½ oz (42 g) butter
1½ oz (42 g) all-purpose flour
16 fl oz (4 dl) milk
1 clove
¼ oz (7 g) onion
1 bay leaf
2 parsley stalks*
Freshly ground salt
Freshly ground white pepper

First prepare:

White sauce: Melt butter in a saucepan over moderate heat and stir in flour. Remove pan from heat and gradually stir in milk. Return to heat and bring to a boil, stirring constantly. Place bay leaf, clove, parsley stalks, onion into a piece of muslin, and tie into a bag. Place into simmering sauce, reduce heat to low and cook for 15 minutes. Season with salt and pepper. Remove spice bag. Set aside until required.

Wash chicken livers and remove white cords. Measure dry and liquid ingredients. Wash, dry and finely chop parsley. Finely chop pimento. Dice onion. Coarsely chop washed and dried chicken livers and place in a hot pan on high heat with 2 tbs hot clarified butter. Season with salt and pepper and just cook through. Do not overcook or they become dry and crumbly. Stir in 10 fl oz (3 dl) of the white sauce and add oregano and brandy. Pour mixture into a blender and puree. Add ½ oz (14 g) butter. After 4 minutes, pour into a bowl and chill until required. Heat a serving platter in warm oven.

Now cook!

1. Cut trimmed tenderloin through center but not completely through. Open out steak and beat it flat with a rolling pin.

2. Spread 1 oz (28 g) diced onion on open steak. Pat down. Cover with half the pimento and then spread with 2 oz (56 g) of chilled chicken liver pâté. Roll steak up like a jelly roll.

3. Cover rolled steak with thin slices of prosciutto ham.

4. With 4 pieces of string, tie butcher knots around roll every 1½ inches (4 cm). Cut between strings to make 4 even-sized steaks.

5. Pour 2 tbs clarified butter into a large frypan on medium heat and fry roll-ups 2 minutes on each side. Remove from pan and keep warm on serving platter.

6. Drain off as much fatty juice as possible. Add remaining diced onion and sauté quickly in meat residue.

7. Pour in red wine and let cook down for 1 minute. Add remaining 2 oz (56 g) of pimento.

8. Cut strings off roll-ups and place on preheated serving platter.

9. Stir 1½ oz (42 g) butter into residue in frypan and add parsley. Pour over the fillets.

CARNE ASADA TAMPIQUENA

For 2 servings, you will need:

12 oz (340 g) beef tenderloin
8 oz (227 g) onion
2 bay leaves
4 whole cloves
8 white peppercorns
1 tsp cayenne pepper
3 fl oz (8 cl) white wine
    vinegar
3 fl oz (8 cl) white wine
1 lb (0.5 kg) dried black beans*
48 fl oz (1.4 l) cold water

2 green peppers (capsicum)
12 tbs clarified butter*
6 oz (170 g) Camembert cheese
3 oz (85 g) Parmesan cheese
2 oz (56 g) butter
Freshly ground salt
Freshly ground black pepper
Yorkshire pudding:
20 fl oz (6 dl) milk
4 eggs
8 oz (227 g) all-purpose flour

First prepare:

Soak beans overnight in 24 fl oz (7 dl) cold water. Make Yorkshire pudding. Beat eggs and milk with a whisk until smooth. Gradually whisk in flour and salt. Beat well. Set aside for 1 hour in a cool place. Finely slice onions. Slice top from peppers, remove seeds and cut flesh into 1 inch (2.5 cm) pieces. Chop Camembert cheese into ½ inch (1.3 cm) cubes. Grate Parmesan cheese. Measure vinegar and wine. Preheat oven to 450°F (232°C). Now for beef: roll fillet while cutting and turn your knife at the same time so as to get a long strip. Flatten out a little with the back of the knife and cut in half lengthwise, to get 2 pieces, 6 oz (170 g).

Now cook!

1. Drain beans and place in a pan with another 24 fl oz (7 dl) cold water. Bring to a boil and gently simmer for 1 hour or until tender. Drain.

2. Place 16 fl oz (4 dl) of chilled Yorkshire pudding batter into a blender and add Camembert and Parmesan cheese. Gently blend together. Stir into remaining Yorkshire pudding batter.

3. Pour 8 tbs clarified butter into a shallow 9 x 13 x 2 (22 x 32 x 5 cm) pan (or suitable baking dish) and place over a high heat (beef drippings would be even better). Pour the "cheesy batter" into pan and place in the preheated oven set at 450°F (232°C) for 40 minutes.

4. Pour a little clarified butter into a saucepan to just cover bottom. Turn heat on high and add 2 oz (56 g) onion, bay leaves, cloves, white peppercorns, cayenne pepper and wine. Bring mixture to a boil. Reduce heat to low.

5. Add peppers to simmering mixture.

6. Pour 4 tbs of clarified butter into a large frypan and add 6 oz (170 g) finely sliced onion and sauté until soft, but not colored. To this, add drained peppers from which bay leaves, cloves and peppercorns have been removed.

7. Stir everything well together and pour mixture from frypan back into a saucepan.

8. Place strips of beef into frypan on high heat and season generously with salt and black pepper. Let the natural fats of meats ooze out. Turn meat, using tongs, and let fry on the other side. Remove and place on serving platter. (It will have a "scorched" taste.)

9. Place cooked onions and peppers in meat pan and stir in the meat drippings quickly to loosen all particles and pour sauce onto a serving dish.

10. Add 2 oz (56 g) butter to drained beans, reheat and serve in a vegetable dish.

11. Remove cooked Yorkshire pudding from oven, cut into slices and arrange around meat. Serve piping hot.

BOATSHED BEEF

For 4 servings, you will need:

1 lb (0.5 kg) beef tenderloin
Clarified butter*
Freshly ground salt
Freshly ground black pepper
2 fl oz (5.6 cl) brandy

4 tbs sour cream
1 medium onion
1 tbs horseradish
4 tbs parsley
6 tsp Danish lumpfish roe
 (a mock caviar)

First prepare:

Cut meat into very thin slices and dry with a cloth. Measure sour cream. Finely dice onion. Heat brandy. Roughly chop parsley. Rinse lumpfish roe thoroughly under cold water.

Now cook!

1. Place some clarified butter in a frypan to just cover bottom and when hot add beef. Fry quickly, turning with a pair of tongs as soon as beef is slightly browned on one side. Season with salt and pepper. Tilt pan forward, add warmed brandy and set alight.

2. When flames die, add sour cream and horseradish and combine with pan juices. Add parsley.

3. Place on a serving dish, sprinkle with lumpfish roe and serve chopped onion separately.

A special hint:

Chop the onion finely if you haven't eaten raw onion before.

PUNTAS DE FILETE SONORENSE

For 4 servings, you will need:

1½ lbs (680 g) beef tenderloin tips
1 avocado
½ lime
2 medium onions
1 green pepper (capsicum)
6 oz (170 g) fresh button mushrooms
1 serrano chili*

2 fl oz (5.6 cl) port
1 oz (28 g) butter
Clarified butter*
Freshly ground salt
Freshly ground white pepper
Freshly ground black pepper
7 oz (198 g) can pimiento

First prepare:

Cut off "silver skin" from tenderloin tips and then cut meat into ½ inch (1.2 cm) slices. Finely slice one onion and finely cube the other. Juice the half lime. Slice tip from pepper and after removing seeds cut flesh into ¼ inch (7 mm) cubes. Wash, dry and finely slice mushrooms (stalks as well). Core tomatoes and blanch in boiling water for 2 minutes. Cool, remove skin and seeds and chop flesh into small cubes. Carefully take out seeds from serrano chili and discard. Finely dice chili. Measure butter and port. Halve avocado and remove seed. Scoop out flesh using a melon baller. Mix with juice of ½ lime to stop discoloration (see hint) and set aside. Dice pimiento.

Now cook!

1. Into a small frypan on low heat put 1 tbs clarified butter and pop in the finely sliced onion and allow to brown. Over them place cubed green peppers and mushrooms. Season generously with salt and white pepper and continue cooking very slowly.

2. In a large frypan on high heat place 2 tbs clarified butter and when heated add pieces of beef. Toss in butter and season with salt and black pepper. Cook for 5 minutes, remove from heat and put meat on a plate.

3. Stir cubes of onion into meat residue and return frypan to heat. Add serrano chili and moisten with port. Scrape pan to remove all particles. Simmer 2 minutes.

4. Add pimiento to sauce and cook another 2 minutes. Stir in tomato.

5. Toss beef back into sauce and stir thoroughly to intermingle flavors. Simmer 2 minutes.

6. Add avocado balls to vegetables in small frypan. Season with white pepper. Pour this into meat mixture and stir gently.

7. With a slotted spoon place meat and vegetables on a serving platter. Stir butter into pan juices to thicken them slightly. Spoon sauce over meat and vegetables.

A special hint:

Place the avocado "seed" in with the flesh—it keeps it from turning brown—but add the lime juice and cover with plastic. Make into avocado balls at the last moment.

TARTARBURGER

For 2 servings, you will need:

8 oz (227 g) beef tenderloin
(beef fillet) (trimmed weight)
2 tsp capers
2 oz (56 g) onion
2 sweet gherkins
1 fl oz (2.8 cl) brandy
2 tsp Worcestershire sauce

1 tbs parsley
1 tsp strong French mustard
Freshly ground salt
Freshly ground black pepper
1 egg yolk
Clarified butter*
2 fl oz (5.6 cl) dry red wine

First prepare:

Slice and then chop meat very fine using two knives. Continue chopping until meat "melts." (Melt means to reduce the meat to a smooth pulp.) Finely chop onion, gherkins and parsley. Measure red wine.

Now cook!

1. Combine meat with onion, capers, gherkins, brandy, Worcestershire sauce, parsley and mustard. Season highly with salt and pepper. Add egg and mix. Drain off any excess juices and reserve. Form meat into 2 patties.

2. Lightly flour burgers. Heat enough clarified butter in a frypan to just cover bottom and when hot, brown burgers 3 minutes on each side. Remove to a heated serving dish and deglaze pan with red wine and reserved juices. Pour this sauce over meat.

LAMB ROLLS ARNEB

64

For 6 servings, you will need:

1 lamb loin	4 tbs clarified butter*
Garlic salt	1 small bunch fresh mint
Freshly ground black pepper	

First prepare:

Remove loin meat from bone, remove outer skin and surplus fat. Season inside of meat with garlic salt and pepper. Roll up loin and tie at 1½ inch (4 cm) intervals. Cut lamb rolls in between the strings. Preheat oven to 375°F (190°C). Finely chop mint.

Now cook!

1. Season lamb rolls again with salt and pepper. Place in frypan with a little clarified butter and sear both sides.

2. Transfer lamb rolls to a shallow roasting pan, brush with butter and sprinkle with mint. Place in oven for 10 minutes. Turn lamb rolls. Brush again with butter and sprinkle with mint. Bake another 10–15 minutes.

GOLDEN MOUNTAIN LAMB ROLLS

66

For 6 servings, you will need:

1 lamb loin	8 canned peach halves
Garlic salt	16 fl oz (4 dl) heavy cream
Freshly ground black pepper	2 fl oz (5.6 cl) brandy
6 tbs clarified butter*	1 tbs parsley leaves

First prepare:

Remove loin meat from bone, remove fell and surplus fat. Season inside of meat with garlic salt and pepper. Roll up loin and tie at 1½ inch (4 cm) intervals. Cut 8 lamb rolls in between the strings. Measure cream and brandy. Warm brandy. Chop parsley finely. Drain peaches. Heat serving dish.

Now cook!

1. Season lamb rolls before cooking with garlic salt and pepper.

2. Melt clarified butter in frypan, add lamb rolls and brown quickly on both sides. Turn down heat for 15-20 minutes, turning rolls if one side becomes overcrisp.

3. Pour off fat when lamb rolls are cooked and place them on serving dish. Remove strings and keep warm.

4. Increase heat of pan and add peaches. Pour over heated brandy and set alight. Add cream and scrape residue up into cream. Reduce heat under pan and simmer until reduced to half.

5. Place peach halves on lamb rolls and top with sauce.

6. Dust with parsley and serve.

A special hint:

The cream must be heavily reduced to get it thick enough to cover.

1. NOISETTES. A basic butchery task.

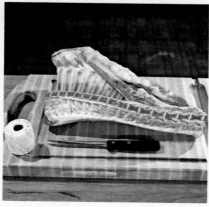

2. First remove the suet and kidney.

3. Make long shallow cuts in the fell 4 inches (10 cm) apart.

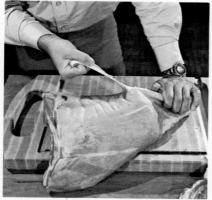

4. Outer skin is loosened and pulled off from leg to head.

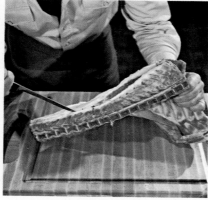

5. Cut close to the vertebrae under eye meat of the cutlets.

6. Slice rib cage away. Be careful not to cut outer fat area.

7. Remove the tip of shoulder blade from the neck end.

8. Cut away the heavy sinew that lies next to the vertebrae.

9. Measure a hand's width from eye meat. Cut off surplus breast.

10. Season inside with salt and pepper. Some also like garlic.

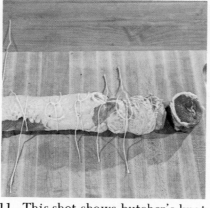

11. This shot shows butcher's knot from right to left.

12. Cut between the strings. You will get at least 9 plump cutlets.

LAMBATY

For 4 servings, you will need:

1 loin of lamb
Garlic salt
Black peppercorns
6 tbs clarified butter*
6 fl oz (1.6 dl) tomato sauce
6 fl oz (1.6 dl) dry white wine

2 cloves garlic
8 rounds bread
8 rounds pâté or good liver
  sausage
2 parsley stalks*
1 tbs parsley

First prepare:

Bone lamb, roll and tie, as in Lamb Rolls Arneb. Cut loin into 1½ inch (4 cm) lamb rolls. Roughly chop or grind peppercorns. Measure sauce and wine, warm wine. Smash or squeeze garlic. Cut bread to same size as lamb rolls and fry. Slice pâté thinly to cover bread rounds (or use liver sausage sliced). Finely chop parsley stalks and parsley. Heat a serving dish.

Now cook!

1. Season lamb rolls before cooking with garlic salt and ground peppercorns.
2. Melt butter in heavy frypan. Add lamb rolls. Brown quickly on both sides, turn down heat, and cook uncovered for 15-20 minutes, turning if one side becomes overcrisp.
3. When cooked, pour off excess fat; pour tomato sauce over lamb rolls. Turn lamb in this sauce, add garlic and warmed wine. Stir well. Simmer to reduce volume, about 15 minutes.
4. Place fried bread on a hot serving dish; spread with pâté.
5. Remove lamb rolls from sauce, cut off string. Place on bread rounds.
6. Add parsley stalks to sauce, skim excess fat and pour over lamb rolls. Dust with parsley and serve.

Service:

Asparagus tips, broiled tomatoes, and french fried potatoes make a delightful combination.

Lamb Rolls

(Overleaf)
Scallopine Don Quixote

1. SCALLOPINE DON QUIXOTE.

2. Infinite care is taken with the garnish.

3. All vegetables are trimmed and cut into same small dice.

4. The garnish is fried gently.

5. The veal is trimmed of outside skin to prevent bunching.

6. Place in lightly buttered pan (for papillote see page 247).

SCALLOPINE DON QUIXOTE

For 2 servings, you will need:

2 slices leg of veal
2 oz (56 g) spring onions
3 oz (85 g) fresh carrots
4 tbs clarified butter*
2 oz (56 g) fresh mushrooms
Freshly ground salt
Freshly ground black pepper

3 oz (85 g) petits pois
4 slices Mozzarella cheese
2 large tomatoes
4 slices prosciutto ham
4 sheets vegetable parchment
  paper

First prepare:

Pound veal slices until thin. Chop carrots into ¼ inch (7 mm) dice. Cut mushrooms into halves. Cut parchment into a heart shape large enough so that when folded in half there is a 1½ inch (4 cm) margin between veal and paper edge. Peel and seed tomatoes and chop roughly. Slice cheese. Preheat oven to 500⁰F (260⁰C). Paint paper with clarified butter.

Now cook!

1. Place enough clarified butter in a saucepan to just cover bottom and when hot add onions. Brown gently, add carrots and then mushrooms. Fry gently until browned. Add peas and remove from heat.

2. Season veal slices that have been pounded thin with salt and pepper. Place a little clarified butter in a pan ¼ inch deep and sauté veal for 1 minute on each side over high heat.

3. Place veal slices on sheets of paper. Cover with slices of prosciutto, Mozzarella cheese and tomatoes. Season with salt and pepper and place vegetable mixture on top. Crimp edges of paper to seal in meat, paint top of paper with clarified butter and place in oven for 10 minutes. Serve in paper.

461

CHICKEN CHICKEN ITZA

62

For 4 servings, you will need:

  3¼ lb (1.5 kg) chicken
  2 pellets achiote **
  1 lemon
  7 tbs clarified butter*

Freshly ground salt
Freshly ground white pepper
4 sheets vegetable parchment
 paper

 ** Achiote can also be purchased in red and brown blocks. If so use 1 oz (28 g) brown and ½ oz (14 g) red.

First prepare:

With a sharp knife cut legs and thighs from chicken and then cut along breast and backbone. Leave outer skin on, scraping against bone all the way to get every morsel of flesh. Scrape thigh and drumstick flesh away from bone and remove both bones from leg. (Be careful to keep flesh in one piece!) Save bones for stock. You should now have 4 portions—2 breasts, 2 legs and thighs. Preheat oven to 425ºF (218ºC). Warm a serving platter.

Now cook!

1. Place a large frypan on medium heat and add 2 tbs clarified butter.
2. Lay 4 portions of chicken into frypan (skin side down) and season generously with salt and white pepper. Pour 1 tbs clarified butter over top and let cook.
3. Into a small frypan on medium heat pour 4 tbs clarified butter, add achiote pieces and let them color and flavor butter.
4. With a pair of tongs turn pieces of chicken over and increase heat to high. Cover with a lid and let fry away.
5. Turn chicken pieces once again (allow five minutes each side). Strain a little of the achiote butter over chicken and the flesh will turn a bright yellow.
6. Squeeze juice of ½ lemon over chicken and stir briskly into pan residue.
7. Brush vegetable paper with a little achiote butter and place a breast and thigh and leg on it skin side up. Repeat using remaining chicken.
8. Pour remaining achiote mixture from small frypan into a bowl, add a cube of ice and stir. This will solidify butter. Spread over chicken. Fold paper over to form a package, like a papillote (see page 247). (This is traditionally done with banana leaves—see hint.)
9. Place chicken in a baking dish and brush with some of the excess achiote juice. Pop into preheated oven set at 425ºF (218ºC) for 30 minutes.
10. After this cooking period, remove from oven and place on a heated serving platter.

A special hint:

Banana leaves should only be used when absolutely fresh from the trees.

TOM MUIR'S KIDNEYS

For 4 servings, you will need:

12 lambs' kidneys
6 spring onions*
2 oz (56 g) mushrooms
1 green pepper (capsicum)
8 tbs clarified butter*
8 oz (227 g) raw rice

Freshly ground salt
Freshly ground black pepper
3 fl oz (8 cl) whisky
8 fl oz (2 dl) chicken stock
2 tsp arrowroot
Parsley

First prepare:

Remove skin from kidneys, cut in half, remove core and then cut into quarters. Dice green pepper. Cut spring onions into ½ inch (1.2 cm) cubes. Slice mushrooms finely. Measure whisky and heat. Measure chicken stock. Measure rice and wash well. Roughly chop parsley.

Now cook!

1. Heat clarified butter in a frypan and add green pepper and spring onions. Fry gently for 3 minutes. Add mushrooms and season with salt and pepper.
2. Place kidneys on vegetable bed and add 1 fl oz (2.8 cl) whisky. Stir all ingredients together, turning mixture over from time to time. This should take approximately 2 minutes.
3. Scrape mixture to side of pan and add 1 fl oz (2.8 cl) whisky. Set alight. Add chicken stock, cover pan and simmer for 2 minutes.
4. Mix arrowroot with a little water and stir into kidney mixture, thickening it instantly. Remove from heat.
5. Place cooked rice on a heated serving dish. Make a well in center and fill with kidneys. Stir 1 fl oz (2.8 cl) whisky into kidneys and then garnish rice with chopped parsley.
6. To cook rice: rain rice into salted boiling water and allow to boil gently for 10 minutes. Drain rice in a metal colander. Place a little hot water in the saucepan, set the rice in the colander on top, cover with a lid and allow rice to steam for 5 minutes.

A special hint:

If you wish to remove the strong taste in the kidneys, place them (after cutting) into a hot buttered pan and fry for 2 minutes, then turn them onto a board to bleed. Dry them and proceed with recipe. The bleeding removes a possible ammonia taste.

*Logic is only a dirty word in kitchens
where you employ others to do the work.*

LAMBS' KIDNEYS MANAWATU

$●
⊠●

GG
62

For 4 servings, you will need:

1 lb (0.5 kg) thin beef sausages*
6 lambs' kidneys
Clarified butter*
4 slices white bread (crust removed)
1 medium onion
1 clove garlic

6 fl oz (1.6 dl) tomato ketchup
4 fl oz (1.2 dl) dry white wine
4 fl oz (1.2 dl) veal stock
1 tbs parsley stalks*
1 tbs parsley leaves
Freshly ground salt
Freshly ground black pepper

First prepare:

Cut sausages into 1½ inch (4 cm) pieces. Remove center core of kidneys, cut into quarters. Peel garlic and smash. Cut bread into heart shapes. Finely slice onion. Measure wine, veal stock and tomato sauce. Chop parsley stalks and leaves.

Now cook!

1. Place clarified butter into a frypan and fry sausages until brown. Remove and set aside.
2. Add kidneys to pan juices and fry. Remove kidneys and discard fat. Add fresh butter to pan and fry bread until golden on each side. Drain and keep warm.
3. Add onion and garlic to pan in which bread was fried and fry gently. When onion is golden add kidneys, sausages and tomato ketchup. Stir until ketchup deepens in color and add stock, wine, parsley stalks. Season with salt and pepper. Simmer for 5 minutes.
4. Place on a shallow dish. Dip tops of fried bread croutons into chopped parsley. Set them around dish.

A special hint:

Pinch and tie sausages so that you get at least 16 to 1 lb (0.5 kg).

KUKU SCHNITZEL AND GOLDEN COAST SAUCE

$●
⊠●
☀
🐑

GG
62

For 4 servings, you will need:

4 veal sweetbreads
2 oz (56 g) all-purpose flour
1 egg
1½ oz (42 g) bread crumbs*
Clarified butter*

Golden Coast sauce:

4 fl oz (1.2 dl) mayonnaise
2 sweet gherkins
1 tbs chopped parsley
2 tbs capers
1 pinch cayenne pepper

First prepare:

Soak sweetbreads, blanch, peel off skin and press between 2 dinner plates under a table leg. Season flour. Beat egg. Place bread crumbs on a plate. Measure sauce ingredients. Preheat frypan to 300ºF (149ºC).

Now cook!

1. Dip sweetbreads in flour, egg, then in bread crumbs and shallow fry in butter in frypan at 300ºF (149ºC). Cook for 3 minutes on either side.
2. Mix sauce ingredients together and pour into a sauceboat.
3. Garnish sweetbreads with chilled watercress, lemon wedges and Bennet potatoes.

ROGNONS DE VEAU MEXICAN

For 4 servings, you will need:

2 lbs (0.9 kg) veal kidneys
8 pepperoni (small spicy hot sausages)
3 tbs clarified butter*
4 oz (113 g) button mushrooms
6 oz (170 g) tomato paste
1 large clove garlic
1 tsp cayenne pepper
16 fl oz (4 dl) beef bouillon
8 fl oz (2 dl) red wine

1 tbs parsley
1½ oz (42 g) all-purpose flour
Clarified butter*
Flour
Tortillas:
10 oz (283 g) white cornmeal
4 oz (113 g) all-purpose flour
8 fl oz (2 dl) warm water
¾ tsp freshly ground salt

70

First prepare:

Wash, cut and devein kidneys. Slice pepperoni in halves, crosswise. Measure tomato paste, beef bouillon, red wine, flour and cayenne pepper. Wash, dry and chop parsley. Cut mushrooms in half. Measure cornmeal, water and flour for tortillas. Heat a shallow serving dish in warming oven.

Now cook!

1. Into a heated frypan pour a little clarified butter to just cover bottom.
2. Cut veal kidneys in 1 inch (2.5 cm) cubes and dust with flour.
3. Put kidneys into hot butter and stir over high heat.
4. Turn kidneys constantly and when they are brown drain off juice.
5. Add smashed clove of garlic.
6. Place 3 tbs clarified butter in a saucepan and melt. Stir in 1½ oz (42 g) flour and cook until pale brown. (This is a roux base for a brown sauce.)
7. Add tomato paste to browning roux and stir thoroughly. Add cayenne pepper.
8. Pour beef bouillon into roux and blend. Pour simmering sauce over kidneys.
9. Pour a little clarified butter into another small frypan to just cover bottom and fry mushrooms over low heat. Add mushrooms and pepperoni to kidneys in sauce.
10. Blend in 4 fl oz (1.2 dl) red wine and bring mixture to a fast boil. Allow sauce to reduce for 10 minutes.
11. *Tortillas:* Place cornmeal, flour and salt into a bowl. Pour warm water into the center and mix with a fork to form a ball. Turn out onto a floured board and knead until the mixture is pliable, dampening hands constantly.
12. Roll out on a floured surface to form a thin sheet.
13. Cut the mixture into 8 tortillas (using a small bowl) and put them in a dry pan over low heat.
14. Stir another 4 fl oz (1.2 dl) red wine into kidneys.
15. Place kidneys into heated serving dish, dust with parsley. Serve piping hot with tortillas.

RIS DE VEAU EN CASSEROLE

For 4 servings, you will need:

4 calves' sweetbreads, 6 oz (170 g) each
1 small tomato
16 fl oz (4 dl) beef stock
8 small onions
4 oz (113 g) button mushrooms
2 fl oz (5.6 cl) brandy
4 fl oz (1.2 dl) red wine
1 bay leaf
3 truffles and juice
1 tsp sugar
3 tsp arrowroot
2 tbs red wine
10 oz (283 g) jar kumquats
2 fl oz (5.6 cl) kumquat juice
Clarified butter*
Freshly ground salt
Freshly ground white pepper

First prepare:

Soak sweetbreads in cold water for one hour, then place in lukewarm water and bring to a boil. This will harden sinew on the outside and whiten flesh. Drain and plunge into a bowl of cold water. Remove hardened outside sinews and skin. Dry naked sweetbreads with a paper towel. Place tomato in boiling water for 1 minute. Remove, peel off skin and remove seeds. Measure beef stock, red wine, brandy and kumquat juice. Finely slice truffles. Blend arrowroot with 2 tbs red wine. Trim stems from button mushrooms. Preheat oven to 350°F (177°C). Heat a serving dish in warming oven.

Now cook!

1. Place a heatproof casserole on heat and pour in enough clarified butter to just cover bottom. Add onions and brown over a moderate heat.

2. In another pan, place tomato flesh and cook over a medium heat until it browns lightly. (Don't burn it!) Keep stirring all the time (see hint).

3. When browned add beef stock, stir and bring to a boil.

4. To browned onions, add trimmed mushrooms and sprinkle with sugar.

5. Add sweetbreads and stir gently to combine.

6. Clear an area in pan by tilting mixture to one side. Pour in brandy and set it alight.

7. When flame goes out, add red wine.

8. Add beef stock, bay leaf and truffle juice. Skim surface of all fat and cover casserole, placing it in a preheated oven set at 350°F (177°C) for 15 minutes.

9. After 15 minutes remove sweetbreads from casserole and keep them hot.

10. Bring liquid in casserole to a boil. Stir in blended arrowroot and red wine until sauce is thick and glossy. Remove bay leaf and add truffles.

11. Return sweetbreads to sauce and finally add preserved kumquats—heat through and serve at once.

A special hint:

Refer Step 2. The reason for cooking tomato flesh until it browns is to make an edible brown color to darken sauce.

Ris de Veau en Casserole

VEAL KIDNEYS ANTONIN CAREME

For 2 servings, you will need:

4 veal kidneys	Black peppercorns
2 tbs clarified butter*	Freshly ground salt
1 tbs cognac	1 tsp port
2 tsp Dijon mustard	2½ oz (70 g) foie gras
2 fl oz (5.6 cl) heavy cream	(goose liver paste)

First prepare:

Remove fat from kidneys and core. Heat cognac. Measure cream and port.

Now cook!

1. Place whole kidneys into hot clarified butter and sauté 1 minute.
2. Add cognac and set alight. Remove kidneys and place on dish to cool.
3. Add mustard and foie gras to pan—mash with a fork. Add cream and stir to combine.
4. Slice slightly cooled kidneys into thick slices—place them in sauce together with their juices and port. Season with salt and pepper and place on serving dish.

A special hint:

The veal kidneys must be fresh and small.

KALBSNIERENTRANCHEN

For 4 servings, you will need:

3 veal kidneys
4 fl oz (1.2 dl) beef stock
3 shallots
1 red pepper (capsicum)
1½ oz (42 g) dried Galco
    mushrooms*
4 fl oz (1.2 dl) cold water
2 fl oz (5.6 cl) brandy
2 tsp tomato paste

4 fl oz (1.2 dl) white wine
1 tsp Dijon mustard
1 tsp English mustard
1 lemon
2 fl oz (5.6 cl) heavy cream
Clarified butter*
Flour
Freshly ground salt
Freshly ground white pepper

First prepare:

Soak dried mushrooms in cold water for 10 minutes. Trim suet from veal kidneys and cut kidneys into bite size portions—about 1 inch (2.5 cm). Cover kidney pieces with a dusting of flour. Finely chop shallots. Slice top from pepper, remove seeds and center core. Measure tomato paste, white wine, brandy, cream and mustard. Squeeze juice of lemon.

Now cook!

1. Pour some clarified butter into a heated saucepan to just cover bottom.
2. Fry kidney pieces in hot butter. Turn them over when they become red on the outside. Drain cooked kidneys.
3. Heat beef stock and allow to reduce to half.
4. Drain mushrooms and add liquid to reduced beef stock.
5. Into a pan pour some clarified butter, add pepper and shallots and gently shallow fry.
6. Add drained kidneys and stir, then add mushrooms.
7. Stir in tomato paste. Raise heat, add brandy and flame.
8. Blend in white wine and reduced beef stock. Stir thoroughly and cook over moderate heat.
9. Add to that the mustards and lemon juice and simmer for 12 minutes.
10. Lastly, stir in cream and reheat.

Service:

I serve this with saffron flavored rice: 8 oz (227 g) boiled, then steamed and seasoned with chopped gherkins, chopped white onion and about 1½ oz (42 g) (soaked weight) Galco mushrooms.

ELMWOOD CHICKEN LIVERS

For 4 small servings, you will need:

1 lb (0.5 kg) chicken livers
1 oz (28 g) clove garlic
1 medium onion
4 oz (113 g) fresh mushrooms
3 tbs clarified butter*
1½ oz (42 g) all-purpose flour

1 tsp oregano
2 fl oz (5.6 cl) dry white wine
4 slices rye toast
Watercress
Freshly ground salt
Freshly ground black pepper

First prepare:

Peel and slightly bruise garlic. Finely slice onion and mushrooms (if the mushrooms are not wild then you need only wash them—no peeling needed). Cut chicken livers into even 1 inch (2.5 cm) pieces. Have rye bread ready for toasting. Rinse and pick over watercress and keep it in iced cold water. Measure wine.

Now cook!

1. Place clarified butter in a heated frypan to just cover bottom and add garlic, onions and mushrooms. Toss all together.
2. Allow to fry gently until just browned. Remove clove of garlic.
3. Meanwhile, put cut chicken livers into a bag in which you have placed the flour and some salt and pepper. Shake well, turn the livers into a colander and toss to remove excess flour.
4. Remove fried vegetables from pan and keep them warm. Add more clarified butter to pan (without cleaning pan—you need the retained flavors). Fry the livers on high heat for 2 minutes on either side. Do not overcook.
5. When livers are done, return previously fried onions and mushrooms to the pan and heat through.
6. Add wine and stir gently to combine. Toast rye bread. Cut off crusts, butter lightly and place on a long dish.
7. Taste the liver mixture, adjust seasoning and spoon it onto buttered rye toast.
8. Garnish with ice cold watercress.

A special hint:

Please don't overcook chicken livers. They need 2 minutes on either side at the most.

BELL BLOCK CHICKEN LIVERS

For 4 servings, you will need:

8 oz (227 g) chicken livers
½ oz (14 g) fresh mushrooms
5 oz (142 g) all-purpose flour
4 oz (113 g) onion
1 lemon
2 tbs parsley

4 slices whole wheat bread
4 tbs clarified butter*
Freshly ground salt
Freshly ground white pepper
4 fl oz (1.2 dl) red wine

65

First prepare:

Season livers and roll in flour. Slice onion finely. Juice lemon. Slice mushrooms and finely chop parsley. Toast bread and butter it.

Now cook!

1. Fry livers in butter with onions (about 5 minutes).
2. Add mushrooms and lemon juice and season with salt and pepper.
3. Stir in wine, heat and spoon onto toast.
4. Sprinkle with parsley.

A special hint:

Don't overcook the livers. Five minutes is the absolute maximum.

TUNISIAN TRIPE

For 4 servings, you will need:

1¼ lbs (566 g) tripe
1 pickled pig's trotter*
1¼ lbs (566 g) fresh tomatoes
2 red peppers (capsicum)
2 medium carrots
2 onions
1 leek
2 cloves garlic
1 sprig thyme

1 bay leaf
Freshly ground salt
Freshly ground black pepper
3 fl oz (8 cl) olive oil
1 tsp cumin
2 tsp paprika
6 bacon slices
Parsley

First prepare:

Finely slice onions. Cut leek and carrots into ¼ inch (7 mm) slices. Peel tomatoes and cut into chunks. Cut tripe into 2 inch (5 cm) squares. Split pig's trotter in half. Slice pepper into ½ inch (1.2 cm) strips. Smash garlic cloves. Roughly chop parsley.

Now cook!

1. Cover bottom of a pan on medium heat with olive oil. Add onions and allow them to fry gently. Add leek, carrots and pepper. Toss vegetables together and add garlic and tomatoes. Season with salt, pepper, cumin and paprika and add thyme and bay leaf. Allow vegetable mixture to cook gently for 2 minutes.
2. Blanch tripe in boiling salted water. Drain and add with pig's trotter to vegetable mixture and cover with bacon slices. Cover pan and allow to simmer for an hour and three quarters.
3. Remove lid, stir bacon into vegetable and tripe mixture. Strain juice through a sieve and reserve. Remove pig's trotter and bay leaf.
4. Place drained vegetables and tripe into a serving dish. Pour over half the strained juice and garnish dish with parsley.

A special hint:

To blanch tripe: place it in cold water and bring gradually to a boil. The moment it boils pour off water and place tripe in clear cold water until ready to use.

FILLET STEAK WASHINGTON

$●
✕●
🐾

G̶G
67

For 4 servings, you will need:

2 lbs (0.9 kg) beef tenderloin cut into 4 steaks (trimmed)	1 lb (0.5 kg) puff pastry*
	1 tsp lemon juice
4 tbs clarified butter*	Cayenne pepper
Black peppercorns	1 egg
Freshly ground salt	120 fl oz (3.4 l) corn oil
4 large mushrooms	

First prepare:

Roll out puff pastry. Take a cup or bowl that just fits over steak and use this to mark out a circle on your pastry. Repeat four times, cutting pastry about ½ inch (1.2 cm) wider than cup measurement. Now, take a saucer and cut rounds a good 1 inch (2.5 cm) wider than the size previously cut out. Repeat four times. Beat egg, squeeze lemon juice, peel mushrooms and remove stalks.

Now cook!

1. Heat frypan, season steaks, add clarified butter to pan. When hot sear steaks on both sides and around edges. (4 minutes for well done each side, 2 minutes for rare). Remove steaks and cool.

2. Place mushrooms into pan (vein side uppermost). Season with lemon juice, salt and cayenne pepper. Turn mushrooms to cook till just darkened on seasoned side. Remove mushrooms and place on top of cooled steaks. Dry with cloth.

3. Put small round of pastry on a board and brush lightly with beaten egg. Place steak in center with a mushroom on top. Brush larger pastry round with egg. Place pastry (egg-brushed side downwards) on top of mushroom and steak. Press edges of pastry and crimp together with a fork to seal completely. Place in a paper bag (or aluminum foil) and refrigerate overnight. Remove from refrigerator for 30 minutes before cooking.

4. Heat oil in deep fryer to 400°F (205°C) and lower pastries into oil very gently with a slotted spoon. Fry for 7 minutes. Drain on absorbent paper.

5. Serve accompanied by small minted potatoes.

A special hint:

The secret is to dry steak and mushrooms thoroughly before wrapping and storing under refrigeration.

G̶G
---

*With more than eight people at dinner
it is hard to hold a conversation.
Without conversation there is no
justification for the dinner.*

1. FILLET STEAK WASHINGTON.

2. Fillet is trimmed of sinew and cut into 8-oz pieces.

3. Seal all sides over high heat. Then lower heat for well-done.

4. Set steaks on a rack to cool. Cook mushrooms lightly.

5. Cut out puff pastry in two sizes using a cup.

6. Brush the pastry with beaten egg.

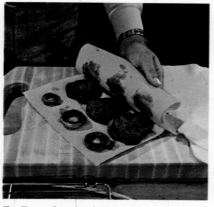

7. Dry the cooled steak and mushrooms thoroughly.

8. Place steak and mushroom on smaller round; cover with larger.

9. Turn package; seal and crimp the edges.

10. Cut away the surplus pastry.

11. Packets can be stored in a paper bag in refrigerator.

12. Cook in deep fat for 7 minutes at 400°F (205°C).

DUCKLING CHASSIGNAT

For 2 servings, you will need:

4 lb (1.8 kg) duck (Aylesbury,
　　Long Island or Brome Lake)
4 fl oz (1.2 dl) dry red wine
3 tbs brandy
1 tsp Marmite (meat flavored
　　yeast concentrate)*
2 oz (56 g) sugar
32 fl oz (1 l) vegetable oil
4 fl oz (1.2 dl) red wine vinegar

1 28 oz (793 g) can cling
　　peach halves
8 fl oz (2 dl) peach juice
Clarified butter*
1 tsp arrowroot
1 tsp red wine
Freshly ground salt
Freshly ground black pepper

First prepare:

Cut duck into pieces: 2 legs and thighs and 2 breasts. Remove wings (and chop them for stock pot) and detach legs at joint next to body. Cut horizontally through center of duck, leaving two halves, the top half being the breasts. Bone the breast and cut into two pieces. Chop carcass bones. Measure brandy, red wine, peach juice, red wine vinegar. Measure Marmite. Heat a serving platter in warming oven. Blend arrowroot and 1 tsp red wine in a small bowl. Heat oil in deep fat fryer to 350°F (177°C).

Now cook!

1. Place pieces of duck in deep fat fryer and cook for 15 minutes.
2. Pour red wine vinegar, peach juice and sugar into a saucepan on medium heat and stir well.
3. Add Marmite and let sauce come to a boil.
4. Add finely chopped carcass bones and joints to give extra flavor.
5. Skim frequently and allow sauce to reduce to half. Add wine.
6. Remove duck from fryer, drain on absorbent paper and cool. Trim protruding bones, season with salt and black pepper and add to simmering sauce for 15 minutes.
7. Remove from sauce and drain.
8. In a heated frypan add enough clarified butter to just cover bottom and fry duck pieces for a few moments to reheat.
9. Allow sauce to keep reducing for 5 minutes. Strain to remove bones and return to saucepan.
10. Add arrowroot to sauce and stir until thickened. Simmer.
11. Place four peach halves in the frypan with duck. Pour on 2 tbs brandy and flame, shaking pan carefully.
12. Add remaining 1 tbs of brandy to sauce.
13. Turn peach halves.
14. Finally, dip duck portions into sauce and arrange on heated platter. Pour sauce over duck and arrange peach halves around it.
15. Serve piping hot.

A special hint:

Be careful at Step 8 when you fry the duck—it can color very quickly and burn if you don't watch it.

Fillet Steak Washington (page 472)

PACKETS OF CHICKEN IN THE CHINESE MANNER

For 2 servings, you will need:

2 chicken breasts
3 tbs soya sauce
4 tbs cooked rice
Fresh root ginger*

2 tsp chopped chives
Cinnamon
Peanut oil for deep frying
2 10-inch (25 cm) squares clear
  cellophane

First prepare:

Remove skin and bones from chicken breasts and cut meat into thin strips. Cook rice in plenty of boiling salted water for 10 minutes, drain and place in a colander above a little boiling water. Cover and allow to steam for 5 minutes. Finely chop chives. Peel root ginger and cut 6 paper-thin pieces. Brush cellophane squares with peanut oil. Pre-heat deep fryer to 400°F (205°C).

Now cook!

1. Place strips of chicken in a bowl and cover with soya sauce. Allow to marinate 1 hour.
2. Place 2 tbs of rice in center of each cellophane square, cover with half of the marinated chicken. Put 3 slices of ginger on top and sprinkle with chives. Dust with a little cinnamon and wrap up like a bonbon, twisting each end tightly.
3. Place into deep fryer basket in hot oil and cook for 5 minutes until cellophane is brown and crisp. Remove and serve immediately.

CHICKEN KIEV—OR BUTTERED BREAST OF CHICKEN

For 2 servings, you will need:

1 whole chicken breast from a
  2 lb (0.9 kg) chicken
4 oz (113 g) parsley butter
2 eggs
1 oz (28 g) bread crumbs*
2½ oz (70 g) all-purpose flour
Peanut oil for deep frying

Parsley butter:
4 oz (113 g) butter
2 tbs parsley
½ tsp cayenne pepper
2 tbs lemon juice
1 clove garlic

First prepare:

Skin chicken breasts. Cut and remove bones from breasts, beat breast with rolling pin to flatten to about ⅛ inch (3 mm) thickness. Beat eggs. Place bread crumbs and flour onto separate plates. Heat oil in deep fryer to 325°F (163°C).
Parsley butter: Finely chop parsley and garlic and add with other ingredients to softened butter. Roll in waxed paper to form a roll 1 inch (2.5 cm) in diameter. Freeze.

Now cook!

1. Cut frozen parsley butter into 4 rounds. Chill 2 rounds to place on cooked chicken. Put one piece inside each breast. Fold ends over and roll up. Seal with beaten egg.
2. Flour each breast, dip in egg, then in bread crumbs.
3. Lower breasts carefully into hot oil and deep fry until golden brown, about 6 minutes.
4. Drain on absorbent paper and place on serving dish. Put chilled parsley butter on chicken.
5. Accompany with green salad and Moreland potatoes.

A special hint:

The parsley butter must be frozen solid before it is placed on the chicken.

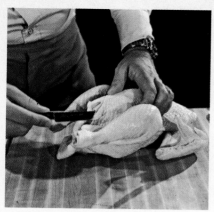

1. TO BONE A CHICKEN. Begin by cutting either side of the vent between the breast and the rib cage.

2. Put your fingers down either side, separating the flesh right down to the wishbone and right underneath along the backbone.

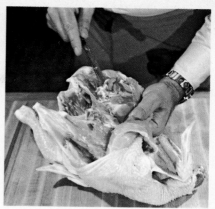

3. Fold the breast forward carefully so as not to stretch or tear the skin. Cut through the socket joints that attach the legs to the body.

4. Trim around the leg area under the parson's nose.

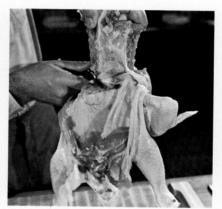

5. Having detached the back area just trim away until you reach the wishbone.

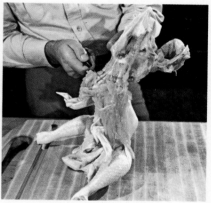

6. As you literally peel the bones out of the flesh let the natural weight be the pulling agent.

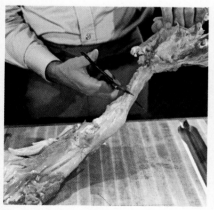

7. Detach at the neck.

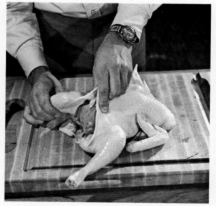

8. Stuff as per recipe, and tie as shown on page 358.

9. Place on a trivet, baste and roast. Doesn't look so hard, does it?

MURRAY BRIDGE CHICKEN

68

For 4 servings, you will need:

1 chicken, 3 lb (1.4 kg)	2 fl oz (5.6 cl) dry white wine
1 lb (0.5 kg) pratwurst sausage*	2 tbs clarified butter*
Freshly ground salt	12 oz (340 g) grapes, peeled
White peppercorns	1 tsp arrowroot

First prepare:

Bone chicken (see below), poach sausage in cold water, bringing it slowly to the boil. Poach for two minutes. Remove and peel off skin. Preheat oven to 350°F (177°C).

Now cook!

1. Stuff chicken with sausage. Sew or skewer openings. Season with salt and pepper and place in ovenproof dish with white wine and clarified butter. Bake in oven for 1 hour.

2. Take chicken from oven and remove string or skewers. Skim excess fat from pan juices and put juices into a saucepan. Heat, add grapes. Mix arrowroot with additional dry white wine to thicken gravy.

3. Pour sauce with grapes over chicken.

A special hint:

To bone a chicken. For this dish it is necessary to remove the entire rib cage and backbone without puncturing the skin. You do this by inserting a small sharp knife in the vent. Cut into the area between the breastbone and the breast meat. Fold the breast forward as it is cut away. Detach the wings from the wishbone from the inside and continue to pull the flesh over as you cut back down the backbone. Leave wing and leg bones in chicken.

FILLETED CHICKEN KEMPSEY

For 4 small servings, you will need:

1 chicken, 3 lb (1.4 kg)	10 fl oz (3 dl) sour cream
6 fl oz (1.6 dl) white wine	2 tsp tomato paste
6 fl oz (1.6 dl) water	1 tbs arrowroot
12 jumbo shrimp (cooked)	2 oz (56 g) peas (shelled)
Freshly ground salt	Fresh mint
Freshly ground black pepper	

First prepare:

Peel shrimp, reserving heads and shells. (Some seafood markets may still sell shrimp with heads.) Cook peas in boiling salted water together with pinch of sugar and sprig of mint.

Now cook!

1. Skin, bone and fillet chicken. Season with salt and pepper. Place the chicken in a bowl (legs, then breasts). Place this bowl in a large pot containing the wine and water and shrimp heads and shells. Cover pot tightly and steam for 1 hour.

2. Remove chicken from bowl and keep warm. Add shrimp to chicken.

3. Place juice from chicken in a pan and reduce to a syrupy consistency. Add chicken and shrimp.

4. Stir in sour cream and tomato paste. Thicken sauce with arrowroot mixed with dry white wine. Serve sprinkled with peas.

Murray Bridge Chicken

Lapin Farci Provencale (page 482)

POULET COTE D'AZUR

For 4 servings, you will need:

3 lb (1.4 kg) chicken
5 oz (142 g) onion
3 oz (85 g) green beans
2 oz (56 g) turnip
4 oz (113 g) parsnip
2 oz (56 g) carrot
2 oz (56 g) green peas
7 oz (198 g) chicken livers
4 oz (113 g) beef sausages*
1¾ oz (50 g) bacon fat

1¼ oz (35 g) white bread crumbs*
8 fl oz (2 dl) dry white wine
1 tsp sage
1 egg
1¼ oz (35 g) foie gras
    (goose liver)
Freshly ground salt
Freshly ground white pepper
Clarified butter*

First prepare:

Bone chicken completely and set aside. Chop carcass bones. Cube parsnips, turnips, onions, carrots and beans. Wash and clean chicken livers. Remove meat from sausage casings. Measure wine. Break egg into a small bowl. Preheat oven to 350⁰F (177⁰C). Heat a serving dish in warming oven. You will need poultry pins and trussing string.

Now cook!

1. Place a large casserole and a frypan on heat and add clarified butter to both to just cover bottom.
2. In casserole place cubed onion and sauté gently. Add beans, turnips, parsnips, carrots and peas. Stir to cover vegetables evenly with hot butter. The finely chopped carcass of the boned chicken can also be added to enhance flavor.
3. Place chicken livers in heated frypan and allow to brown gently in butter. Season generously with salt and pepper.
4. Constantly stir both mixtures.
5. Add beef sausage meat and bacon fat to cooked chicken livers, stir in the bread crumbs and continue cooking over low heat.
6. Add 4 fl oz (1.2 dl) of wine to simmering vegetables and chicken bones. Continue to simmer.
7. Remove chicken liver pan from heat and stir in rubbed sage, foie gras and egg. Allow it to cool completely.
8. Lay boned chicken on a board and stuff with chicken liver mixture. Reassemble chicken to its original shape.
9. Secure with poultry pins and truss firmly with string.
10. Remove bones from pot containing vegetables and put vegetables into a casserole to form a bed on which to cook chicken.
11. Lay chicken on top of vegetables, sprinkle with 4 fl oz (1.2 dl) of wine and place uncovered in preheated oven 350⁰F (177⁰C).
12. At completion of cooking period when chicken is tender, remove from oven. Cut away string and pop under broiler for 3 minutes to make it crisp and golden brown.

A special hint:

Refer to Step 7: it is better to cool this kind of mixture quickly in order to distribute the fats finely throughout the "farce." To do this, set one mixing bowl inside a larger one containing crushed ice. Stir the mixture constantly in the bowl until it is thick and chilled (about four to five minutes only).

LAPIN FARCI PROVENCALE

For 6 servings, you will need:
1 rabbit, 3 lb (1.4 kg)
1 lb (0.5 kg) smoked bacon
    (in one piece) with rind
Freshly ground salt
Freshly ground black pepper
2 fl oz (5.6 cl) brandy
1 tsp thyme
1 lb (0.5 kg) veal tenderloin
    (fillet of veal)

1 lb (0.5 kg) pork tenderloin
    (fillet of pork)
2 eggs
2 large cloves garlic
3 tbs parsley
2 tsp thyme
Clarified butter*

First prepare:

Bone rabbit—not all the bones—just rib cage, saddle and backbone. You can leave shoulder and thigh bones in. Remove bones without cutting through outer skin. Remove outer rind from bacon and cut into ½-inch (1.2 cm) square strips. Add to rabbit tenderloin which you have removed while boning out and cut into ½-inch-strips. Add 2 fl oz (5.6 cl) brandy, plenty of salt and black pepper and 1 tsp thyme and allow to stand for at least 1 hour (gets better if left in marinade for up to 12 hours). Grind veal and pork tenderloin and kidneys and liver from rabbit. Chop parsley. Preheat oven to 350°F (177°C).

Now cook!

1. Combine ground veal, pork, and rabbit liver and kidneys with eggs.
2. Season mixture highly with salt and black pepper.
3. Smash, chop and add garlic.
4. Stir in finely chopped parsley and thyme.
5. Drain brandy from marinated strips of bacon into stuffing and beat thoroughly.
6. Open out boned rabbit and put half the "forcemeat" into cavity. Press it down but keep a clear area 2 inches (5 cm) from either end.
7. Lay bacon and rabbit tenderloin strips onto this layer of forcemeat and cover with remainder.
8. Sew or truss rabbit together with poultry pins.
9. Tie it loosely every 2 inches (5 cm) (the stuffing expands during cooking). Place the rabbit in a roasting pan, spread with clarified butter and roast at 350°F (177°C) for 1½ hours.

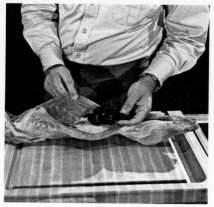

1. TO BONE A RABBIT first check that the liver is a good, dense, dark, even color. Remove it.

2. Cut either side between the breast and rib cage.

3. Continue right around up and under the shoulder.

4. Carry on down the backbone. Be careful at the point of the spine.

5. Break the leg at the ball and socket joint on the hip. Cut through.

6. This is the only way to get the spine clear. You *leapfrog* each vertebra with a fine knife.

7. Pull the carcass back through the rear legs. Be gentle!

8. This is what you should have left. I usually leave the leg and shoulder bones in.

9. A good stuffing can now be enclosed in the boned body and tied up.

PART VII
SAUCES

From top left counterclockwise: Hollandaise Sauce (page 500), Tomato Sauce
(page 506), White Sauce (page 491), Brown Sauce (page 494), Mayonnaise
(page 501).

PART VII
SAUCES

Idiots claim that the French invented sauces to mask the inferior quality of their meat. There was a time, it is true, when early marinades did perform this function, and even worse, there was an era in which cooks appeared to consider the sauce more important than the meat. Critics today are, however, not dealing in the past but the present. They accuse the French sauce artists of smothering good food while they live in a glass house full of such culinary stones as ketchup, Worcestershire, mint and parsley sauces.

Good sauce uplifts the main dish like an athlete on the shoulders of the crowd. It must never compete with the star performer. The more delicate the star, the greater should be the sense of family. A sauce for chicken should be based upon chicken stock; fish, fish stock; veal, veal stock. The more robust the meat the greater the nonfamily intrusion may be. BUT they must still be friends!

It is extremely difficult to explain the proper taste relationship between the meat and the sauce. As a Scot I prefer to relate the problem to one of cost; at least it underscores the need for the evaluation, if not the manipulatory technique.

I regard taste relationships as a pyramid of flavor. Side A is the flavor of the meat and Side B the sauce. Point C, the apex of the pyramid, is one's own sense of taste.

Let us therefore assume that the meat costs 100 units, and the sauce 40 units. When both flavors harmonize and reach Point C *together*, then you have 140 units of *value*. Less than perfect harmony and you can achieve the effect of the lesser value sauce *masking* the value of the meat, thereby causing a flavor/value debit. You actually lose money!

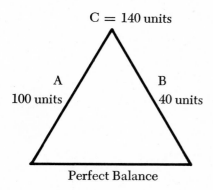

C = 140 units

A
100 units

B
40 units

Perfect Balance

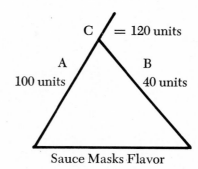

C = 120 units

A
100 units

B
40 units

Sauce Masks Flavor

Value/Flavor Loss = 20 units

I believe this really hits home on the *need*, but in practice how is it achieved? Only by always thinking about the problem. You must reach, through constant practice, what is called "flavor recall." That is to say, you can memory-match the flavor of beef with that of horseradish, turbot with hollandaise, shrimp with remoulade—and know if one will overwhelm the other. If this seems like oversimplification, then I can only say that the most classic, artistic endeavors *are* simple. It is only constant practice that makes perfection.

In this Part, I have divided sauces under Fruit, White, Brown, Butter, Mayonnaise, Kitchen, Tomato and Salad. All the sauces rely, for their absolute success, upon the use of the very best possible materials, especially when the recipe calls for a stock.

CUMBERLAND SAUCE

For 2 servings, you will need:

2 oz (56 gl) glace cherries*
4 fl oz (1.2 dl) chicken stock
Arrowroot
½ orange
1 lemon
1 tbs castor sugar*
1 medium onion
12 fl oz (3.2 dl) cold water

2 tbs red currant jelly
3 fl oz (8 cl) tawny port
2 tbs red wine vinegar
1½ tsp English mustard
Cayenne pepper
1½ bay leaves
Clarified butter*

First prepare:

Pare rind of ½ orange and 1 lemon with a vegetable scraper. Squeeze juice of lemon and orange. Finely slice onion and wash glacé cherries. Measure chicken stock, cold water, port and red wine vinegar. Open jar of red currant jelly and English mustard. Warm serving dish. In small pan add some water and pop in peel of orange and lemon to blanch. This removes the bitterness from the skins and also softens them. Takes only a couple of minutes. Strain and set aside rinds to cool, then slice them into fine strips.

Now cook!

1. Into a saucepan pour enough clarified butter to just cover bottom. Add finely sliced onion and allow to fry gently.

2. If available add pheasant or other poultry giblets (liver, kidney, heart, neck, tips of wings) and continue to fry.

3. To browning onions, add sugar and stir thoroughly until richly browned. (This will not sweeten the mixture but it will caramelize and darken it.)

4. Remove pan from heat and pour in cold water. Return to the heat and bring almost to a boil. Add bay leaves and reduce heat. Strain stock.

5. In a frypan place cooled skins of orange and lemon which have been finely sliced.

6. To this add port, red wine vinegar, juice of lemon and orange and red currant jelly.

7. To add further pep, stir in mustard and a dash of cayenne and allow this aromatic sauce to come to a boil and reduce gently.

8. At this point strained stock may be added, to further enhance sauce.

9. Mix 1 tsp arrowroot with a little water. Stir into sauce to thicken.

10. Pop in glacé cherries and continue to allow the Cumberland sauce to simmer gently.

APRICOT SAUCE I

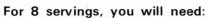

For 8 servings, you will need:

1 lb (0.5 kg) canned apricot halves
2 oz (56 g) butter
¼ tsp cinnamon
2 fl oz (5.6 cl) Slivovitz

3 fl oz (8 cl) heavy cream
2 tbs Calvados
1 egg yolk
Grated rind of ½ lemon

Now cook!

1. Place apricots in a pan on high heat. Add the butter and allow to melt. Flavor with cinnamon.

2. Pour in Slivovitz and light. When flames have almost died down, add Calvados. Add grated lemon rind and then stir in cream. Puree mixture in blender and then pour back into pan on heat. Add egg yolk, whisk into sauce and serve in a sauceboat.

APRICOT SAUCE II

For 6 servings, you will need:

10 canned apricot halves
2 fl oz (5.6 cl) apricot juice

2 fl oz (5.6 cl) brandy

Now cook!

1. Place apricot halves with brandy and apricot juice into a blender and puree. Pour mixture into a pan on gentle heat.

YARRADARRA SAUCE

6 fl oz (1.6 dl) fish stock
   (for recipe see page 50)
6 fl oz (1.6 dl) milk
1 oz (28 g) butter

1 oz (28 g) flour
Freshly ground salt
Freshly ground pepper
Nutmeg

Now cook!

1. Melt butter and stir in flour. Cook gently for 1 minute, then gradually stir in hot milk and fish stock. Stir constantly over low heat to make a smooth sauce. Season with salt, pepper and nutmeg.

2. Cook gently for 15 minutes stirring from time to time.

HAZELNUT SAUCE

For 2 servings, you will need:

10 fl oz (3 dl) chicken stock
1 oz (28 g) hazelnuts roasted
   whole and ground
1 oz (28 g) butter
3 fl oz (8 cl) heavy cream

Juice of ¼ lemon
Freshly ground salt
Freshly ground white pepper
1 fl oz (2.8 cl) brandy
2 heaped tsp arrowroot

Now cook!

1. Reduce chicken stock to two-thirds. Mix arrowroot with a little additional chicken stock. Stir into stock until thickened. Melt butter in a saucepan and slowly add stock stirring all the time. Add cream slowly, then hazelnuts and brandy. Season with salt, pepper and lemon juice.

ONION SAUCE

For 4 servings, you will need:

2 medium onions
4 tbs clarified butter*
2 oz (56 g) all-purpose flour
20 fl oz (6 dl) cold milk

4 fl oz (1.2 dl) dry white wine
Freshly ground salt
Freshly ground white pepper

First prepare:

Slice onions finely. Measure flour, butter, milk and wine.

Now cook!

1. Shallow fry onion in clarified butter; but don't brown. When onion begins to soften, add flour and stir well over low heat.

2. Add milk slowly, whisking to form a smooth sauce. Cook over a very gentle heat for 10 minutes, stirring constantly. Add wine and season to taste with salt and pepper.

CIDER SAUCE

For 2 servings, you will need:

4 fl oz (1.2 dl) hard cider
4 fl oz (1.2 dl) milk
1½ oz (42 g) butter
1½ oz (42 g) all-purpose flour
Freshly ground salt
Freshly ground white pepper

Fish fumet:
1 lb (0.5 kg) fish bones
1 small onion
1 bay leaf
1 small leek
4 white peppercorns
4 celery tops
Pinch of thyme
24 fl oz (7 dl) cold water

First prepare:

Measure cider and allow to become flat. Measure milk. Sift flour.
Fish fumet: To water in saucepan, add fish bones, celery tops, leek, onion, bay leaf, peppercorns and thyme. Place over moderate heat and bring to a boil, then simmer for 20 minutes, skimming frequently. Reduce to 6 fl oz (1.6 dl). Strain.

Now cook!

1. Melt butter in a slighty warmed saucepan, remove from heat and stir in flour. Return to heat and cook, stirring constantly, for 3 minutes over a low heat.

2. Add milk and cider to roux in saucepan. Stir thoroughly. Increase heat to boiling point, cook for 3 minutes, then reduce heat.

3. Add reduced fish fumet to sauce and stir. Reduce heat and allow to simmer gently to the desired consistency.

1. WHITE SAUCE. Make roux of butter and flour, cooked gently.

2. Add onion seasoning to roux to release natural onion oil.

3. Add milk, stir to thicken. Add herbs and cook 15 minutes.

4. Strain gently through a fine sieve. No solids, please.

WHITE SAUCE

For 2 servings, you will need:
- 1 oz (28 g) butter
- 1 oz (28 g) flour
- 6 fl oz (1.6 dl) milk
- ½ oz (14 g) onion

- 2 parsley stalks*
- 1 bay leaf
- Pinch of mace

First prepare:

Measure milk. Sift flour and weigh butter. Finely chop onion. Wash parsley stalks.

Now cook!

1. Melt butter in a heated saucepan, remove from heat and stir in flour. Return to a moderate heat to cook for 5 minutes without coloring. Again remove from heat and gradually stir in milk. Add bay leaf, onion, mace and parsley stalks. Increase heat and stir until sauce thickens. Boil for 3 minutes, stirring constantly, then simmer. Remove herbs before sauce is needed.

MUSTARD SAUCE

For 6 servings, you will need:

2 oz (56 g) butter
1½ oz (42 g) all-purpose flour
2 level tbs dry mustard
20 fl oz (6 dl) veal stock
   (see page 234)

Freshly ground salt
Freshly ground white pepper
1 tbs lemon juice
2 egg yolks

First prepare:

Measure butter, flour, veal stock, mustard and lemon juice. Separate eggs.

Now cook!

1. Heat veal stock. Place butter in a saucepan and when melted stir in flour to form a roux. Allow to cook on low heat for 1 minute. Gradually add hot veal stock, whisking to form a smooth sauce. Add mustard and lemon juice. Allow sauce to cook over low heat for 12 minutes, stirring occasionally. Season with salt and pepper.

2. Beat egg yolks with a little of the hot sauce and return mixture to saucepan. Whisk over gentle heat until sauce is hot. Do not boil.

TOMATO AND CHEESE SAUCE

For 2 servings, you will need:

1 small leek (you will need
   only 1 oz: 28 g)
1 medium onion
1 red pepper (capsicum)
1 lb (0.5 kg) fresh tomatoes
6 fl oz (1.6 dl) dry white wine
¼ tsp dried sweet basil
1½ oz (42 g) butter
1½ oz (42 g) all-purpose flour

8 fl oz (2 dl) chicken stock
6 oz (170 g) Emmenthal cheese
1 black truffle*
1 large mushroom
2 oz (56 g) cooked ham
Clarified butter*
Freshly ground salt
Freshly ground white pepper

First prepare:

Finely slice onion and leek. Chop red pepper. Measure wine and chicken stock. Finely slice truffle, ham, mushroom and leek. (Cut leek into matchsticks 1 inch (2.5 cm) long and ¹⁄₁₆ inch (2 mm) thick.) Roughly slice tomatoes. Cube Emmenthal cheese.

Now cook!

1. Pour a little clarified butter into a frypan to just cover bottom and add onion. Allow to fry gently. Add red pepper and tomatoes and moisten with wine. Season generously with salt and white pepper and add basil.

2. Place mushrooms into this simmering tomato sauce and allow to poach gently for 5 minutes.

3. Melt 1½ oz (42 g) butter in a small saucepan. Stir in flour and cook over moderate heat for a few moments.

4. Gradually stir in chicken stock and bring to a boil, stirring constantly. Reduce heat and add Emmenthal cheese, a handful at a time. Stir until smooth.

5. Add leek, truffle and ham to cheese sauce.

6. Strain tomato mixture into cheese sauce but don't force vegetables through sieve.

GREEN PEPPERCORN SAUCE

For 4 servings, you will need:

2 tbs green peppercorns*
4 fl oz (1.2 dl) jellied veal
  and duck stock
2 tbs white wine
1 fl oz (2.8 cl) cognac
2 red peppers (capsicum)
Rind of ½ lemon
Clarified butter*

White sauce:
1 oz (28 g) all-purpose flour
1 oz (28 g) butter

10 fl oz (3 dl) milk
Freshly ground salt
Freshly ground white pepper
Nutmeg

Duck and veal jelly:
Wings and neck of duck
Clarified butter*
1 veal knuckle
1 onion
40 fl oz (1.2 l) water
Freshly ground salt

68

First prepare:

Duck and veal jelly: Chop duck wings and neck finely. Place enough clarified butter in a saucepan to just cover bottom. When hot, add duck meat and brown. Add veal knuckle and onion, cover with water and allow to simmer for 3 hours. Season with salt and pepper. Strain and refrigerate.

Drain peppercorns and reserve juice. Remove rind of lemon using a potato parer. Blanch in boiling water for 1 minute. Remove and cut into fine strips. Finely dice red peppers.

White sauce: Melt butter in a saucepan and stir in flour to form a roux. Allow to cook on a gentle heat for 1 minute, then add milk, whisking until smooth. Season with selt, pepper and nutmeg. Bring to the boil and allow to simmer for 12 minutes.

Now cook!

1. Place green peppercorn juice into a small saucepan. Add blanched lemon rind, white wine and cognac. Allow to reduce to half. Add green peppercorns and veal and duck jelly. Simmer gently for 5 minutes.

2. Put enough clarified butter in a frypan to just cover bottom and add red peppers. Allow to soften in butter and then add to white sauce. Add reduced peppercorn juice mixture and peppercorns to sauce. Allow the sauce to simmer on a low heat.

---

*One compliment is often enough
to justify an entire day in the kitchen.*

BROWN SAUCE AND BROWN STOCK

Brown stock:
- ½ lb (227 g) gravy beef
  (cheap lean beef chuck)
- 6 beef bones
- 1 medium carrot
- 2 medium onions
- 1 bouquet garni

Brown sauce:
- 8 tbs clarified butter*
- 4 oz (113 g) all-purpose flour
- 40 fl oz (1.2 l) brown stock
- 1 carrot
- 1 onion
- 2 rashers bacon*
- 2 tbs tomato puree

First prepare:

Brown stock: Cut carrot and onions into chunks. Cut gravy beef into 1 inch (2.5 cm) cubes.

Brown sauce: Cut carrot and onion and bacon into ¼ inch (7 mm) cubes.

Now cook!

1. *Brown stock:* Place beef, bones, and vegetables for stock in a hot oven, 425°F (218°C). Roast until bones and vegetables are golden brown—about 30 minutes.
2. Transfer to a saucepan, add bouquet garni and water to cover.
3. Simmer for 6 hours.
4. Strain through muslin or several layers of cheesecloth.
5. *Brown sauce:* Melt butter, add flour and cook until a good dark brown.
6. Stir in brown stock gradually and bring to boil.
7. Sauté chopped vegetables and bacon for sauce in a little additional clarified butter until tender. Add to sauce. Add tomato puree.
8. Simmer sauce gently until reduced by half.
9. Strain sauce through muslin.

A special hint:

When you make brown sauce make at least 60 fl oz (2.3 l) and freeze the surplus for another day.

1. BROWN SAUCE. This method is fairly quick.

2. Chopped seeded tomato is fried in butter oil until brown.

3. Keep lifting tomato so it is dark brown but *not* scorched.

4. Add a really good clarified beef stock.

5. Thicken boiling stock with paste of arrowroot and water.

6. Sieve to remove tomato solids. Adjust the seasoning.

BROWN SAUCE

1 lb (454 g) tomatoes
1 oz (28 g) clarified butter*
1 oz (28 g) corn oil
24 fl oz (6.5 dl) beef stock

½ oz (14 g) arrowroot
Freshly ground salt
Freshly ground pepper

First prepare:

Chop tomatoes. Mix arrowroot with 2 tbs water.

Now cook!

1. Heat butter and oil in a saucepan. Add tomatoes.
2. Cook tomatoes over medium heat until tomatoes are dark brown but not scorched.
3. Stir in beef stock and scrape to loosen all particles.
4. Bring to a boil and stir in arrowroot mixture. Cook until thickened.
5. Sieve to remove tomato solids. Season to taste with salt and pepper. Refrigerate until needed. Makes about 24 fl oz (6.5 dl).

BOLOGNAISE SAUCE

For 4 servings, you will need:

2 tbs clarified butter*
12 oz (340 g) minced sirloin
   or round steak
4 oz (113 g) finely chopped
   shoulder bacon*
2 bay leaves
1 oz (28 g) celery
3 oz (85 g) onion

2 oz (56 g) carrot
1 clove garlic
3 tsp tomato paste
3 fl oz (8 cl) dry white wine
12 fl oz (3.2 dl) beef stock
Freshly ground salt
Freshly ground black pepper
2 oz (56 g) Parmesan cheese

Now cook!

1. Grind bacon and meat. Finely chop carrot, celery and onion. Peel and smash garlic. Measure wine and beef stock. Grate cheese.

2. Melt butter in a frypan and when hot add onion and garlic. When they are golden add meat and brown.

3. Add carrot, celery and white wine. Stir to combine.

4. Add tomato paste, beef stock and bay leaves. Season with salt and pepper.

5. Simmer in an open pot for 1 hour. Adjust seasoning. Stir in cheese.

SAUCE PERIGORD

For 6 servings, you will need:

6 fl oz (1.6 dl) beef stock
1½ oz (42 g) black truffles*
   (and the juice)
2 tsp arrowroot

2 tbs meat glaze*(or roast jelly)
Freshly ground salt
Freshly ground white pepper

First prepare:

Blend arrowroot with a little meat glaze (the jelly from the bottom of the roast beef drippings), just before making sauce. Finely chop black truffles. Save truffle juice.

Now cook!

1. Pour beef stock into a pan and add truffle juice. Boil and stir in arrowroot mixture. Cook while stirring until thickened. Add finely chopped truffles and simmer. Do not reboil after truffles have been added. Season to taste with salt and pepper.

1. BOLOGNAISE SAUCE is justifiably one of the great sauces of the world.

2. The vegetables are first finely ground. This is so much easier (and better) than hand cutting for this particular dish.

3. The vegetables are cooked slowly in clarified butter (used in Bologna) to release the natural aromatic oils—not to brown them.

4. During this time the meats are also finely ground.

5. Increase the pan temperature and add the meats. Cook until browned.

6. To help the color add good quality tomato paste. Stir in well.

7. Add wine and good beef stock.

8. When the meat is cooked add some stiff white sauce and beaten eggs.

9. Stir well and use for canneloni (see page 78).

LEMON BUTTER SAUCE

For 2 servings, you will need:

2 egg yolks
Freshly ground salt
Freshly ground white pepper
Nutmeg
½ tsp lemon juice

1 tbs water
Extra lemon juice if necessary
1 tbs horseradish sauce*
1 tbs chopped chives
4 oz (113 g) softened butter

Now cook!

1. Place lemon juice, grated nutmeg and water in top of double boiler.

2. Add egg yolks with 1 oz (28 g) butter and whisk together. When smooth, add another 1 oz piece of butter, beating well. The sauce at this stage will have thickened considerably. Continue adding 1 oz (28 g) pieces of butter, whisking smooth. When all the butter has been added remove pan from heat and whisk for 1 minute.

3. Return pan to a very low heat and add lemon juice, chives and horseradish sauce. Season to taste with salt and pepper. Keep on low heat until ready to serve.

CHORON SAUCE

For 4 servings, you will need:

2 fl oz (5.6 cl) tarragon vinegar
2 shallots
2 tbs chives
2 tbs parsley
4 egg yolks

8 oz (227 g) butter
Clarified butter*
Freshly ground salt
Freshly ground black pepper
2 fl oz (5.6 cl) tomato puree

First prepare:

Finely chop chives and parsley. Measure vinegar. Separate eggs. Cut butter into four equal pieces. Measure tomato puree. Finely chop shallots.

Now cook!

1. Place vinegar, shallots, 1 tbs chives and 1 tbs parsley in a saucepan and boil until reduced to a syrup.

2. Place syrup in a pan over a pot of boiling water. Add 2 oz (56 g) butter and egg yolks, whisking until mixture thickens. Add another 2 oz (56 g) butter, whisking it in, and continue until all the butter is absorbed. Whisk in the tomato puree. Season with salt and pepper. Sieve sauce. Add 1 tbs chives and parsley and place sauce in top of double boiler to keep warm. Do not allow water in bottom pot to boil.

A special hint:

If sauce should curdle take an ice cube, drop it into sauce and whisk until cube melts completely. The sauce will then become smooth.

EDEN SAUCE

For 2 servings, you will need:

2 fl oz (5.6 cl) tarragon vinegar
1 tsp dried tarragon
2 egg yolks
4 oz (113 g) butter

Freshly ground salt
Freshly ground white pepper
2 tbs parsley

First prepare:

Chop parsley. Measure vinegar. Slightly soften butter.

Now cook!

1. Into a small frypan pour vinegar and add dried tarragon and a little salt and pepper. Bring to a boil and keep your eye on it until the liquid has almost completely reduced (you need only 1 tbs).

2. In the top of a double boiler place tarragon liquid and egg yolks. Gradually whisk in butter so that all ingredients are blended well together and texture is light and creamy. Season to taste with salt and pepper.

POVLIK SAUCE

For 2 servings, you will need:

2 cloves garlic
1 medium onion
1 tsp rosemary
6 fl oz (1.6 dl) dry white wine

Clarified butter*
Freshly ground salt
Freshly ground white pepper

First prepare:

Lightly bruise garlic cloves. Finely slice onion. Measure dry white wine and rosemary.

Now cook!

1. Pour enough clarified butter into the heated frypan to just cover bottom and add onion. Fry gently.

2. Add bruised garlic cloves and simmer.

3. Add rosemary and wine.

4. Allow sauce to bubble gently over moderate heat. Season to taste with salt and pepper.

MEURICE SAUCE

For 2 servings, you will need:

32 fl oz (1 l) veal stock
  (for recipe see page 234)
½ oz (14 g) butter

1 egg yolk
2 fl oz (5.6 cl) heavy cream
½ lemon

First prepare:

Squeeze lemon. Measure cream.

Now cook!

1. Reduce veal stock to 2 fl oz (5.6 cl). This reduction produces a very stiff, delicious glaze.

2. Place 2 tbs of reduced veal stock in a small saucepan. When it boils take it off the heat and add butter and egg yolk. Whisk furiously. Add lemon juice and cream and continue beating until smooth and creamy. (This all happens very quickly so prepare sauce just before you serve it.)

1. HOLLANDAISE SAUCE. Simple made in a glass double boiler.

2. The water below must have *no bubbles*.

3. Add eggs all at once to heated seasonings; whisk.

4. Add the butter in four equal portions, one at a time.

5. As each stick of butter is absorbed the sauce thickens.

6. If sauce curdles add ice cube, reheat gently, beat till smooth.

HOLLANDAISE SAUCE

¼ tsp mace
4 egg yolks
8 oz (227 g) butter
1 tbs water

1 tsp lemon juice
Freshly ground salt
Freshly ground white pepper

Now cook!

1. In double boiler place 1 tsp lemon juice, freshly ground salt, freshly ground white pepper and the mace.

2. Add 1 tbs water and gently stir in egg yolks and 2 oz (56 g) butter. Beat with a whisk over low heat. Slowly add remaining 6 oz (170 g) butter in 3 portions, beating in each 2 oz (56 g) completely before adding next.

3. Sauce will thicken; remove from heat and whisk for 1 minute. Return to very low heat and add a little lemon juice to taste. Set aside until required.

A special hint:

Hollandaise sauce has a habit of curdling when left to stand, as is frequently the case. To rectify, simply add an ice cube and beat into the hollandaise.

1. MAYONNAISE WITHOUT A BLENDER.

2. Dried mustard powder goes in first.

3. Add egg yolks and drizzle a little oil on top. Beat well.

4. As each addition of oil is absorbed you can add more.

5. If mixture begins to curdle add whipped egg white.

6. For bottling, add 1 tbs boiling water. Stir in well.

MAYONNAISE

1 tsp dry mustard
2 tbs lemon juice
¼ tsp cayenne pepper
5 fl oz (1.5 dl) oil

1 egg
Freshly ground salt
Freshly ground white pepper

First prepare:

Measure dry ingredients and oil.

Now assemble!

1. Pour some hot water into your blender to warm it, then drain.
2. Put mustard, lemon juice, cayenne pepper, oil and egg into warmed blender. Mix at high speed for 30 seconds.
3. Spoon stiff mayonnaise into a bowl. Season to taste with salt and white pepper and refrigerate until required.

CAFE DE PARIS SAUCE

For 2 servings, you will need:

½ oz (14 g) spring onions❋
2 anchovy fillets
3 oz (85 g) butter
1 tbs parsley
5 sage leaves
Pinch dried tarragon

1 small clove garlic
1 tsp lemon juice
2 tsp mild French mustard
Dash of paprika
Freshly ground white pepper
1 tsp cognac

First prepare:

Finely chop spring onions, anchovy fillets, parsley and sage. Allow butter to soften. Smash garlic.

Now assemble!

1. Place softened butter in a bowl, add spring onions, anchovy fillets, parsley, sage leaves, tarragon, garlic, lemon juice, mild mustard, paprika and some white pepper. Flavor with the cognac and mix until creamy.

WATERCRESS SAUCE

For 8 servings, you will need:

10 fl oz (3 dl) mayonnaise
1 tbs chopped shallot
1 bunch watercress

1 tbs white wine vinegar
1 stiffly beaten egg white
1 egg yolk

67

Now assemble!

1. Finely chop watercress discarding thick stalks.
2. Add shallot and watercress to mayonnaise, add vinegar, 1 egg yolk and fold in stiffly beaten egg white. Chill.

LEGAL SAUCE

For 4 servings, you will need:

4 oz (113 g) cooked, shelled and
    deveined shrimp
8 pitted black olives

1 tbs dill
4 fl oz (1.2 dl) mayonnaise
Freshly ground black pepper

71

First prepare:

Chop olives. Finely chop dill and shrimp. Measure mayonnaise.

Now assemble!

1. Combine olives, shrimp and dill with mayonnaise, season with pepper. Chill.

CHIVE SAUCE

For 2 servings, you will need:

1 large shallot, sliced
1 tbs veal jelly
2 fl oz (5.6 cl) dry vermouth
2 fl oz (5.6 cl) fish stock
2 tbs heavy cream
1 oz (28 g) butter
1 tbs finely chopped chives
Juice of ½ lemon
Clarified butter*
Freshly ground salt
Freshly ground white pepper
Fish stock:
  1 red snapper head
  1 medium onion
  1 bouquet garni

20 fl oz (6 dl) water
2 fl oz (5.6 cl) dry white wine
Freshly ground salt
8 peppercorns
Veal jelly:
  1 veal knuckle
  1 onion
  1 carrot
  1 bouquet garni (2 sprigs thyme,
    3 inch (7.6 cm) stalk celery,
    1 bay leaf, 6 stalks parsley*)
Freshly ground salt
Black peppercorns
Water to cover

First prepare:

Fish stock: Place all ingredients into a saucepan, bring to the boil and skim surface. Allow stock to boil gently for 25 minutes.

Veal jelly: Combine all ingredients in a saucepan. Bring to a boil, skim and allow to simmer 6 hours or until reduced to ½ cup (4 fl oz: 1.2 dl). Strain and refrigerate.

Now cook!

1. Place clarified butter into saucepan to just cover bottom. Heat, add shallots and fry until translucent but not brown.

2. Add 1 tbs veal jelly. Allow to melt, add vermouth and 2 fl oz (5.6 cl) fish stock. Boil and reduce to a syrupy consistency.

3. Beat in cream. Remove from heat and beat in butter. Stir in chives and lemon juice. Season to taste with salt and pepper.

CHICKEN EGGS SAUCE

For 4 servings, you will need:

4 fl oz (1.2 dl) mayonnaise
2 gherkins

½ tsp curry powder

Now assemble!

1. Mix mayonnaise, curry powder and finely chopped gherkins. Chill. Serve in a sauceboat.

62

GOLDEN COAST SAUCE

For 4 servings, you will need:

4 fl oz (1.2 dl) mayonnaise
2 sweet gherkins, chopped
1 tbs parsley, chopped

2 tbs capers
1 pinch cayenne pepper

Now assemble!

1. Mix ingredients together and pour into a sauceboat. Chill.

67

KITCHEN TOMATO SAUCE

4 fl oz (1.2 dl) cider vinegar
2 tsp freshly ground salt
1 tsp freshly ground pepper
1 tsp paprika
4 fl oz (1.2 dl) olive oil

3 lb red ripe tomatoes
1 lb (454 g) onions
1 clove garlic
2 cans pimento, each 4 oz (113 g)

First prepare:

Chop tomatoes, onions and garlic. Drain and chop pimento.

Now cook!

1. Heat vinegar, salt, pepper and paprika to just boiling. Cool.
2. In a large frypan heat olive oil and sauté tomatoes, onions and garlic until mushy.
3. Add pimento and press mixture through a sieve or food mill.
4. Replace in frypan and simmer until thick. Cover sauce with a spatter screen and strain vinegar through it into sauce.
5. Simmer sauce until thick. Strain sauce again and spoon into jars. Add a spoonful of olive oil to surface to seal it. Refrigerate until needed. Makes about 32 fl oz (1 l).

1. KITCHEN TOMATO SAUCE begins with spiced vinegar mix.

2. It also helps to have the very best red tomatoes.

3. Good olive oil must, in this case, replace butter.

4. Canned red pimento gives good color and flavor.

5. When tomato has cooked with the onion, add pimento.

6. Stir well and check that everything is soft.

7. Pass everything through a fine sieve.

8. Cook sauce down to thicken, but use screen to lessen splatter.

9. Add the spiced vinegar through screen.

10. Once again strain thick sauce—easier this time.

11. Pour the sauce into sterilized jars.

12. Add a spoonful of olive oil to seal surface.

TOMATO SAUCE

For 4 servings, you will need:

1½ lbs (680 g) fresh tomatoes
1 clove garlic
1 tsp sugar
Freshly ground salt

Freshly ground black pepper
2 tbs dry white wine
Clarified butter*

First prepare:

Core tomatoes and quarter. Smash garlic. Measure dry white wine.

Now cook!

1. Place enough clarified butter in a saucepan to cover bottom and when hot add garlic and tomatoes. Add sugar and dry white wine and allow sauce to boil gently un-covered for 10 minutes. Season to taste with salt and pepper.

2. Press tomato sauce through a sieve before serving.

KAREWAI SAUCE

For 4 servings, you will need:

1 clove garlic
Clarified butter*
4 oz (113 g) fresh mushrooms

6 fl oz (1.6 dl) tomato sauce
6 fl oz (1.6 dl) dry white wine
1 tbs parsley stalks*

First prepare:

Peel garlic. Finely slice mushrooms. Measure tomato sauce and wine. Finely chop parsley stalks.

62

Now cook!

1. Smash garlic and put in saucepan, add a little butter and fry gently. Add mush-rooms and toss in butter. Add tomato sauce, cook for 2 minutes, then add wine and parsley stalks. Simmer sauce for 5 minutes.

COCKTAIL SAUCE

For 4 servings, you will need:

4 fl oz (1.2 dl) mayonnaise
1 fl oz (2.8 cl) tomato paste

1 fl oz (2.8 cl) heavy cream

First prepare:

Measure mayonnaise. Whip cream.

Now assemble!

1. Make sauce by folding cream into mayonnaise. Add tomato paste until light pink in color. Chill.

CURRY SAUCE

For 4 servings, you will need:

1 medium onion
1 tbs clarified butter*
3 tsp hot Madras curry powder*

1 large clove garlic
2 tsp flour
8 fl oz (2 dl) coconut stock
(see page 50)

First prepare:

Finely slice onion. Lightly bruise garlic (keep it in one piece). Measure curry powder. Make coconut stock.

Now cook!

1. Into a hot frypan put butter and sliced onion. Toss. Reduce heat and add curry powder. Stir and allow to cook gently.

2. Add garlic and flour to curry mixture. Stir well and allow to cook for 4 minutes over the same low heat. Stir occasionally.

3. Stir 8 fl oz (2 dl) coconut stock into curry mixture. Let sauce cook for 5 minutes at low heat.

THOUSAND ISLAND DRESSING

For 4 servings, you will need:

8 fl oz (2 dl) mayonnaise
1 tsp chili sauce
1 tsp chopped pimento
1 tsp chopped chives

1 tsp chopped green pepper
(capsicum)
1 chopped hard-boiled egg
1 tsp chopped green limes

Now assemble!

1. Mix all ingredients together in a bowl and chill until required.

PROVENCALE DRESSING

4 fl oz (1.2 dl) wine vinegar
1 tsp crumbled thyme
1 tsp crumbled rosemary

1 bay leaf
5 fl oz (1.5 dl) heavy cream

Now assemble!

1. Place all the ingredients into a pan and gradually bring to a boil. Lower heat and simmer for ten minutes. Chill.

PART VIII
VEGETABLES

509

PART VIII
VEGETABLES

Each time I begin one of these Part introductions, it seems that I overstress the vital importance of the subject. I would like to avoid being accused of crying wolf. But perhaps it is because every stage in a menu is vital. Vegetables are certainly vital (here I go again!). I consider them of equal importance to any other menu factor. Home cooks and professional chefs alike tend to fall down, to sidestep the vegetable as a matter of little creative interest.

In my experience of visiting restaurants, I have found that the successful ones are those that serve fresh vegetables with a different seasoning that literally makes the *interest* sit up and beg! There is no real substitute for fresh vegetables and I really mean *fresh* fresh. They take time, apparently endless time, to prepare and they are not easy to cook to perfection, but when all the labor and the care have been exercised the result is justification alone. I should like to emphasize that my comments relate solely to dinner-party planning and not to the day-to-day family kitchen. Exactly the same factors apply, of course; the result is better and usually costs less, but the labor is probably not so easily related to the potential level of recognition (see page 25, "First Catch Your Appreciation"). All my comments from now on relate to the fresh vegetable and the dinner party.

Find yourself a good vegetable retailer. Buy his recommendation, work up some mutual trust (see page 37, "Shopping Guide"). To give yourself the maximum chance of success:

- Buy on the day you serve.

- Change your first-choice vegetable rather than accept second quality.

- Prepare and keep chilled. DON'T leave standing in cold water. (Potatoes are an exception to this rule.)

- Cut vegetables in an even shape.

- Use less water and a lower heat than that to which you may be accustomed.

- Always cover the saucepan.

- Avoid precooking and reheating.

- Do all you can except using bicarbonate of soda (an old-fashioned technique that promotes good green color, but kills Vitamin C) to keep the maximum bright natural color.

- Don't overseason but be sure to make the most creative use you can of herbs and spices. A little nutmeg on buttered carrots is a good example. Use herbs like an expensive perfume; one touch will excite, too much and you'll clobber the senses!

- Purchase a good table or table-side heater to insure that the vegetables are served hot—hot!

MUSHROOM SALAD I

For 4 servings, you will need:

1 lb (0.5 kg) fresh small white
    button mushrooms
Freshly ground salt
Freshly ground black pepper
Nutmeg
1 lemon
½ tbs parsley

½ tbs chives
Small sprig lemon thyme*
French dressing:
3 fl oz (8 cl) olive oil
1 fl oz (2.8 cl) white wine
    vinegar
Freshly ground salt
Freshly ground black pepper

First prepare:

Wash mushrooms. Slice them thinly. Juice lemon. Finely chop parsley and chives. Shake all French dressing ingredients together.

Now assemble!

1. Season mushrooms with salt, pepper and nutmeg.
2. Add French dressing and lemon juice and allow to marinate for a while.
3. Serve chilled in a salad bowl garnished with the parsley, chives and lemon thyme.

MUSHROOM SALAD II

For 2 servings, you will need:

8 oz (227 g) small fresh mushrooms
4 bacon rashers*
Clarified butter*
Lemon juice

Cayenne pepper
1 tbs chives
Freshly ground salt
Freshly ground black pepper

First prepare:

Remove mushroom stalks and finely slice mushrooms. Place into a bowl. Finely slice bacon rashers. Finely chop chives.

Now cook!

1. Place enough clarified butter in a frypan to just cover bottom. When hot add bacon and sauté until crisp.
2. Put mushrooms in a salad bowl, season with salt, pepper, lemon juice and a dusting of cayenne pepper. Sprinkle with chives.
3. Pour bacon and pan juices over mushrooms and toss together. Serve hot.

WATERCRESS SALAD

For 4 servings, you will need:

1 bunch of watercress, trimmed
4 fl oz (1.2 dl) tarragon wine
vinegar
2 fl oz (5.6 cl) olive oil
¼ tsp dry mustard

2 tsp sugar
Finely chopped mint
Freshly ground salt
Freshly ground black pepper

First prepare:

Measure vinegar, oil, mustard and sugar. Chop mint finely.

Now assemble!

1. Mix mustard and sugar with oil and vinegar. Season to taste with salt and black pepper.
2. Toss watercress in salad bowl with dressing and sprinkle with finely chopped mint.

ZUCCHINI SALAD

For 4 servings, you will need:

4 zucchini (baby marrow)
2 medium tomatoes
1 green pepper (capsicum)
Parsley

Chives
Marjoram
French dressing

First prepare:

Cook zucchini in boiling salted water for 10 minutes. Drain and slice and place in salad bowl. Cut tomatoes into quarters. Chop capsicum finely.

Now assemble!

1. Toss all ingredients in a salad bowl with French dressing and garnish with chopped herbs. Chill.

BEAN SALAD

For 4 servings, you will need:

1 lb (0.5 kg) fresh green beans
Freshly ground salt
Freshly ground black pepper
Nutmeg
1 medium onion

French dressing
Parsley
Chives
Black olives

First prepare:

Drop whole beans into salted boiling water and cook for 10 minutes. Drain. Finely chop parsley, chives and onion.

Now assemble!

1. While beans are still warm, season with salt, pepper and nutmeg. Mix with onion.
2. Toss with French dressing and serve garnished with chopped parsley and chives and a few black olives.

CUCUMBER AND CHIVE SALAD

For 4 servings, you will need:

2 cucumbers
4 tbs chives
8 fl oz (2 dl) heavy cream
2 tsp sugar

4 tbs olive oil
Freshly ground salt
Freshly ground black pepper
1 tbs tarragon vinegar

First prepare:

Peel cucumber and slice into paper-thin slices. Sprinkle with salt and leave for 1 hour. Wash with cold water and drain. Finely chop chives.

Now assemble!

1. Mix sugar with vinegar and add cream and olive oil. Beat well.
2. Toss cucumbers in a salad bowl with dressing. Season to taste with salt and pepper. Garnish with chives.

TUNUNDA SALAD

For 4 servings, you will need:

3 tbs sour cream
2 tsp red currant jelly

1½ oz (42 g) walnuts
½ lb (227 g) sultana grapes

First prepare:

67

Chop walnuts roughly. Measure sour cream and jelly. Mash jelly.

Now assemble!

1. Combine sour cream with red currant jelly. Fold in walnuts. Chill. Mix through grapes.

Tununda Salad

BROCCOLI WITH FRENCH DRESSING

For 4 servings, you will need:

1½ lbs (680 g) fresh broccoli
Freshly ground salt

Freshly ground black pepper
French dressing

First prepare:

Cut off broccoli heads together with a few inches (centimeters) of the stem. Wash and drain. Place in boiling salted water and cook for 8-10 minutes. Drain and cool.

Now assemble!

1. Place broccoli in a serving dish, season with salt and pepper and toss with French dressing (made with lemon juice). Chill.

A special hint:

For additional seasoning, I add 1 tbs finely sliced blanched lemon peel and a little nutmeg.

SALADE NICOISE

For 4 servings, you will need:

1 head lettuce
2 hard-boiled eggs
2 medium tomatoes
6 flat anchovy fillets
10 pitted black olives
2 tsp capers
1 red pepper (capsicum)

8 oz (227 g) green beans
2 tbs white wine vinegar
4 tbs olive oil
Freshly ground salt
Freshly ground black pepper
Finely chopped parsley
1 smashed clove garlic

First prepare:

Wash lettuce and dry. Hard-boil eggs and cut in halves. Cut tomatoes into quarters. Make vinaigrette dressing by combining vinegar, oil, garlic, salt and pepper. Finely slice red pepper. Cut beans into 1 inch lengths and cook in boiling salted water for 6 minutes. Drain and chill.

Now assemble!

1. Arrange lettuce in salad bowl, add eggs, tomatoes, anchovy fillets, olives and capers, red pepper and beans. Toss with dressing just before serving. Dust with finely chopped parsley.

PEAS A L'ETOUFFEE

For 4 servings, you will need:

1 lb (0.5 kg) fresh peas
2 tiny white onions
1 small sprig parsley
1 small sprig chervil
1 small sprig mint

½ oz (14 g) butter
Freshly ground salt
Freshly ground black pepper
1 tsp sugar
4 fl oz (1.2 dl) water

First prepare:

Shell peas. Peel and cut onions into quarters.

Now cook!

1. Place peas with onions, herbs, butter, salt and pepper, sugar and water in a saucepan. Bring to a boil, cover tightly and boil hard, shaking pan from time to time until peas are soft (15 minutes).

2. Look at peas occasionally and if they are getting too dry, add a few drops of hot water. There should be just a little juice at the end of cooking.

BROAD BEANS WITH BACON

For 4 servings, you will need:

1 lb (0.5 kg) broad beans*
Freshly ground salt
Freshly ground pepper

Nutmeg
4 bacon rashers*
3 tbs heavy cream

First prepare:

Dice bacon. Fry until crisp. Drain bacon on absorbent paper.

Now cook!

1. Drop broad beans into salted boiling water and cook until tender. Drain.

2. Place beans in another pan, pour over cream, bring to a boil and season with salt and pepper. Add crisp bacon and serve.

SPICED RED CABBAGE

For 4 servings, you will need:

½ head red cabbage
4 fl oz (1.2 dl) white wine vinegar
4 whole cloves
4 peppercorns
2 bay leaves
2 tsp coriander seed

Freshly ground salt
Freshly ground black pepper
3 tbs sugar
1 onion
2 tbs clarified butter*
1 Granny Smith apple*

First prepare:

Cut cabbage into halves and remove core. Finely slice cabbage and mix with vinegar, cloves, peppercorns, salt, bay leaves and sugar. Allow to stand for 1 hour. Finely dice onion. Peel and core apple and slice.

Now cook!

1. Heat clarified butter in a saucepan, add onion and allow it to fry gently until soft but not brown. Add cabbage and marinade and simmer covered for 30 minutes.

2. After 25 minutes add apple slices and cook another 5 minutes. Remove cloves and bay leaves.

CREAMED SPINACH

For 4 servings, you will need:

2 lbs (0.9 kg) fresh spinach
1 oz (28 g) butter
1 tsp sugar

3 tbs heavy cream
Freshly ground salt
Freshly ground pepper

First prepare:

Remove stalks from spinach and wash several times. Place in a saucepan with 1 fl oz (2.8 cl) water and butter, season with salt and pepper, cover and cook over low heat for 5 minutes. Puree in a blender.

Now assemble!

1. Heat puree and add sugar and cream. Season if necessary.

Spiced Red Cabbage

CARROTS CHANTILLY

For 6 servings, you will need:

2 lb (0.9 kg) fresh carrots, scraped
1 lb (0.5 kg) fresh peas, shelled
4 fl oz (1.2 dl) heavy cream

Freshly ground salt
Freshly ground white pepper
2 tbs butter

First prepare:

Slice carrots in rounds, cover with salted water and cook at a boil for 15 minutes. (If baby carrots cook whole.) Drain carrots and measure cream. Cook peas and drain.

Now cook!

1. Place carrots in a saucepan with butter, heat and then add the cream. Season with salt and pepper.
2. Place carrots in a serving dish. Toss peas with butter, salt and pepper. Spoon around carrots.

GLAZED RUM CARROTS

For 4 servings, you will need:

1 lb (0.5 kg) small fresh carrots
Freshly ground salt
Freshly ground pepper
Coriander

1 tbs rum
2 tbs sugar
2 tbs butter

First prepare:

Scrape carrots and dice.

Now cook!

1. Place carrots in water just to cover, add sugar, rum, butter, salt, pepper and coriander to taste. Cook at a boil until water has evaporated, leaving carrots glazed. Stir occasionally to prevent sticking.

GLAZED CARROTS IN TONIC

For 4 servings, you will need:

1 lb (0.5 kg) baby carrots
2 oz (56 g) butter
12 fl oz (3.2 dl) tonic water*
Parsley

1 tbs sugar
Pinch nutmeg
Freshly ground salt
1 tbs butter

64

First prepare:

Scrape and wash carrots. Wash and chop parsley. Measure butter and sugar.

Now cook!

1. Trim each carrot to same size and cut in rounds about 1 inch (2.5 cm) long.
2. In a heated pan melt butter, add tonic water and about 6 parsley stalks. Pop in salt and sugar and grate in nutmeg.
3. Place carrots in liquid and cook uncovered for 15 minutes on medium heat.
4. Drain if necessary (tonic boils down with lid off) and add 1 tbs butter. Toss and fry to develop an attractive glaze. Adjust seasoning so that you can just taste nutmeg.

BEANS IN GARLIC FLAVORED BUTTER

For 4 servings, you will need:

1 lb (0.5 kg) green beans
   (long, French)
1 clove garlic
4 fl oz (1.2 dl) ice cold water

1 oz (28 g) butter
Pinch of nutmeg
Freshly ground salt
Freshly ground white pepper

First prepare:

Trim beans and wash. Smash garlic. Measure butter. Put some ice in a bowl of cold water. Heat a vegetable dish in warming oven.

Now cook!

1. Place a small amount of water in a small saucepan and bring it to a boil.
2. Pop beans into boiling water and cook for 2 minutes.
3. Drain beans and immediately plunge them into iced water. This prevents them from losing their beautiful green color.
4. Return pan to heat, add garlic and butter and allow to sizzle.
5. Drain beans and toss them in garlic butter. Add salt and pepper and a pinch of nutmeg. Heat through and toss to cover the now glistening beans in garlic butter. Serve in heated vegetable dish.

CHOU A LA CREME

For 4 servings, you will need:

1 lb (0.5 kg) green cabbage
2 oz (56 g) bacon
Clarified butter*
1 medium onion
1 oz (28 g) butter
1 oz (28 g) all-purpose flour

10 fl oz (3 dl) milk
Freshly ground salt
Freshly ground pepper
Nutmeg
1 fl oz (2.8 cl) heavy cream

First prepare:

Remove core from cabbage and slice very finely. Finely dice bacon and onion. Sift flour, measure butter, milk and cream. Place cabbage in salted boiling water and cook for 5 minutes. Drain.

Now cook!

1. Place a little clarified butter into a saucepan to just cover bottom. Add bacon and onion and fry for 1 minute. Add 1 oz (28 g) butter and stir in flour to form a roux. Cook stirring for 1 minute.

2. Whisk in milk gradually to form a smooth sauce. Bring to a boil and stir until thickened. Season with salt, pepper and grated nutmeg. Add cabbage and allow to cook gently for 10 minutes.

3. Just before serving stir in cream. Reheat but do not boil.

ENGLISH SPINACH

For 4 servings, you will need:

2 lbs (0.9 kg) fresh spinach
2 oz (56 g) butter

Freshly ground salt
Freshly ground pepper

First prepare:

Wash spinach thoroughly several times.

Now cook!

1. Place spinach in a large pot. Cook slowly (the water remaining on the leaves will be enough liquid) with ½ oz (14 g) butter for 8 minutes. Drain and cool.

2. Press out moisture with your hands. Chop spinach and add remaining butter. Reheat. Season with salt and pepper.

1. IMPROVISED ASPARAGUS COOKER. Scrape woody stalks.

2. Boil the asparagus in a large tin can over moderate heat.

3. Fill can until water level is just under the tender tips.

4. Reserve the cooking liquid—it positively teems with goodness.

5. Note the can base—not a trace of melted solder.

6. Decapitate for recipes calling for asparagus tips.

ASPARAGUS WITH HERB BUTTER

For 4 servings, you will need:
1 bunch of asparagus
4 oz (113 g) butter
1 tbs parsley
1 tbs chives

Lemon juice
Freshly ground salt
Freshly ground black pepper

First prepare:

Break off woody part of asparagus stem and remove green scales from stem. Tie asparagus together in a bunch. Juice lemon. Chop parsley and chives finely. Melt butter.

Now cook!

1. Place asparagus in boiling salted water leaving tender heads to steam above level of water. Cook for 20 to 35 minutes. Drain.
2. Mix herbs with butter and season with salt, pepper and lemon juice.
3. Place asparagus on a serving dish and cover with butter sauce.

BUTTERED SPRING ONIONS

65

For 4 servings, you will need:
    3 oz (85 g) spring onions*
    12 toasted blanched almonds
    2 oz (56 g) butter

1 lemon
Freshly ground salt

Now cook!

1. Place ½ inch (1.2 cm) water in a saucepan, add butter, salt, lemon juice and the two lemon halves (which have been squeezed). Bring to a boil and drop in spring onions and chopped toasted almonds. Cover saucepan and allow to steam for 10 seconds.

2. With a slotted spoon lift onions onto a dish. Reduce cooking liquid at a fast boil and when well reduced, return onions to saucepan to heat through.

3. Place onto a dish and serve.

GREEN BEANS

For 4 servings, you will need:
    1 lb (0.5 kg) green beans
    1 clove garlic
    2 tbs clarified butter*
    Juice of ½ lemon

Freshly ground salt
Freshly ground pepper
Nutmeg
Parsley

First prepare:

Peel and crush clove of garlic. Keep beans whole. Juice lemon. Chop parsley finely.

Now cook!

1. Place beans, garlic, butter, salt and pepper into a saucepan and cook gently for 10 minutes.

2. Place in a serving dish and season with lemon juice and nutmeg. Garnish with parsley.

CAULIFLOWER WITH BLACK BUTTER

For 4 servings, you will need:

1 cauliflower
4 oz (113 g) butter
1½ oz (42 g) bread crumbs✱

4 tsp cider vinegar
Freshly ground salt

First prepare:

Divide cauliflower into flowerettes and boil in salted boiling water for 8 minutes. Fry bread crumbs in clarified butter (2 tbs) until crisp and golden.

Now cook!

1. Drain cooked cauliflower.
2. Put butter in pan and allow to brown. Remove pan from stove, sprinkle cauliflower with vinegar, pour over black butter and garnish with crisp bread crumbs.

BRAISED HEART OF CELERY — BASIL BUTTER

For 4 servings, you will need:

1 large celery heart
2 tbs butter
Dried basil

Freshly ground salt
Freshly ground black pepper

Now cook!

1. Place celery heart in boiling salted water and simmer for 23 minutes.
2. Remove celery and drain well. Cut into quarters, place on a serving dish, decorate with thin slices of butter and sprinkle with basil, salt and pepper to taste.

67

CHICORY MEUNIERE

For 5 servings, you will need:

6 endives
2 oz (56 g) butter
Freshly ground salt

Freshly ground black pepper
1 oz (28 g) butter
Basil

First prepare:

Wash and dry endive. Trim ends.

Now cook!

1. Bring a small amount of salted water to a boil, add endive and 2 oz (56 g) butter. Cook gently for 15 minutes.

2. Drain and place on a serving dish garnished with pieces of butter and a sprinkle of basil. Season to taste with salt and pepper.

GLAZED ONIONS

For 4 servings, you will need:

1 lb (0.5 kg) tiny onions
Freshly ground salt

2 tbs sugar
2 tbs butter

First prepare:

Peel onions.

Now cook!

1. Put onions in water to just cover, add salt and 2 tbs sugar and butter. Bring to a boil and simmer until water evaporates and the onions caramelize, about 30 minutes. Stir frequently when onions start to brown.

---

*A cup measure, while useful for many things,
cannot replace a weighing scale
whereas a scale can replace the cup.*

MASHED POTATOES

For 4 servings, you will need:

2 lbs (0.9 kg) large potatoes
Freshly ground salt
Clarified butter*
3 oz (85 g) bacon, in one piece
1 egg white

2 tbs butter
Freshly ground salt
Freshly ground pepper
Nutmeg
Juice of ¼ lemon

First prepare:

Wash potatoes, cut a thin slice from end of each, sprinkle with salt and bake in a 350⁰F (177⁰C) oven for 1½ hours. Stiffly beat egg white. Finely chop bacon.

Now cook!

1. Remove potato from skins and put in a bowl.
2. Place 1 tbs clarified butter in a pan and when hot add bacon and fry until crisp. Drain off bacon fat and add bacon to potato.
3. Add butter to potato and mash with a potato masher. Add lemon juice. Season to taste with salt, pepper and nutmeg. Add egg white and whisk together until smooth.
4. Mound on a heated serving dish.

POTATOES WITH LEMON JUICE

For 4 servings, you will need:

2 lbs (0.9 kg) new potatoes
1 lemon
2 tbs butter

2 tbs parsley
Rind of 1 lemon

First prepare:

Wash and scrape new potatoes and parboil them in boiling salted water. Pour off some of the water leaving just enough to cover. Juice lemon. Chop parsley finely. Grate half the lemon rind. Melt butter.

Now cook!

1. Add lemon juice to water and simmer potatoes until cooked. Drain, pour over melted butter and sprinkle with parsley and lemon rind at last minute.

HATEBLIKSEM

For 4 servings, you will need:

2 lbs (0.9 kg) potatoes
4 sour apples
2 sweet apples
4 oz (113 g) butter

32 fl oz (1 l) cold water
Freshly ground salt
Freshly ground white pepper

First prepare:

Peel potatoes. Peel and soak apples in water to cover until required. Measure butter and cold water.

Now cook!

1. Season cold water with 1 tsp. freshly ground salt. Slice potatoes and apples in ¼-inch (7 mm) slices. Place slices in pan and cook covered for 30 minutes.
2. Drain juice off cooked potatoes and apples and mash with a potato masher. Season with salt, white pepper and butter.
3. Return to heat and allow to dry out slightly.
4. Remove and place on warmed serving platter.

MORELAND POTATOES

59

For 4 servings, you will need:

8 medium potatoes
2 tbs chives
2 oz (56 g) butter

7 tbs whole wheat flour
  (use whole meal flour)

First prepare:

Peel potatoes. Chop chives finely. Melt butter. Measure flour into a dish.

Now assemble!

1. Cook potatoes in boiling salted water until tender. Peel.
2. Replace in pan, dry over low heat covered with a tea towel.
3. Brush with melted butter and chopped chives.
4. Dust with flour and serve at once.

BUTTERED AND HERBED NEW POTATOES

For 4 servings, you will need:

2 lb (0.9 kg) tiny new potatoes   Pinch of salt
1 bunch parsley   2 oz (56 g) butter
1 bunch mint

First prepare:

Rinse potatoes. Do not remove skins. Put a pot of water on to boil. Wash mint and parsley and chop. Heat a vegetable dish in warming oven.

Now cook!

1. Pop potatoes into boiling water with a pinch of salt. Add parsley and mint stalk. Cover with a tightly fitting lid.
2. Boil for 20 minutes on high heat.
3. Drain cooked potatoes and submerge in cold, running water. Rub them between your hands and skin will come away more easily than by any other peeling method.
4. Return potatoes to a pan with melted butter and cover with a clean cloth. Place over lowest heat (if gas please use a heat pad to avoid direct contact).
5. Remove cloth and dust potatoes with mint and parsley. Place in the vegetable dish and serve.

HUTSPOT MIT KLAPSTUK

For 6 large servings, you will need:

3 lbs (1.4 kg) smoked boneless   1 lb (0.5 kg) onions
      pork butt   4 oz (113 g) butter
4 lbs (1.8 kg) potatoes   Freshly ground salt
2 lbs (0.9 kg) carrots   Freshly ground black pepper

First prepare:

Slice onions, cube potatoes and carrots. Heat a serving platter in warming oven. Bring smoked corned beef to a boil in cold water. Simmer until tender.

Now cook!

1. Layer vegetables in a big pan seasoning after each addition. First potatoes, carrots, and lastly onions. Add water to just cover and cook until tender (approximately 1 hour).
2. Drain cooked vegetables and roughly mash them. Pop in 4 oz (113 g) butter to make them rich and creamy.
3. Drain meat and slice it thinly.
4. Spoon vegetables (hutspot) on heated serving platter and lay meat slices (klapstuk) over them.

FRIED CAULIFLOWER

For 4 servings, you will need:

1 medium cauliflower	Freshly ground black pepper
4 tbs clarified butter*	2 tbs parsley
Freshly ground salt	1 tbs grated Parmesan cheese

First prepare:

Chop parsley finely and grate cheese.

Now cook!

1. Place a whole cauliflower head into salted boiling water and cook until three-quarters done (15 to 18 minutes).

2. Break cauliflower into small flowerets.

3. Heat clarified butter and fry pieces of cauliflower until browned on all sides. Season with salt and pepper. Place in a serving dish and sprinkle with parsley, cheese and a few pieces of butter.

PEAS BOLOGNA

For 4 servings, you will need:

4 oz (113 g) Hungarian salami	2 tsp mint
8 oz (227 g) green peas	1½ oz (42 g) butter
2 tsp sugar	Freshly ground salt

67

First prepare:

Cook peas in boiling salted water, drain and set aside. Measure sugar. Wash, dry and finely chop mint. Weigh butter. Slice salami (you need 8 pieces about ¹⁄₁₆-inch (2 mm) thick) but do not remove outer skin. Finely cube rest of salami (should be about 2 oz: 56 g) and remove skin.

Now cook!

1. Melt butter in a heated frypan, add cooked peas and season with salt.

2. Add chopped salami and mint.

3. Sprinkle sugar over top.

4. Heat a large skillet and quickly add thin slices of salami—the outer skin will contract forming little cups. Remove and place around whatever food they are used to garnish.

5. Fill little cups with savory pea mixture.

LIMOUSINE POTATOES

For 4 servings, you will need:

2 lbs (0.9 kg) potatoes
4 bacon rashers*

4 tbs clarified butter*
Freshly ground salt

First prepare:

Wash and peel potatoes and soak them in water for 1 hour. Dry and grate. Remove rind from bacon and chop finely.

Now cook!

1. Place clarified butter in large pan, add bacon and grated potato. When potatoes are well browned on one side turn to brown other side. (5 minutes on the first side, 2 minutes on the second, at high heat.) Season with salt.

DANISH SUGAR BROWNED POTATOES

For 3 servings, you will need:

1 lb (0.5 kg) small new potatoes
2 tbs butter

2 oz (56 g) sugar
Freshly ground salt

First prepare:

Measure sugar and butter.

Now cook!

1. Cook potatoes (in their skins) in salted boiling water until tender (15 minutes). Drain and peel.
2. Melt butter in a frypan, add sugar and cook until mixture forms a golden caramel.
3. Add skinned potatoes and roll in caramel. Sauté for 3 to 5 minutes, turning occasionally.

GREEN PEPPER POTATOES

For 4 servings, you will need:

1½ lbs (680 g) potatoes
3 tbs clarified butter*
3 oz (85 g) green pepper (capsicum)
1 oz (28 g) onion

Freshly ground salt
Freshly ground black pepper
Parsley

66

First prepare:

Slice pepper and onion finely. Chop parsley. Peel potatoes.

Now cook!

1. Boil potatoes until tender but still firm. Dry and slice ½-inch (1.2 cm) thick.
2. Shallow fry potato slices in clarified butter.
3. Turn and add pepper and onion rings.
4. When browned lightly, serve dusted with salt, pepper and chopped parsley.

FRIED POTATOES

For 4 servings, you will need:
    1½ lb (680 g) potatoes
    Peanut or corn oil for deep frying

Freshly ground salt
Lemon

First prepare:

Cut potatoes into ⅛-inch (3.5 mm) thick slices and soak for 1 hour in a bowl of warm water with a piece of lemon. Remove and dry thoroughly.

Now cook!

1. Heat fat to 350⁰F (177⁰C) in deep fryer. When hot place potato chips in basket and lower into oil for 10 minutes. Remove and drain.

2. Increase heat to 450⁰F (232⁰C) and return chips to oil. Cook for 3 minutes longer until crisp golden brown. Drain on absorbent paper.

SAUTEED POTATOES

For 2 servings, you will need:
    1 lb (0.5 kg) potatoes

Clarified butter*

Now cook!

1. Boil peeled potatoes until just cooked. Remove them from pan and cut into ½ inch (1.2 cm) thick slices and fry gently in butter in a large frypan. Turn once and fry until golden brown.

FRIED POTATOES PAYSANNE

For 4 servings, you will need:
    2 lbs (0.9 kg) potatoes
    4 tbs bacon fat
    1 clove garlic

Freshly ground salt
Chopped parsley

First prepare:

Peel and cut potatoes into small cubes (½ inch : 1.2 cm). Peel and smash clove garlic. Chop parsley. Dry potatoes well.

Now cook!

1. Melt bacon fat and when hot add potatoes. Stir to cover with fat, then add garlic. Sauté until golden brown and crisp, about 10 to 12 minutes.

2. At last moment add chopped parsley and sprinkle with salt.

NOISETTE POTATOES

For 4 servings, you will need:
1 lb (0.5 kg) large potatoes
4 tbs clarified butter*

Freshly ground salt
Freshly ground pepper

Now cook!

1. Peel potatoes and with a melon baller scoop out small "balls" of potato.
2. Place into cold salted water and bring to a boil. Cook for 2 to 3 minutes. Drain and dry well.
3. Melt butter in pan and cook potatoes, shaking pan occasionally until potatoes are golden and soft, about 7 to 8 minutes. Season with salt and pepper.

SHOESTRING POTATOES

For 2 servings, you will need:
1 lb (0.5 kg) potatoes
Parsley

Freshly ground salt
Deep oil

First prepare:

Grate potatoes on a coarse grater into cold water. Drain and dry.

Now cook!

1. Place potatoes in an even layer in basket of deep fryer and lower into 380°F (193°C) oil. Cook for 1 minute and remove.
2. Heat oil to 500°F (260°C) and place potatoes once more into oil and allow to become golden (about 2 minutes).
3. Remove from deep fryer and drain. Potatoes will now look a little like a bird's nest. Cut in half, season with salt and sprinkle with parsley.

DEEP FRIED BEANS

For 3 servings, you will need:

1 lb (0.5 kg) green beans
2 egg yolks
Flour
¾ oz (21 g) fresh bread crumbs*

Freshly ground salt
Nutmeg
Juice of ½ lemon
Oil

First prepare:

Trim green beans and cut each into halves. Beat egg yolks and put on dish. Place flour and bread crumbs on dishes.

Now cook!

1. Lightly flour beans. Dip into beaten egg and then into bread crumbs. Fry in hot oil for 2 minutes. Place on a serving dish covered with a paper doily. Dust with salt and nutmeg. Add a squeeze of lemon juice.

BENNET POTATOES

For 6 servings, you will need:

1½ lbs (680 g) potatoes
3 egg whites
3 tbs chives
Freshly ground salt

Freshly ground white pepper
Parsley
Deep oil

59

First prepare:

Peel and cook potatoes and mash well. Season with salt and pepper. Whip egg whites until stiff. Finely chop chives and parsley. Preheat oil to 400°F (205°C).

Now cook!

1. Add chives to mashed potatoes and fold in egg whites. Fill pastry bag; fitted with ½-inch (1.2 cm) plain nozzle.
2. Pipe 2-inch lengths of potato into hot oil and cook for 2 minutes until crisp and golden brown. Drain.
3. Serve on a dish covered with a paper doily and dust with parsley.

STUFFED SAVORY MUSHROOMS "GRAVETYE"

For 4 servings, you will need:

16 mushrooms each 2 inch (5 cm)
   diameter (must be even sized)
1 green pepper (capsicum)
1 red pepper (capsicum)
Clarified butter*
1 oz (28 g) spring onions*
Freshly ground salt
Freshly ground black pepper
4 oz (113 g) smoked ham
2 fl oz (5.6 cl) dry white wine
All-purpose flour
1 egg

Fresh white bread crumbs*
Deep oil
Sauce:
10 fl oz (3 dl) milk
1 oz (28 g) all-purpose flour
1 oz (28 g) butter
Freshly ground salt
Freshly ground white pepper
Nutmeg
4 oz (113 g) Cheddar cheese
   (finely grated)

First prepare:

Preheat oil in deep fryer to 350°F (177°C). Remove stems from mushrooms. Finely dice red and green peppers. Finely chop spring onions. Finely dice ham. Measure white wine.

Sauce: Melt butter in a saucepan and add flour. Stir to form a roux and cook over low heat for 1 minute. Add milk gradually, stirring until smooth. Season with salt, pepper and nutmeg. Bring sauce to a boil while stirring and then allow to cook gently for 15 minutes. Gradually add cheese and stir until melted. Cover surface with a piece of buttered paper to avoid a skin forming and cool.

Now cook!

1. Place enough clarified butter to just cover bottom into a frypan and when hot add peppers. Fry gently and then add onions and ham. Season with salt and pepper and allow to fry for a few minutes. Add wine, cook for 1 minute and cool.

2. Mix sauce with vegetable and ham mixture. Place a large spoonful of mixture on 1 mushroom. Sandwich with another mushroom exactly same size, placing it stem side down on top of filling. Dip in flour, then egg and then bread crumbs. Place mushrooms into a deep fryer basket and deep fry for 5 minutes.

3. After 5 minutes remove, drain and arrange on a serving dish.

A special hint:

The mushrooms are all important to this dish. They should be cultivated, very fresh, firm and white with deep rounded caps on the inside.

TOMATO FILLED WITH CREAMED CORN MAITRE D'HOTEL BUTTER

For 4 servings, you will need:

2 large tomatoes
4 tbs creamed corn
Maitre d'hotel butter:
2 oz (56 g) butter

1 tbs parsley
Freshly ground salt
Freshly ground pepper
Dash lemon juice

First prepare:

Maitre d'hotel butter: Soften butter, add finely chopped parsley. Season with salt and pepper and add lemon juice to taste.

Now cook!

1. Halve tomatoes crosswise and scoop out seeds. Fill each half with 1 tbs creamed corn. Place under broiler for 4 minutes.
2. Top with a piece of maitre d'hotel butter.

STUFFED ONIONS

For 4 servings, you will need:

4 large onions
½ lb (227 g) ground beef
4 oz (113 g) bacon slices
2 eggs
Clarified butter*
1 tbs parsley stalks*
½ tsp allspice

Freshly ground salt
Freshly ground black pepper
1 tsp dried basil
1 tsp dried oregano or
20 fresh leaves
Parsley leaves

First prepare:

Peel onions and place them in salted boiling water for 10 minutes. Drain. Remove insides of onions leaving 2 outer skins. Reserve pulp of 1 onion. Cut bacon into thin slices. Finely cut parsley stalks. Roughly chop parsley. Preheat oven to 350°F (177°C).

Now cook!

1. Heat some clarified butter in a pan and add finely chopped pulp of 1 onion and ground beef crumbled roughly. Allow meat to brown and reduce pan heat. Add bacon and season with salt, pepper and allspice. Stir mixture together and allow to fry gently for 2 minutes.
2. Place meat mixture into a bowl, add eggs, parsley, basil and oregano. Fill onions.
3. Bake onions in an ovenproof dish for 20 minutes at 350°F (177°C).
4. After 20 minutes remove from oven and place onions on a serving dish.

ARTICHOKES MORAN

For 2 servings, you will need:

2 artichokes	1 oz (28 g) Gentleman's Relish*
2 fl oz (5.6 cl) olive oil	1 fl oz (2.8 cl) white wine vinegar
1 clove garlic	2 fl oz (5.6 cl) white wine
3 shallots	2 oz (56 g) butter
24 fl oz (7 dl) cold water	1 egg yolk
1 tsp oregano	1 level tsp hot English mustard
1 lemon	1 level tsp horseradish
4 oz (113 g) fresh bread crumbs*	2 tsp chives
2 oz (56 g) grated Parmesan cheese	Freshly ground salt
1 oz (28 g) parsley	Freshly ground white pepper
1 egg	Freshly ground black pepper

First prepare:

Measure oil, water, wine and white wine vinegar. Smash garlic clove. Cut shallots into quarters. Juice lemon. Wash, dry and finely chop parsley. Measure remaining dry ingredients. Thoroughly wash artichokes under running water. With a pair of scissors clip pointed end off every leaf. Reserve trimmings. Cut off stem and rub base with lemon. Pour juice over both artichokes to prevent discoloration. Finely chop chives. Make English mustard by adding water to dry mustard.

Now cook!

1. Put olive oil into a pan on low heat, then stir in garlic and shallots and continue cooking for 2 minutes.

2. Add cold water to garlic mixture and add artichoke trimmings. Season with oregano and add lemon pieces. Season with salt and white pepper to taste. Cover pan and simmer to create a court bouillon.

3. Mix bread crumbs in a bowl with Parmesan cheese and season generously with salt and lots of white pepper. Stir in parsley. Make a well in center and add egg and Gentleman's Relish. Blend until everything is well mixed (takes about 2 minutes).

4. Stir vinegar into bread crumb mixture. Then carefully press this mixture between the leaves of artichokes.

5. Place artichokes into court bouillon (it should reach one-third up vegetable) and replace lid. Cook for about 40 minutes, until leaves can be pulled out easily.

6. Place drained artichokes on a heatproof serving platter and slide under broiler for 3 minutes to dry and brown stuffing.

7. Pour white wine into court bouillon and bring to a boil. Reduce almost completely, then strain into top of a double boiler placed over simmering water. Use only 1 tsp.

8. Blend in butter, egg yolk, mustard, horseradish and chives. Keep beating until sauce thickens. Do not allow water to boil or it will curdle. Season with black pepper.

9. Spoon sauce over the top of the artichokes and serve.

STUFFED TOMATOES

For 4 servings, you will need:

4 large tomatoes
1 green pepper (capsicum)
Freshly ground salt

Freshly ground pepper
2 tbs clarified butter*

First prepare:

Cut tomatoes into halves crosswise and season with salt and pepper. Finely chop green pepper. Preheat broiler.

Now cook!

1. Make a semi-circular cut in each tomato. Lift up pulp with a teaspoon and fill pocket with finely chopped pepper. Season again. Replace pulp over pepper.
2. Brush tomatoes with clarified butter and slide under a hot broiler. Broil for 3-4 minutes or until tender but still firm.

TOMATO CREVETTES

For 2 servings, you will need:

4 oz (113 g) tiny shrimp
    (fresh or good canned ones)
2 large tomatoes
2 tbs parsley
1 small Boston lettuce
Mayonnaise:
½ tsp dry mustard

2 tbs lemon juice
¼ tsp cayenne pepper
5 fl oz (1.5 dl) oil
1 egg
Freshly ground salt
Freshly ground white pepper

First prepare:

Measure dry ingredients. Wash and dry lettuce and chill. Wash and chop parsley. Measure oil. Remove tops from two tomatoes in a zigzag fashion and scoop out seeds being careful not to break outer shell. Reserve tops. Press pulp and seeds through a sieve and keep tomato pulp ready for use.

Now assemble!

1. Warm your blender with hot water, drain.
2. Put mustard, lemon juice, 2 tsp tomato pulp, cayenne pepper, oil and egg into warmed blender. Mix at high speed for 30 seconds.
3. Pour stiff mayonnaise into a bowl, season to taste with salt and white pepper and fold in shrimp. Chill until required.
4. Arrange tomato shells on a bed of crisp lettuce.
5. Fill them with shrimp mixture, top with their caps and dust with parsley.

ARTISCHOCKEN MIT SCHINKSALAT

For 2 servings, you will need:

2 large artichokes
1 lemon
6 oz (170 g) cooked ham
3 oz (85 g) Emmenthal cheese
2 tsp capers
6 small gherkins
1 tsp dill
2 tsp Dijon mustard

1 red bell pepper (capsicum)
3 tbs mayonnaise
Freshly ground salt
Freshly ground white pepper
Sauce:
2 tbs oil
2 tbs tarragon vinegar

First prepare:

Wash artichokes thoroughly. Cut off bottom stem and rub with a fresh lemon. Trim tops from each leaf with a pair of scissors. Cut ham into julienne strips. Dice cheese. Finely chop gherkins and dill. Measure mustard, oil, vinegar and mayonnaise. Dice red pepper. Finger bowls will be required.

Now cook!

1. Fill a pan two-thirds full of water and bring to a boil. Squeeze lemon into boiling water, season with salt and white pepper.

2. Put artichokes in pan. Cover and boil gently for 40 minutes.

3. Drain off water and allow artichokes to cool slightly.

4. Cool artichokes and pull off leaves. Remove fuzzy choke from artichoke heart.

5. With a sharp knife trim top of artichoke bottom that remains after leaves are removed. It will look like a small saucer.

6. Place ham, mayonnaise, cheese, capers, dill, gherkins, mustard and red pepper into a bowl and mix well together.

7. Dip leaves into oil and vinegar sauce and arrange in a circle on a serving dish. Place artichoke bottom in center.

8. Spoon ham and cheese salad into artichoke bottom.

A special hint:

Eat bottom of artichoke with a fork and leaves with fingers.

SEAFOOD ZUCCHINI

For 4 servings, you will need:

¾ oz (21 g) butter
¾ oz (21 g) flour
2 fl oz (5.6 cl) dry white wine
3 fl oz (8 cl) fish stock
6 oz (170 g) scallops
1 bay leaf

6 oz (170 g) king crab
4 zucchinis
1 tbs Parmesan cheese
Freshly ground salt
Freshly ground white pepper

First prepare:

Measure butter, wine and fish stock. Sift flour. Grate Parmesan cheese. Weigh scallops then poach in white wine for 4 minutes. Weigh crab. Put zucchinis into boiling salted water, cook for 6 minutes, then drain. (They must be firm.) Preheat broiler.

Now cook!

1. Make a roux: melt butter in a pan, stir in flour and cook for 3 minutes.
2. Gradually stir in fish stock and bring to a boil.
3. Stir in white wine and simmer sauce gently over low heat.
4. Slice top off zucchinis lengthwise and scoop out center seeds, leaving a firm outer casing.
5. Place prepoached scallops into wine sauce and add crab.
6. Spoon mixture into zucchinis.
7. Sprinkle grated Parmesan cheese over top and slide under preheated broiler until golden brown.

TOMATOES PROVENCAL

For 4 servings, you will need:

4 medium tomatoes
1½ oz (42 g) fresh bread crumbs*
3 cloves garlic
Olive oil

Freshly ground salt
Freshly ground pepper
2 tbs parsley

First prepare:

Make bread crumbs. Cut tomatoes in halves crosswise and shake to remove seeds. Peel and finely chop garlic. Finely chop parsley. Preheat broiler.

Now cook!

1. Mix garlic and parsley with bread crumbs. Fill tomato halves with this mixture. Moisten with olive oil, season with salt and pepper.
2. Place in a pan under broiler until tomatoes are soft and the top is browned (about 10-15 minutes).

CHOU FARCI

For 12 servings, you will need:

1 lb 14 oz (850 g) large green cabbage	4 oz (113 g) celery
12 eggs	10 oz (283 g) green peas
2 lbs (0.9 kg) neck of pork	Freshly ground salt
4 oz (113 g) Parmesan cheese	Freshly ground black pepper
8 oz (227 g) onion	Clarified butter*
4 oz (113 g) carrots	

First prepare:

Cabbage: In a large pan boil some water and add a good pinch of salt. Peel cabbage leaf by leaf and cut away heavy center stalks. Drop leaves into boiling water to blanch. Turn with tongs and try to give them even cooking time. Cook for 3 minutes, drain and plunge them into a bowl of ice water (this helps to retain fresh green color and prevents overcooking).

Farci: Cut pork into little cubes, finely slice onions and grate cheese. Hard-boil 4 of the eggs. Roughly chop carrots and celery. Assemble a grinder.

Now cook!

1. Pour enough clarified butter into a pan to just cover bottom and heat.
2. To this add pork and fry until golden brown on all sides.
3. Add sliced onions and stir to cook evenly.
4. Mix in carrots and celery, season and cover. Reduce heat and allow to cook gently for 1 hour.
5. After one hour remove the meat and vegetables from pot and put them through fine blade in a grinder.
6. Put this mixture in a bowl and beat in eight remaining eggs. Stir in cheese, adjust seasoning and add more salt and pepper if necessary.
7. Mix in green peas.
8. In a greased 2-quart ovenproof bowl or casserole place cabbage leaves to form a firm lining.
9. Pour in half ground mixture and on top of this place the four hard-boiled eggs cut in half lengthwise. Cover them with other half of ground mixture.
10. Lay more of the cabbage leaves over the top to form a lid and press down firmly.
11. Cover with a layer of foil and place in preheated oven 350°F (177°C) for 30 minutes.
12. Remove chou farci from oven and loosen cabbage mold from bowl with knife.
13. Place heated serving dish on top of bowl and turn upside down to unmold.
14. Serve either hot or cold.

A special hint:

Be sure to remove the heavy "ribs" from outer leaves. Left in, they spoil this great dish.

MIMOUSSAKA

For 6 servings, you will need:

2 eggplants
1 clove garlic
3 medium tomatoes
1 large onion
1 lb (0.5 kg) cooked lamb
2½ oz (70 g) mushrooms
3 fl oz (8 cl) beef stock
2 fl oz (5.6 cl) tomato puree

Pinch saffron
Freshly ground salt
Freshly ground black pepper
1 oz (28 g) bread crumbs*
2 oz (56 g) grated cheese
1 tbs lemon peel
Clarified butter*

First prepare:

Skin and slice tomatoes. Pare skin off eggplants in long thin strips. Peel one clove garlic and smash. Finely slice onion. Finely slice mushrooms. Dice cooked lamb. Finely grate cheese. Finely slice lemon peel. Mix lemon peel, cheese, bread crumbs and remaining 2 cloves of garlic. Blanch eggplant skins in boiling water for 2 minutes. Butter an ovenproof dish. Cut one eggplant into 1 inch (2.5 cm) dice. Preheat oven to 400ºF (205ºC).

Now cook!

1. Line base and sides of round 2-quart ovenproof dish with eggplant skins, black side against sides of dish. Overlap skins lengthwise slightly so that they form a complete casing and hang over edge.

2. Place clarified butter in heated frypan. Add onion, garlic, mushrooms and eggplant cubes. Season with salt and pepper and allow to sweat.

3. Place bread crumb mixture on eggplant skins, add half lamb, half vegetable mixture and then a layer of sliced tomatoes. Now add the rest of the vegetable mixture, the lamb and some sliced tomatoes.

4. Fold eggplant skins over top of casserole to encase mixture and gently add stock and tomato puree mixed with saffron.

5. Place in oven for 20 minutes. When cooked pour off excess juice. Invert onto serving dish, unmold and serve.

A special hint:

Can be prepared in advance. In this case leave in ovenproof dish, do not drain the mixture and reheat altogether when required.

BAKED POTATOES—SOUR CREAM CHIVES

For 4 servings, you will need:

4 large potatoes	2 tbs chives
4 tbs sour cream	Freshly ground salt

First prepare:

Measure sour cream. Chop chives finely. Preheat oven to 350°F (177°C).

Now cook!

1. Scrub potatoes well and dust thoroughly with salt. Trim a thin slice from one end.
2. Place in oven and bake for 1½ hours or until potatoes are soft.
3. Fold a cloth so that it can be slipped like a noose around potato and cut deeply into center to form a cross. Squeeze cloth gently at first, then harder until the cut opens out. Fluff potato with a fork.
4. Place a tablespoon of sour cream in center of each potato and dust with chives.

BLUE SPUR POTATOES

For 4 servings, you will need:

4 large potatoes	Nutmeg
2 tbs sour cream	1 tbs butter
Freshly ground salt	4 tbs chives
Freshly ground white pepper	

First prepare:

Chop chives finely.

Now cook!

1. Bake potatoes in their jackets in 350°F (177°C) oven for 1½ hours. Break open and scoop out centers.
2. Cream potatoes with butter and sour cream. Season with salt, pepper and nutmeg. Whisk until smooth.
3. At last minute add chopped chives.